The Best Of
Alex
2012

Charles Peattie & Russell Taylor

Masterley Publishing

H46 555 589 X

The Best Of Alex

2012

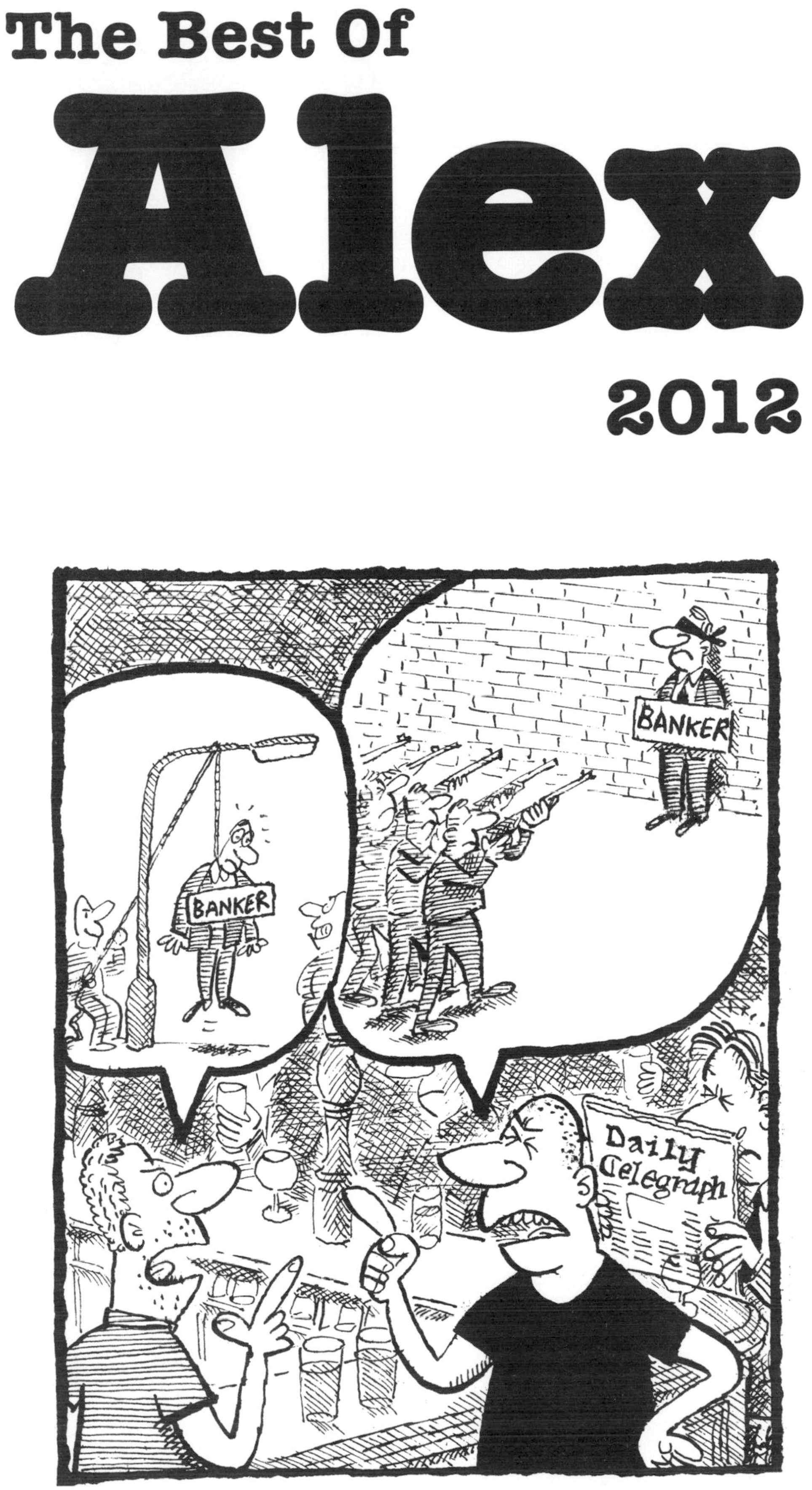

BANKER
BANKER
Daily Telegraph

First Published in 2012 by MASTERLEY PUBLISHING

Layout and Artwork: Suzette Field

ISBN: 978 1 85375 859 1

Printed and bound by CPI Group (UK) Ltd, Croydon, CR0 4YY

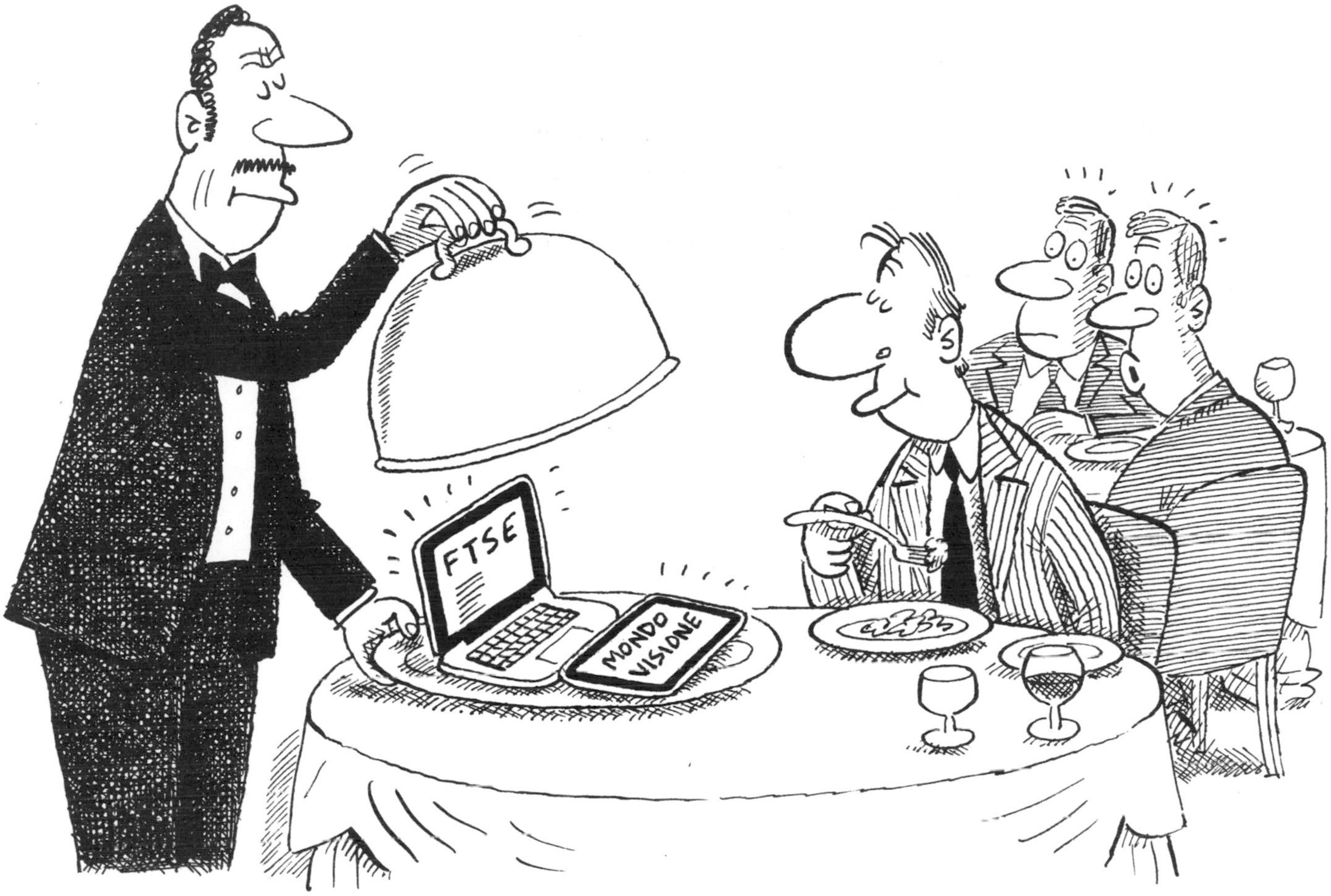
FTSE
MONDO VISIONE

Our usual gratitude goes to our generous sponsors.

FTSE Group (FTSE) is the world-leader in the creation and management of index solutions.

Mondo Visione provides vital knowledge about the world's exchanges and trading venues.

FOREWORD

2012 will be remembered as the year that the Queen celebrated her Diamond Jubilee and Team GB won a proud swathe of gold medals at the London Olympics.

Slightly less feted was the fact that 2012 also saw us, the humble chroniclers of Alex's lifestyle, attain a silver of our own: February of this year marked the 25th anniversary of Alex's first appearance in a newspaper. The cartoon has now been running for well over a mile (we calculate it as about 2,300 yards if all the strips were laid end to end) and would probably take over 90 hours of reading time to get through, which would be quite a Marathon (and a long time to spend on the loo).

The sit-down disciplines are of course the ones at which the British traditionally excel and Alex is disappointed that his own favoured event (the Luncheon Heptathlon) is still yet to be recognised by the Olympic committee. He contends that lunching is a genuine test of stamina, co-ordination and physical endurance, not to mention the sheer dumb courage needed to stay the course (and in fact all the other courses, including the cheese course, when competitors are permitted to talk business) and deserves wider public recognition. Moreover there is much home grown talent in this field (remember the furore over those empty corporate seats in the Olympic stadium, whose rightful occupiers were giving it their all in the hospitality tents?)

But until such a time as lunching is allowed to take its place alongside other comparable competitive activities as an Olympic sport, Alex will be continuing his training schedule in a series of unofficial 'paralytic' events, probably in a restaurant near you. Try not to mind him throwing the bread rolls: he's only in preparation for Rio in 2016.

So, as Alex starts to research Brazilian companies to justify an extended business trip there in four years' time, read on to see if there will still be a global economy by then.

Charles Peattie Russell Taylor

Charles Peattie and Russell Taylor

Alex - Investment banker

Penny - Alex's wife

Christopher - their son

Clive - Alex's colleague

Bridget - Clive's wife

Rupert - Senior banker

Cyrus - Alex's boss

Jessica - Alex's PA

Hardcastle - Alex's client

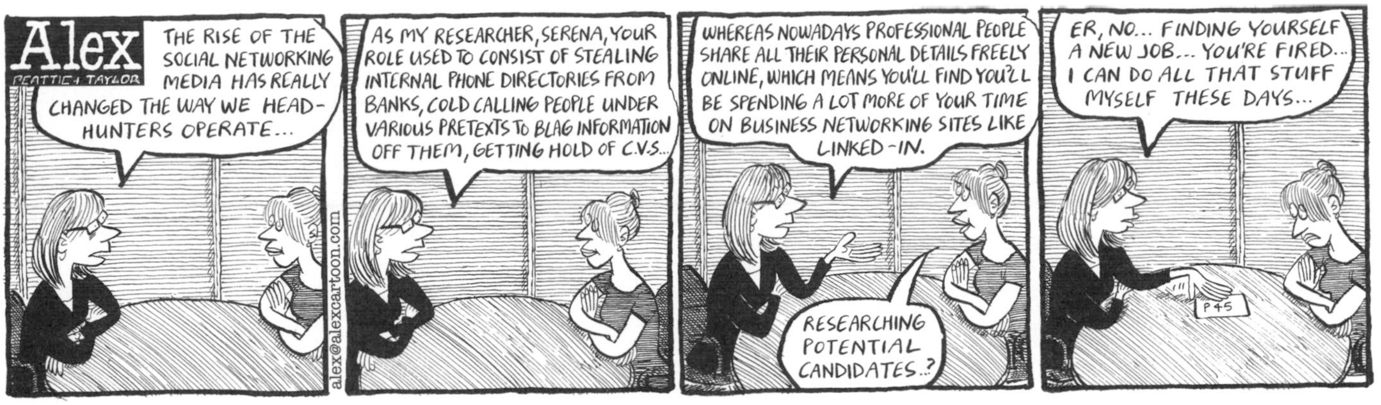
Alex
PEATTIE + TAYLOR
THE RISE OF THE SOCIAL NETWORKING MEDIA HAS REALLY CHANGED THE WAY WE HEAD-HUNTERS OPERATE...
alex@alexcartoon.com
AS MY RESEARCHER, SERENA, YOUR ROLE USED TO CONSIST OF STEALING INTERNAL PHONE DIRECTORIES FROM BANKS, COLD CALLING PEOPLE UNDER VARIOUS PRETEXTS TO BLAG INFORMATION OFF THEM, GETTING HOLD OF C.V.S...
WHEREAS NOWADAYS PROFESSIONAL PEOPLE SHARE ALL THEIR PERSONAL DETAILS FREELY ONLINE, WHICH MEANS YOU'LL FIND YOU'LL BE SPENDING A LOT MORE OF YOUR TIME ON BUSINESS NETWORKING SITES LIKE LINKED-IN.
RESEARCHING POTENTIAL CANDIDATES..?
ER, NO... FINDING YOURSELF A NEW JOB... YOU'RE FIRED... I CAN DO ALL THAT STUFF MYSELF THESE DAYS...
P45

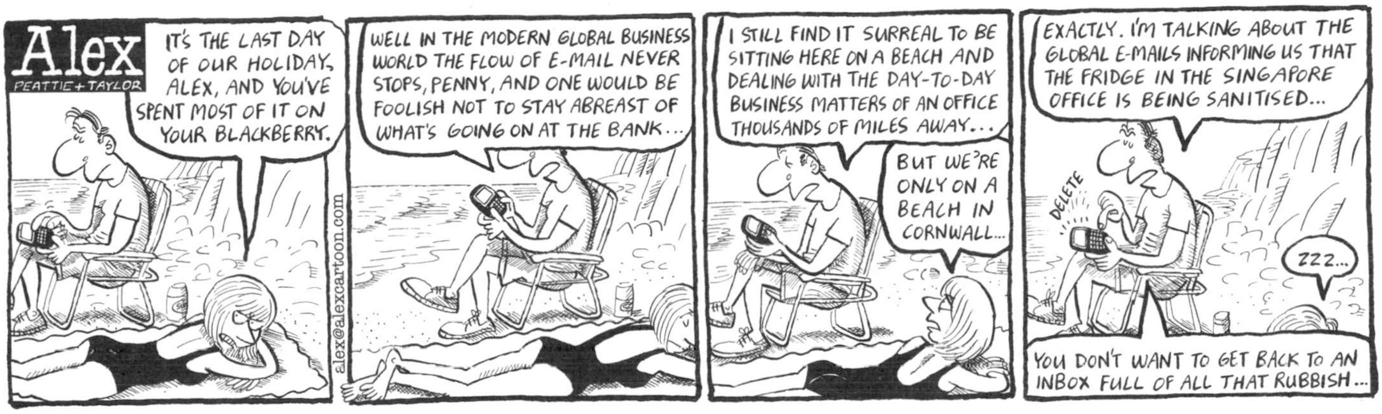
Alex
PEATTIE + TAYLOR
IT'S THE LAST DAY OF OUR HOLIDAY, ALEX, AND YOU'VE SPENT MOST OF IT ON YOUR BLACKBERRY.
alex@alexcartoon.com
WELL IN THE MODERN GLOBAL BUSINESS WORLD THE FLOW OF E-MAIL NEVER STOPS, PENNY, AND ONE WOULD BE FOOLISH NOT TO STAY ABREAST OF WHAT'S GOING ON AT THE BANK...
I STILL FIND IT SURREAL TO BE SITTING HERE ON A BEACH AND DEALING WITH THE DAY-TO-DAY BUSINESS MATTERS OF AN OFFICE THOUSANDS OF MILES AWAY...
BUT WE'RE ONLY ON A BEACH IN CORNWALL...
EXACTLY. I'M TALKING ABOUT THE GLOBAL E-MAILS INFORMING US THAT THE FRIDGE IN THE SINGAPORE OFFICE IS BEING SANITISED...
DELETE
ZZZ...
YOU DON'T WANT TO GET BACK TO AN INBOX FULL OF ALL THAT RUBBISH...

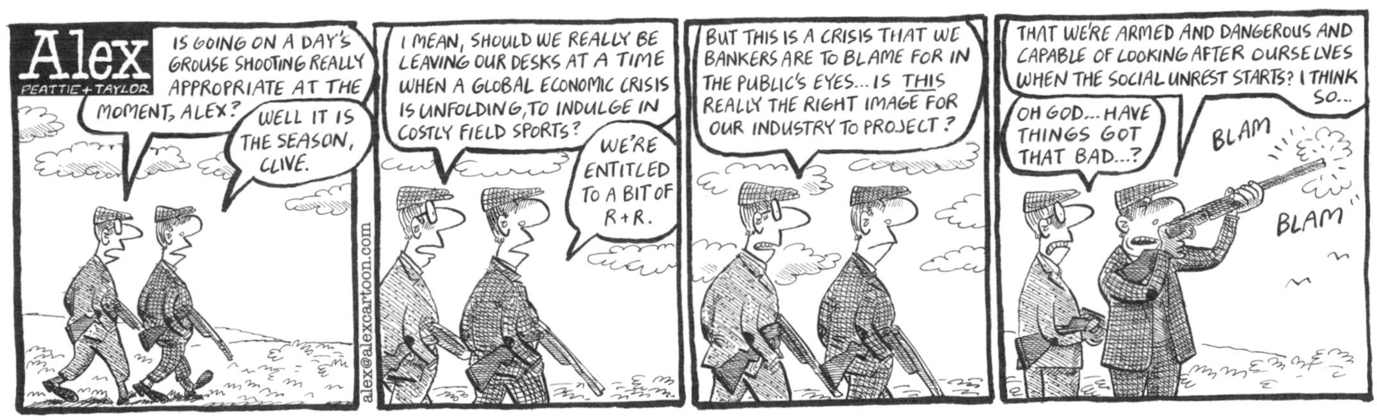
Alex
PEATTIE + TAYLOR
IS GOING ON A DAY'S GROUSE SHOOTING REALLY APPROPRIATE AT THE MOMENT, ALEX?
WELL IT IS THE SEASON, CLIVE.
alex@alexcartoon.com
I MEAN, SHOULD WE REALLY BE LEAVING OUR DESKS AT A TIME WHEN A GLOBAL ECONOMIC CRISIS IS UNFOLDING, TO INDULGE IN COSTLY FIELD SPORTS?
WE'RE ENTITLED TO A BIT OF R+R.
BUT THIS IS A CRISIS THAT WE BANKERS ARE TO BLAME FOR IN THE PUBLIC'S EYES... IS THIS REALLY THE RIGHT IMAGE FOR OUR INDUSTRY TO PROJECT?
THAT WE'RE ARMED AND DANGEROUS AND CAPABLE OF LOOKING AFTER OURSELVES WHEN THE SOCIAL UNREST STARTS? I THINK SO...
OH GOD... HAVE THINGS GOT THAT BAD...?
BLAM
BLAM

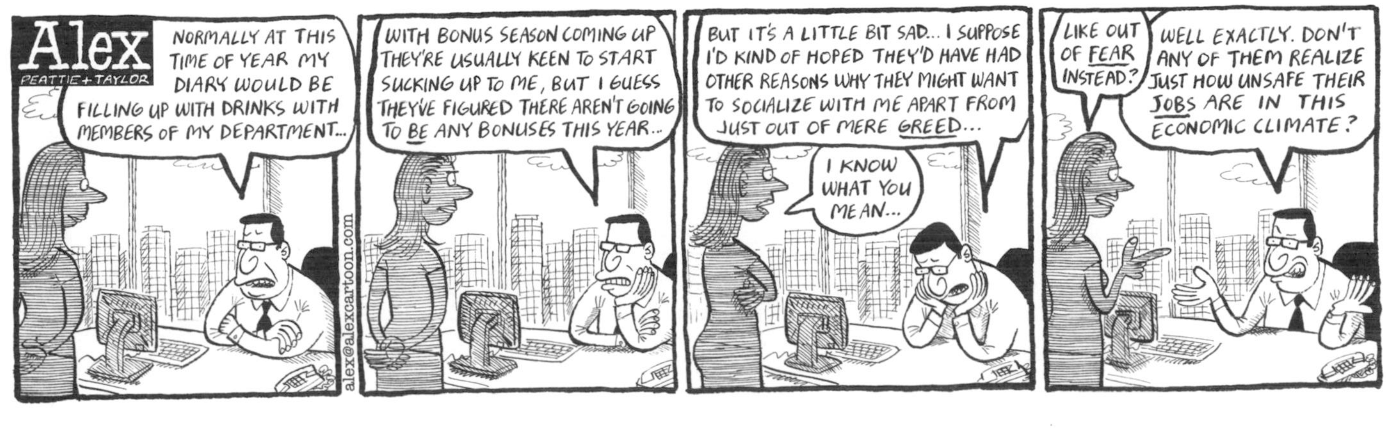
Alex
PEATTIE + TAYLOR
NORMALLY AT THIS TIME OF YEAR MY DIARY WOULD BE FILLING UP WITH DRINKS WITH MEMBERS OF MY DEPARTMENT...
alex@alexcartoon.com
WITH BONUS SEASON COMING UP THEY'RE USUALLY KEEN TO START SUCKING UP TO ME, BUT I GUESS THEY'VE FIGURED THERE AREN'T GOING TO BE ANY BONUSES THIS YEAR...
BUT IT'S A LITTLE BIT SAD... I SUPPOSE I'D KIND OF HOPED THEY'D HAVE HAD OTHER REASONS WHY THEY MIGHT WANT TO SOCIALIZE WITH ME APART FROM JUST OUT OF MERE GREED...
I KNOW WHAT YOU MEAN...
LIKE OUT OF FEAR INSTEAD?
WELL EXACTLY. DON'T ANY OF THEM REALIZE JUST HOW UNSAFE THEIR JOBS ARE IN THIS ECONOMIC CLIMATE?

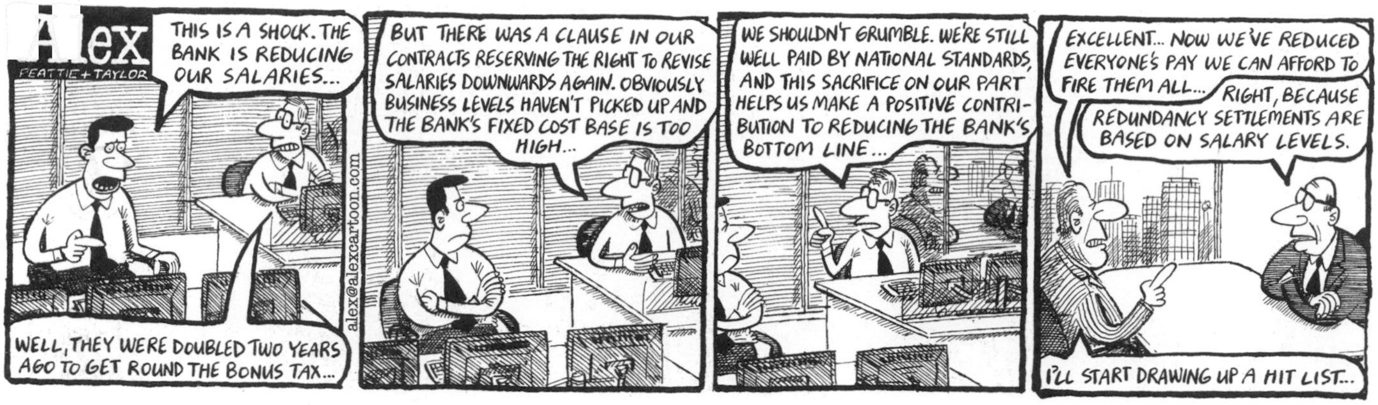
Alex
PEATTIE+TAYLOR
THIS IS A SHOCK. THE BANK IS REDUCING OUR SALARIES...
WELL, THEY WERE DOUBLED TWO YEARS AGO TO GET ROUND THE BONUS TAX...
alex@alexcartoon.com
BUT THERE WAS A CLAUSE IN OUR CONTRACTS RESERVING THE RIGHT TO REVISE SALARIES DOWNWARDS AGAIN. OBVIOUSLY BUSINESS LEVELS HAVEN'T PICKED UP AND THE BANK'S FIXED COST BASE IS TOO HIGH...
WE SHOULDN'T GRUMBLE. WE'RE STILL WELL PAID BY NATIONAL STANDARDS, AND THIS SACRIFICE ON OUR PART HELPS US MAKE A POSITIVE CONTRIBUTION TO REDUCING THE BANK'S BOTTOM LINE...
EXCELLENT... NOW WE'VE REDUCED EVERYONE'S PAY WE CAN AFFORD TO FIRE THEM ALL...
RIGHT, BECAUSE REDUNDANCY SETTLEMENTS ARE BASED ON SALARY LEVELS.
I'LL START DRAWING UP A HIT LIST...

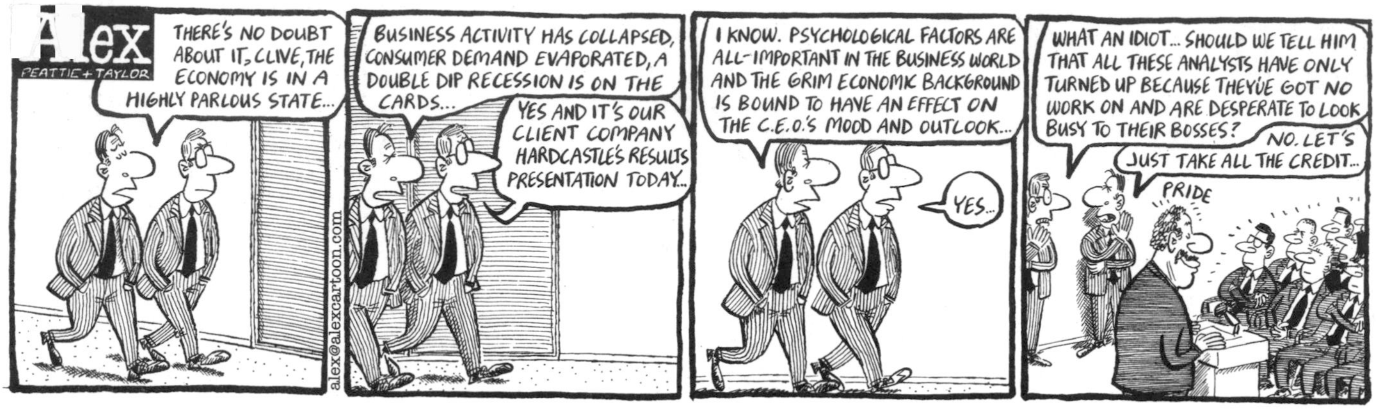
Alex
PEATTIE+TAYLOR
THERE'S NO DOUBT ABOUT IT, CLIVE, THE ECONOMY IS IN A HIGHLY PARLOUS STATE...
alex@alexcartoon.com
BUSINESS ACTIVITY HAS COLLAPSED, CONSUMER DEMAND EVAPORATED, A DOUBLE DIP RECESSION IS ON THE CARDS...
YES AND IT'S OUR CLIENT COMPANY HARDCASTLE'S RESULTS PRESENTATION TODAY...
I KNOW. PSYCHOLOGICAL FACTORS ARE ALL-IMPORTANT IN THE BUSINESS WORLD AND THE GRIM ECONOMIC BACKGROUND IS BOUND TO HAVE AN EFFECT ON THE C.E.O.'S MOOD AND OUTLOOK...
YES...
WHAT AN IDIOT... SHOULD WE TELL HIM THAT ALL THESE ANALYSTS HAVE ONLY TURNED UP BECAUSE THEY'VE GOT NO WORK ON AND ARE DESPERATE TO LOOK BUSY TO THEIR BOSSES?
NO. LET'S JUST TAKE ALL THE CREDIT...
PRIDE

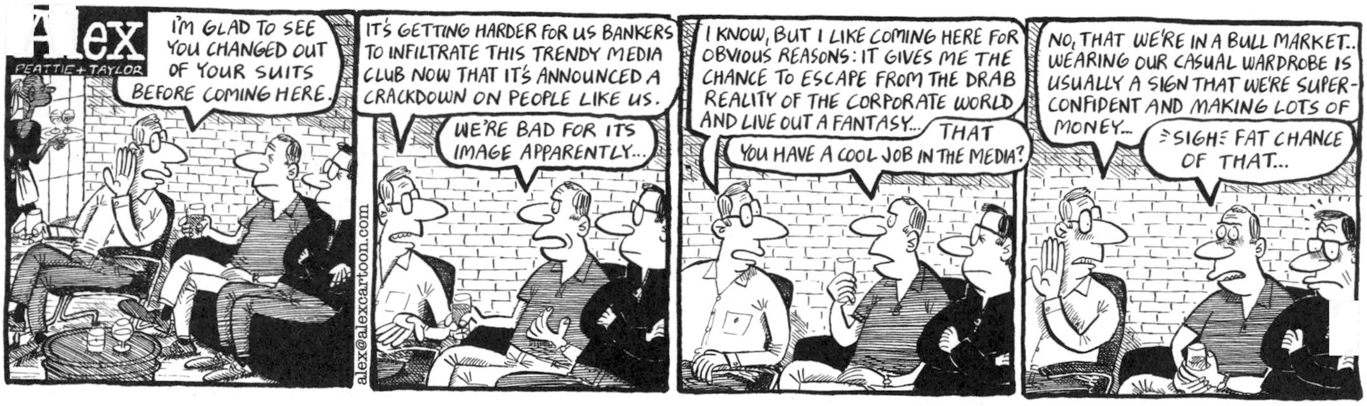
Alex
PEATTIE+TAYLOR
I'M GLAD TO SEE YOU CHANGED OUT OF YOUR SUITS BEFORE COMING HERE.
alex@alexcartoon.com
IT'S GETTING HARDER FOR US BANKERS TO INFILTRATE THIS TRENDY MEDIA CLUB NOW THAT IT'S ANNOUNCED A CRACKDOWN ON PEOPLE LIKE US.
WE'RE BAD FOR ITS IMAGE APPARENTLY...
I KNOW, BUT I LIKE COMING HERE FOR OBVIOUS REASONS: IT GIVES ME THE CHANCE TO ESCAPE FROM THE DRAB REALITY OF THE CORPORATE WORLD AND LIVE OUT A FANTASY...
THAT YOU HAVE A COOL JOB IN THE MEDIA?
NO, THAT WE'RE IN A BULL MARKET.. WEARING OUR CASUAL WARDROBE IS USUALLY A SIGN THAT WE'RE SUPER-CONFIDENT AND MAKING LOTS OF MONEY...
≡SIGH≡ FAT CHANCE OF THAT...

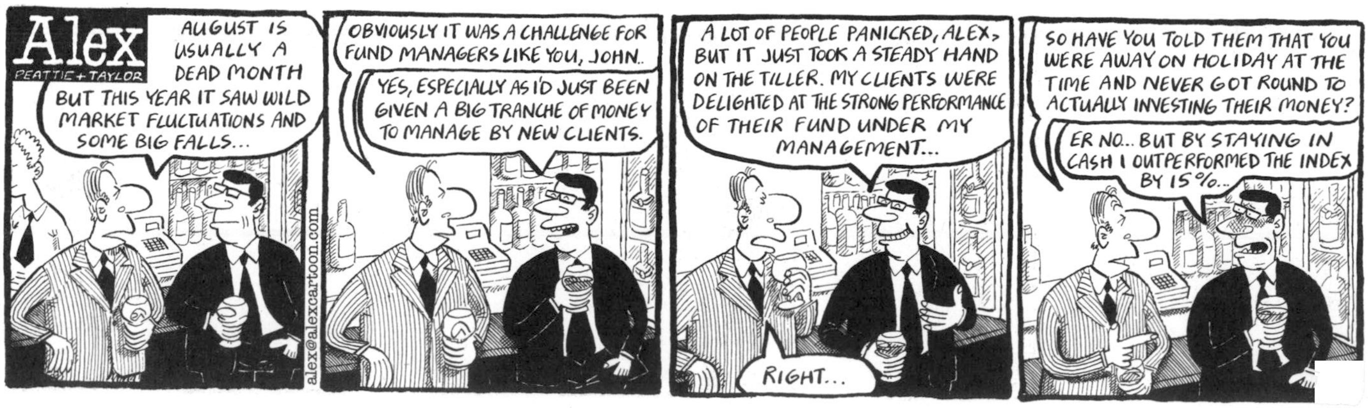
Alex
PEATTIE+TAYLOR
AUGUST IS USUALLY A DEAD MONTH BUT THIS YEAR IT SAW WILD MARKET FLUCTUATIONS AND SOME BIG FALLS...
alex@alexcartoon.com
OBVIOUSLY IT WAS A CHALLENGE FOR FUND MANAGERS LIKE YOU, JOHN..
YES, ESPECIALLY AS I'D JUST BEEN GIVEN A BIG TRANCHE OF MONEY TO MANAGE BY NEW CLIENTS.
A LOT OF PEOPLE PANICKED, ALEX, BUT IT JUST TOOK A STEADY HAND ON THE TILLER. MY CLIENTS WERE DELIGHTED AT THE STRONG PERFORMANCE OF THEIR FUND UNDER MY MANAGEMENT...
RIGHT...
SO HAVE YOU TOLD THEM THAT YOU WERE AWAY ON HOLIDAY AT THE TIME AND NEVER GOT ROUND TO ACTUALLY INVESTING THEIR MONEY?
ER NO... BUT BY STAYING IN CASH I OUTPERFORMED THE INDEX BY 15%...

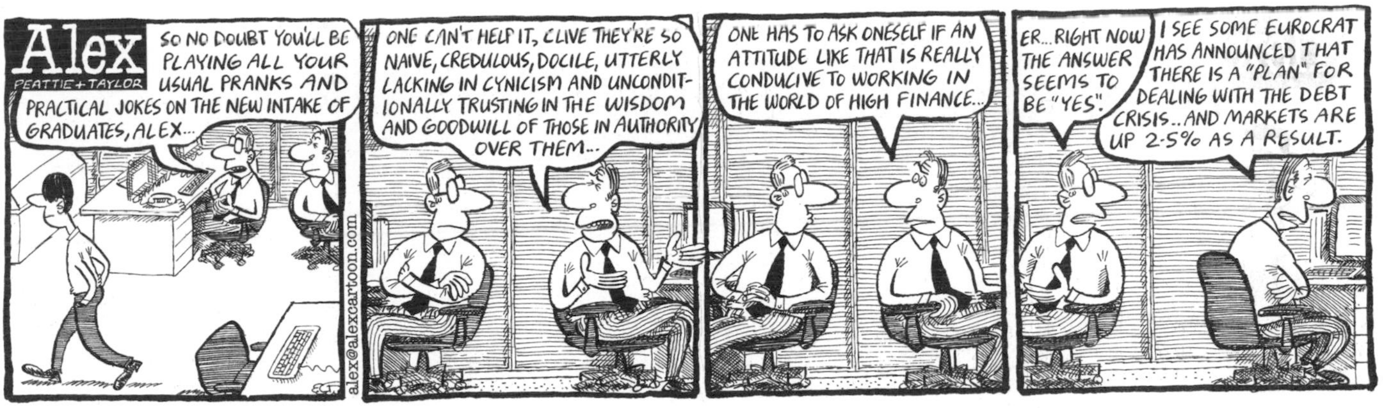
Alex
PEATTIE+TAYLOR
SO NO DOUBT YOU'LL BE PLAYING ALL YOUR USUAL PRANKS AND PRACTICAL JOKES ON THE NEW INTAKE OF GRADUATES, ALEX...
alex@alexcartoon.com
ONE CAN'T HELP IT, CLIVE THEY'RE SO NAIVE, CREDULOUS, DOCILE, UTTERLY LACKING IN CYNICISM AND UNCONDITIONALLY TRUSTING IN THE WISDOM AND GOODWILL OF THOSE IN AUTHORITY OVER THEM...
ONE HAS TO ASK ONESELF IF AN ATTITUDE LIKE THAT IS REALLY CONDUCIVE TO WORKING IN THE WORLD OF HIGH FINANCE...
ER...RIGHT NOW THE ANSWER SEEMS TO BE "YES".
I SEE SOME EUROCRAT HAS ANNOUNCED THAT THERE IS A "PLAN" FOR DEALING WITH THE DEBT CRISIS...AND MARKETS ARE UP 2·5% AS A RESULT.

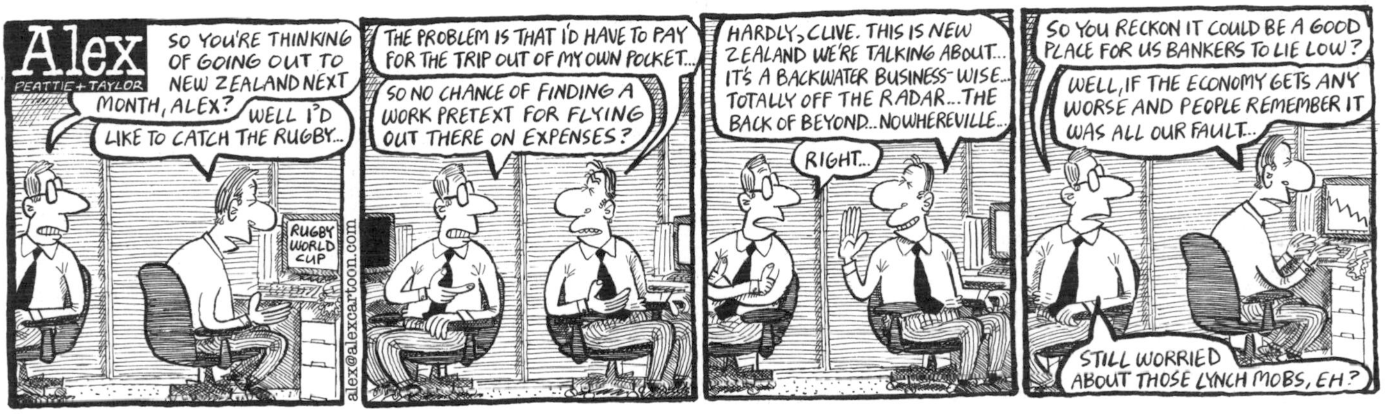
Alex
PEATTIE+TAYLOR
SO YOU'RE THINKING OF GOING OUT TO NEW ZEALAND NEXT MONTH, ALEX?
WELL I'D LIKE TO CATCH THE RUGBY...
RUGBY WORLD CUP
alex@alexcartoon.com
THE PROBLEM IS THAT I'D HAVE TO PAY FOR THE TRIP OUT OF MY OWN POCKET...
SO NO CHANCE OF FINDING A WORK PRETEXT FOR FLYING OUT THERE ON EXPENSES?
HARDLY, CLIVE. THIS IS NEW ZEALAND WE'RE TALKING ABOUT... IT'S A BACKWATER BUSINESS-WISE... TOTALLY OFF THE RADAR... THE BACK OF BEYOND...NOWHEREVILLE...
RIGHT...
SO YOU RECKON IT COULD BE A GOOD PLACE FOR US BANKERS TO LIE LOW?
WELL, IF THE ECONOMY GETS ANY WORSE AND PEOPLE REMEMBER IT WAS ALL OUR FAULT...
STILL WORRIED ABOUT THOSE LYNCH MOBS, EH?

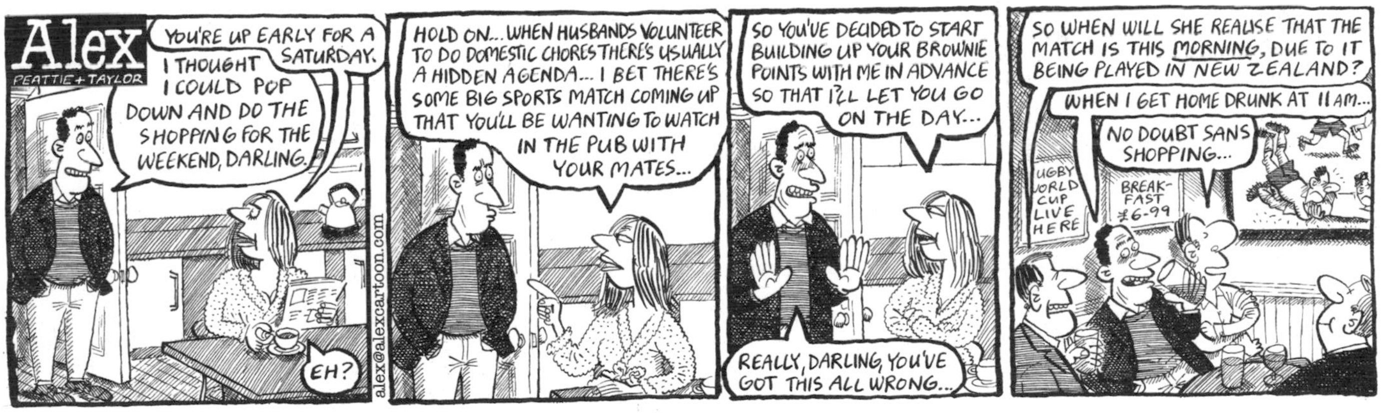
Alex
PEATTIE+TAYLOR
YOU'RE UP EARLY FOR A SATURDAY.
I THOUGHT I COULD POP DOWN AND DO THE SHOPPING FOR THE WEEKEND, DARLING.
EH?
alex@alexcartoon.com
HOLD ON... WHEN HUSBANDS VOLUNTEER TO DO DOMESTIC CHORES THERE'S USUALLY A HIDDEN AGENDA... I BET THERE'S SOME BIG SPORTS MATCH COMING UP THAT YOU'LL BE WANTING TO WATCH IN THE PUB WITH YOUR MATES...
SO YOU'VE DECIDED TO START BUILDING UP YOUR BROWNIE POINTS WITH ME IN ADVANCE SO THAT I'LL LET YOU GO ON THE DAY...
REALLY, DARLING, YOU'VE GOT THIS ALL WRONG...
SO WHEN WILL SHE REALISE THAT THE MATCH IS THIS MORNING, DUE TO IT BEING PLAYED IN NEW ZEALAND?
WHEN I GET HOME DRUNK AT 11 AM...
NO DOUBT SANS SHOPPING...
UGBY ORLD CUP LIVE HERE
BREAK-FAST £6·99

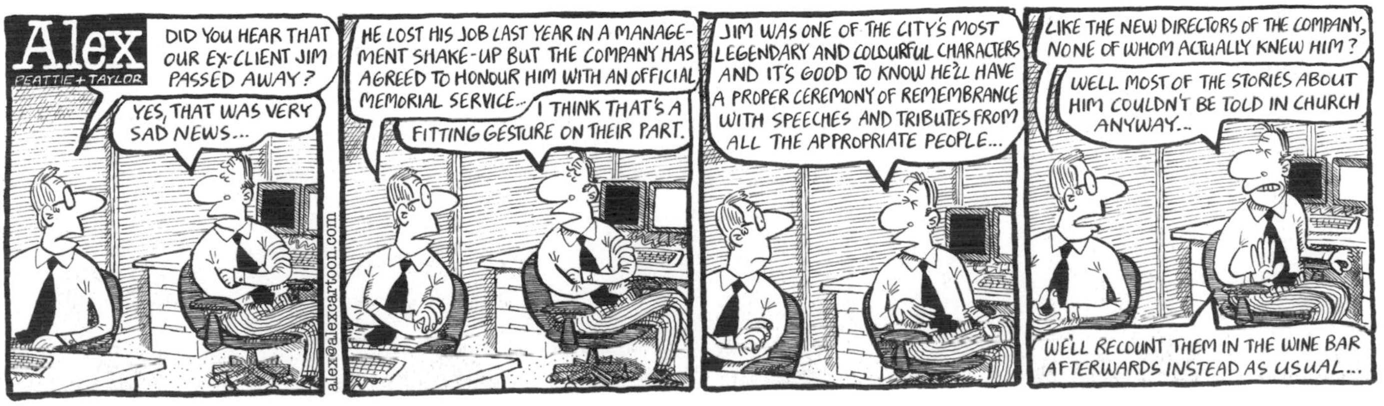
Alex
PEATTIE+TAYLOR
DID YOU HEAR THAT OUR EX-CLIENT JIM PASSED AWAY?
YES, THAT WAS VERY SAD NEWS...
alex@alexcartoon.com
HE LOST HIS JOB LAST YEAR IN A MANAGEMENT SHAKE-UP BUT THE COMPANY HAS AGREED TO HONOUR HIM WITH AN OFFICIAL MEMORIAL SERVICE...
I THINK THAT'S A FITTING GESTURE ON THEIR PART.
JIM WAS ONE OF THE CITY'S MOST LEGENDARY AND COLOURFUL CHARACTERS AND IT'S GOOD TO KNOW HE'LL HAVE A PROPER CEREMONY OF REMEMBRANCE WITH SPEECHES AND TRIBUTES FROM ALL THE APPROPRIATE PEOPLE...
LIKE THE NEW DIRECTORS OF THE COMPANY, NONE OF WHOM ACTUALLY KNEW HIM?
WELL MOST OF THE STORIES ABOUT HIM COULDN'T BE TOLD IN CHURCH ANYWAY...
WE'LL RECOUNT THEM IN THE WINE BAR AFTERWARDS INSTEAD AS USUAL...

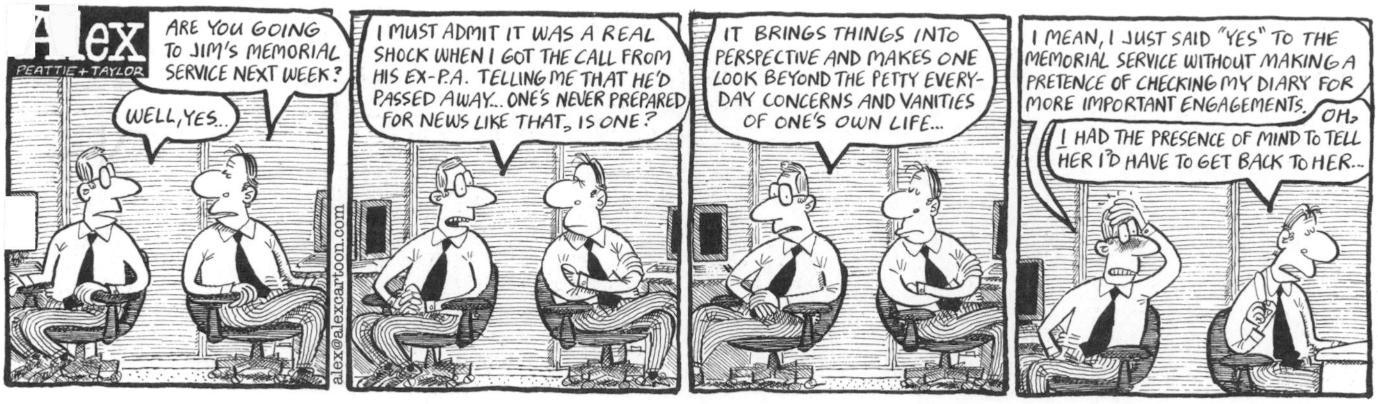
Alex
PEATTIE + TAYLOR
ARE YOU GOING TO JIM'S MEMORIAL SERVICE NEXT WEEK?
WELL, YES...
I MUST ADMIT IT WAS A REAL SHOCK WHEN I GOT THE CALL FROM HIS EX-P.A. TELLING ME THAT HE'D PASSED AWAY... ONE'S NEVER PREPARED FOR NEWS LIKE THAT, IS ONE?
alex@alexcartoon.com
IT BRINGS THINGS INTO PERSPECTIVE AND MAKES ONE LOOK BEYOND THE PETTY EVERY-DAY CONCERNS AND VANITIES OF ONE'S OWN LIFE...
I MEAN, I JUST SAID "YES" TO THE MEMORIAL SERVICE WITHOUT MAKING A PRETENCE OF CHECKING MY DIARY FOR MORE IMPORTANT ENGAGEMENTS.
OH, I HAD THE PRESENCE OF MIND TO TELL HER I'D HAVE TO GET BACK TO HER...

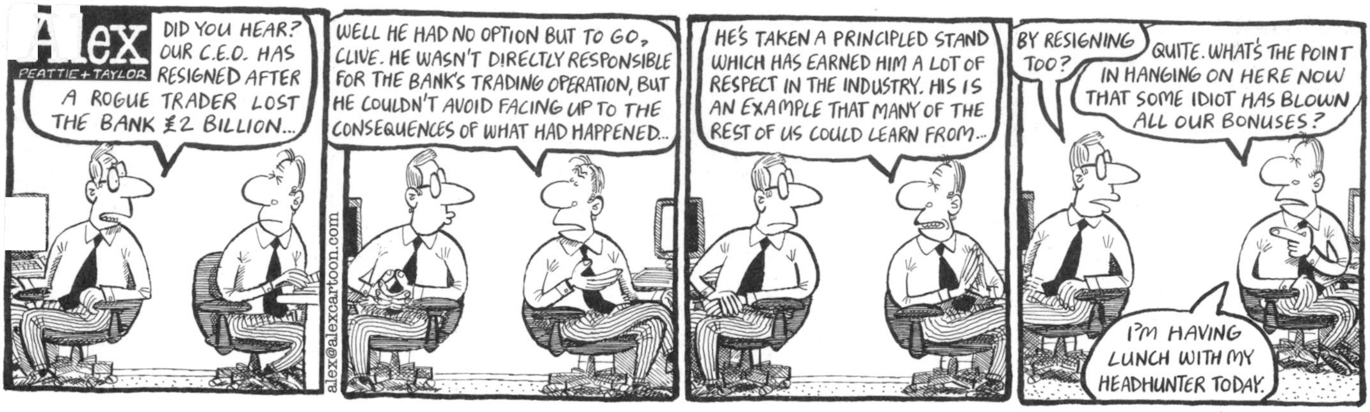
Alex
PEATTIE + TAYLOR
DID YOU HEAR? OUR C.E.O. HAS RESIGNED AFTER A ROGUE TRADER LOST THE BANK £2 BILLION...
WELL HE HAD NO OPTION BUT TO GO, CLIVE. HE WASN'T DIRECTLY RESPONSIBLE FOR THE BANK'S TRADING OPERATION, BUT HE COULDN'T AVOID FACING UP TO THE CONSEQUENCES OF WHAT HAD HAPPENED...
alex@alexcartoon.com
HE'S TAKEN A PRINCIPLED STAND WHICH HAS EARNED HIM A LOT OF RESPECT IN THE INDUSTRY. HIS IS AN EXAMPLE THAT MANY OF THE REST OF US COULD LEARN FROM...
BY RESIGNING TOO?
QUITE. WHAT'S THE POINT IN HANGING ON HERE NOW THAT SOME IDIOT HAS BLOWN ALL OUR BONUSES?
I'M HAVING LUNCH WITH MY HEADHUNTER TODAY.

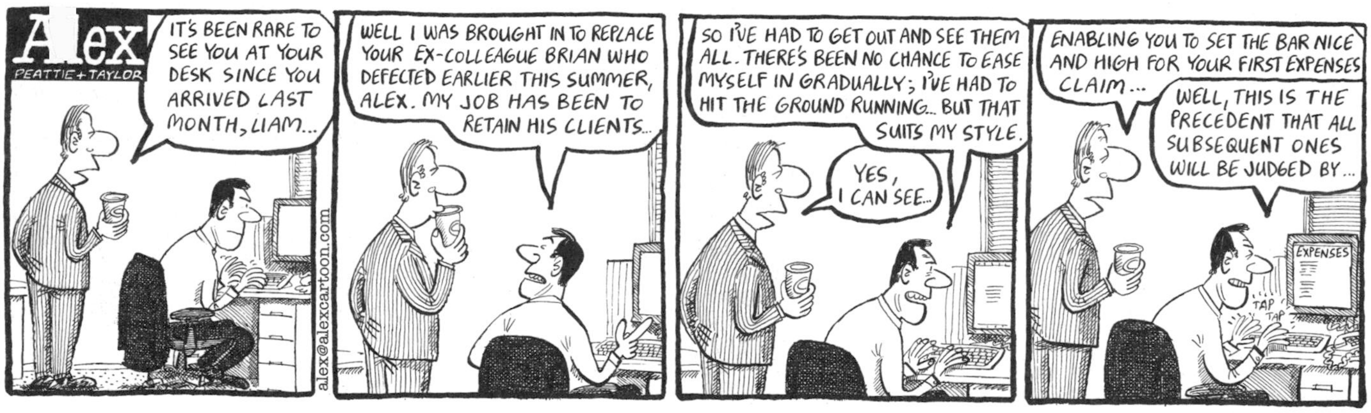
Alex
PEATTIE + TAYLOR
IT'S BEEN RARE TO SEE YOU AT YOUR DESK SINCE YOU ARRIVED LAST MONTH, LIAM...
alex@alexcartoon.com
WELL I WAS BROUGHT IN TO REPLACE YOUR EX-COLLEAGUE BRIAN WHO DEFECTED EARLIER THIS SUMMER, ALEX. MY JOB HAS BEEN TO RETAIN HIS CLIENTS...
SO I'VE HAD TO GET OUT AND SEE THEM ALL. THERE'S BEEN NO CHANCE TO EASE MYSELF IN GRADUALLY; I'VE HAD TO HIT THE GROUND RUNNING... BUT THAT SUITS MY STYLE.
YES, I CAN SEE...
ENABLING YOU TO SET THE BAR NICE AND HIGH FOR YOUR FIRST EXPENSES CLAIM...
WELL, THIS IS THE PRECEDENT THAT ALL SUBSEQUENT ONES WILL BE JUDGED BY...
EXPENSES
TAP TAP

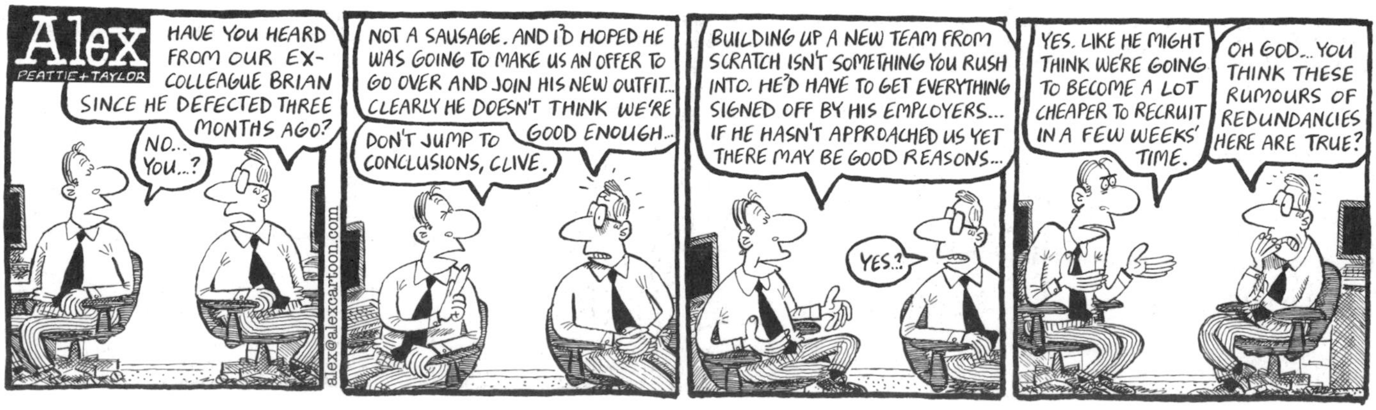
Alex
PEATTIE + TAYLOR
HAVE YOU HEARD FROM OUR EX-COLLEAGUE BRIAN SINCE HE DEFECTED THREE MONTHS AGO?
NO... YOU...?
alex@alexcartoon.com
NOT A SAUSAGE. AND I'D HOPED HE WAS GOING TO MAKE US AN OFFER TO GO OVER AND JOIN HIS NEW OUTFIT... CLEARLY HE DOESN'T THINK WE'RE GOOD ENOUGH...
DON'T JUMP TO CONCLUSIONS, CLIVE.
BUILDING UP A NEW TEAM FROM SCRATCH ISN'T SOMETHING YOU RUSH INTO. HE'D HAVE TO GET EVERYTHING SIGNED OFF BY HIS EMPLOYERS... IF HE HASN'T APPROACHED US YET THERE MAY BE GOOD REASONS...
YES..?
YES. LIKE HE MIGHT THINK WE'RE GOING TO BECOME A LOT CHEAPER TO RECRUIT IN A FEW WEEKS' TIME.
OH GOD... YOU THINK THESE RUMOURS OF REDUNDANCIES HERE ARE TRUE?

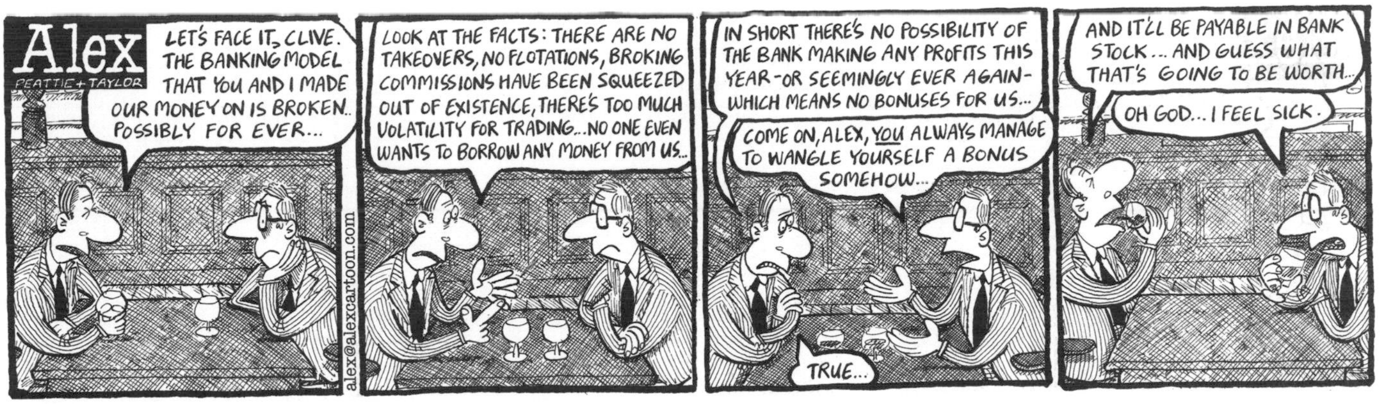
Alex
PEATTIE + TAYLOR
LET'S FACE IT, CLIVE. THE BANKING MODEL THAT YOU AND I MADE OUR MONEY ON IS BROKEN.. POSSIBLY FOR EVER...
alex@alexcartoon.com
LOOK AT THE FACTS: THERE ARE NO TAKEOVERS, NO FLOTATIONS, BROKING COMMISSIONS HAVE BEEN SQUEEZED OUT OF EXISTENCE, THERE'S TOO MUCH VOLATILITY FOR TRADING... NO ONE EVEN WANTS TO BORROW ANY MONEY FROM US...
IN SHORT THERE'S NO POSSIBILITY OF THE BANK MAKING ANY PROFITS THIS YEAR - OR SEEMINGLY EVER AGAIN - WHICH MEANS NO BONUSES FOR US...
COME ON, ALEX, YOU ALWAYS MANAGE TO WANGLE YOURSELF A BONUS SOMEHOW...
TRUE...
AND IT'LL BE PAYABLE IN BANK STOCK... AND GUESS WHAT THAT'S GOING TO BE WORTH...
OH GOD... I FEEL SICK.

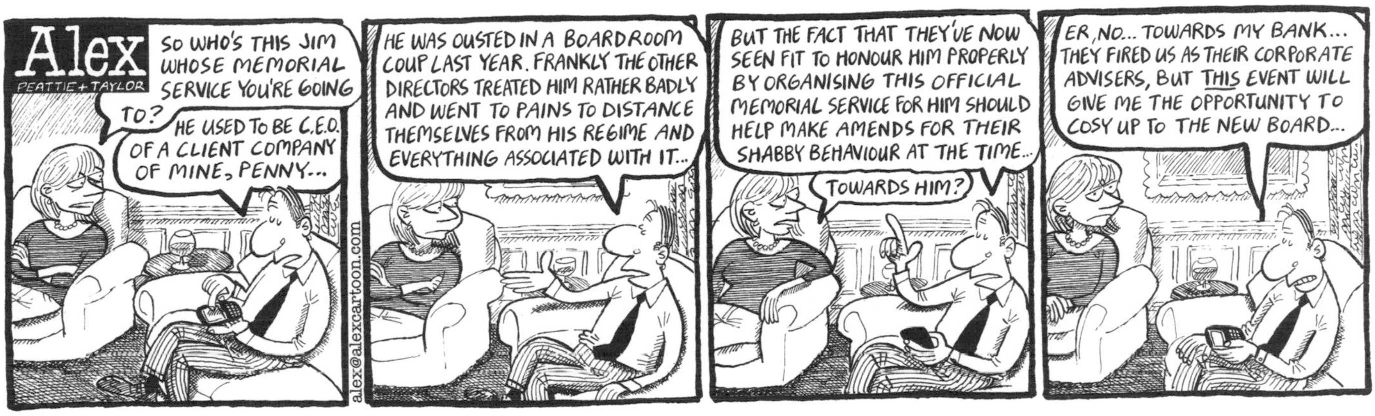
Alex
PEATTIE + TAYLOR
SO WHO'S THIS JIM WHOSE MEMORIAL SERVICE YOU'RE GOING TO?
HE USED TO BE C.E.O. OF A CLIENT COMPANY OF MINE, PENNY...
alex@alexcartoon.com
HE WAS OUSTED IN A BOARDROOM COUP LAST YEAR. FRANKLY THE OTHER DIRECTORS TREATED HIM RATHER BADLY AND WENT TO PAINS TO DISTANCE THEMSELVES FROM HIS REGIME AND EVERYTHING ASSOCIATED WITH IT...
BUT THE FACT THAT THEY'VE NOW SEEN FIT TO HONOUR HIM PROPERLY BY ORGANISING THIS OFFICIAL MEMORIAL SERVICE FOR HIM SHOULD HELP MAKE AMENDS FOR THEIR SHABBY BEHAVIOUR AT THE TIME...
TOWARDS HIM?
ER, NO... TOWARDS MY BANK... THEY FIRED US AS THEIR CORPORATE ADVISERS, BUT THIS EVENT WILL GIVE ME THE OPPORTUNITY TO COSY UP TO THE NEW BOARD...

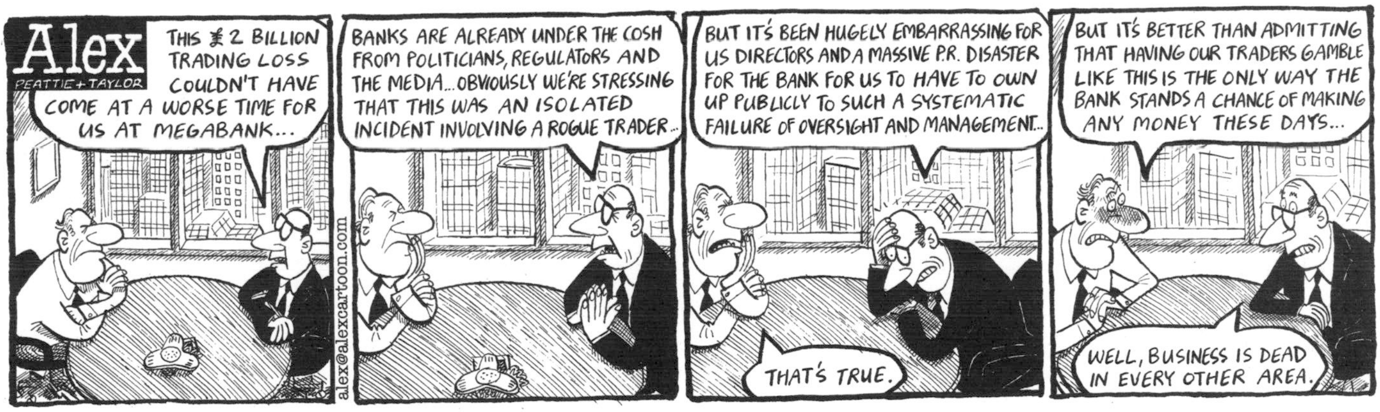
Alex
PEATTIE + TAYLOR
THIS ¥2 BILLION TRADING LOSS COULDN'T HAVE COME AT A WORSE TIME FOR US AT MEGABANK...
alex@alexcartoon.com
BANKS ARE ALREADY UNDER THE COSH FROM POLITICIANS, REGULATORS AND THE MEDIA... OBVIOUSLY WE'RE STRESSING THAT THIS WAS AN ISOLATED INCIDENT INVOLVING A ROGUE TRADER...
BUT IT'S BEEN HUGELY EMBARRASSING FOR US DIRECTORS AND A MASSIVE P.R. DISASTER FOR THE BANK FOR US TO HAVE TO OWN UP PUBLICLY TO SUCH A SYSTEMATIC FAILURE OF OVERSIGHT AND MANAGEMENT...
THAT'S TRUE.
BUT IT'S BETTER THAN ADMITTING THAT HAVING OUR TRADERS GAMBLE LIKE THIS IS THE ONLY WAY THE BANK STANDS A CHANCE OF MAKING ANY MONEY THESE DAYS...
WELL, BUSINESS IS DEAD IN EVERY OTHER AREA.

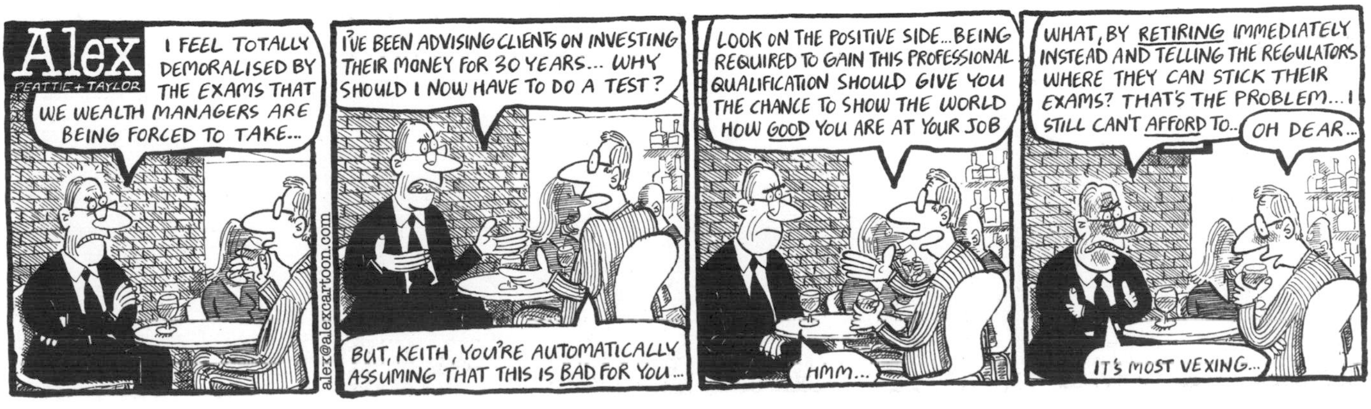
Alex
PEATTIE + TAYLOR
I FEEL TOTALLY DEMORALISED BY THE EXAMS THAT WE WEALTH MANAGERS ARE BEING FORCED TO TAKE...
alex@alexcartoon.com
I'VE BEEN ADVISING CLIENTS ON INVESTING THEIR MONEY FOR 30 YEARS... WHY SHOULD I NOW HAVE TO DO A TEST?
BUT, KEITH, YOU'RE AUTOMATICALLY ASSUMING THAT THIS IS BAD FOR YOU...
LOOK ON THE POSITIVE SIDE... BEING REQUIRED TO GAIN THIS PROFESSIONAL QUALIFICATION SHOULD GIVE YOU THE CHANCE TO SHOW THE WORLD HOW GOOD YOU ARE AT YOUR JOB
HMM...
WHAT, BY RETIRING IMMEDIATELY INSTEAD AND TELLING THE REGULATORS WHERE THEY CAN STICK THEIR EXAMS? THAT'S THE PROBLEM... I STILL CAN'T AFFORD TO...
OH DEAR...
IT'S MOST VEXING...

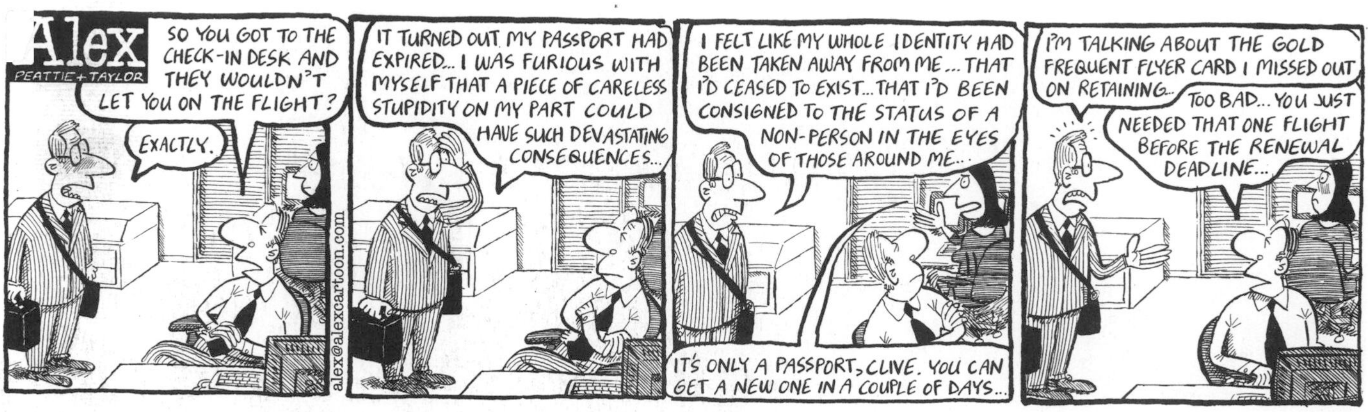
Alex
PEATTIE + TAYLOR
SO YOU GOT TO THE CHECK-IN DESK AND THEY WOULDN'T LET YOU ON THE FLIGHT?
EXACTLY.
alex@alexcartoon.com
IT TURNED OUT MY PASSPORT HAD EXPIRED... I WAS FURIOUS WITH MYSELF THAT A PIECE OF CARELESS STUPIDITY ON MY PART COULD HAVE SUCH DEVASTATING CONSEQUENCES...
I FELT LIKE MY WHOLE IDENTITY HAD BEEN TAKEN AWAY FROM ME... THAT I'D CEASED TO EXIST... THAT I'D BEEN CONSIGNED TO THE STATUS OF A NON-PERSON IN THE EYES OF THOSE AROUND ME...
IT'S ONLY A PASSPORT, CLIVE. YOU CAN GET A NEW ONE IN A COUPLE OF DAYS...
I'M TALKING ABOUT THE GOLD FREQUENT FLYER CARD I MISSED OUT ON RETAINING...
TOO BAD... YOU JUST NEEDED THAT ONE FLIGHT BEFORE THE RENEWAL DEADLINE...

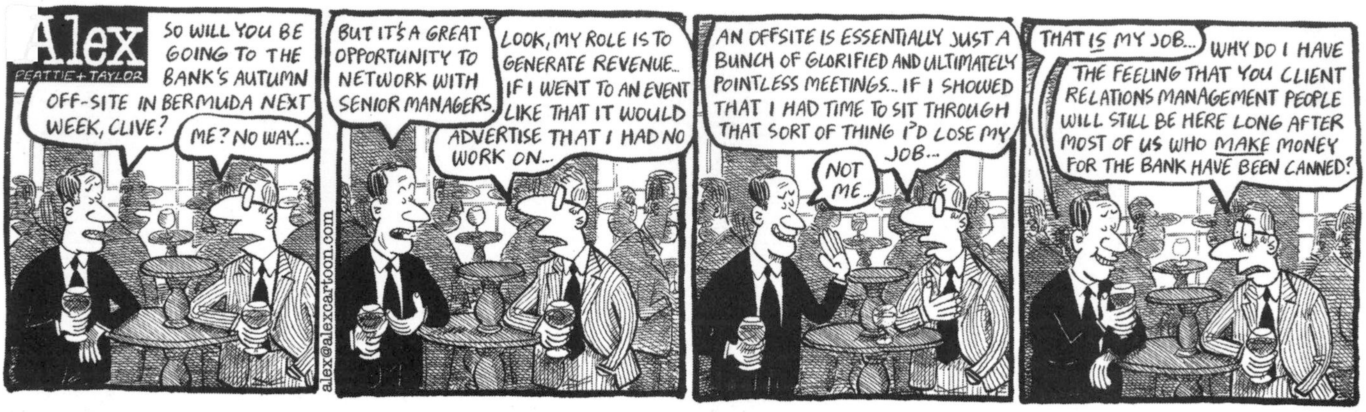
Alex
PEATTIE + TAYLOR
SO WILL YOU BE GOING TO THE BANK'S AUTUMN OFF-SITE IN BERMUDA NEXT WEEK, CLIVE?
ME? NO WAY...
alex@alexcartoon.com
BUT IT'S A GREAT OPPORTUNITY TO NETWORK WITH SENIOR MANAGERS.
LOOK, MY ROLE IS TO GENERATE REVENUE.. IF I WENT TO AN EVENT LIKE THAT IT WOULD ADVERTISE THAT I HAD NO WORK ON...
AN OFFSITE IS ESSENTIALLY JUST A BUNCH OF GLORIFIED AND ULTIMATELY POINTLESS MEETINGS... IF I SHOWED THAT I HAD TIME TO SIT THROUGH THAT SORT OF THING I'D LOSE MY JOB...
NOT ME...
THAT IS MY JOB...
WHY DO I HAVE THE FEELING THAT YOU CLIENT RELATIONS MANAGEMENT PEOPLE WILL STILL BE HERE LONG AFTER MOST OF US WHO MAKE MONEY FOR THE BANK HAVE BEEN CANNED?

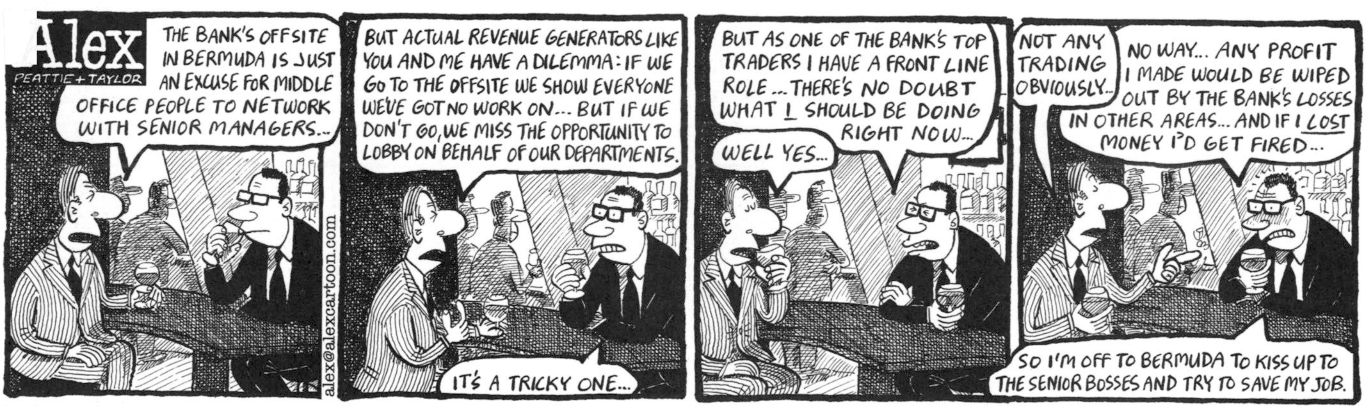
Alex
PEATTIE + TAYLOR
THE BANK'S OFFSITE IN BERMUDA IS JUST AN EXCUSE FOR MIDDLE OFFICE PEOPLE TO NETWORK WITH SENIOR MANAGERS...
alex@alexcartoon.com
BUT ACTUAL REVENUE GENERATORS LIKE YOU AND ME HAVE A DILEMMA: IF WE GO TO THE OFFSITE WE SHOW EVERYONE WE'VE GOT NO WORK ON... BUT IF WE DON'T GO, WE MISS THE OPPORTUNITY TO LOBBY ON BEHALF OF OUR DEPARTMENTS.
IT'S A TRICKY ONE...
BUT AS ONE OF THE BANK'S TOP TRADERS I HAVE A FRONT LINE ROLE... THERE'S NO DOUBT WHAT I SHOULD BE DOING RIGHT NOW...
WELL YES...
NOT ANY TRADING OBVIOUSLY...
NO WAY... ANY PROFIT I MADE WOULD BE WIPED OUT BY THE BANK'S LOSSES IN OTHER AREAS... AND IF I LOST MONEY I'D GET FIRED...
SO I'M OFF TO BERMUDA TO KISS UP TO THE SENIOR BOSSES AND TRY TO SAVE MY JOB.

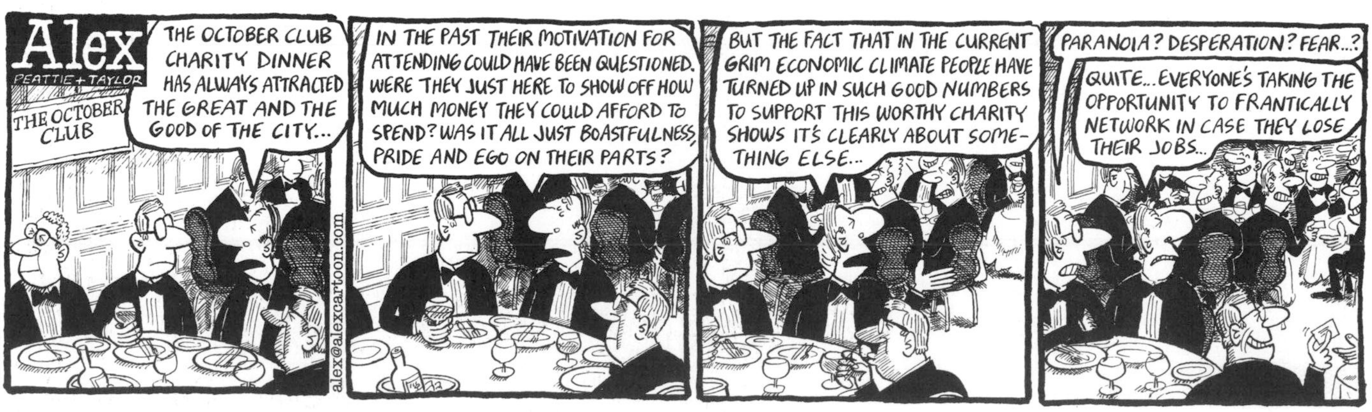
Alex
PEATTIE + TAYLOR
THE OCTOBER CLUB
THE OCTOBER CLUB CHARITY DINNER HAS ALWAYS ATTRACTED THE GREAT AND THE GOOD OF THE CITY...
alex@alexcartoon.com
IN THE PAST THEIR MOTIVATION FOR ATTENDING COULD HAVE BEEN QUESTIONED. WERE THEY JUST HERE TO SHOW OFF HOW MUCH MONEY THEY COULD AFFORD TO SPEND? WAS IT ALL JUST BOASTFULNESS, PRIDE AND EGO ON THEIR PARTS?
BUT THE FACT THAT IN THE CURRENT GRIM ECONOMIC CLIMATE PEOPLE HAVE TURNED UP IN SUCH GOOD NUMBERS TO SUPPORT THIS WORTHY CHARITY SHOWS IT'S CLEARLY ABOUT SOMETHING ELSE...
PARANOIA? DESPERATION? FEAR...?
QUITE... EVERYONE'S TAKING THE OPPORTUNITY TO FRANTICALLY NETWORK IN CASE THEY LOSE THEIR JOBS...

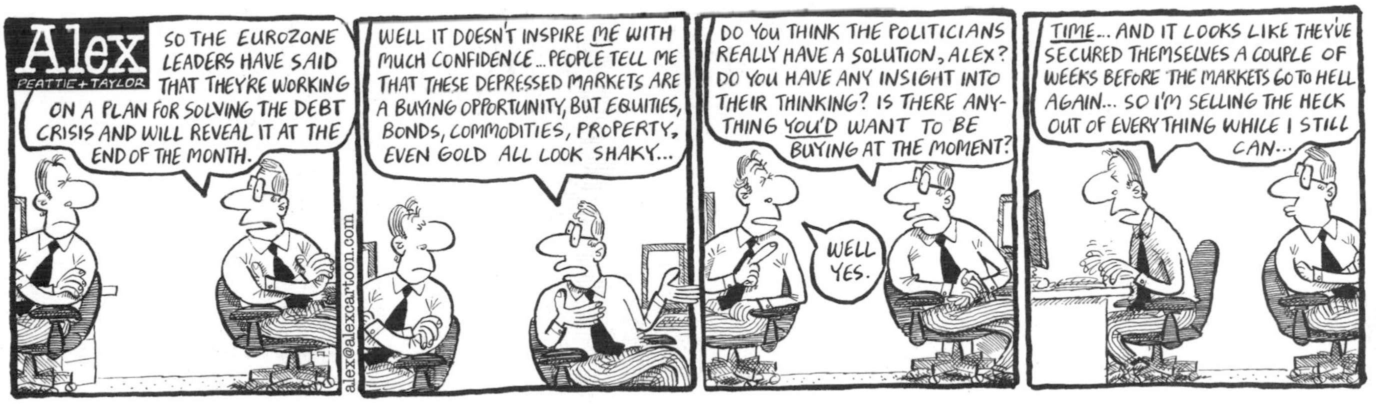
Alex
PEATTIE + TAYLOR
SO THE EUROZONE LEADERS HAVE SAID THAT THEY'RE WORKING ON A PLAN FOR SOLVING THE DEBT CRISIS AND WILL REVEAL IT AT THE END OF THE MONTH.
alex@alexcartoon.com
WELL IT DOESN'T INSPIRE ME WITH MUCH CONFIDENCE... PEOPLE TELL ME THAT THESE DEPRESSED MARKETS ARE A BUYING OPPORTUNITY, BUT EQUITIES, BONDS, COMMODITIES, PROPERTY, EVEN GOLD ALL LOOK SHAKY...
DO YOU THINK THE POLITICIANS REALLY HAVE A SOLUTION, ALEX? DO YOU HAVE ANY INSIGHT INTO THEIR THINKING? IS THERE ANYTHING YOU'D WANT TO BE BUYING AT THE MOMENT?
WELL YES.
TIME... AND IT LOOKS LIKE THEY'VE SECURED THEMSELVES A COUPLE OF WEEKS BEFORE THE MARKETS GO TO HELL AGAIN... SO I'M SELLING THE HECK OUT OF EVERYTHING WHILE I STILL CAN...

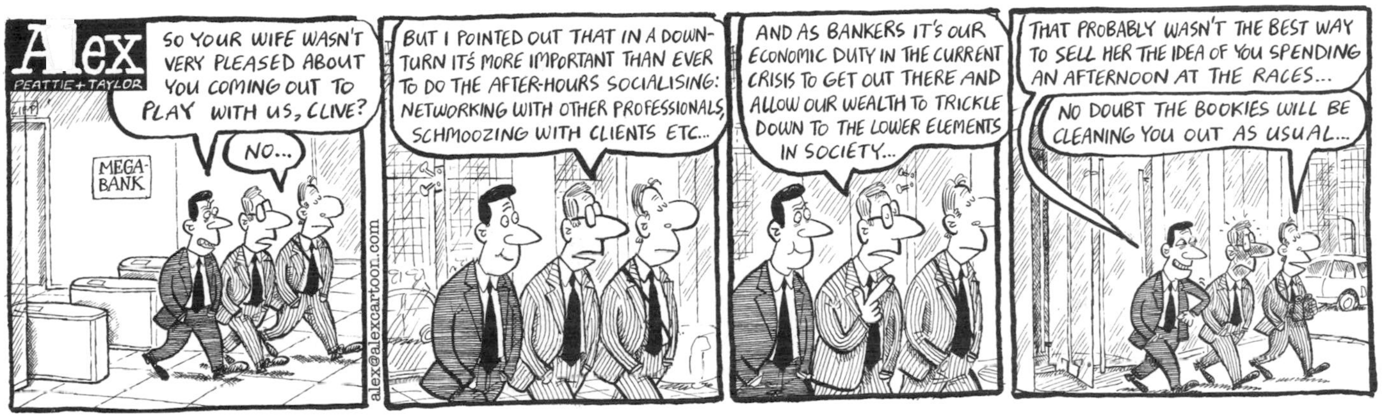
Alex
PEATTIE + TAYLOR
SO YOUR WIFE WASN'T VERY PLEASED ABOUT YOU COMING OUT TO PLAY WITH US, CLIVE?
NO...
MEGA-BANK
alex@alexcartoon.com
BUT I POINTED OUT THAT IN A DOWNTURN IT'S MORE IMPORTANT THAN EVER TO DO THE AFTER-HOURS SOCIALISING: NETWORKING WITH OTHER PROFESSIONALS, SCHMOOZING WITH CLIENTS ETC...
AND AS BANKERS IT'S OUR ECONOMIC DUTY IN THE CURRENT CRISIS TO GET OUT THERE AND ALLOW OUR WEALTH TO TRICKLE DOWN TO THE LOWER ELEMENTS IN SOCIETY...
THAT PROBABLY WASN'T THE BEST WAY TO SELL HER THE IDEA OF YOU SPENDING AN AFTERNOON AT THE RACES...
NO DOUBT THE BOOKIES WILL BE CLEANING YOU OUT AS USUAL...

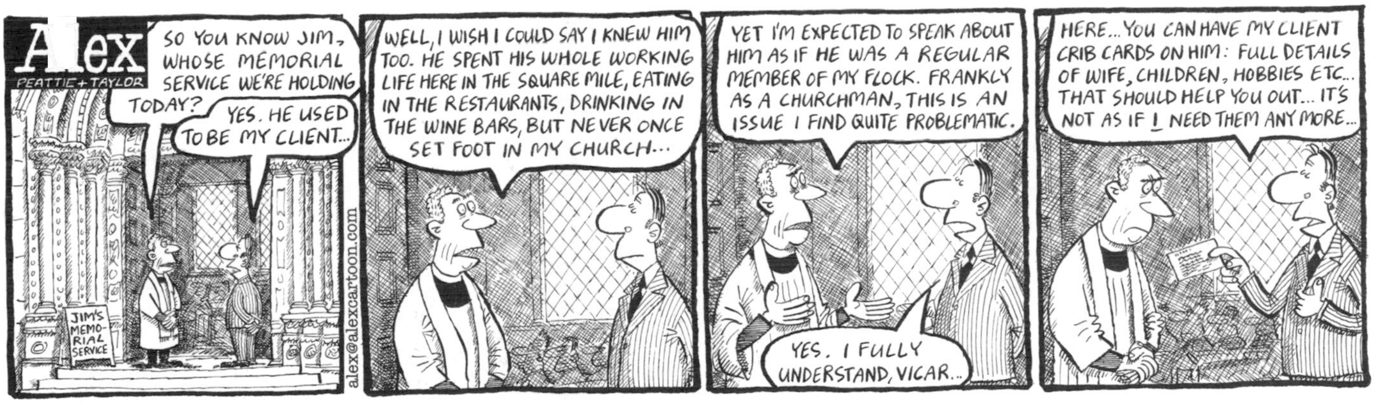
Alex
PEATTIE + TAYLOR
SO YOU KNOW JIM, WHOSE MEMORIAL SERVICE WE'RE HOLDING TODAY?
YES. HE USED TO BE MY CLIENT...
JIM'S MEMORIAL SERVICE
alex@alexcartoon.com
WELL, I WISH I COULD SAY I KNEW HIM TOO. HE SPENT HIS WHOLE WORKING LIFE HERE IN THE SQUARE MILE, EATING IN THE RESTAURANTS, DRINKING IN THE WINE BARS, BUT NEVER ONCE SET FOOT IN MY CHURCH...
YET I'M EXPECTED TO SPEAK ABOUT HIM AS IF HE WAS A REGULAR MEMBER OF MY FLOCK. FRANKLY AS A CHURCHMAN, THIS IS AN ISSUE I FIND QUITE PROBLEMATIC.
YES. I FULLY UNDERSTAND, VICAR...
HERE... YOU CAN HAVE MY CLIENT CRIB CARDS ON HIM: FULL DETAILS OF WIFE, CHILDREN, HOBBIES ETC... THAT SHOULD HELP YOU OUT... IT'S NOT AS IF I NEED THEM ANY MORE...

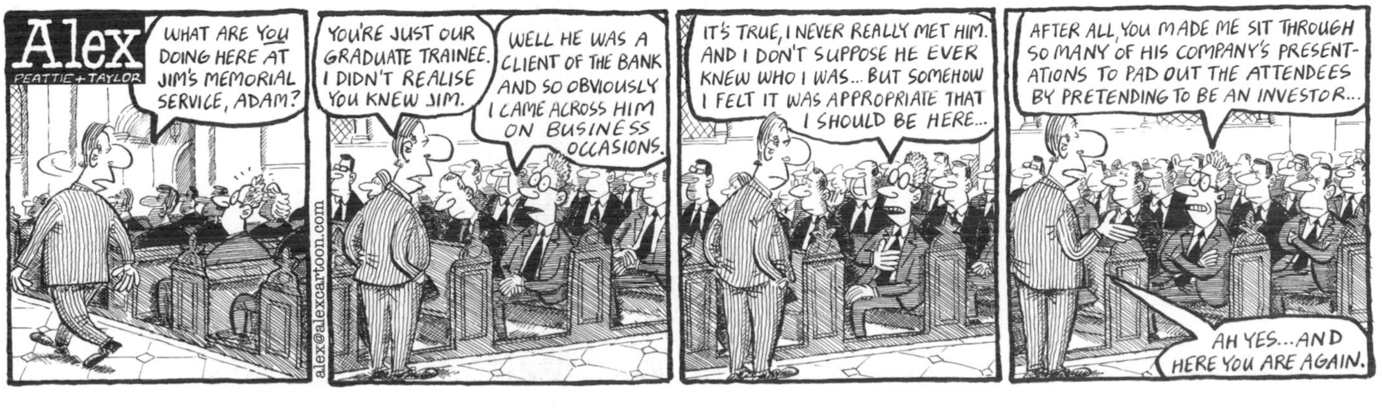
Alex
PEATTIE + TAYLOR
WHAT ARE YOU DOING HERE AT JIM'S MEMORIAL SERVICE, ADAM?
alex@alexcartoon.com
YOU'RE JUST OUR GRADUATE TRAINEE. I DIDN'T REALISE YOU KNEW JIM.
WELL HE WAS A CLIENT OF THE BANK AND SO OBVIOUSLY I CAME ACROSS HIM ON BUSINESS OCCASIONS.
IT'S TRUE, I NEVER REALLY MET HIM. AND I DON'T SUPPOSE HE EVER KNEW WHO I WAS... BUT SOMEHOW I FELT IT WAS APPROPRIATE THAT I SHOULD BE HERE...
AFTER ALL, YOU MADE ME SIT THROUGH SO MANY OF HIS COMPANY'S PRESENTATIONS TO PAD OUT THE ATTENDEES BY PRETENDING TO BE AN INVESTOR...
AH YES... AND HERE YOU ARE AGAIN.

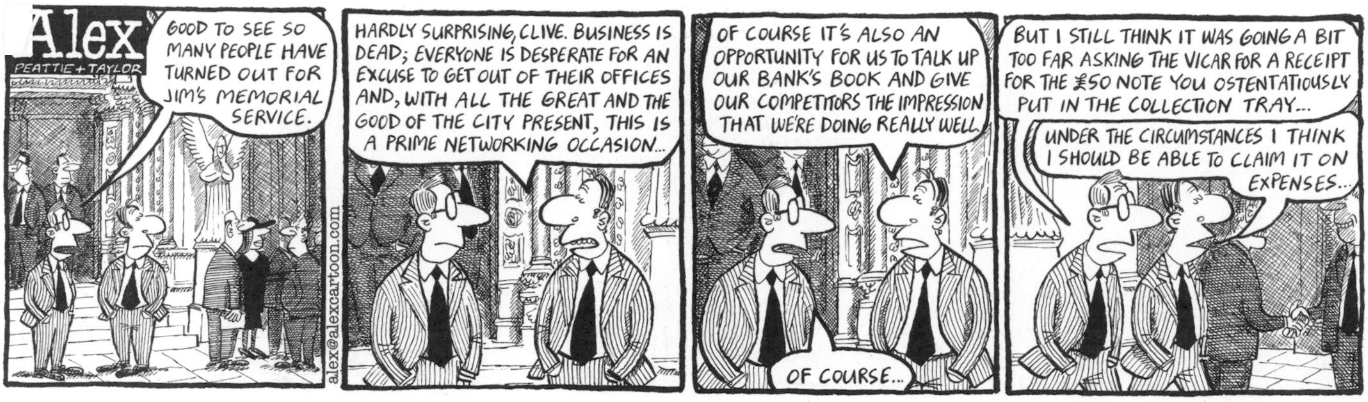
Alex
PEATTIE + TAYLOR
GOOD TO SEE SO MANY PEOPLE HAVE TURNED OUT FOR JIM'S MEMORIAL SERVICE.
alex@alexcartoon.com
HARDLY SURPRISING, CLIVE. BUSINESS IS DEAD; EVERYONE IS DESPERATE FOR AN EXCUSE TO GET OUT OF THEIR OFFICES AND, WITH ALL THE GREAT AND THE GOOD OF THE CITY PRESENT, THIS IS A PRIME NETWORKING OCCASION...
OF COURSE IT'S ALSO AN OPPORTUNITY FOR US TO TALK UP OUR BANK'S BOOK AND GIVE OUR COMPETITORS THE IMPRESSION THAT WE'RE DOING REALLY WELL.
OF COURSE...
BUT I STILL THINK IT WAS GOING A BIT TOO FAR ASKING THE VICAR FOR A RECEIPT FOR THE £50 NOTE YOU OSTENTATIOUSLY PUT IN THE COLLECTION TRAY...
UNDER THE CIRCUMSTANCES I THINK I SHOULD BE ABLE TO CLAIM IT ON EXPENSES...

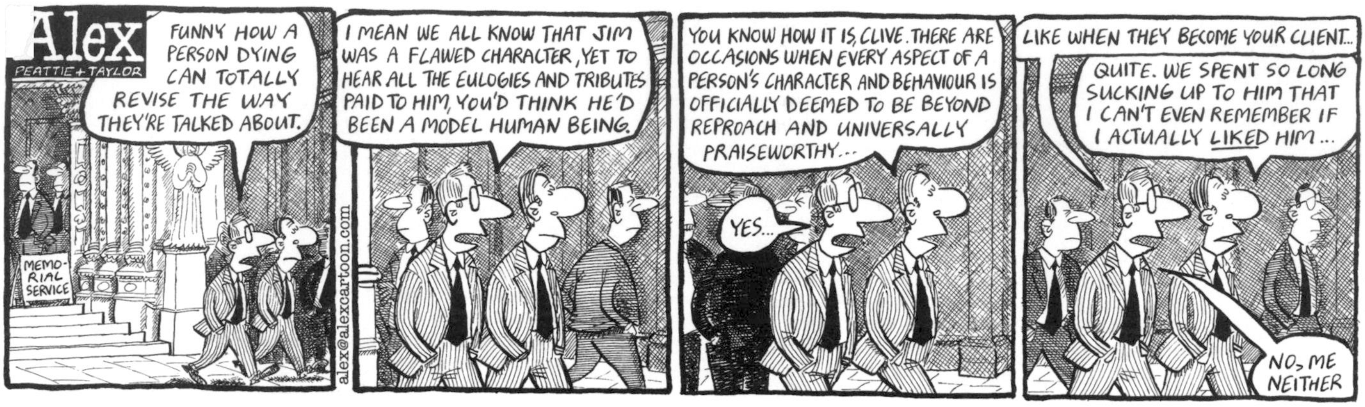
Alex
PEATTIE + TAYLOR
FUNNY HOW A PERSON DYING CAN TOTALLY REVISE THE WAY THEY'RE TALKED ABOUT.
MEMO-RIAL SERVICE
alex@alexcartoon.com
I MEAN WE ALL KNOW THAT JIM WAS A FLAWED CHARACTER, YET TO HEAR ALL THE EULOGIES AND TRIBUTES PAID TO HIM, YOU'D THINK HE'D BEEN A MODEL HUMAN BEING.
YOU KNOW HOW IT IS, CLIVE. THERE ARE OCCASIONS WHEN EVERY ASPECT OF A PERSON'S CHARACTER AND BEHAVIOUR IS OFFICIALLY DEEMED TO BE BEYOND REPROACH AND UNIVERSALLY PRAISEWORTHY...
YES...
LIKE WHEN THEY BECOME YOUR CLIENT...
QUITE. WE SPENT SO LONG SUCKING UP TO HIM THAT I CAN'T EVEN REMEMBER IF I ACTUALLY LIKED HIM...
NO, ME NEITHER

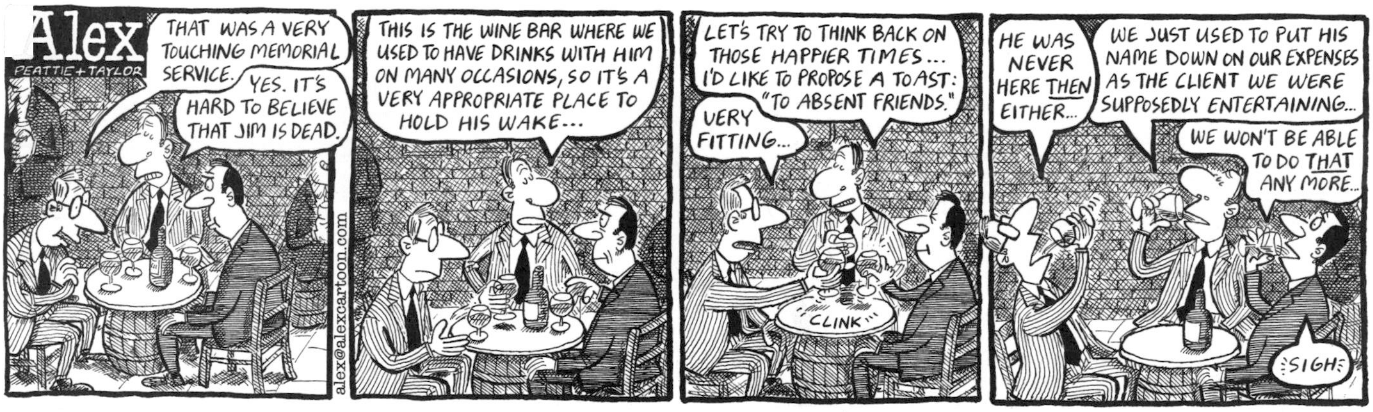
Alex
PEATTIE + TAYLOR
THAT WAS A VERY TOUCHING MEMORIAL SERVICE.
YES. IT'S HARD TO BELIEVE THAT JIM IS DEAD.
alex@alexcartoon.com
THIS IS THE WINE BAR WHERE WE USED TO HAVE DRINKS WITH HIM ON MANY OCCASIONS, SO IT'S A VERY APPROPRIATE PLACE TO HOLD HIS WAKE...
LET'S TRY TO THINK BACK ON THOSE HAPPIER TIMES... I'D LIKE TO PROPOSE A TOAST: "TO ABSENT FRIENDS."
VERY FITTING...
CLINK
HE WAS NEVER HERE THEN EITHER...
WE JUST USED TO PUT HIS NAME DOWN ON OUR EXPENSES AS THE CLIENT WE WERE SUPPOSEDLY ENTERTAINING...
WE WON'T BE ABLE TO DO THAT ANY MORE...
SIGH

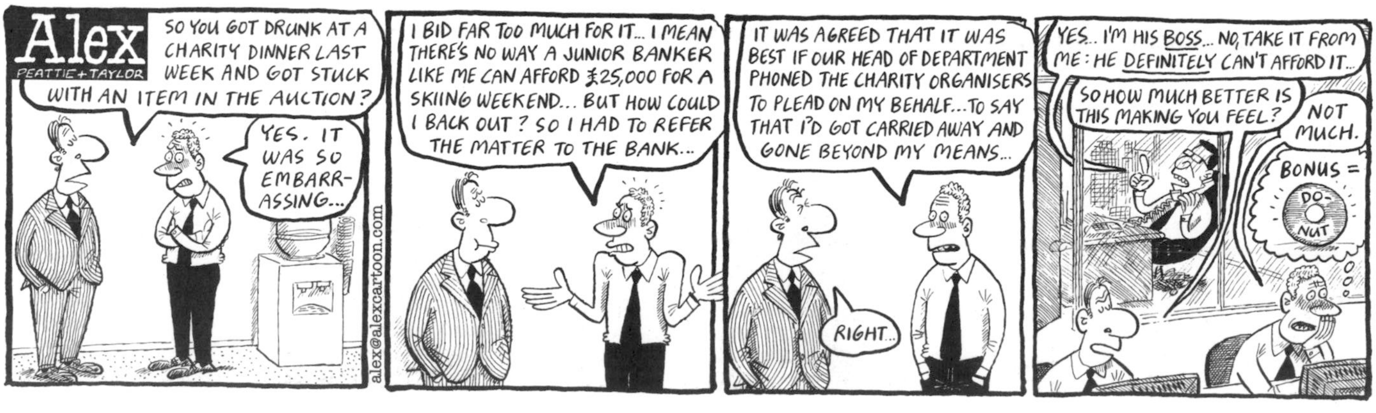
Alex
PEATTIE + TAYLOR
SO YOU GOT DRUNK AT A CHARITY DINNER LAST WEEK AND GOT STUCK WITH AN ITEM IN THE AUCTION?
YES. IT WAS SO EMBARR-ASSING...
alex@alexcartoon.com
I BID FAR TOO MUCH FOR IT... I MEAN THERE'S NO WAY A JUNIOR BANKER LIKE ME CAN AFFORD £25,000 FOR A SKIING WEEKEND... BUT HOW COULD I BACK OUT? SO I HAD TO REFER THE MATTER TO THE BANK...
IT WAS AGREED THAT IT WAS BEST IF OUR HEAD OF DEPARTMENT PHONED THE CHARITY ORGANISERS TO PLEAD ON MY BEHALF... TO SAY THAT I'D GOT CARRIED AWAY AND GONE BEYOND MY MEANS...
RIGHT...
YES... I'M HIS BOSS... NO, TAKE IT FROM ME: HE DEFINITELY CAN'T AFFORD IT...
SO HOW MUCH BETTER IS THIS MAKING YOU FEEL?
NOT MUCH.
BONUS = DO-NUT

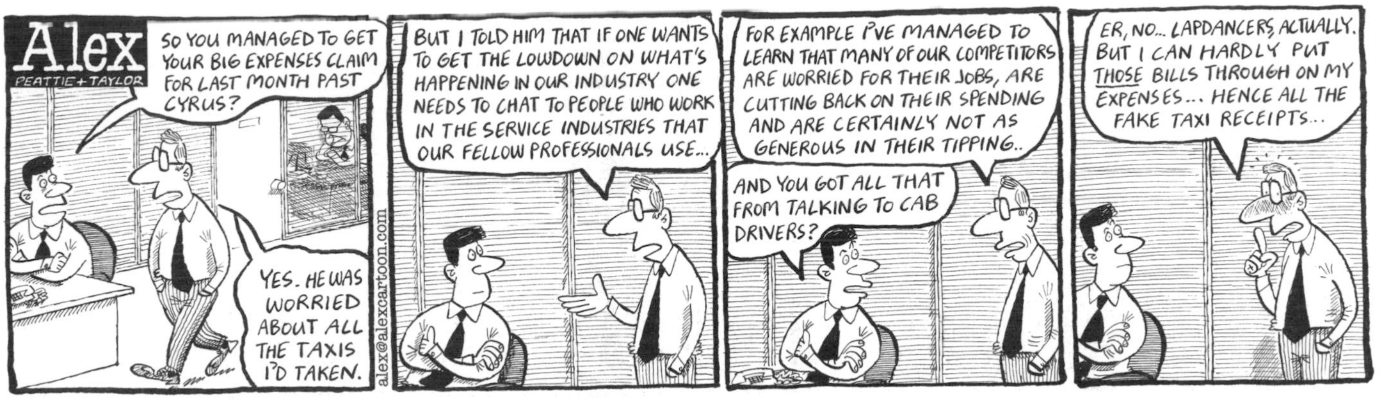
Alex
PEATTIE + TAYLOR
SO YOU MANAGED TO GET YOUR BIG EXPENSES CLAIM FOR LAST MONTH PAST CYRUS?
YES. HE WAS WORRIED ABOUT ALL THE TAXIS I'D TAKEN.
alex@alexcartoon.com
BUT I TOLD HIM THAT IF ONE WANTS TO GET THE LOWDOWN ON WHAT'S HAPPENING IN OUR INDUSTRY ONE NEEDS TO CHAT TO PEOPLE WHO WORK IN THE SERVICE INDUSTRIES THAT OUR FELLOW PROFESSIONALS USE...
FOR EXAMPLE I'VE MANAGED TO LEARN THAT MANY OF OUR COMPETITORS ARE WORRIED FOR THEIR JOBS, ARE CUTTING BACK ON THEIR SPENDING AND ARE CERTAINLY NOT AS GENEROUS IN THEIR TIPPING..
AND YOU GOT ALL THAT FROM TALKING TO CAB DRIVERS?
ER, NO... LAPDANCERS ACTUALLY. BUT I CAN HARDLY PUT THOSE BILLS THROUGH ON MY EXPENSES... HENCE ALL THE FAKE TAXI RECEIPTS...

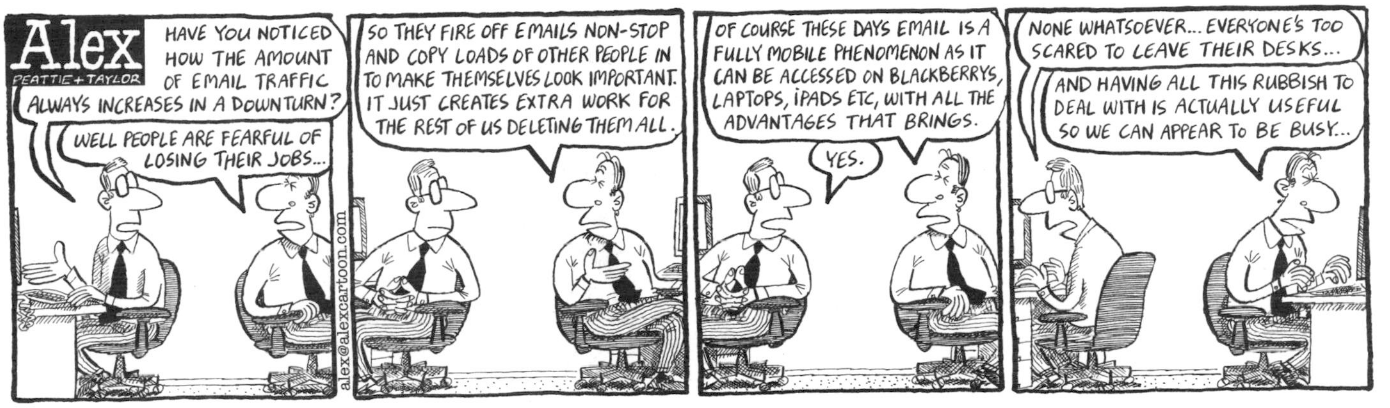
Alex
PEATTIE + TAYLOR
HAVE YOU NOTICED HOW THE AMOUNT OF EMAIL TRAFFIC ALWAYS INCREASES IN A DOWNTURN?
WELL PEOPLE ARE FEARFUL OF LOSING THEIR JOBS...
alex@alexcartoon.com
SO THEY FIRE OFF EMAILS NON-STOP AND COPY LOADS OF OTHER PEOPLE IN TO MAKE THEMSELVES LOOK IMPORTANT. IT JUST CREATES EXTRA WORK FOR THE REST OF US DELETING THEM ALL.
OF COURSE THESE DAYS EMAIL IS A FULLY MOBILE PHENOMENON AS IT CAN BE ACCESSED ON BLACKBERRYS, LAPTOPS, IPADS ETC, WITH ALL THE ADVANTAGES THAT BRINGS.
YES.
NONE WHATSOEVER... EVERYONE'S TOO SCARED TO LEAVE THEIR DESKS...
AND HAVING ALL THIS RUBBISH TO DEAL WITH IS ACTUALLY USEFUL SO WE CAN APPEAR TO BE BUSY...

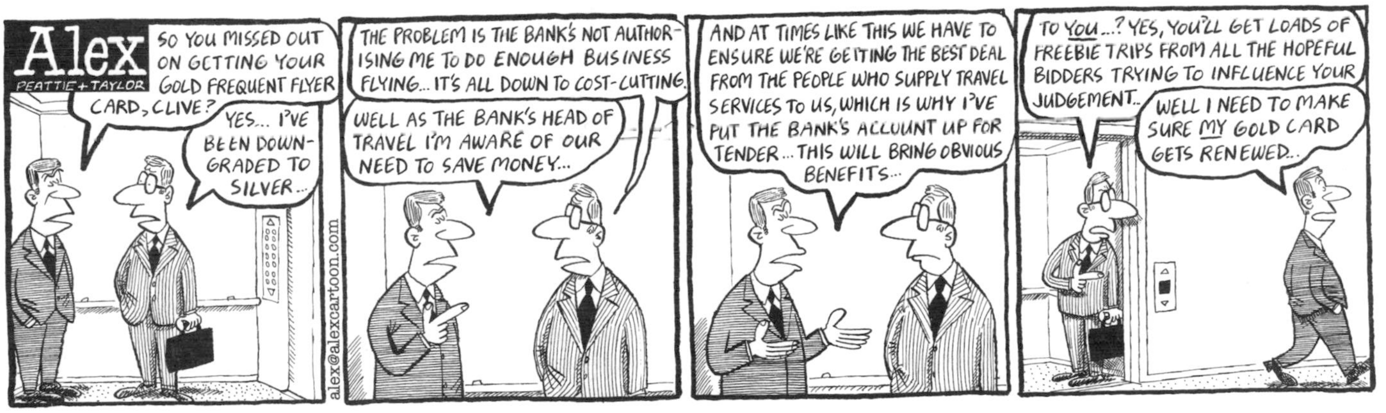
Alex
PEATTIE + TAYLOR
SO YOU MISSED OUT ON GETTING YOUR GOLD FREQUENT FLYER CARD, CLIVE?
YES... I'VE BEEN DOWN-GRADED TO SILVER...
alex@alexcartoon.com
THE PROBLEM IS THE BANK'S NOT AUTHOR-ISING ME TO DO ENOUGH BUSINESS FLYING... IT'S ALL DOWN TO COST-CUTTING.
WELL AS THE BANK'S HEAD OF TRAVEL I'M AWARE OF OUR NEED TO SAVE MONEY...
AND AT TIMES LIKE THIS WE HAVE TO ENSURE WE'RE GETTING THE BEST DEAL FROM THE PEOPLE WHO SUPPLY TRAVEL SERVICES TO US, WHICH IS WHY I'VE PUT THE BANK'S ACCOUNT UP FOR TENDER... THIS WILL BRING OBVIOUS BENEFITS...
TO YOU...? YES, YOU'LL GET LOADS OF FREEBIE TRIPS FROM ALL THE HOPEFUL BIDDERS TRYING TO INFLUENCE YOUR JUDGEMENT...
WELL I NEED TO MAKE SURE MY GOLD CARD GETS RENEWED...

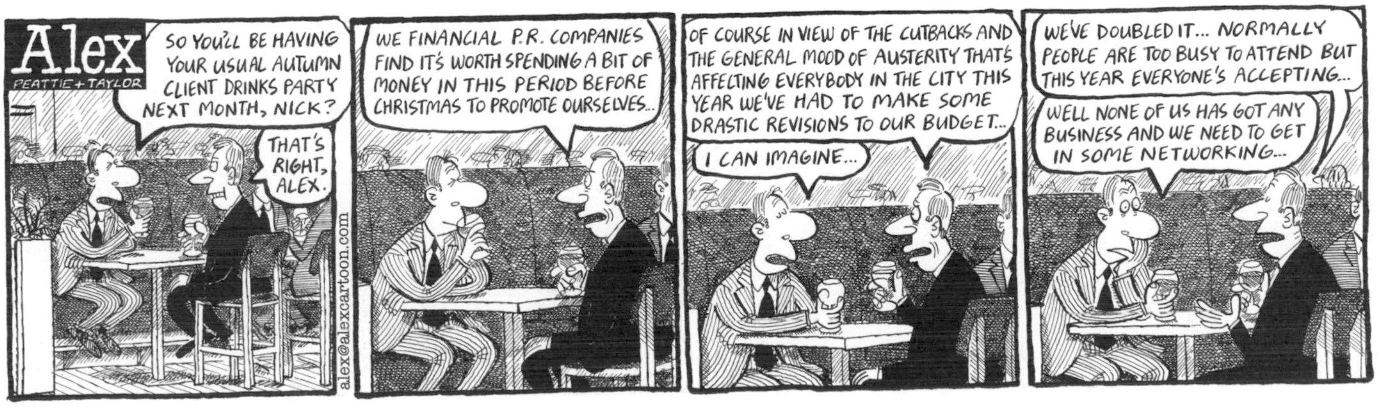
Alex
PEATTIE + TAYLOR
SO YOU'LL BE HAVING YOUR USUAL AUTUMN CLIENT DRINKS PARTY NEXT MONTH, NICK?
THAT'S RIGHT, ALEX.
alex@alexcartoon.com
WE FINANCIAL P.R. COMPANIES FIND IT'S WORTH SPENDING A BIT OF MONEY IN THIS PERIOD BEFORE CHRISTMAS TO PROMOTE OURSELVES...
OF COURSE IN VIEW OF THE CUTBACKS AND THE GENERAL MOOD OF AUSTERITY THAT'S AFFECTING EVERYBODY IN THE CITY THIS YEAR WE'VE HAD TO MAKE SOME DRASTIC REVISIONS TO OUR BUDGET...
I CAN IMAGINE...
WE'VE DOUBLED IT... NORMALLY PEOPLE ARE TOO BUSY TO ATTEND BUT THIS YEAR EVERYONE'S ACCEPTING...
WELL NONE OF US HAS GOT ANY BUSINESS AND WE NEED TO GET IN SOME NETWORKING...

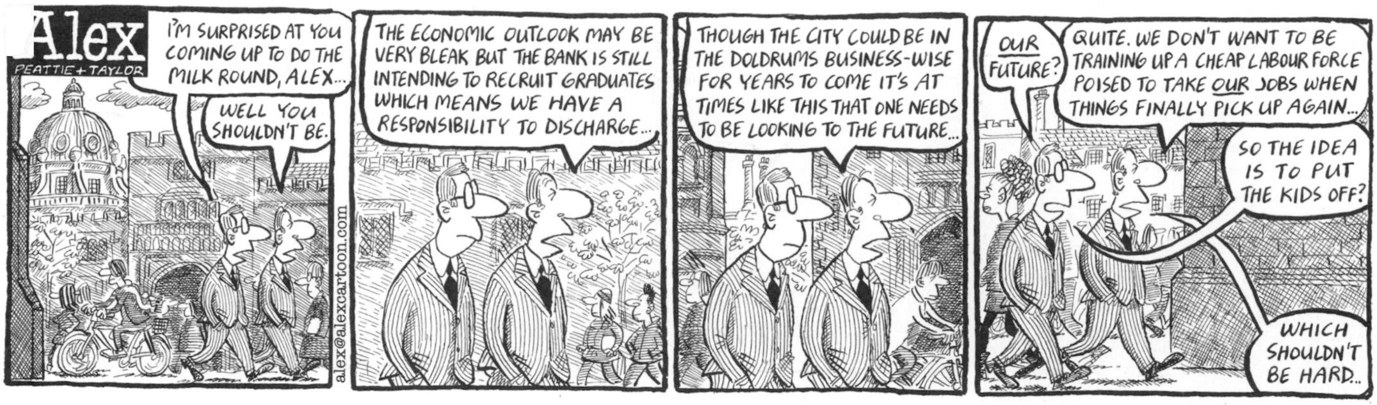
Alex
PEATTIE+TAYLOR
I'M SURPRISED AT YOU COMING UP TO DO THE MILK ROUND, ALEX...
WELL YOU SHOULDN'T BE.
alex@alexcartoon.com
THE ECONOMIC OUTLOOK MAY BE VERY BLEAK BUT THE BANK IS STILL INTENDING TO RECRUIT GRADUATES WHICH MEANS WE HAVE A RESPONSIBILITY TO DISCHARGE...
THOUGH THE CITY COULD BE IN THE DOLDRUMS BUSINESS-WISE FOR YEARS TO COME IT'S AT TIMES LIKE THIS THAT ONE NEEDS TO BE LOOKING TO THE FUTURE...
OUR FUTURE?
QUITE. WE DON'T WANT TO BE TRAINING UP A CHEAP LABOUR FORCE POISED TO TAKE OUR JOBS WHEN THINGS FINALLY PICK UP AGAIN...
SO THE IDEA IS TO PUT THE KIDS OFF?
WHICH SHOULDN'T BE HARD...

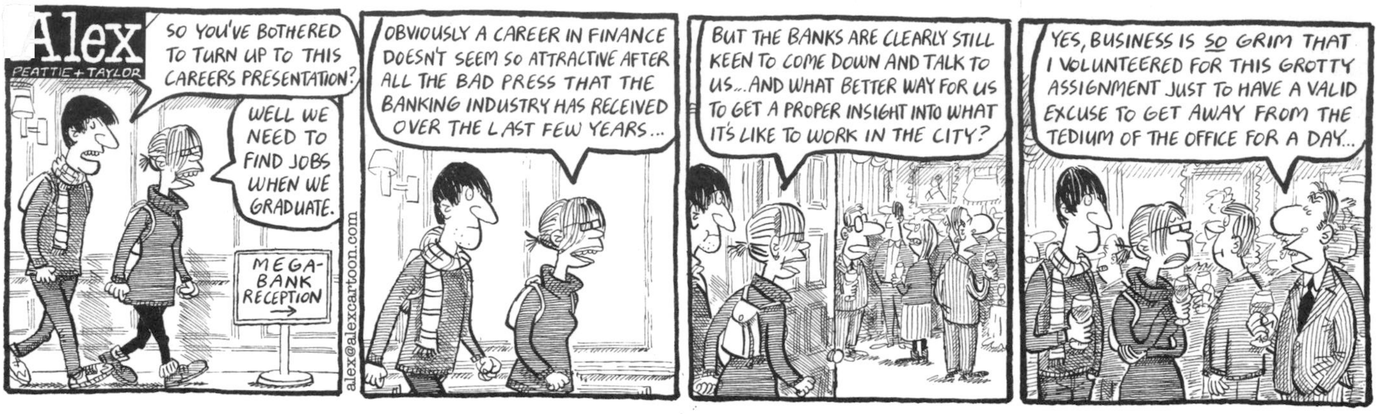
Alex
PEATTIE+TAYLOR
SO YOU'VE BOTHERED TO TURN UP TO THIS CAREERS PRESENTATION?
WELL WE NEED TO FIND JOBS WHEN WE GRADUATE.
MEGA-BANK RECEPTION →
alex@alexcartoon.com
OBVIOUSLY A CAREER IN FINANCE DOESN'T SEEM SO ATTRACTIVE AFTER ALL THE BAD PRESS THAT THE BANKING INDUSTRY HAS RECEIVED OVER THE LAST FEW YEARS...
BUT THE BANKS ARE CLEARLY STILL KEEN TO COME DOWN AND TALK TO US...AND WHAT BETTER WAY FOR US TO GET A PROPER INSIGHT INTO WHAT IT'S LIKE TO WORK IN THE CITY?
YES, BUSINESS IS SO GRIM THAT I VOLUNTEERED FOR THIS GROTTY ASSIGNMENT JUST TO HAVE A VALID EXCUSE TO GET AWAY FROM THE TEDIUM OF THE OFFICE FOR A DAY...

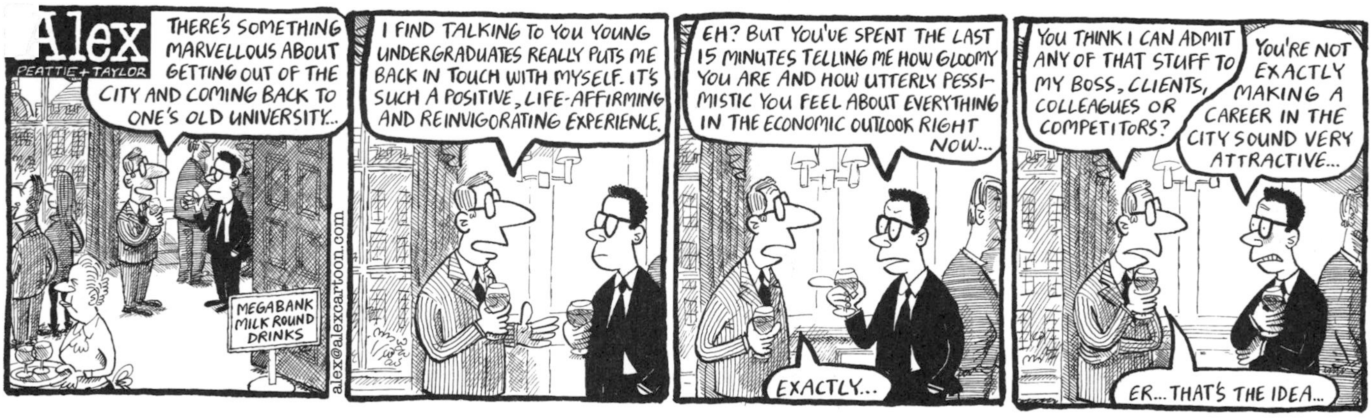
Alex
PEATTIE+TAYLOR
THERE'S SOMETHING MARVELLOUS ABOUT GETTING OUT OF THE CITY AND COMING BACK TO ONE'S OLD UNIVERSITY...
MEGABANK MILK ROUND DRINKS
alex@alexcartoon.com
I FIND TALKING TO YOU YOUNG UNDERGRADUATES REALLY PUTS ME BACK IN TOUCH WITH MYSELF. IT'S SUCH A POSITIVE, LIFE-AFFIRMING AND REINVIGORATING EXPERIENCE.
EH? BUT YOU'VE SPENT THE LAST 15 MINUTES TELLING ME HOW GLOOMY YOU ARE AND HOW UTTERLY PESSIMISTIC YOU FEEL ABOUT EVERYTHING IN THE ECONOMIC OUTLOOK RIGHT NOW...
EXACTLY...
YOU THINK I CAN ADMIT ANY OF THAT STUFF TO MY BOSS, CLIENTS, COLLEAGUES OR COMPETITORS?
YOU'RE NOT EXACTLY MAKING A CAREER IN THE CITY SOUND VERY ATTRACTIVE...
ER... THAT'S THE IDEA...

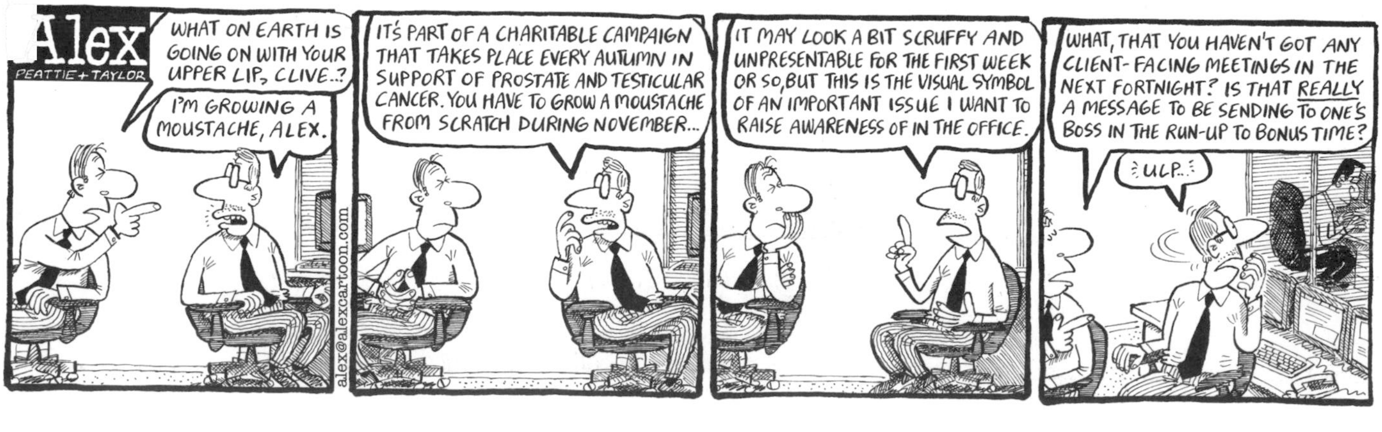
Alex
PEATTIE+TAYLOR
WHAT ON EARTH IS GOING ON WITH YOUR UPPER LIP, CLIVE..?
I'M GROWING A MOUSTACHE, ALEX.
alex@alexcartoon.com
IT'S PART OF A CHARITABLE CAMPAIGN THAT TAKES PLACE EVERY AUTUMN IN SUPPORT OF PROSTATE AND TESTICULAR CANCER. YOU HAVE TO GROW A MOUSTACHE FROM SCRATCH DURING NOVEMBER...
IT MAY LOOK A BIT SCRUFFY AND UNPRESENTABLE FOR THE FIRST WEEK OR SO, BUT THIS IS THE VISUAL SYMBOL OF AN IMPORTANT ISSUE I WANT TO RAISE AWARENESS OF IN THE OFFICE.
WHAT, THAT YOU HAVEN'T GOT ANY CLIENT-FACING MEETINGS IN THE NEXT FORTNIGHT? IS THAT REALLY A MESSAGE TO BE SENDING TO ONE'S BOSS IN THE RUN-UP TO BONUS TIME?
ULP...

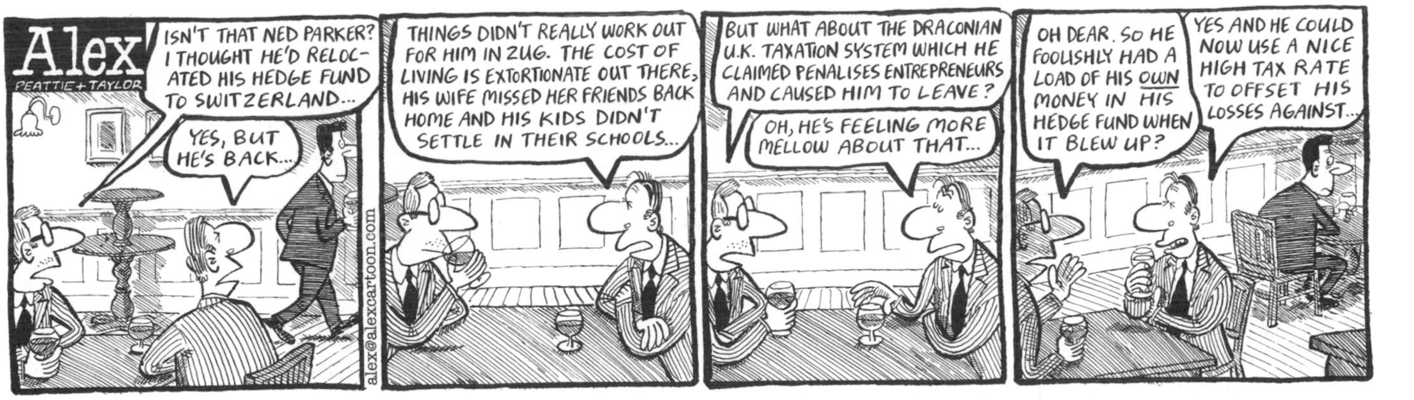
Alex
PEATTIE + TAYLOR
ISN'T THAT NED PARKER? I THOUGHT HE'D RELOCATED HIS HEDGE FUND TO SWITZERLAND...
YES, BUT HE'S BACK...
alex@alexcartoon.com
THINGS DIDN'T REALLY WORK OUT FOR HIM IN ZUG. THE COST OF LIVING IS EXTORTIONATE OUT THERE, HIS WIFE MISSED HER FRIENDS BACK HOME AND HIS KIDS DIDN'T SETTLE IN THEIR SCHOOLS...
BUT WHAT ABOUT THE DRACONIAN U.K. TAXATION SYSTEM WHICH HE CLAIMED PENALISES ENTREPRENEURS AND CAUSED HIM TO LEAVE?
OH, HE'S FEELING MORE MELLOW ABOUT THAT...
OH DEAR. SO HE FOOLISHLY HAD A LOAD OF HIS OWN MONEY IN HIS HEDGE FUND WHEN IT BLEW UP?
YES AND HE COULD NOW USE A NICE HIGH TAX RATE TO OFFSET HIS LOSSES AGAINST...

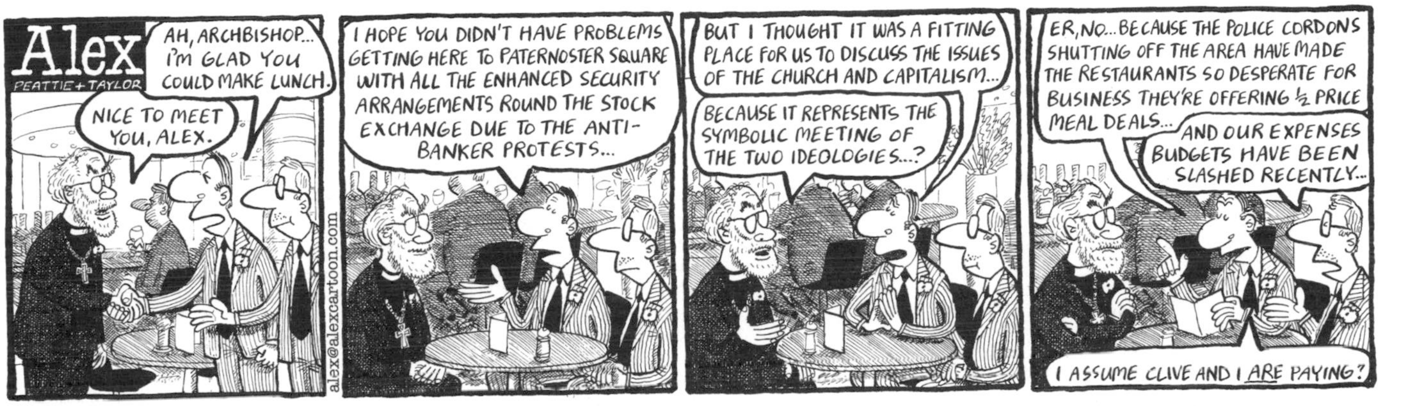
Alex
PEATTIE + TAYLOR
AH, ARCHBISHOP... I'M GLAD YOU COULD MAKE LUNCH.
NICE TO MEET YOU, ALEX.
alex@alexcartoon.com
I HOPE YOU DIDN'T HAVE PROBLEMS GETTING HERE TO PATERNOSTER SQUARE WITH ALL THE ENHANCED SECURITY ARRANGEMENTS ROUND THE STOCK EXCHANGE DUE TO THE ANTI-BANKER PROTESTS...
BUT I THOUGHT IT WAS A FITTING PLACE FOR US TO DISCUSS THE ISSUES OF THE CHURCH AND CAPITALISM...
BECAUSE IT REPRESENTS THE SYMBOLIC MEETING OF THE TWO IDEOLOGIES...?
ER, NO... BECAUSE THE POLICE CORDONS SHUTTING OFF THE AREA HAVE MADE THE RESTAURANTS SO DESPERATE FOR BUSINESS THEY'RE OFFERING ½ PRICE MEAL DEALS...
AND OUR EXPENSES BUDGETS HAVE BEEN SLASHED RECENTLY...
I ASSUME CLIVE AND I ARE PAYING?

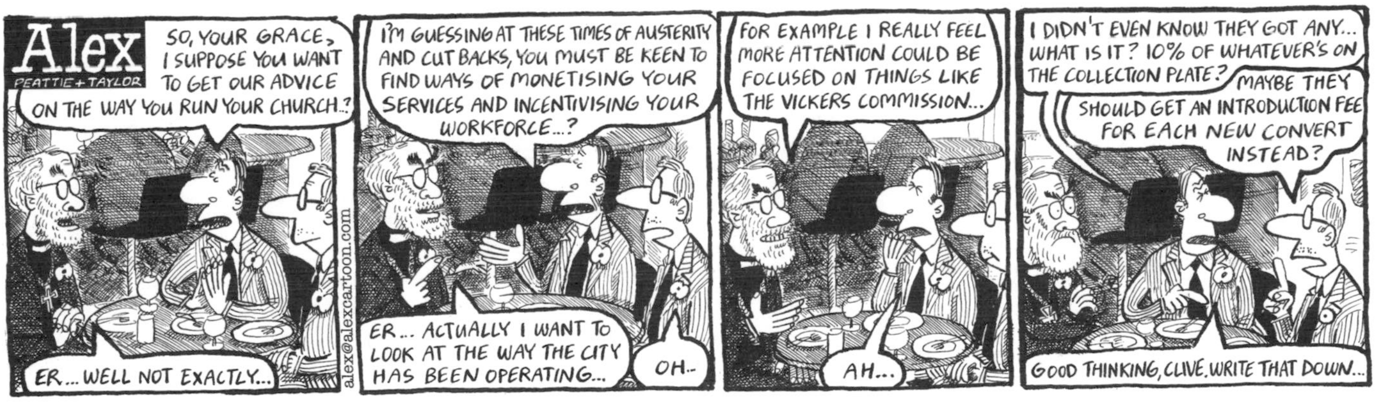
Alex
PEATTIE + TAYLOR
SO, YOUR GRACE, I SUPPOSE YOU WANT TO GET OUR ADVICE ON THE WAY YOU RUN YOUR CHURCH..?
ER... WELL NOT EXACTLY...
alex@alexcartoon.com
I'M GUESSING AT THESE TIMES OF AUSTERITY AND CUT BACKS, YOU MUST BE KEEN TO FIND WAYS OF MONETISING YOUR SERVICES AND INCENTIVISING YOUR WORKFORCE...?
ER... ACTUALLY I WANT TO LOOK AT THE WAY THE CITY HAS BEEN OPERATING...
OH..
FOR EXAMPLE I REALLY FEEL MORE ATTENTION COULD BE FOCUSED ON THINGS LIKE THE VICKERS COMMISSION...
AH...
I DIDN'T EVEN KNOW THEY GOT ANY... WHAT IS IT? 10% OF WHATEVER'S ON THE COLLECTION PLATE?
MAYBE THEY SHOULD GET AN INTRODUCTION FEE FOR EACH NEW CONVERT INSTEAD?
GOOD THINKING, CLIVE. WRITE THAT DOWN...

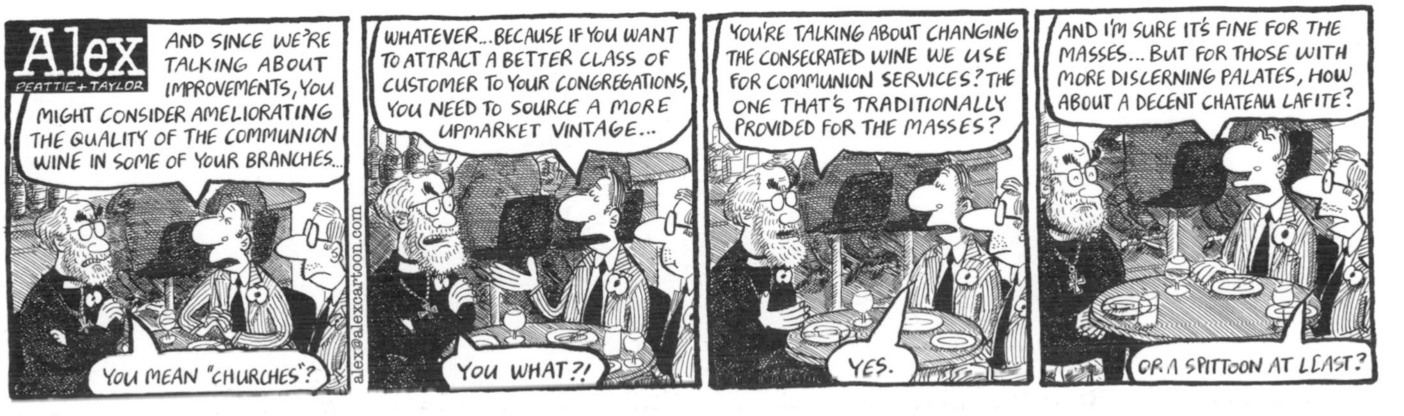
Alex
PEATTIE + TAYLOR
AND SINCE WE'RE TALKING ABOUT IMPROVEMENTS, YOU MIGHT CONSIDER AMELIORATING THE QUALITY OF THE COMMUNION WINE IN SOME OF YOUR BRANCHES...
YOU MEAN "CHURCHES"?
alex@alexcartoon.com
WHATEVER... BECAUSE IF YOU WANT TO ATTRACT A BETTER CLASS OF CUSTOMER TO YOUR CONGREGATIONS, YOU NEED TO SOURCE A MORE UPMARKET VINTAGE...
YOU WHAT?!
YOU'RE TALKING ABOUT CHANGING THE CONSECRATED WINE WE USE FOR COMMUNION SERVICES? THE ONE THAT'S TRADITIONALLY PROVIDED FOR THE MASSES?
YES.
AND I'M SURE IT'S FINE FOR THE MASSES... BUT FOR THOSE WITH MORE DISCERNING PALATES, HOW ABOUT A DECENT CHATEAU LAFITE?
OR A SPITTOON AT LEAST?

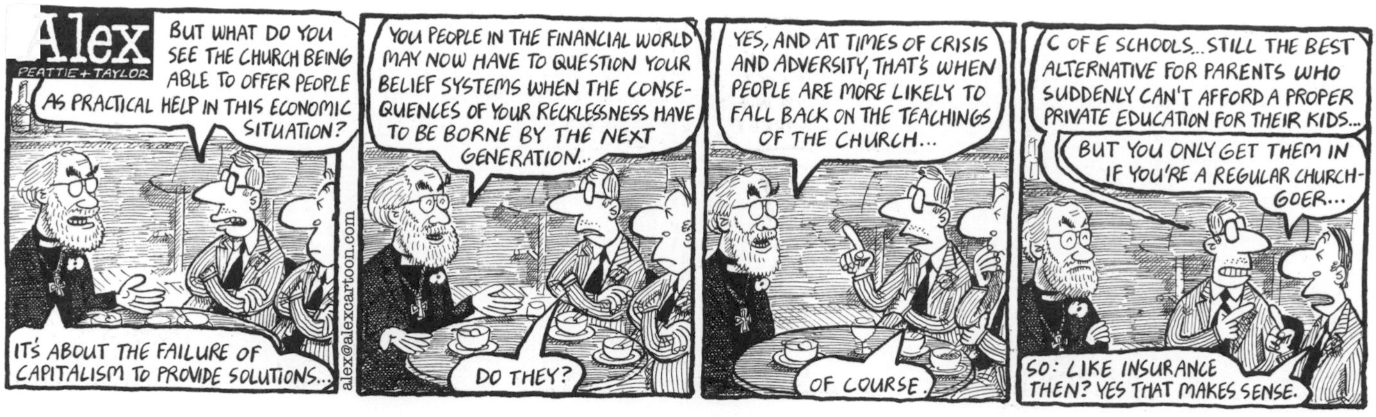
Alex
PEATTIE + TAYLOR
BUT WHAT DO YOU SEE THE CHURCH BEING ABLE TO OFFER PEOPLE AS PRACTICAL HELP IN THIS ECONOMIC SITUATION?
IT'S ABOUT THE FAILURE OF CAPITALISM TO PROVIDE SOLUTIONS...
alex@alexcartoon.com
YOU PEOPLE IN THE FINANCIAL WORLD MAY NOW HAVE TO QUESTION YOUR BELIEF SYSTEMS WHEN THE CONSEQUENCES OF YOUR RECKLESSNESS HAVE TO BE BORNE BY THE NEXT GENERATION...
DO THEY?
YES, AND AT TIMES OF CRISIS AND ADVERSITY, THAT'S WHEN PEOPLE ARE MORE LIKELY TO FALL BACK ON THE TEACHINGS OF THE CHURCH...
OF COURSE.
C OF E SCHOOLS... STILL THE BEST ALTERNATIVE FOR PARENTS WHO SUDDENLY CAN'T AFFORD A PROPER PRIVATE EDUCATION FOR THEIR KIDS...
BUT YOU ONLY GET THEM IN IF YOU'RE A REGULAR CHURCH-GOER...
SO: LIKE INSURANCE THEN? YES THAT MAKES SENSE.

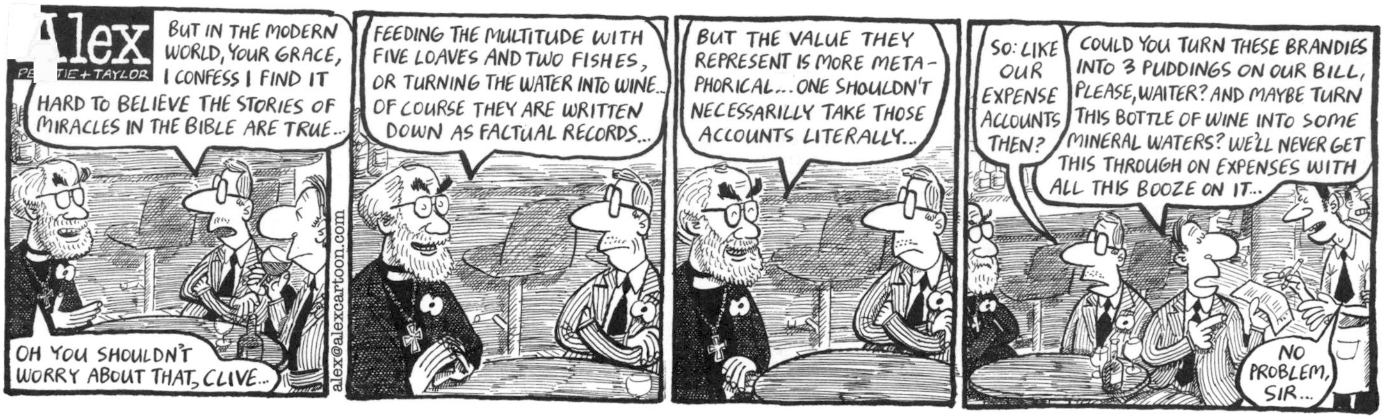
Alex
PEATTIE + TAYLOR
BUT IN THE MODERN WORLD, YOUR GRACE, I CONFESS I FIND IT HARD TO BELIEVE THE STORIES OF MIRACLES IN THE BIBLE ARE TRUE...
OH YOU SHOULDN'T WORRY ABOUT THAT, CLIVE...
alex@alexcartoon.com
FEEDING THE MULTITUDE WITH FIVE LOAVES AND TWO FISHES, OR TURNING THE WATER INTO WINE... OF COURSE THEY ARE WRITTEN DOWN AS FACTUAL RECORDS...
BUT THE VALUE THEY REPRESENT IS MORE METAPHORICAL... ONE SHOULDN'T NECESSARILLY TAKE THOSE ACCOUNTS LITERALLY...
SO: LIKE OUR EXPENSE ACCOUNTS THEN?
COULD YOU TURN THESE BRANDIES INTO 3 PUDDINGS ON OUR BILL, PLEASE, WAITER? AND MAYBE TURN THIS BOTTLE OF WINE INTO SOME MINERAL WATERS? WE'LL NEVER GET THIS THROUGH ON EXPENSES WITH ALL THIS BOOZE ON IT...
NO PROBLEM, SIR...

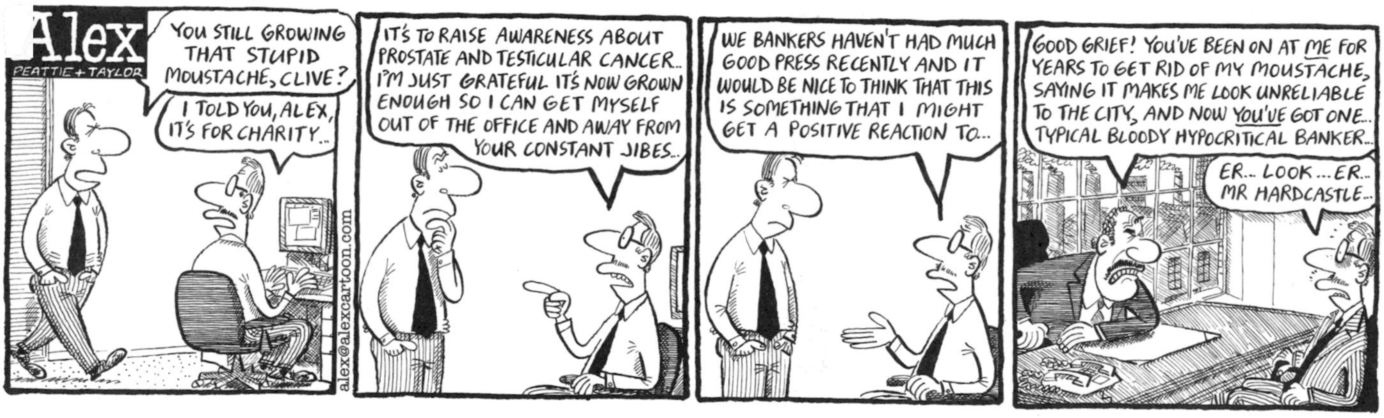
Alex
PEATTIE + TAYLOR
YOU STILL GROWING THAT STUPID MOUSTACHE, CLIVE?
I TOLD YOU, ALEX, IT'S FOR CHARITY...
alex@alexcartoon.com
IT'S TO RAISE AWARENESS ABOUT PROSTATE AND TESTICULAR CANCER... I'M JUST GRATEFUL IT'S NOW GROWN ENOUGH SO I CAN GET MYSELF OUT OF THE OFFICE AND AWAY FROM YOUR CONSTANT JIBES...
WE BANKERS HAVEN'T HAD MUCH GOOD PRESS RECENTLY AND IT WOULD BE NICE TO THINK THAT THIS IS SOMETHING THAT I MIGHT GET A POSITIVE REACTION TO...
GOOD GRIEF! YOU'VE BEEN ON AT ME FOR YEARS TO GET RID OF MY MOUSTACHE, SAYING IT MAKES ME LOOK UNRELIABLE TO THE CITY, AND NOW YOU'VE GOT ONE... TYPICAL BLOODY HYPOCRITICAL BANKER...
ER... LOOK... ER... MR HARDCASTLE...

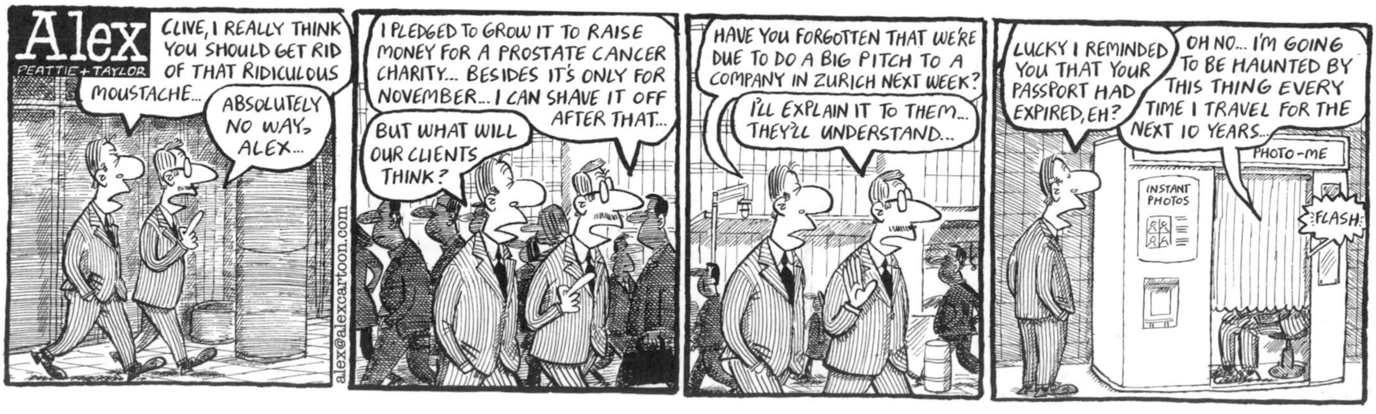
Alex
PEATTIE + TAYLOR
CLIVE, I REALLY THINK YOU SHOULD GET RID OF THAT RIDICULOUS MOUSTACHE...
ABSOLUTELY NO WAY, ALEX...
alex@alexcartoon.com
I PLEDGED TO GROW IT TO RAISE MONEY FOR A PROSTATE CANCER CHARITY... BESIDES IT'S ONLY FOR NOVEMBER... I CAN SHAVE IT OFF AFTER THAT...
BUT WHAT WILL OUR CLIENTS THINK?
HAVE YOU FORGOTTEN THAT WE'RE DUE TO DO A BIG PITCH TO A COMPANY IN ZURICH NEXT WEEK?
I'LL EXPLAIN IT TO THEM... THEY'LL UNDERSTAND...
LUCKY I REMINDED YOU THAT YOUR PASSPORT HAD EXPIRED, EH?
OH NO... I'M GOING TO BE HAUNTED BY THIS THING EVERY TIME I TRAVEL FOR THE NEXT 10 YEARS...
PHOTO-ME
INSTANT PHOTOS
FLASH!

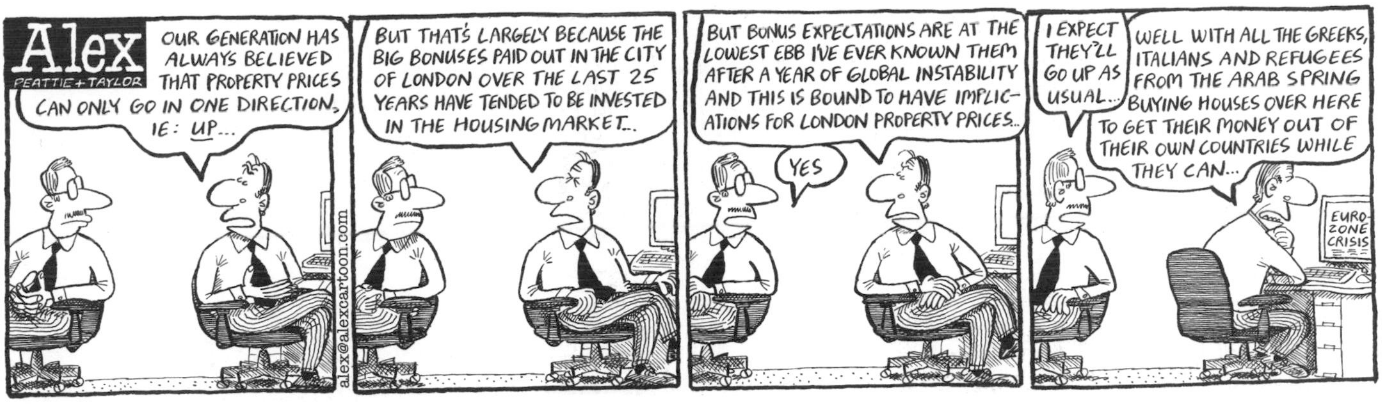
Alex
PEATTIE + TAYLOR
OUR GENERATION HAS ALWAYS BELIEVED THAT PROPERTY PRICES CAN ONLY GO IN ONE DIRECTION, IE: UP...
BUT THAT'S LARGELY BECAUSE THE BIG BONUSES PAID OUT IN THE CITY OF LONDON OVER THE LAST 25 YEARS HAVE TENDED TO BE INVESTED IN THE HOUSING MARKET...
alex@alexcartoon.com
BUT BONUS EXPECTATIONS ARE AT THE LOWEST EBB I'VE EVER KNOWN THEM AFTER A YEAR OF GLOBAL INSTABILITY AND THIS IS BOUND TO HAVE IMPLICATIONS FOR LONDON PROPERTY PRICES...
YES
I EXPECT THEY'LL GO UP AS USUAL...
WELL WITH ALL THE GREEKS, ITALIANS AND REFUGEES FROM THE ARAB SPRING BUYING HOUSES OVER HERE TO GET THEIR MONEY OUT OF THEIR OWN COUNTRIES WHILE THEY CAN...
EURO-ZONE CRISIS

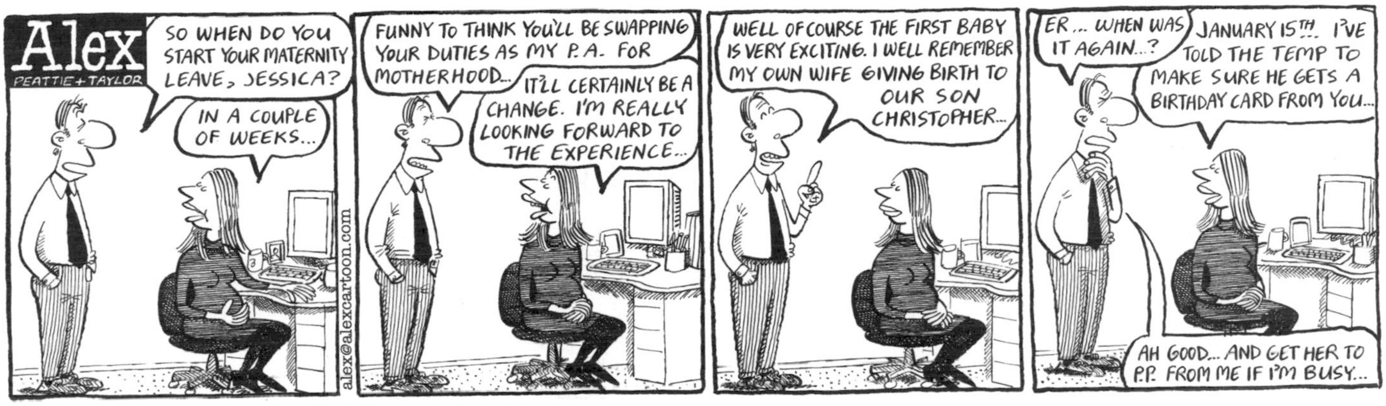
Alex
PEATTIE + TAYLOR
SO WHEN DO YOU START YOUR MATERNITY LEAVE, JESSICA?
IN A COUPLE OF WEEKS...
FUNNY TO THINK YOU'LL BE SWAPPING YOUR DUTIES AS MY P.A. FOR MOTHERHOOD...
IT'LL CERTAINLY BE A CHANGE. I'M REALLY LOOKING FORWARD TO THE EXPERIENCE...
alex@alexcartoon.com
WELL OF COURSE THE FIRST BABY IS VERY EXCITING. I WELL REMEMBER MY OWN WIFE GIVING BIRTH TO OUR SON CHRISTOPHER...
ER... WHEN WAS IT AGAIN...?
JANUARY 15TH... I'VE TOLD THE TEMP TO MAKE SURE HE GETS A BIRTHDAY CARD FROM YOU...
AH GOOD... AND GET HER TO P.P. FROM ME IF I'M BUSY...

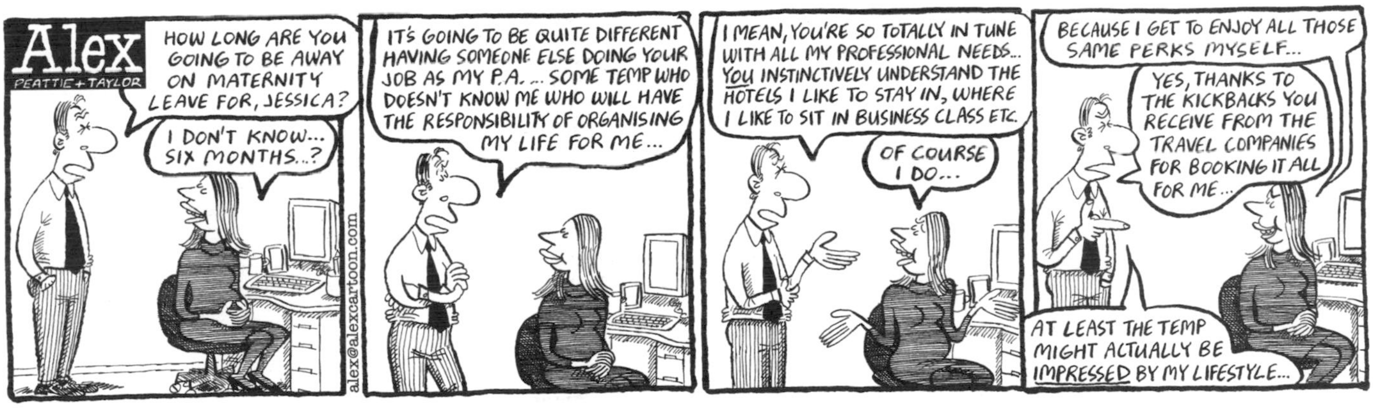
Alex
PEATTIE + TAYLOR
HOW LONG ARE YOU GOING TO BE AWAY ON MATERNITY LEAVE FOR, JESSICA?
I DON'T KNOW... SIX MONTHS...?
IT'S GOING TO BE QUITE DIFFERENT HAVING SOMEONE ELSE DOING YOUR JOB AS MY P.A. ... SOME TEMP WHO DOESN'T KNOW ME WHO WILL HAVE THE RESPONSIBILITY OF ORGANISING MY LIFE FOR ME...
alex@alexcartoon.com
I MEAN, YOU'RE SO TOTALLY IN TUNE WITH ALL MY PROFESSIONAL NEEDS... YOU INSTINCTIVELY UNDERSTAND THE HOTELS I LIKE TO STAY IN, WHERE I LIKE TO SIT IN BUSINESS CLASS ETC.
OF COURSE I DO...
BECAUSE I GET TO ENJOY ALL THOSE SAME PERKS MYSELF...
YES, THANKS TO THE KICKBACKS YOU RECEIVE FROM THE TRAVEL COMPANIES FOR BOOKING IT ALL FOR ME...
AT LEAST THE TEMP MIGHT ACTUALLY BE IMPRESSED BY MY LIFESTYLE...

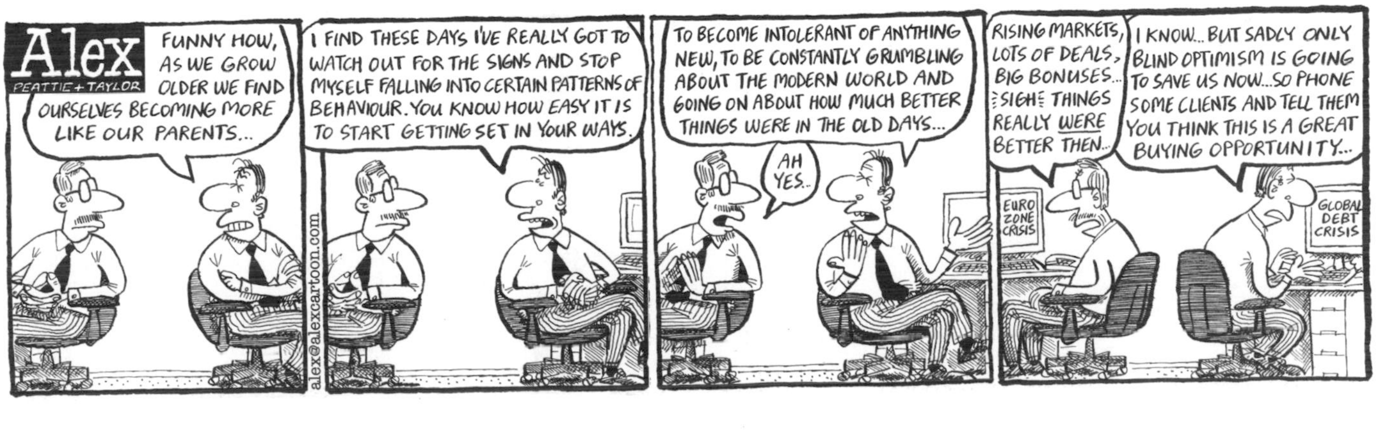
Alex
PEATTIE + TAYLOR
FUNNY HOW, AS WE GROW OLDER WE FIND OURSELVES BECOMING MORE LIKE OUR PARENTS...
I FIND THESE DAYS I'VE REALLY GOT TO WATCH OUT FOR THE SIGNS AND STOP MYSELF FALLING INTO CERTAIN PATTERNS OF BEHAVIOUR. YOU KNOW HOW EASY IT IS TO START GETTING SET IN YOUR WAYS.
alex@alexcartoon.com
TO BECOME INTOLERANT OF ANYTHING NEW, TO BE CONSTANTLY GRUMBLING ABOUT THE MODERN WORLD AND GOING ON ABOUT HOW MUCH BETTER THINGS WERE IN THE OLD DAYS...
AH YES...
RISING MARKETS, LOTS OF DEALS, BIG BONUSES... SIGH THINGS REALLY WERE BETTER THEN...
I KNOW... BUT SADLY ONLY BLIND OPTIMISM IS GOING TO SAVE US NOW... SO PHONE SOME CLIENTS AND TELL THEM YOU THINK THIS IS A GREAT BUYING OPPORTUNITY...
EURO ZONE CRISIS
GLOBAL DEBT CRISIS

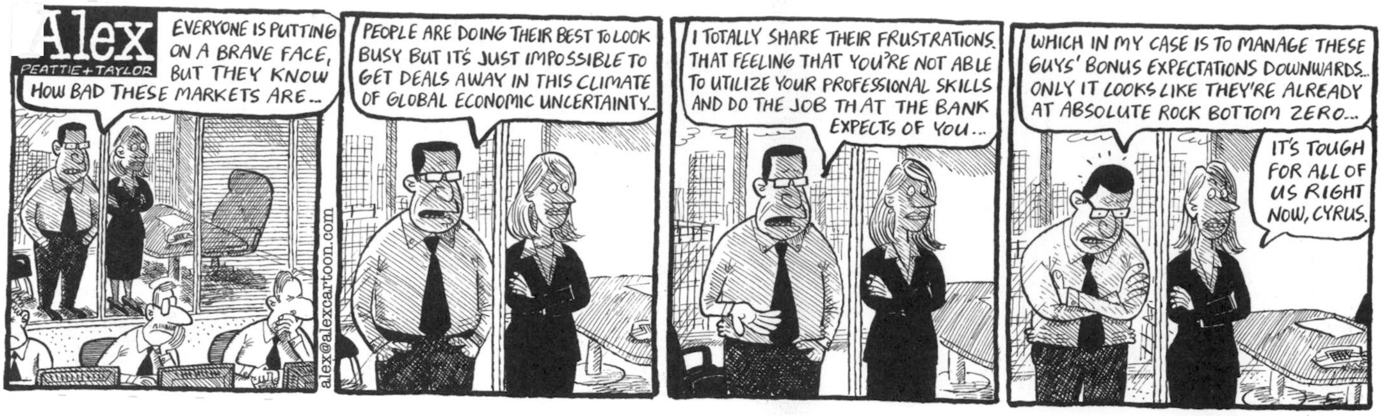
Alex
PEATTIE + TAYLOR
EVERYONE IS PUTTING ON A BRAVE FACE, BUT THEY KNOW HOW BAD THESE MARKETS ARE...
alex@alexcartoon.com
PEOPLE ARE DOING THEIR BEST TO LOOK BUSY BUT IT'S JUST IMPOSSIBLE TO GET DEALS AWAY IN THIS CLIMATE OF GLOBAL ECONOMIC UNCERTAINTY...
I TOTALLY SHARE THEIR FRUSTRATIONS. THAT FEELING THAT YOU'RE NOT ABLE TO UTILIZE YOUR PROFESSIONAL SKILLS AND DO THE JOB THAT THE BANK EXPECTS OF YOU...
WHICH IN MY CASE IS TO MANAGE THESE GUYS' BONUS EXPECTATIONS DOWNWARDS... ONLY IT LOOKS LIKE THEY'RE ALREADY AT ABSOLUTE ROCK BOTTOM ZERO...
IT'S TOUGH FOR ALL OF US RIGHT NOW, CYRUS.

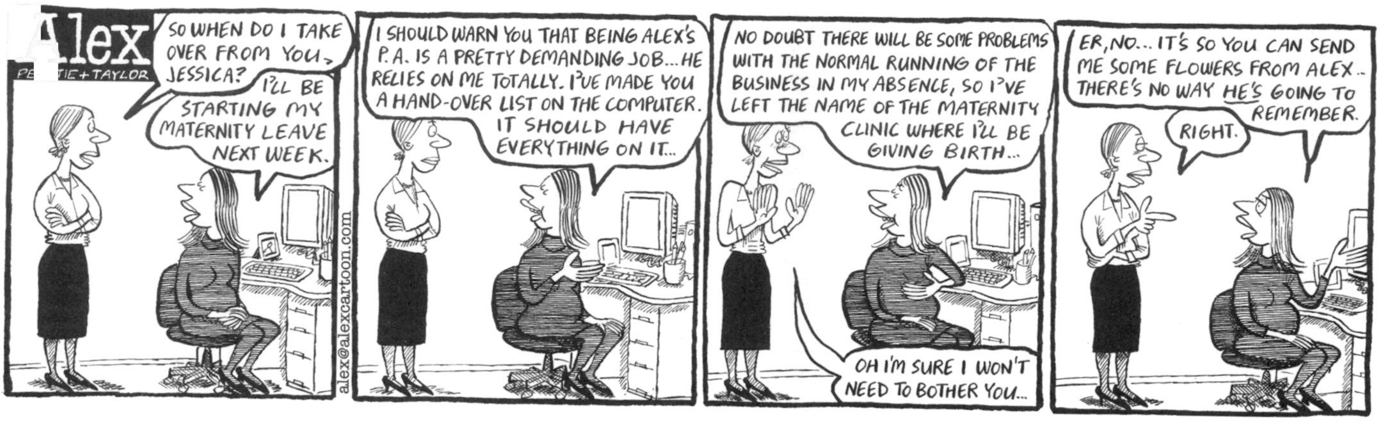
Alex
PEATTIE + TAYLOR
SO WHEN DO I TAKE OVER FROM YOU, JESSICA?
I'LL BE STARTING MY MATERNITY LEAVE NEXT WEEK.
alex@alexcartoon.com
I SHOULD WARN YOU THAT BEING ALEX'S P.A. IS A PRETTY DEMANDING JOB... HE RELIES ON ME TOTALLY. I'VE MADE YOU A HAND-OVER LIST ON THE COMPUTER. IT SHOULD HAVE EVERYTHING ON IT...
NO DOUBT THERE WILL BE SOME PROBLEMS WITH THE NORMAL RUNNING OF THE BUSINESS IN MY ABSENCE, SO I'VE LEFT THE NAME OF THE MATERNITY CLINIC WHERE I'LL BE GIVING BIRTH...
OH I'M SURE I WON'T NEED TO BOTHER YOU...
ER, NO... IT'S SO YOU CAN SEND ME SOME FLOWERS FROM ALEX... THERE'S NO WAY HE'S GOING TO REMEMBER.
RIGHT.

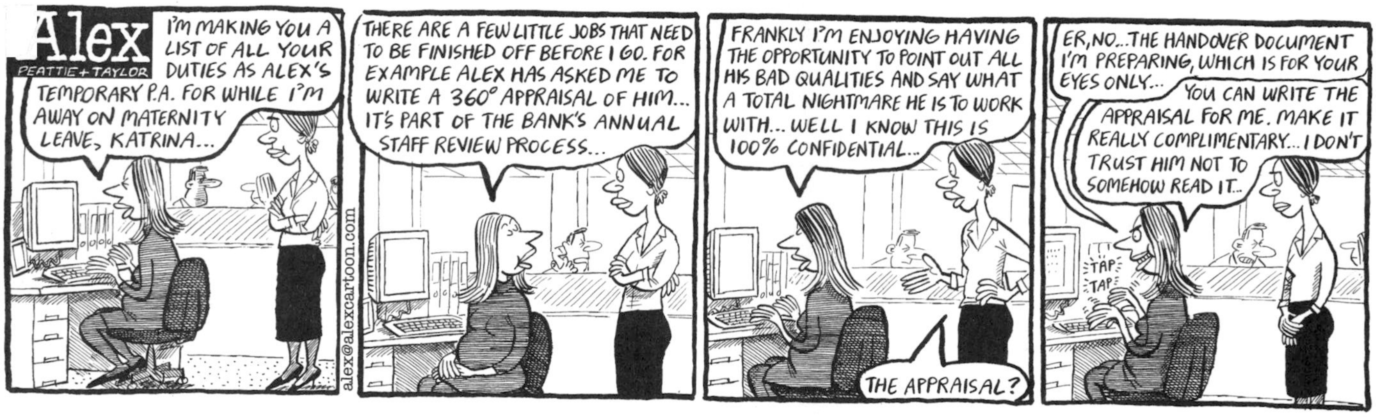
Alex
PEATTIE + TAYLOR
I'M MAKING YOU A LIST OF ALL YOUR DUTIES AS ALEX'S TEMPORARY P.A. FOR WHILE I'M AWAY ON MATERNITY LEAVE, KATRINA...
alex@alexcartoon.com
THERE ARE A FEW LITTLE JOBS THAT NEED TO BE FINISHED OFF BEFORE I GO. FOR EXAMPLE ALEX HAS ASKED ME TO WRITE A 360° APPRAISAL OF HIM... IT'S PART OF THE BANK'S ANNUAL STAFF REVIEW PROCESS...
FRANKLY I'M ENJOYING HAVING THE OPPORTUNITY TO POINT OUT ALL HIS BAD QUALITIES AND SAY WHAT A TOTAL NIGHTMARE HE IS TO WORK WITH... WELL I KNOW THIS IS 100% CONFIDENTIAL...
THE APPRAISAL?
ER, NO... THE HANDOVER DOCUMENT I'M PREPARING, WHICH IS FOR YOUR EYES ONLY...
YOU CAN WRITE THE APPRAISAL FOR ME. MAKE IT REALLY COMPLIMENTARY... I DON'T TRUST HIM NOT TO SOMEHOW READ IT...
TAP TAP

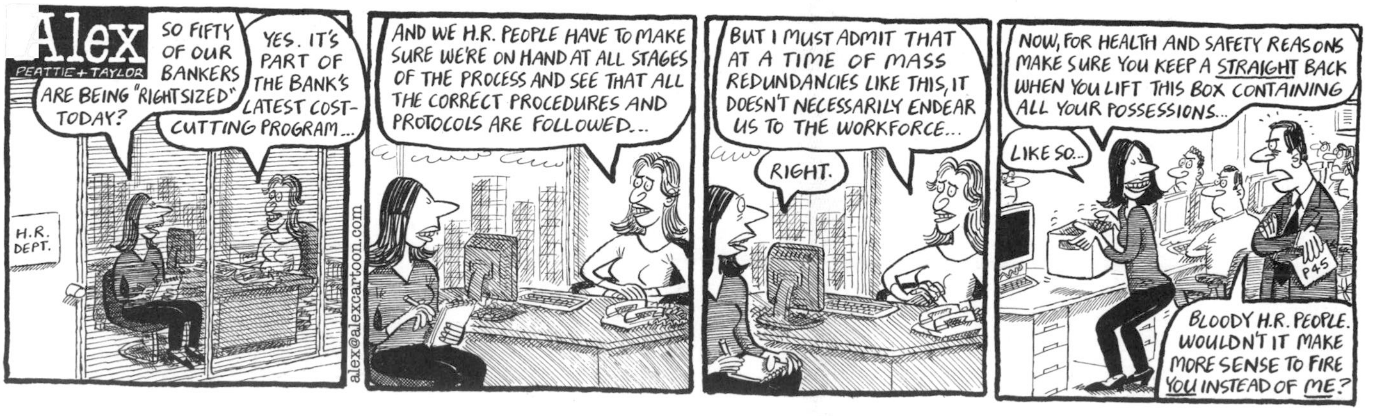
Alex
PEATTIE + TAYLOR
SO FIFTY OF OUR BANKERS ARE BEING "RIGHTSIZED" TODAY?
YES. IT'S PART OF THE BANK'S LATEST COST-CUTTING PROGRAM...
H.R. DEPT.
alex@alexcartoon.com
AND WE H.R. PEOPLE HAVE TO MAKE SURE WE'RE ON HAND AT ALL STAGES OF THE PROCESS AND SEE THAT ALL THE CORRECT PROCEDURES AND PROTOCOLS ARE FOLLOWED...
BUT I MUST ADMIT THAT AT A TIME OF MASS REDUNDANCIES LIKE THIS, IT DOESN'T NECESSARILY ENDEAR US TO THE WORKFORCE...
RIGHT.
NOW, FOR HEALTH AND SAFETY REASONS MAKE SURE YOU KEEP A STRAIGHT BACK WHEN YOU LIFT THIS BOX CONTAINING ALL YOUR POSSESSIONS...
LIKE SO...
P45
BLOODY H.R. PEOPLE. WOULDN'T IT MAKE MORE SENSE TO FIRE YOU INSTEAD OF ME?

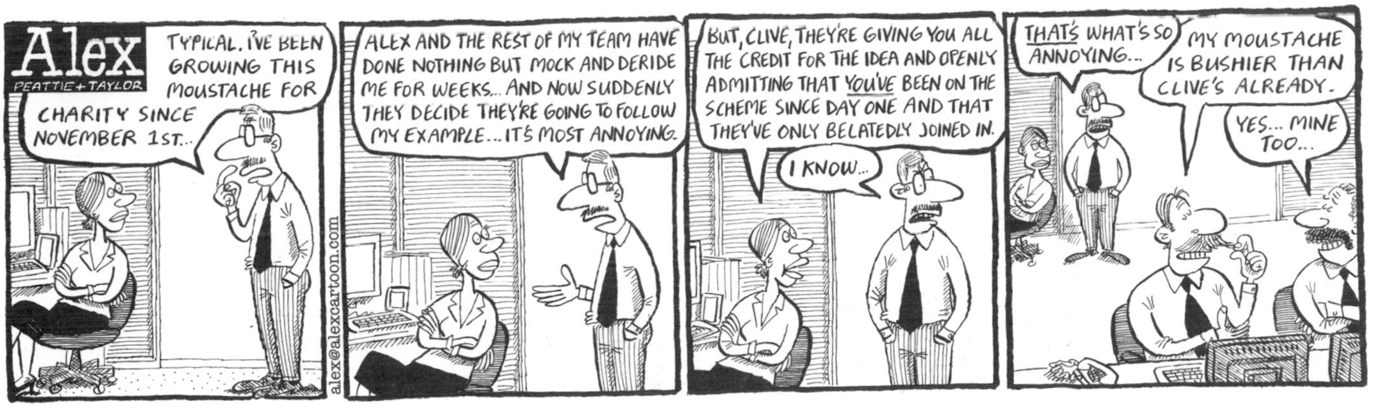
Alex
PEATTIE + TAYLOR
TYPICAL. I'VE BEEN GROWING THIS MOUSTACHE FOR CHARITY SINCE NOVEMBER 1ST...
alex@alexcartoon.com
ALEX AND THE REST OF MY TEAM HAVE DONE NOTHING BUT MOCK AND DERIDE ME FOR WEEKS... AND NOW SUDDENLY THEY DECIDE THEY'RE GOING TO FOLLOW MY EXAMPLE... IT'S MOST ANNOYING.
BUT, CLIVE, THEY'RE GIVING YOU ALL THE CREDIT FOR THE IDEA AND OPENLY ADMITTING THAT YOU'VE BEEN ON THE SCHEME SINCE DAY ONE AND THAT THEY'VE ONLY BELATEDLY JOINED IN.
I KNOW...
THAT'S WHAT'S SO ANNOYING...
MY MOUSTACHE IS BUSHIER THAN CLIVE'S ALREADY.
YES... MINE TOO...

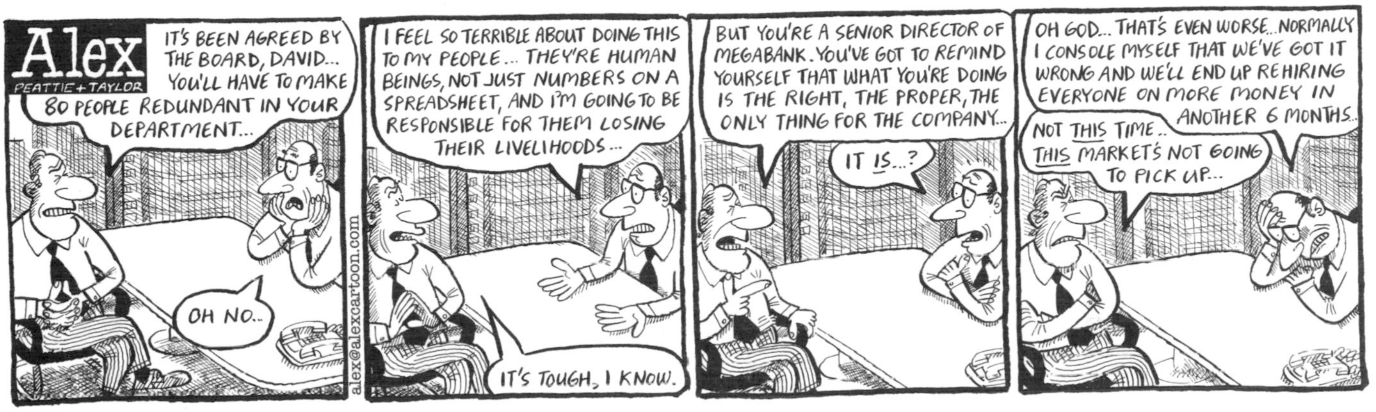
Alex
PEATTIE + TAYLOR
IT'S BEEN AGREED BY THE BOARD, DAVID... YOU'LL HAVE TO MAKE 80 PEOPLE REDUNDANT IN YOUR DEPARTMENT...
OH NO...
alex@alexcartoon.com
I FEEL SO TERRIBLE ABOUT DOING THIS TO MY PEOPLE... THEY'RE HUMAN BEINGS, NOT JUST NUMBERS ON A SPREADSHEET, AND I'M GOING TO BE RESPONSIBLE FOR THEM LOSING THEIR LIVELIHOODS...
IT'S TOUGH, I KNOW.
BUT YOU'RE A SENIOR DIRECTOR OF MEGABANK. YOU'VE GOT TO REMIND YOURSELF THAT WHAT YOU'RE DOING IS THE RIGHT, THE PROPER, THE ONLY THING FOR THE COMPANY...
IT IS...?
OH GOD... THAT'S EVEN WORSE... NORMALLY I CONSOLE MYSELF THAT WE'VE GOT IT WRONG AND WE'LL END UP REHIRING EVERYONE ON MORE MONEY IN ANOTHER 6 MONTHS...
NOT THIS TIME... THIS MARKET'S NOT GOING TO PICK UP...

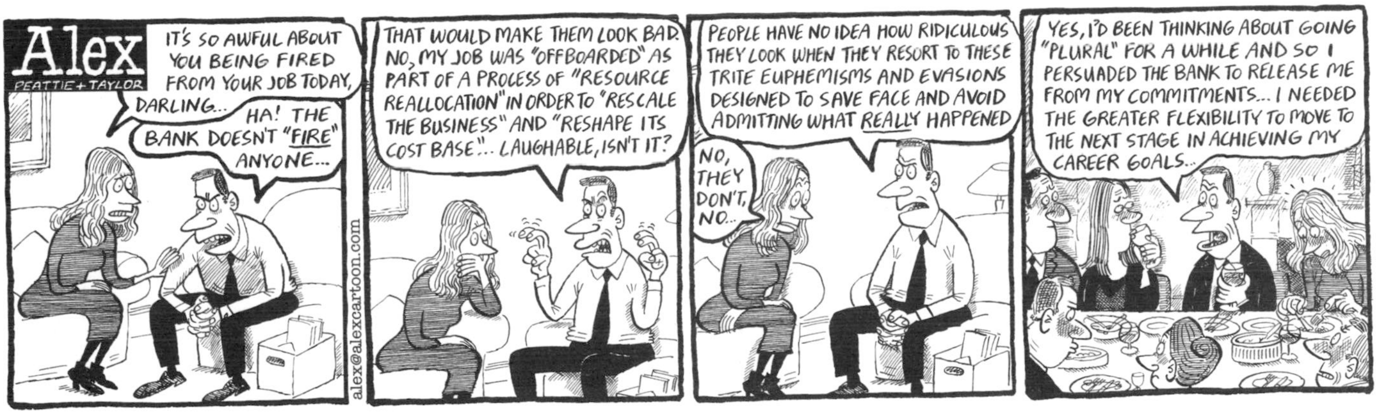
Alex
PEATTIE + TAYLOR
IT'S SO AWFUL ABOUT YOU BEING FIRED FROM YOUR JOB TODAY, DARLING...
HA! THE BANK DOESN'T "FIRE" ANYONE...
alex@alexcartoon.com
THAT WOULD MAKE THEM LOOK BAD. NO, MY JOB WAS "OFFBOARDED" AS PART OF A PROCESS OF "RESOURCE REALLOCATION" IN ORDER TO "RESCALE THE BUSINESS" AND "RESHAPE ITS COST BASE"... LAUGHABLE, ISN'T IT?
PEOPLE HAVE NO IDEA HOW RIDICULOUS THEY LOOK WHEN THEY RESORT TO THESE TRITE EUPHEMISMS AND EVASIONS DESIGNED TO SAVE FACE AND AVOID ADMITTING WHAT REALLY HAPPENED
NO, THEY DON'T, NO...
YES, I'D BEEN THINKING ABOUT GOING "PLURAL" FOR A WHILE AND SO I PERSUADED THE BANK TO RELEASE ME FROM MY COMMITMENTS... I NEEDED THE GREATER FLEXIBILITY TO MOVE TO THE NEXT STAGE IN ACHIEVING MY CAREER GOALS...

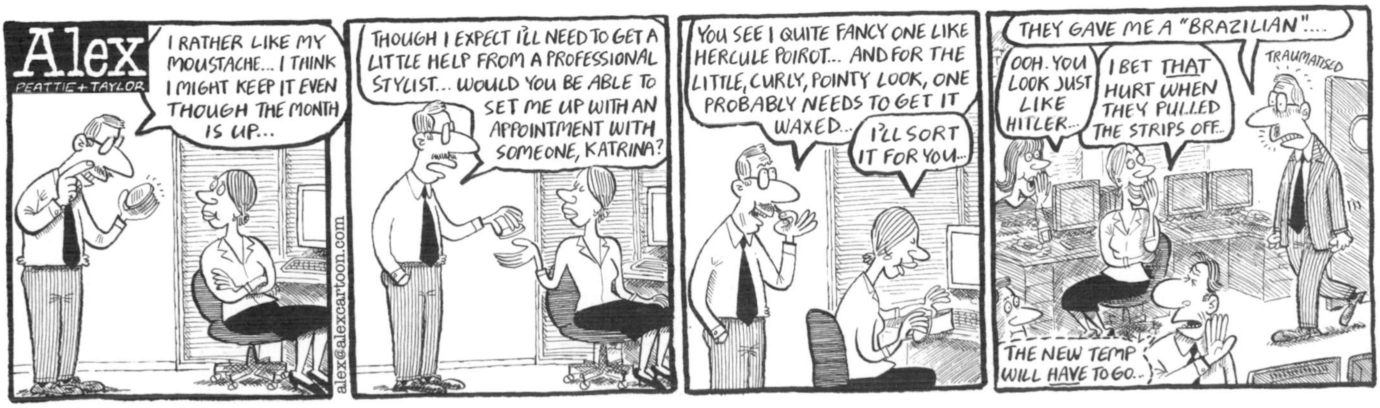
Alex
PEATTIE + TAYLOR
I RATHER LIKE MY MOUSTACHE... I THINK I MIGHT KEEP IT EVEN THOUGH THE MONTH IS UP...
alex@alexcartoon.com
THOUGH I EXPECT I'LL NEED TO GET A LITTLE HELP FROM A PROFESSIONAL STYLIST... WOULD YOU BE ABLE TO SET ME UP WITH AN APPOINTMENT WITH SOMEONE, KATRINA?
YOU SEE I QUITE FANCY ONE LIKE HERCULE POIROT... AND FOR THE LITTLE, CURLY, POINTY LOOK, ONE PROBABLY NEEDS TO GET IT WAXED...
I'LL SORT IT FOR YOU...
THEY GAVE ME A "BRAZILIAN"...
OOH. YOU LOOK JUST LIKE HITLER...
I BET THAT HURT WHEN THEY PULLED THE STRIPS OFF...
TRAUMATISED
THE NEW TEMP WILL HAVE TO GO...

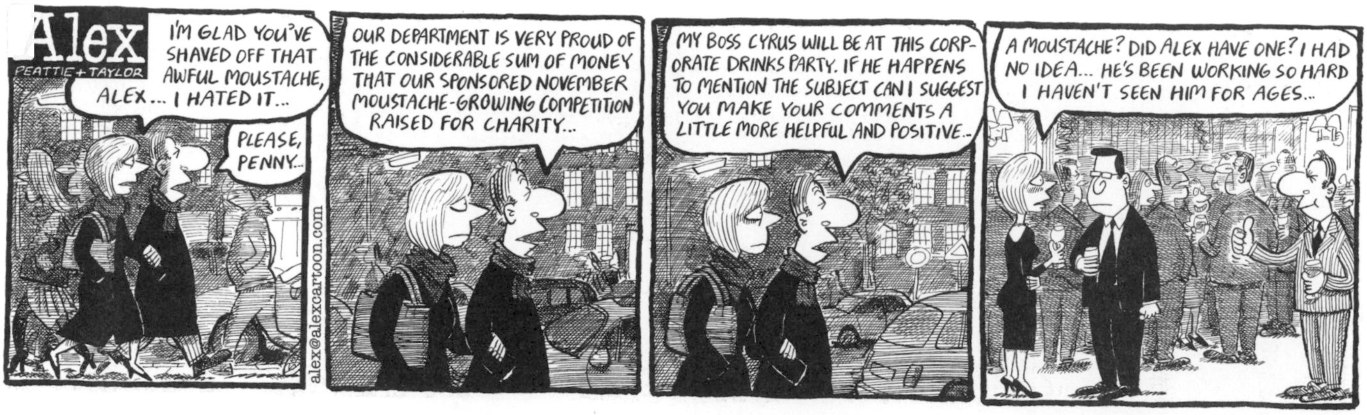
Alex
PEATTIE+TAYLOR
I'M GLAD YOU'VE SHAVED OFF THAT AWFUL MOUSTACHE, ALEX... I HATED IT...
PLEASE, PENNY...
alex@alexcartoon.com
OUR DEPARTMENT IS VERY PROUD OF THE CONSIDERABLE SUM OF MONEY THAT OUR SPONSORED NOVEMBER MOUSTACHE-GROWING COMPETITION RAISED FOR CHARITY...
MY BOSS CYRUS WILL BE AT THIS CORPORATE DRINKS PARTY. IF HE HAPPENS TO MENTION THE SUBJECT CAN I SUGGEST YOU MAKE YOUR COMMENTS A LITTLE MORE HELPFUL AND POSITIVE...
A MOUSTACHE? DID ALEX HAVE ONE? I HAD NO IDEA... HE'S BEEN WORKING SO HARD I HAVEN'T SEEN HIM FOR AGES...

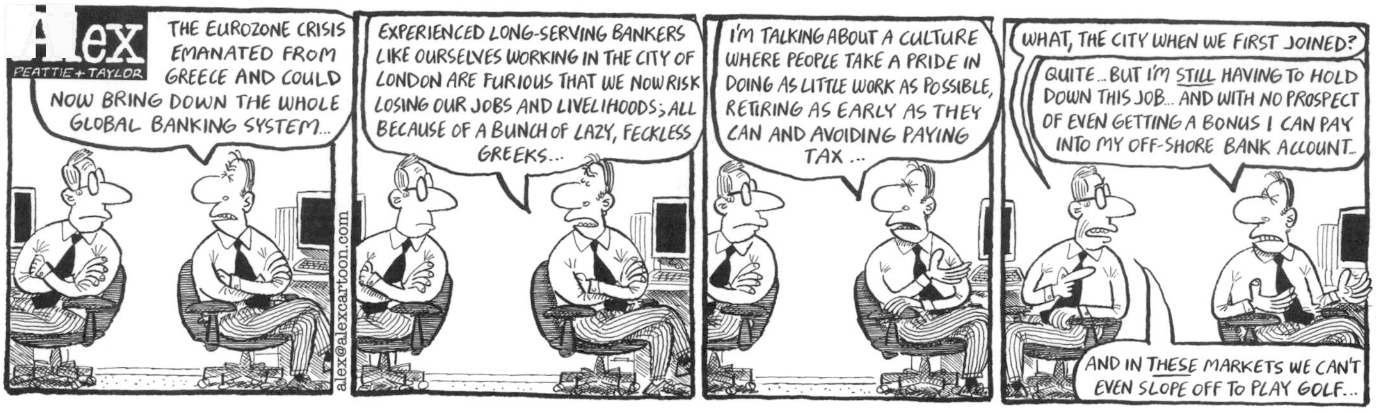
Alex
PEATTIE+TAYLOR
THE EUROZONE CRISIS EMANATED FROM GREECE AND COULD NOW BRING DOWN THE WHOLE GLOBAL BANKING SYSTEM...
alex@alexcartoon.com
EXPERIENCED LONG-SERVING BANKERS LIKE OURSELVES WORKING IN THE CITY OF LONDON ARE FURIOUS THAT WE NOW RISK LOSING OUR JOBS AND LIVELIHOODS; ALL BECAUSE OF A BUNCH OF LAZY, FECKLESS GREEKS...
I'M TALKING ABOUT A CULTURE WHERE PEOPLE TAKE A PRIDE IN DOING AS LITTLE WORK AS POSSIBLE, RETIRING AS EARLY AS THEY CAN AND AVOIDING PAYING TAX ...
WHAT, THE CITY WHEN WE FIRST JOINED?
QUITE... BUT I'M STILL HAVING TO HOLD DOWN THIS JOB... AND WITH NO PROSPECT OF EVEN GETTING A BONUS I CAN PAY INTO MY OFF-SHORE BANK ACCOUNT...
AND IN THESE MARKETS WE CAN'T EVEN SLOPE OFF TO PLAY GOLF...

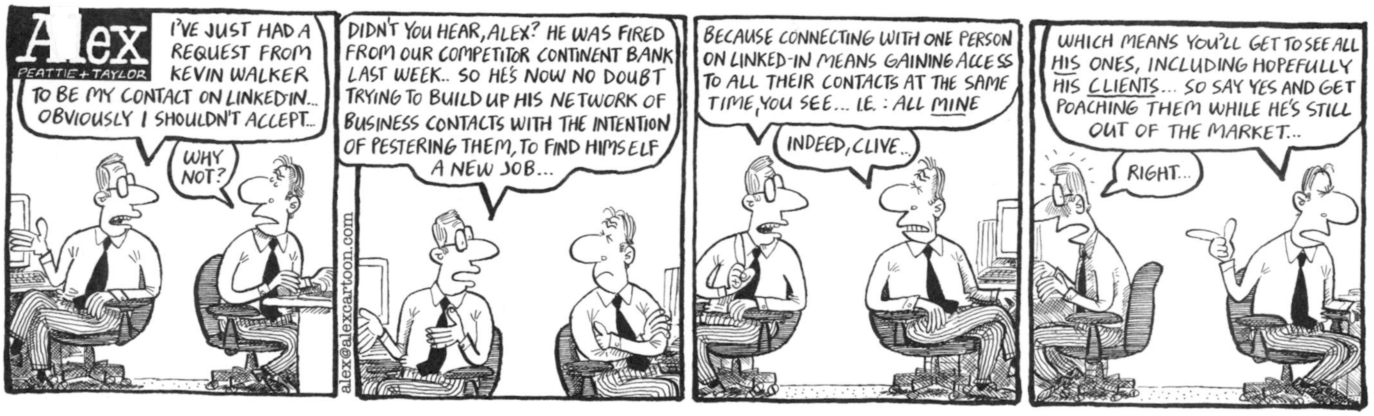
Alex
PEATTIE+TAYLOR
I'VE JUST HAD A REQUEST FROM KEVIN WALKER TO BE MY CONTACT ON LINKED-IN... OBVIOUSLY I SHOULDN'T ACCEPT...
WHY NOT?
alex@alexcartoon.com
DIDN'T YOU HEAR, ALEX? HE WAS FIRED FROM OUR COMPETITOR CONTINENT BANK LAST WEEK.. SO HE'S NOW NO DOUBT TRYING TO BUILD UP HIS NETWORK OF BUSINESS CONTACTS WITH THE INTENTION OF PESTERING THEM, TO FIND HIMSELF A NEW JOB...
BECAUSE CONNECTING WITH ONE PERSON ON LINKED-IN MEANS GAINING ACCESS TO ALL THEIR CONTACTS AT THE SAME TIME, YOU SEE... I.E. : ALL MINE
INDEED, CLIVE...
WHICH MEANS YOU'LL GET TO SEE ALL HIS ONES, INCLUDING HOPEFULLY HIS CLIENTS... SO SAY YES AND GET POACHING THEM WHILE HE'S STILL OUT OF THE MARKET...
RIGHT...

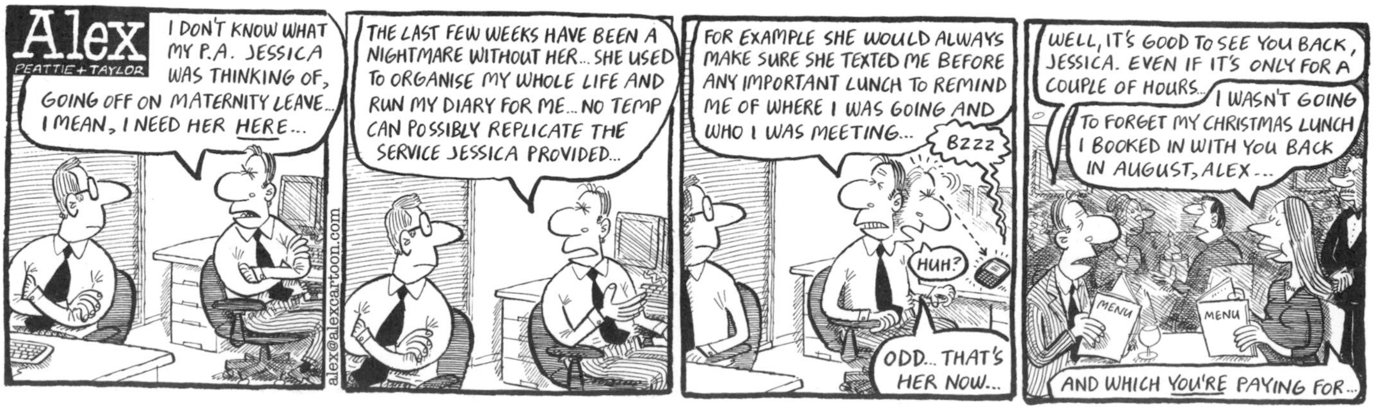
Alex
PEATTIE+TAYLOR
I DON'T KNOW WHAT MY P.A. JESSICA WAS THINKING OF, GOING OFF ON MATERNITY LEAVE... I MEAN, I NEED HER HERE...
alex@alexcartoon.com
THE LAST FEW WEEKS HAVE BEEN A NIGHTMARE WITHOUT HER... SHE USED TO ORGANISE MY WHOLE LIFE AND RUN MY DIARY FOR ME... NO TEMP CAN POSSIBLY REPLICATE THE SERVICE JESSICA PROVIDED...
FOR EXAMPLE SHE WOULD ALWAYS MAKE SURE SHE TEXTED ME BEFORE ANY IMPORTANT LUNCH TO REMIND ME OF WHERE I WAS GOING AND WHO I WAS MEETING...
BZZZ
HUH?
ODD... THAT'S HER NOW...
WELL, IT'S GOOD TO SEE YOU BACK, JESSICA. EVEN IF IT'S ONLY FOR A COUPLE OF HOURS...
I WASN'T GOING TO FORGET MY CHRISTMAS LUNCH I BOOKED IN WITH YOU BACK IN AUGUST, ALEX...
MENU
MENU
AND WHICH YOU'RE PAYING FOR...

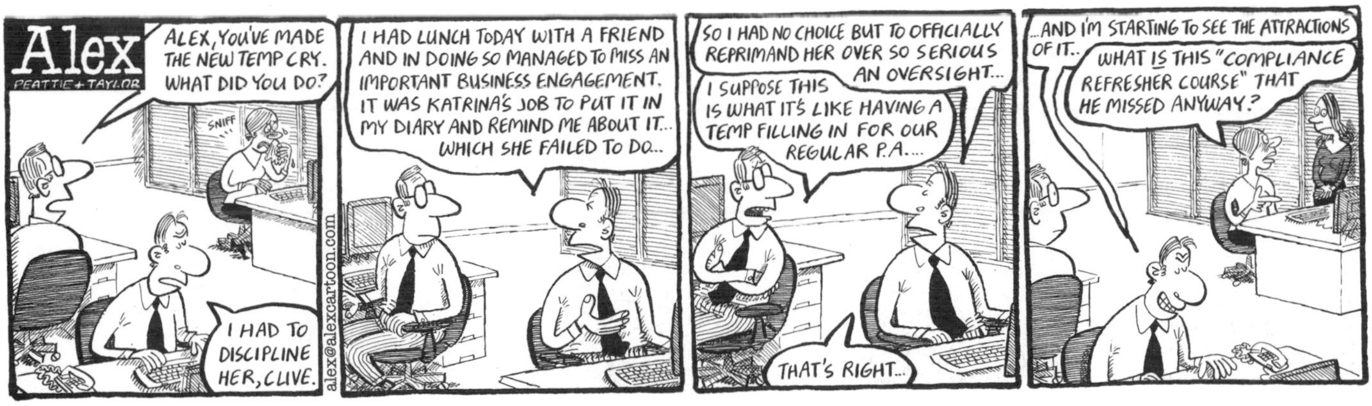
Alex
PEATTIE+TAYLOR
ALEX, YOU'VE MADE THE NEW TEMP CRY. WHAT DID YOU DO?
SNIFF
I HAD TO DISCIPLINE HER, CLIVE.
alex@alexcartoon.com
I HAD LUNCH TODAY WITH A FRIEND AND IN DOING SO MANAGED TO MISS AN IMPORTANT BUSINESS ENGAGEMENT. IT WAS KATRINA'S JOB TO PUT IT IN MY DIARY AND REMIND ME ABOUT IT... WHICH SHE FAILED TO DO...
SO I HAD NO CHOICE BUT TO OFFICIALLY REPRIMAND HER OVER SO SERIOUS AN OVERSIGHT...
I SUPPOSE THIS IS WHAT IT'S LIKE HAVING A TEMP FILLING IN FOR OUR REGULAR P.A....
THAT'S RIGHT...
...AND I'M STARTING TO SEE THE ATTRACTIONS OF IT...
WHAT IS THIS "COMPLIANCE REFRESHER COURSE" THAT HE MISSED ANYWAY?

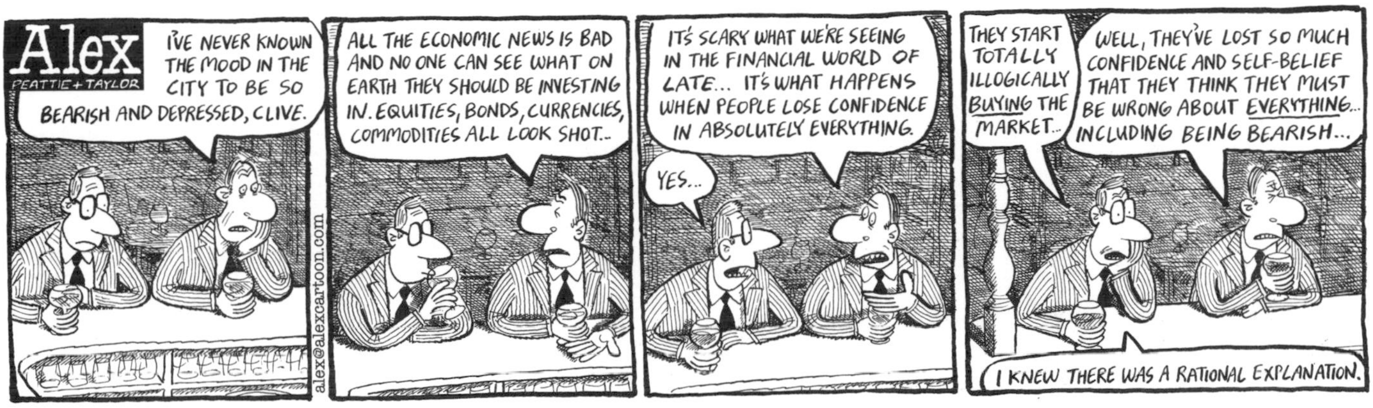
Alex
PEATTIE+TAYLOR
I'VE NEVER KNOWN THE MOOD IN THE CITY TO BE SO BEARISH AND DEPRESSED, CLIVE.
alex@alexcartoon.com
ALL THE ECONOMIC NEWS IS BAD AND NO ONE CAN SEE WHAT ON EARTH THEY SHOULD BE INVESTING IN. EQUITIES, BONDS, CURRENCIES, COMMODITIES ALL LOOK SHOT...
IT'S SCARY WHAT WE'RE SEEING IN THE FINANCIAL WORLD OF LATE... IT'S WHAT HAPPENS WHEN PEOPLE LOSE CONFIDENCE IN ABSOLUTELY EVERYTHING.
YES...
THEY START TOTALLY ILLOGICALLY BUYING THE MARKET...
WELL, THEY'VE LOST SO MUCH CONFIDENCE AND SELF-BELIEF THAT THEY THINK THEY MUST BE WRONG ABOUT EVERYTHING... INCLUDING BEING BEARISH...
I KNEW THERE WAS A RATIONAL EXPLANATION.

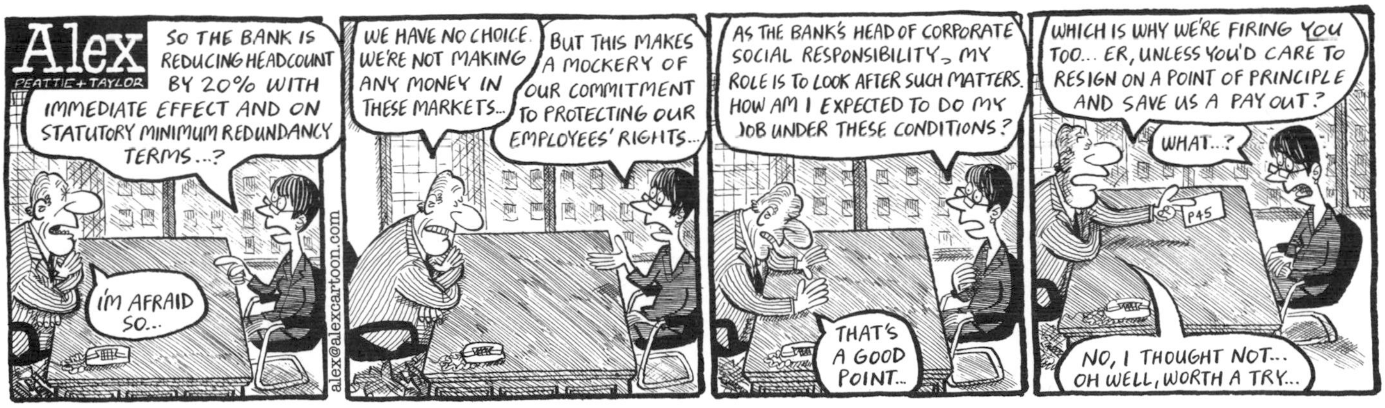
Alex
PEATTIE+TAYLOR
SO THE BANK IS REDUCING HEADCOUNT BY 20% WITH IMMEDIATE EFFECT AND ON STATUTORY MINIMUM REDUNDANCY TERMS...?
I'M AFRAID SO...
alex@alexcartoon.com
WE HAVE NO CHOICE. WE'RE NOT MAKING ANY MONEY IN THESE MARKETS...
BUT THIS MAKES A MOCKERY OF OUR COMMITMENT TO PROTECTING OUR EMPLOYEES' RIGHTS...
AS THE BANK'S HEAD OF CORPORATE SOCIAL RESPONSIBILITY, MY ROLE IS TO LOOK AFTER SUCH MATTERS. HOW AM I EXPECTED TO DO MY JOB UNDER THESE CONDITIONS?
THAT'S A GOOD POINT...
WHICH IS WHY WE'RE FIRING YOU TOO... ER, UNLESS YOU'D CARE TO RESIGN ON A POINT OF PRINCIPLE AND SAVE US A PAY OUT?
WHAT...?
P45
NO, I THOUGHT NOT... OH WELL, WORTH A TRY...

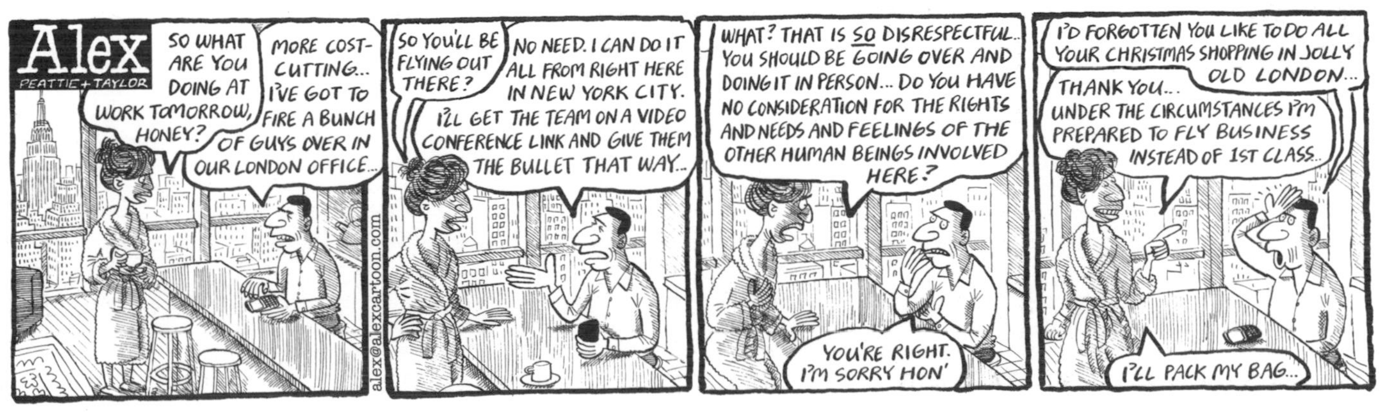
Alex
PEATTIE+TAYLOR
SO WHAT ARE YOU DOING AT WORK TOMORROW, HONEY?
MORE COST-CUTTING... I'VE GOT TO FIRE A BUNCH OF GUYS OVER IN OUR LONDON OFFICE...
alex@alexcartoon.com
SO YOU'LL BE FLYING OUT THERE?
NO NEED. I CAN DO IT ALL FROM RIGHT HERE IN NEW YORK CITY.
I'LL GET THE TEAM ON A VIDEO CONFERENCE LINK AND GIVE THEM THE BULLET THAT WAY...
WHAT? THAT IS SO DISRESPECTFUL... YOU SHOULD BE GOING OVER AND DOING IT IN PERSON... DO YOU HAVE NO CONSIDERATION FOR THE RIGHTS AND NEEDS AND FEELINGS OF THE OTHER HUMAN BEINGS INVOLVED HERE?
YOU'RE RIGHT. I'M SORRY HON'
I'D FORGOTTEN YOU LIKE TO DO ALL YOUR CHRISTMAS SHOPPING IN JOLLY OLD LONDON...
THANK YOU... UNDER THE CIRCUMSTANCES I'M PREPARED TO FLY BUSINESS INSTEAD OF 1ST CLASS...
I'LL PACK MY BAG...

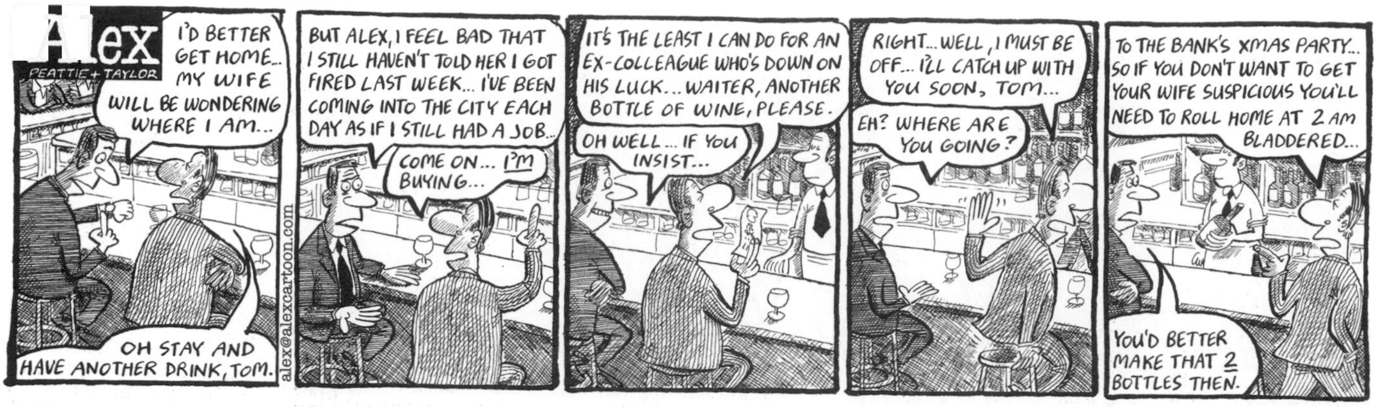
Alex
PEATTIE + TAYLOR
I'D BETTER GET HOME... MY WIFE WILL BE WONDERING WHERE I AM...
OH STAY AND HAVE ANOTHER DRINK, TOM.
alex@alexcartoon.com
BUT ALEX, I FEEL BAD THAT I STILL HAVEN'T TOLD HER I GOT FIRED LAST WEEK... I'VE BEEN COMING INTO THE CITY EACH DAY AS IF I STILL HAD A JOB...
COME ON... I'M BUYING...
IT'S THE LEAST I CAN DO FOR AN EX-COLLEAGUE WHO'S DOWN ON HIS LUCK... WAITER, ANOTHER BOTTLE OF WINE, PLEASE.
OH WELL... IF YOU INSIST...
RIGHT... WELL, I MUST BE OFF... I'LL CATCH UP WITH YOU SOON, TOM...
EH? WHERE ARE YOU GOING?
TO THE BANK'S XMAS PARTY... SO IF YOU DON'T WANT TO GET YOUR WIFE SUSPICIOUS YOU'LL NEED TO ROLL HOME AT 2 AM BLADDERED...
YOU'D BETTER MAKE THAT 2 BOTTLES THEN.

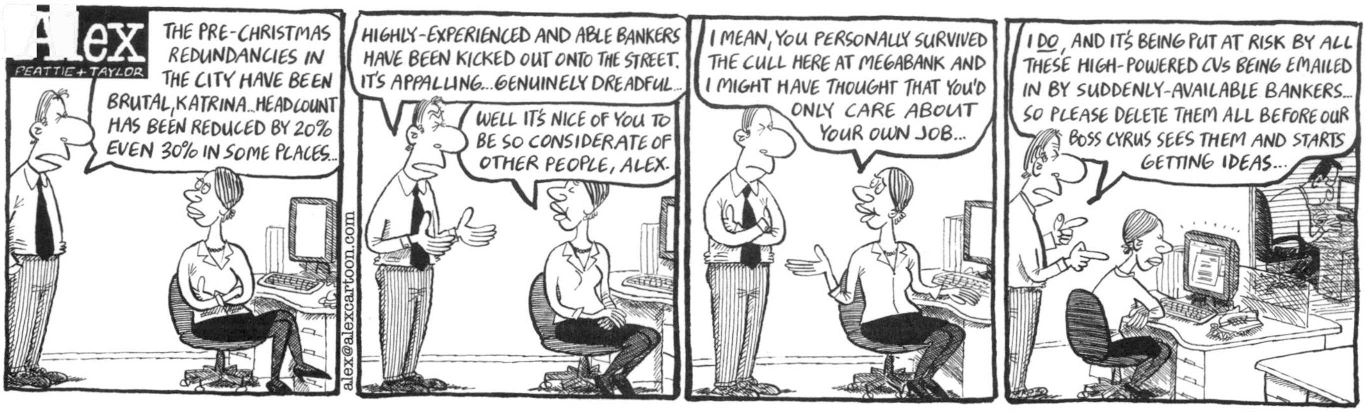
Alex
PEATTIE + TAYLOR
THE PRE-CHRISTMAS REDUNDANCIES IN THE CITY HAVE BEEN BRUTAL, KATRINA... HEADCOUNT HAS BEEN REDUCED BY 20% EVEN 30% IN SOME PLACES...
alex@alexcartoon.com
HIGHLY-EXPERIENCED AND ABLE BANKERS HAVE BEEN KICKED OUT ONTO THE STREET. IT'S APPALLING... GENUINELY DREADFUL...
WELL IT'S NICE OF YOU TO BE SO CONSIDERATE OF OTHER PEOPLE, ALEX.
I MEAN, YOU PERSONALLY SURVIVED THE CULL HERE AT MEGABANK AND I MIGHT HAVE THOUGHT THAT YOU'D ONLY CARE ABOUT YOUR OWN JOB...
I DO, AND IT'S BEING PUT AT RISK BY ALL THESE HIGH-POWERED CVs BEING EMAILED IN BY SUDDENLY-AVAILABLE BANKERS... SO PLEASE DELETE THEM ALL BEFORE OUR BOSS CYRUS SEES THEM AND STARTS GETTING IDEAS...

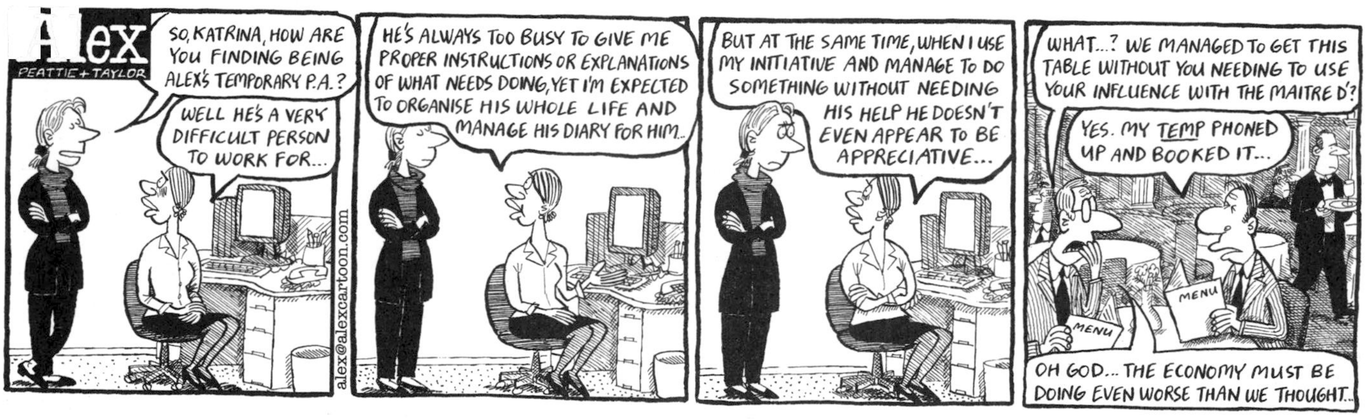
Alex
PEATTIE + TAYLOR
SO, KATRINA, HOW ARE YOU FINDING BEING ALEX'S TEMPORARY P.A.?
WELL HE'S A VERY DIFFICULT PERSON TO WORK FOR...
alex@alexcartoon.com
HE'S ALWAYS TOO BUSY TO GIVE ME PROPER INSTRUCTIONS OR EXPLANATIONS OF WHAT NEEDS DOING, YET I'M EXPECTED TO ORGANISE HIS WHOLE LIFE AND MANAGE HIS DIARY FOR HIM...
BUT AT THE SAME TIME, WHEN I USE MY INITIATIVE AND MANAGE TO DO SOMETHING WITHOUT NEEDING HIS HELP HE DOESN'T EVEN APPEAR TO BE APPRECIATIVE...
WHAT...? WE MANAGED TO GET THIS TABLE WITHOUT YOU NEEDING TO USE YOUR INFLUENCE WITH THE MAITRE D'?
YES. MY TEMP PHONED UP AND BOOKED IT...
MENU
MENU
OH GOD... THE ECONOMY MUST BE DOING EVEN WORSE THAN WE THOUGHT...

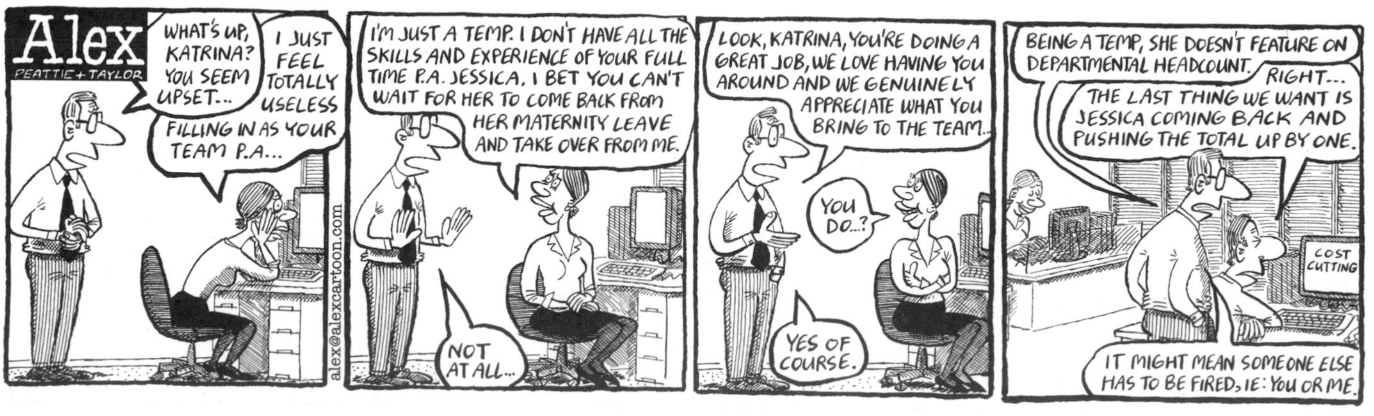
Alex
PEATTIE + TAYLOR
WHAT'S UP, KATRINA? YOU SEEM UPSET...
I JUST FEEL TOTALLY USELESS FILLING IN AS YOUR TEAM P.A...
alex@alexcartoon.com
I'M JUST A TEMP. I DON'T HAVE ALL THE SKILLS AND EXPERIENCE OF YOUR FULL TIME P.A. JESSICA. I BET YOU CAN'T WAIT FOR HER TO COME BACK FROM HER MATERNITY LEAVE AND TAKE OVER FROM ME.
NOT AT ALL...
LOOK, KATRINA, YOU'RE DOING A GREAT JOB, WE LOVE HAVING YOU AROUND AND WE GENUINELY APPRECIATE WHAT YOU BRING TO THE TEAM...
YOU DO...?
YES OF COURSE.
BEING A TEMP, SHE DOESN'T FEATURE ON DEPARTMENTAL HEADCOUNT.
RIGHT... THE LAST THING WE WANT IS JESSICA COMING BACK AND PUSHING THE TOTAL UP BY ONE.
COST CUTTING
IT MIGHT MEAN SOMEONE ELSE HAS TO BE FIRED, IE: YOU OR ME.

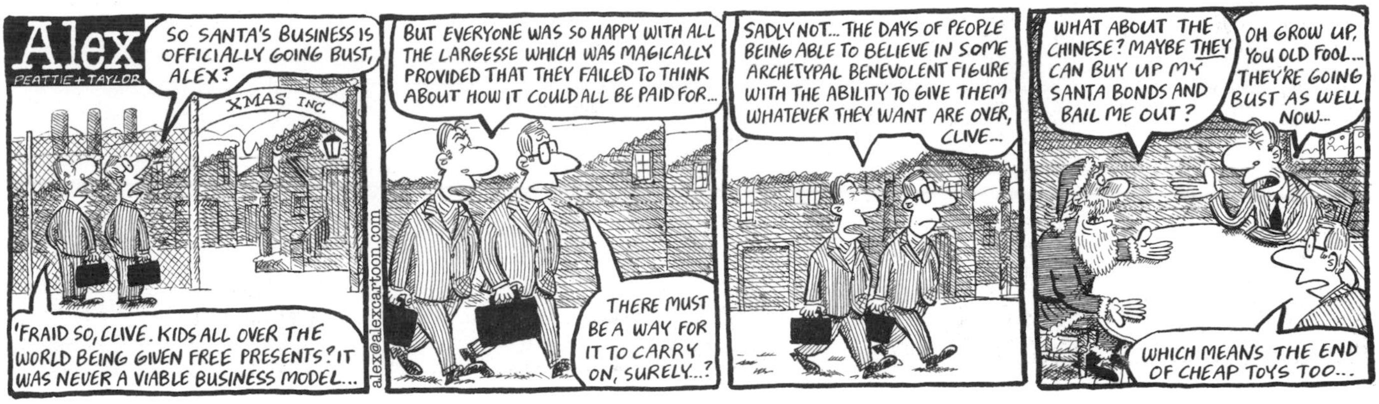
Alex
PEATTIE + TAYLOR
SO SANTA'S BUSINESS IS OFFICIALLY GOING BUST, ALEX?
XMAS INC.
'FRAID SO, CLIVE. KIDS ALL OVER THE WORLD BEING GIVEN FREE PRESENTS? IT WAS NEVER A VIABLE BUSINESS MODEL...
BUT EVERYONE WAS SO HAPPY WITH ALL THE LARGESSE WHICH WAS MAGICALLY PROVIDED THAT THEY FAILED TO THINK ABOUT HOW IT COULD ALL BE PAID FOR...
THERE MUST BE A WAY FOR IT TO CARRY ON, SURELY...?
alex@alexcartoon.com
SADLY NOT... THE DAYS OF PEOPLE BEING ABLE TO BELIEVE IN SOME ARCHETYPAL BENEVOLENT FIGURE WITH THE ABILITY TO GIVE THEM WHATEVER THEY WANT ARE OVER, CLIVE...
WHAT ABOUT THE CHINESE? MAYBE THEY CAN BUY UP MY SANTA BONDS AND BAIL ME OUT?
OH GROW UP, YOU OLD FOOL... THEY'RE GOING BUST AS WELL NOW...
WHICH MEANS THE END OF CHEAP TOYS TOO...

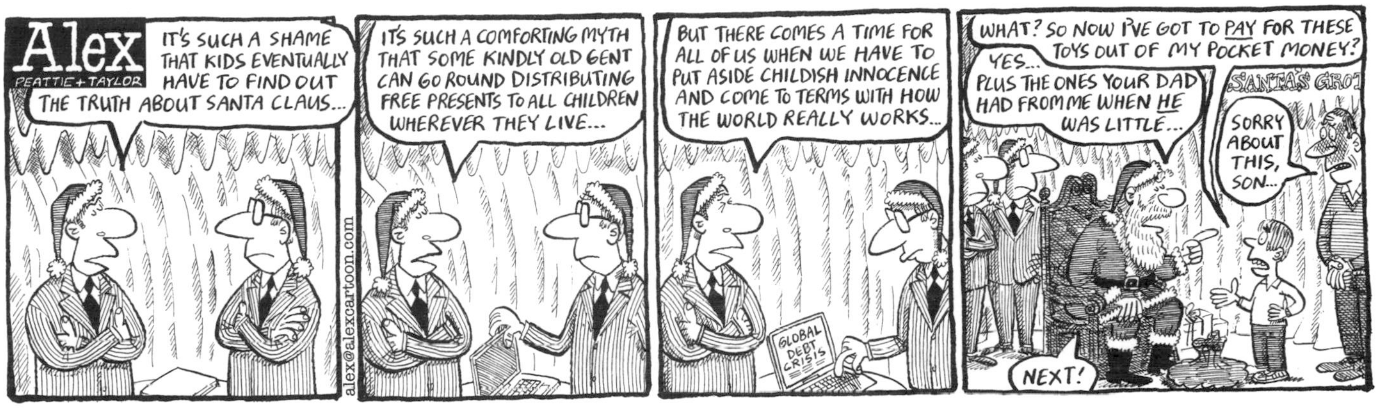
Alex
PEATTIE + TAYLOR
IT'S SUCH A SHAME THAT KIDS EVENTUALLY HAVE TO FIND OUT THE TRUTH ABOUT SANTA CLAUS...
IT'S SUCH A COMFORTING MYTH THAT SOME KINDLY OLD GENT CAN GO ROUND DISTRIBUTING FREE PRESENTS TO ALL CHILDREN WHEREVER THEY LIVE...
alex@alexcartoon.com
BUT THERE COMES A TIME FOR ALL OF US WHEN WE HAVE TO PUT ASIDE CHILDISH INNOCENCE AND COME TO TERMS WITH HOW THE WORLD REALLY WORKS...
GLOBAL DEBT CRISIS
WHAT? SO NOW I'VE GOT TO PAY FOR THESE TOYS OUT OF MY POCKET MONEY?
YES... PLUS THE ONES YOUR DAD HAD FROM ME WHEN HE WAS LITTLE...
SANTA'S GROT
SORRY ABOUT THIS, SON...
NEXT!

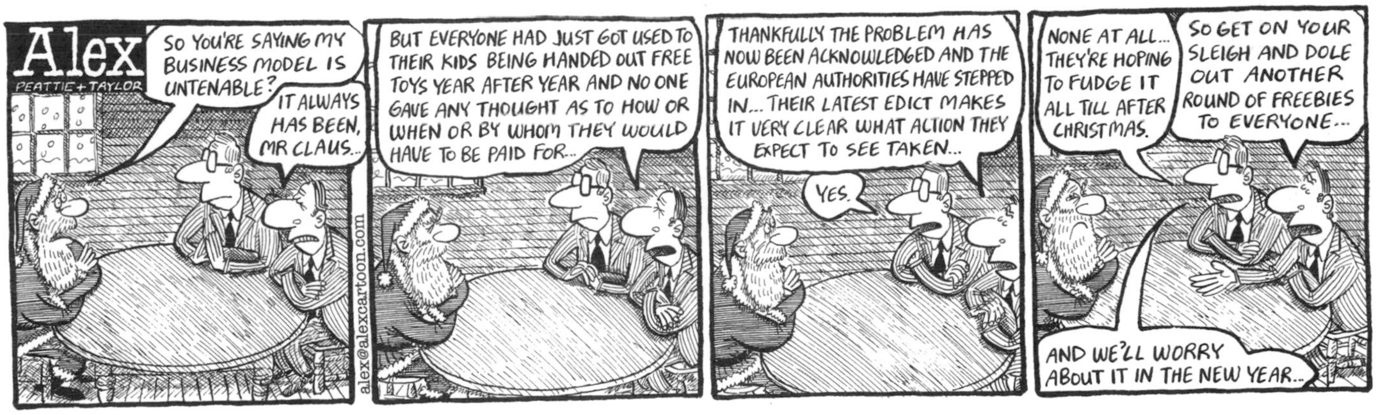
Alex
PEATTIE + TAYLOR
SO YOU'RE SAYING MY BUSINESS MODEL IS UNTENABLE?
IT ALWAYS HAS BEEN, MR CLAUS...
alex@alexcartoon.com
BUT EVERYONE HAD JUST GOT USED TO THEIR KIDS BEING HANDED OUT FREE TOYS YEAR AFTER YEAR AND NO ONE GAVE ANY THOUGHT AS TO HOW OR WHEN OR BY WHOM THEY WOULD HAVE TO BE PAID FOR...
THANKFULLY THE PROBLEM HAS NOW BEEN ACKNOWLEDGED AND THE EUROPEAN AUTHORITIES HAVE STEPPED IN... THEIR LATEST EDICT MAKES IT VERY CLEAR WHAT ACTION THEY EXPECT TO SEE TAKEN...
YES.
NONE AT ALL... THEY'RE HOPING TO FUDGE IT ALL TILL AFTER CHRISTMAS.
SO GET ON YOUR SLEIGH AND DOLE OUT ANOTHER ROUND OF FREEBIES TO EVERYONE...
AND WE'LL WORRY ABOUT IT IN THE NEW YEAR...

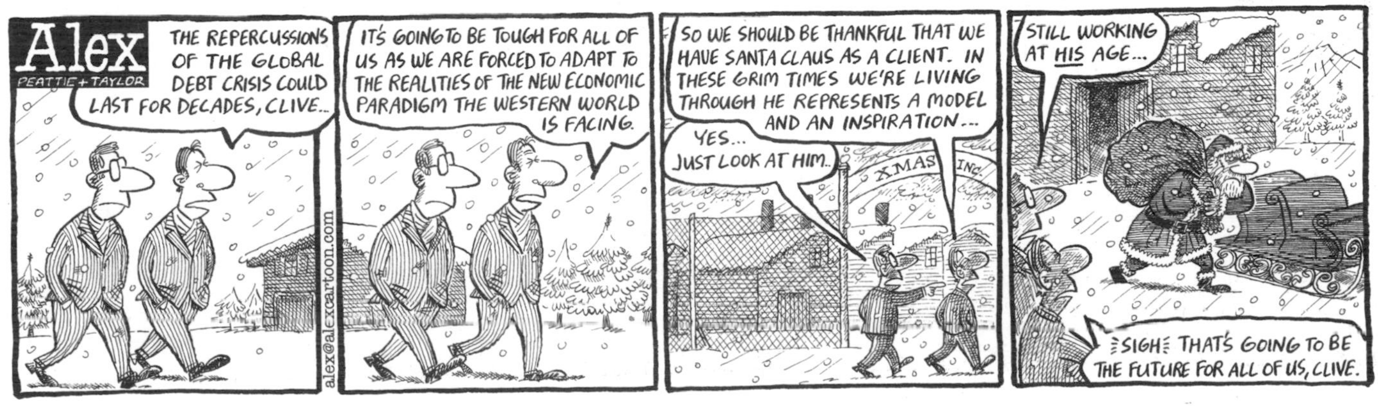
Alex
PEATTIE + TAYLOR
THE REPERCUSSIONS OF THE GLOBAL DEBT CRISIS COULD LAST FOR DECADES, CLIVE...
alex@alexcartoon.com
IT'S GOING TO BE TOUGH FOR ALL OF US AS WE ARE FORCED TO ADAPT TO THE REALITIES OF THE NEW ECONOMIC PARADIGM THE WESTERN WORLD IS FACING.
SO WE SHOULD BE THANKFUL THAT WE HAVE SANTA CLAUS AS A CLIENT. IN THESE GRIM TIMES WE'RE LIVING THROUGH HE REPRESENTS A MODEL AND AN INSPIRATION...
YES... JUST LOOK AT HIM...
XMAS INC.
STILL WORKING AT HIS AGE...
SIGH THAT'S GOING TO BE THE FUTURE FOR ALL OF US, CLIVE.

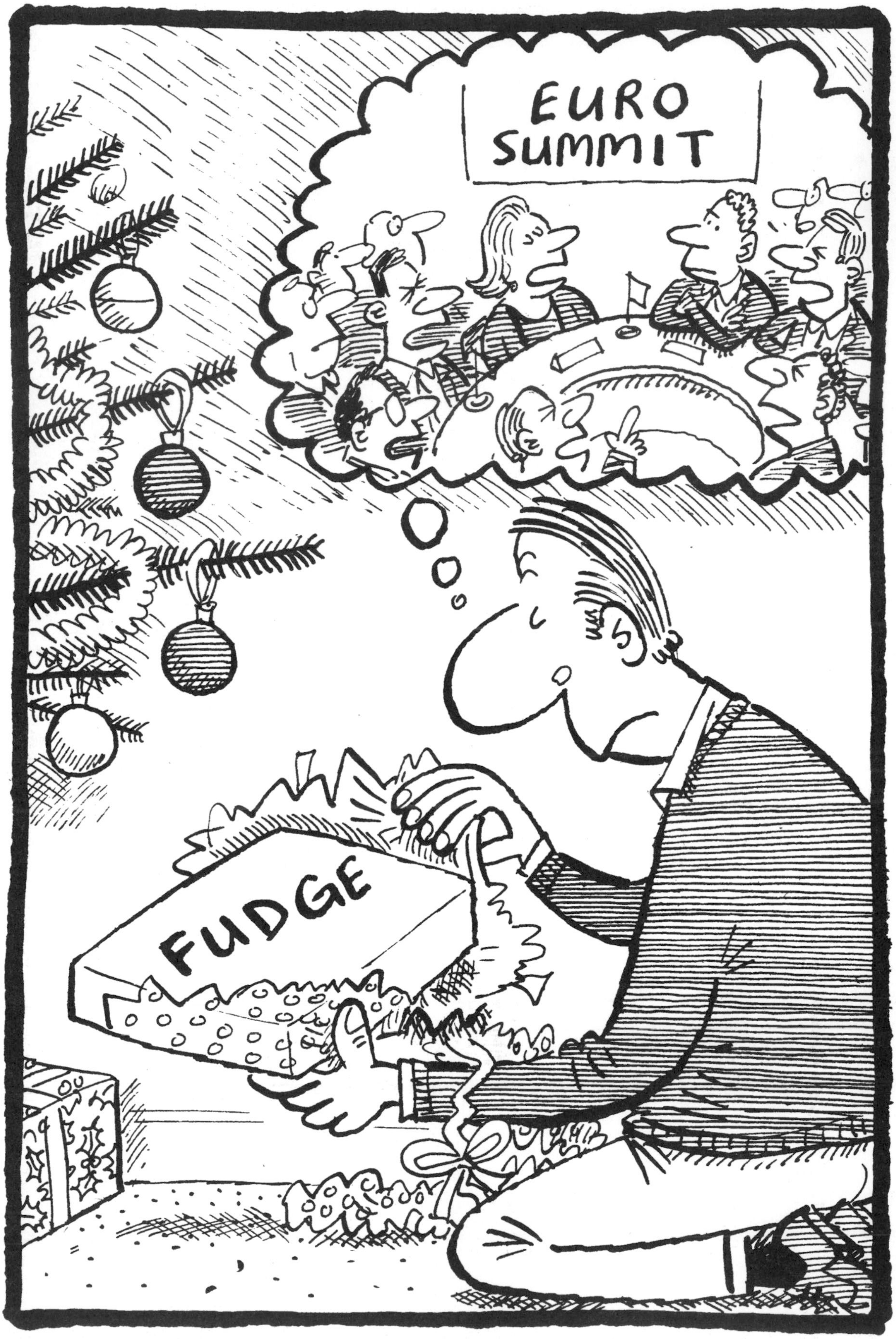
EURO
SUMMIT
FUDGE

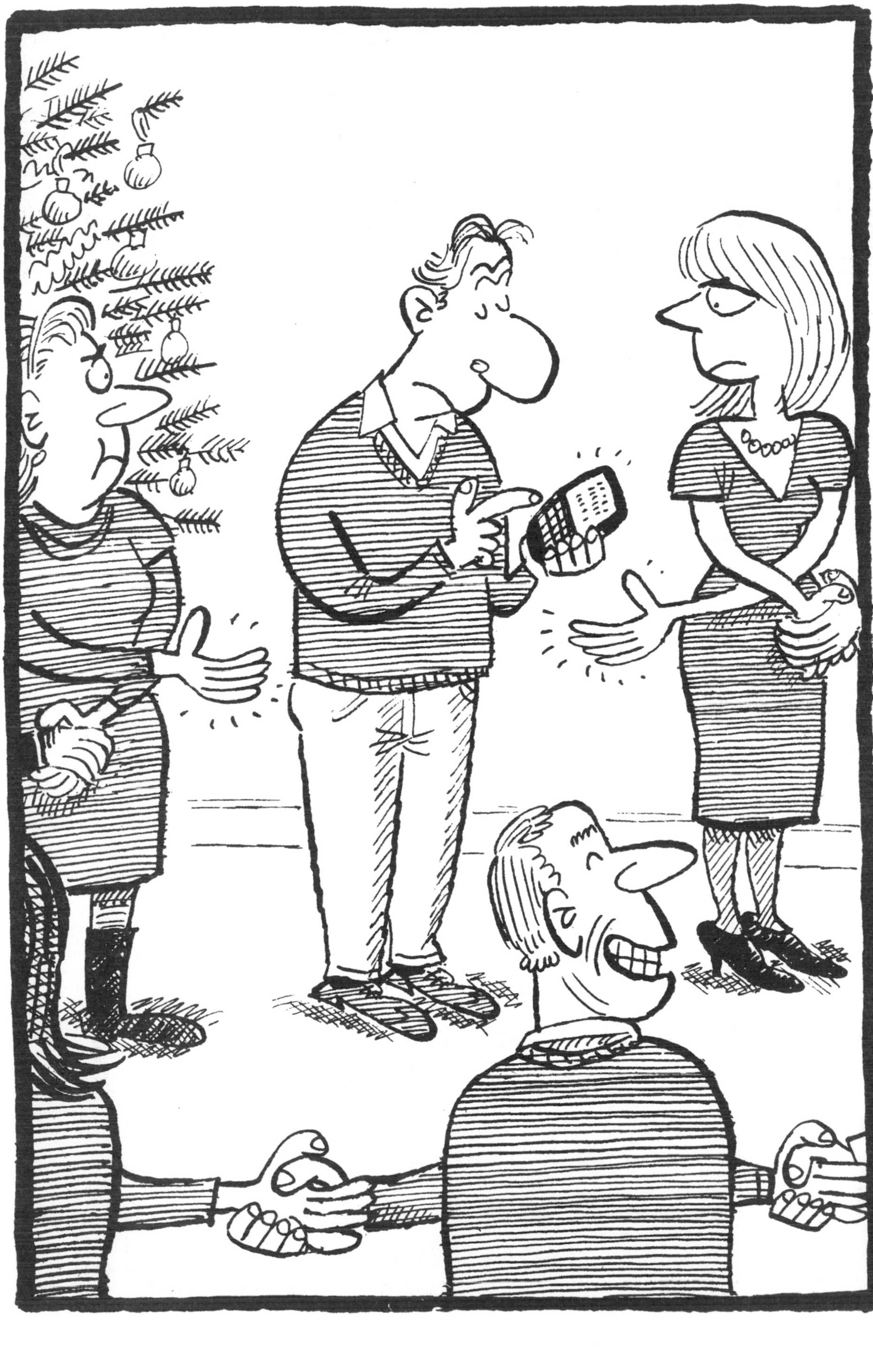

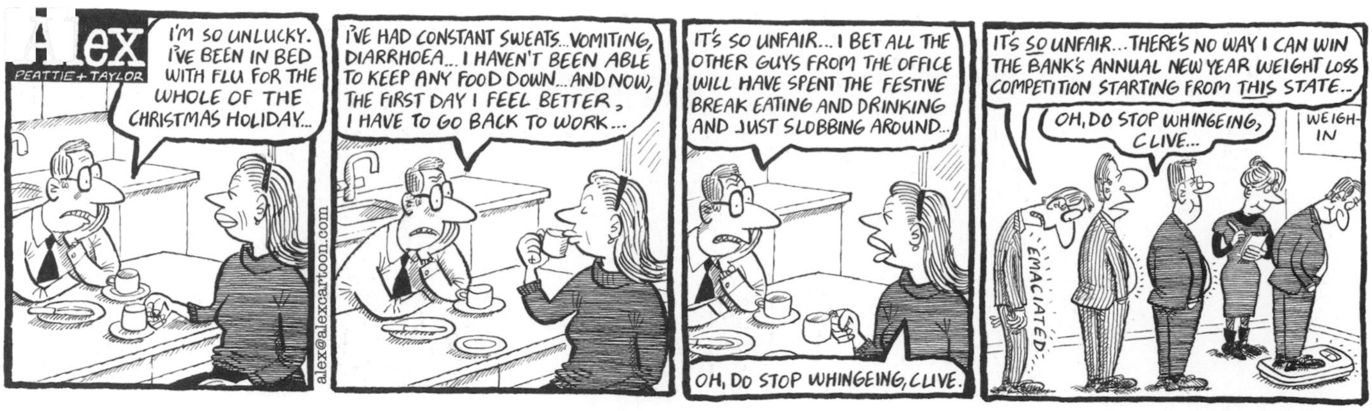
Alex
PEATTIE+TAYLOR
I'M SO UNLUCKY. I'VE BEEN IN BED WITH FLU FOR THE WHOLE OF THE CHRISTMAS HOLIDAY...
I'VE HAD CONSTANT SWEATS...VOMITING, DIARRHOEA... I HAVEN'T BEEN ABLE TO KEEP ANY FOOD DOWN...AND NOW, THE FIRST DAY I FEEL BETTER, I HAVE TO GO BACK TO WORK...
alex@alexcartoon.com
IT'S SO UNFAIR... I BET ALL THE OTHER GUYS FROM THE OFFICE WILL HAVE SPENT THE FESTIVE BREAK EATING AND DRINKING AND JUST SLOBBING AROUND...
OH, DO STOP WHINGEING, CLIVE.
IT'S SO UNFAIR...THERE'S NO WAY I CAN WIN THE BANK'S ANNUAL NEW YEAR WEIGHT LOSS COMPETITION STARTING FROM THIS STATE...
OH, DO STOP WHINGEING, CLIVE...
WEIGH-IN
EMACIATED

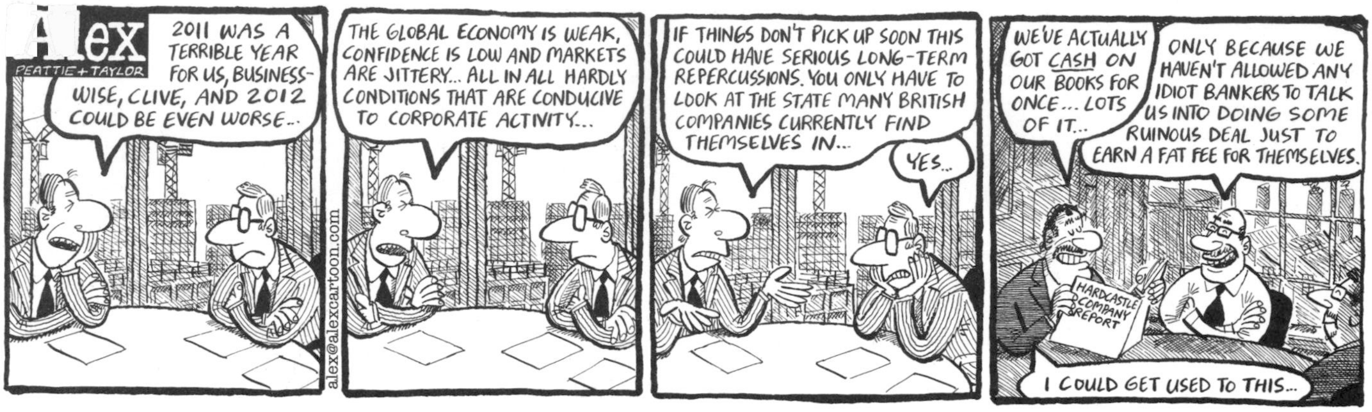
Alex
PEATTIE+TAYLOR
2011 WAS A TERRIBLE YEAR FOR US, BUSINESS-WISE, CLIVE, AND 2012 COULD BE EVEN WORSE...
THE GLOBAL ECONOMY IS WEAK, CONFIDENCE IS LOW AND MARKETS ARE JITTERY... ALL IN ALL HARDLY CONDITIONS THAT ARE CONDUCIVE TO CORPORATE ACTIVITY...
alex@alexcartoon.com
IF THINGS DON'T PICK UP SOON THIS COULD HAVE SERIOUS LONG-TERM REPERCUSSIONS. YOU ONLY HAVE TO LOOK AT THE STATE MANY BRITISH COMPANIES CURRENTLY FIND THEMSELVES IN...
YES...
WE'VE ACTUALLY GOT CASH ON OUR BOOKS FOR ONCE... LOTS OF IT...
ONLY BECAUSE WE HAVEN'T ALLOWED ANY IDIOT BANKERS TO TALK US INTO DOING SOME RUINOUS DEAL JUST TO EARN A FAT FEE FOR THEMSELVES.
HARDCASTLE COMPANY REPORT
I COULD GET USED TO THIS...

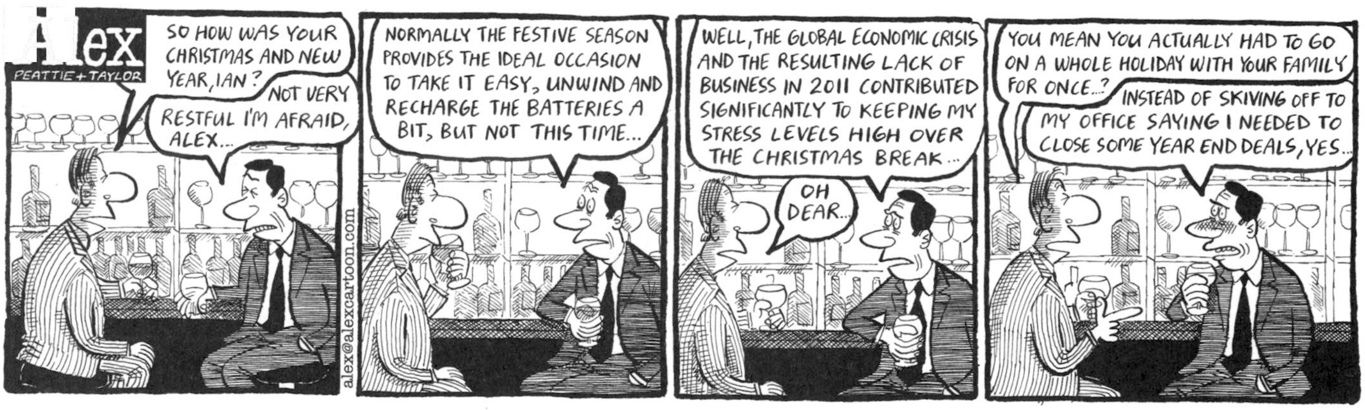
Alex
PEATTIE+TAYLOR
SO HOW WAS YOUR CHRISTMAS AND NEW YEAR, IAN?
NOT VERY RESTFUL I'M AFRAID, ALEX...
NORMALLY THE FESTIVE SEASON PROVIDES THE IDEAL OCCASION TO TAKE IT EASY, UNWIND AND RECHARGE THE BATTERIES A BIT, BUT NOT THIS TIME...
alex@alexcartoon.com
WELL, THE GLOBAL ECONOMIC CRISIS AND THE RESULTING LACK OF BUSINESS IN 2011 CONTRIBUTED SIGNIFICANTLY TO KEEPING MY STRESS LEVELS HIGH OVER THE CHRISTMAS BREAK...
OH DEAR...
YOU MEAN YOU ACTUALLY HAD TO GO ON A WHOLE HOLIDAY WITH YOUR FAMILY FOR ONCE...?
INSTEAD OF SKIVING OFF TO MY OFFICE SAYING I NEEDED TO CLOSE SOME YEAR END DEALS, YES...

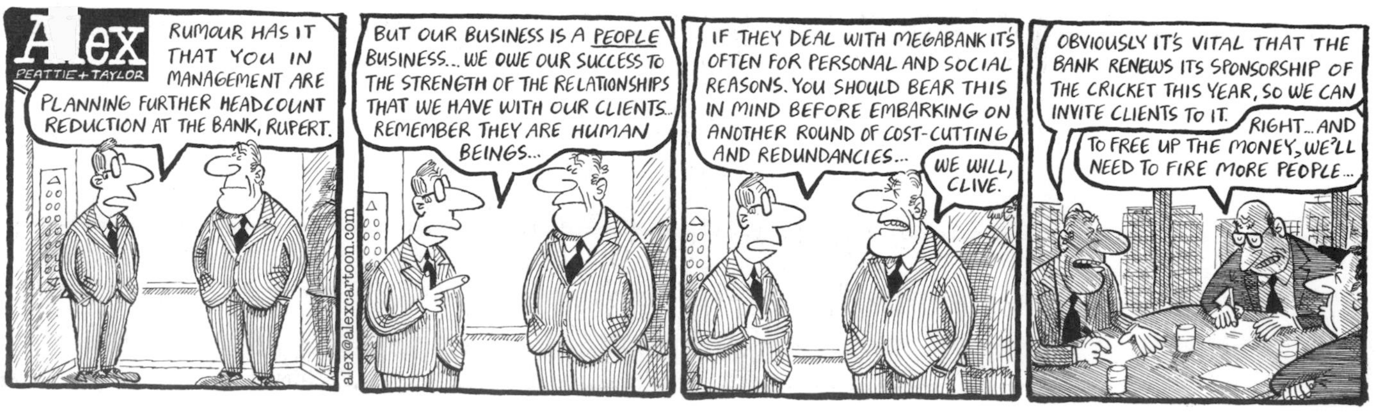
Alex
PEATTIE+TAYLOR
RUMOUR HAS IT THAT YOU IN MANAGEMENT ARE PLANNING FURTHER HEADCOUNT REDUCTION AT THE BANK, RUPERT.
BUT OUR BUSINESS IS A PEOPLE BUSINESS... WE OWE OUR SUCCESS TO THE STRENGTH OF THE RELATIONSHIPS THAT WE HAVE WITH OUR CLIENTS... REMEMBER THEY ARE HUMAN BEINGS...
alex@alexcartoon.com
IF THEY DEAL WITH MEGABANK IT'S OFTEN FOR PERSONAL AND SOCIAL REASONS. YOU SHOULD BEAR THIS IN MIND BEFORE EMBARKING ON ANOTHER ROUND OF COST-CUTTING AND REDUNDANCIES...
WE WILL, CLIVE.
OBVIOUSLY IT'S VITAL THAT THE BANK RENEWS ITS SPONSORSHIP OF THE CRICKET THIS YEAR, SO WE CAN INVITE CLIENTS TO IT.
RIGHT... AND TO FREE UP THE MONEY, WE'LL NEED TO FIRE MORE PEOPLE...

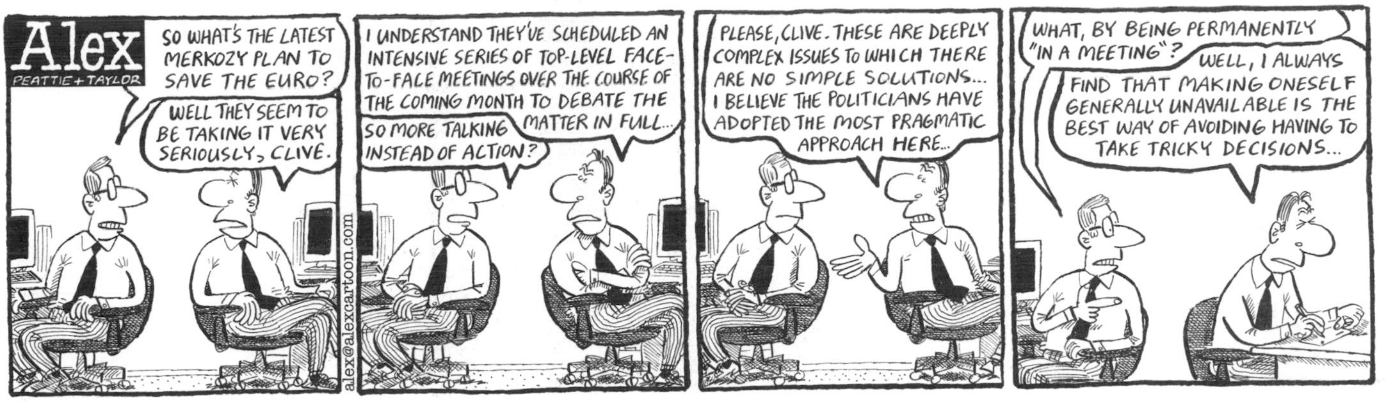
Alex
PEATTIE + TAYLOR
SO WHAT'S THE LATEST MERKOZY PLAN TO SAVE THE EURO?
WELL THEY SEEM TO BE TAKING IT VERY SERIOUSLY, CLIVE.
I UNDERSTAND THEY'VE SCHEDULED AN INTENSIVE SERIES OF TOP-LEVEL FACE-TO-FACE MEETINGS OVER THE COURSE OF THE COMING MONTH TO DEBATE THE MATTER IN FULL...
SO MORE TALKING INSTEAD OF ACTION?
PLEASE, CLIVE. THESE ARE DEEPLY COMPLEX ISSUES TO WHICH THERE ARE NO SIMPLE SOLUTIONS... I BELIEVE THE POLITICIANS HAVE ADOPTED THE MOST PRAGMATIC APPROACH HERE...
WHAT, BY BEING PERMANENTLY "IN A MEETING"?
WELL, I ALWAYS FIND THAT MAKING ONESELF GENERALLY UNAVAILABLE IS THE BEST WAY OF AVOIDING HAVING TO TAKE TRICKY DECISIONS...
alex@alexcartoon.com

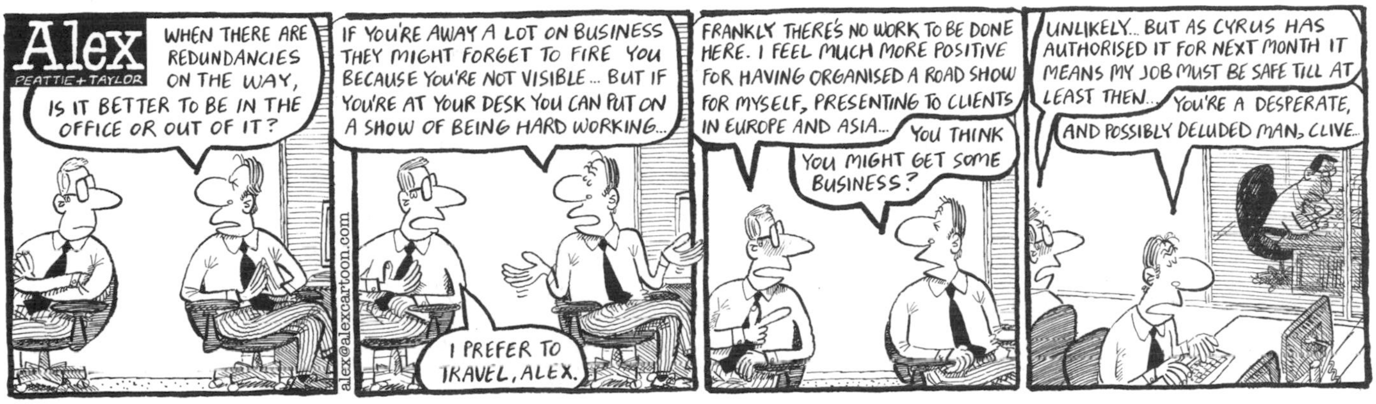
Alex
PEATTIE + TAYLOR
WHEN THERE ARE REDUNDANCIES ON THE WAY, IS IT BETTER TO BE IN THE OFFICE OR OUT OF IT?
IF YOU'RE AWAY A LOT ON BUSINESS THEY MIGHT FORGET TO FIRE YOU BECAUSE YOU'RE NOT VISIBLE... BUT IF YOU'RE AT YOUR DESK YOU CAN PUT ON A SHOW OF BEING HARD WORKING...
I PREFER TO TRAVEL, ALEX.
FRANKLY THERE'S NO WORK TO BE DONE HERE. I FEEL MUCH MORE POSITIVE FOR HAVING ORGANISED A ROAD SHOW FOR MYSELF, PRESENTING TO CLIENTS IN EUROPE AND ASIA...
YOU THINK YOU MIGHT GET SOME BUSINESS?
UNLIKELY... BUT AS CYRUS HAS AUTHORISED IT FOR NEXT MONTH IT MEANS MY JOB MUST BE SAFE TILL AT LEAST THEN...
YOU'RE A DESPERATE, AND POSSIBLY DELUDED MAN, CLIVE...
alex@alexcartoon.com

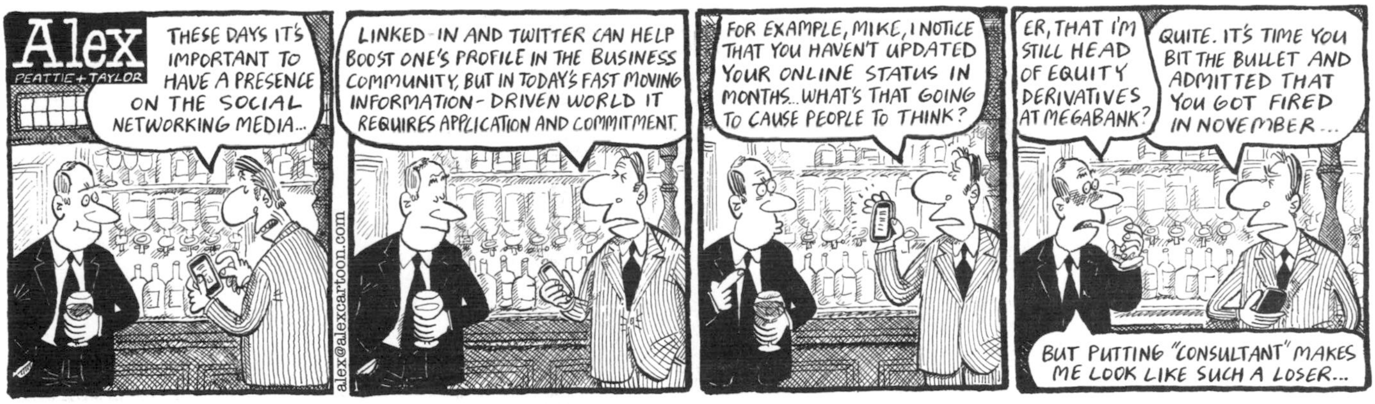
Alex
PEATTIE + TAYLOR
THESE DAYS IT'S IMPORTANT TO HAVE A PRESENCE ON THE SOCIAL NETWORKING MEDIA...
LINKED-IN AND TWITTER CAN HELP BOOST ONE'S PROFILE IN THE BUSINESS COMMUNITY, BUT IN TODAY'S FAST MOVING INFORMATION-DRIVEN WORLD IT REQUIRES APPLICATION AND COMMITMENT.
FOR EXAMPLE, MIKE, I NOTICE THAT YOU HAVEN'T UPDATED YOUR ONLINE STATUS IN MONTHS... WHAT'S THAT GOING TO CAUSE PEOPLE TO THINK?
ER, THAT I'M STILL HEAD OF EQUITY DERIVATIVES AT MEGABANK?
QUITE. IT'S TIME YOU BIT THE BULLET AND ADMITTED THAT YOU GOT FIRED IN NOVEMBER...
BUT PUTTING "CONSULTANT" MAKES ME LOOK LIKE SUCH A LOSER...
alex@alexcartoon.com

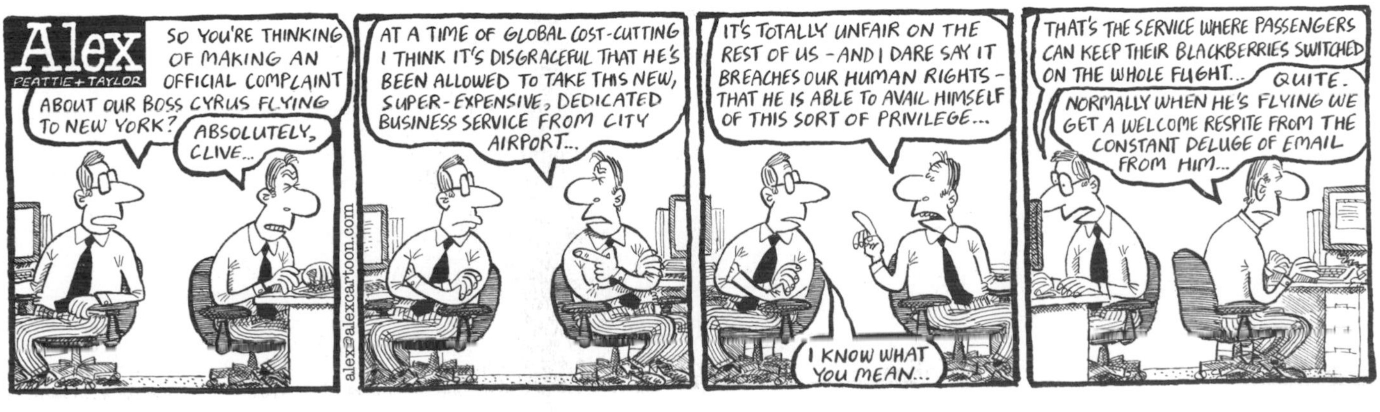
Alex
PEATTIE + TAYLOR
SO YOU'RE THINKING OF MAKING AN OFFICIAL COMPLAINT ABOUT OUR BOSS CYRUS FLYING TO NEW YORK?
ABSOLUTELY, CLIVE...
AT A TIME OF GLOBAL COST-CUTTING I THINK IT'S DISGRACEFUL THAT HE'S BEEN ALLOWED TO TAKE THIS NEW, SUPER-EXPENSIVE, DEDICATED BUSINESS SERVICE FROM CITY AIRPORT...
IT'S TOTALLY UNFAIR ON THE REST OF US - AND I DARE SAY IT BREACHES OUR HUMAN RIGHTS - THAT HE IS ABLE TO AVAIL HIMSELF OF THIS SORT OF PRIVILEGE...
I KNOW WHAT YOU MEAN...
THAT'S THE SERVICE WHERE PASSENGERS CAN KEEP THEIR BLACKBERRIES SWITCHED ON THE WHOLE FLIGHT...
QUITE. NORMALLY WHEN HE'S FLYING WE GET A WELCOME RESPITE FROM THE CONSTANT DELUGE OF EMAIL FROM HIM...
alex@alexcartoon.com

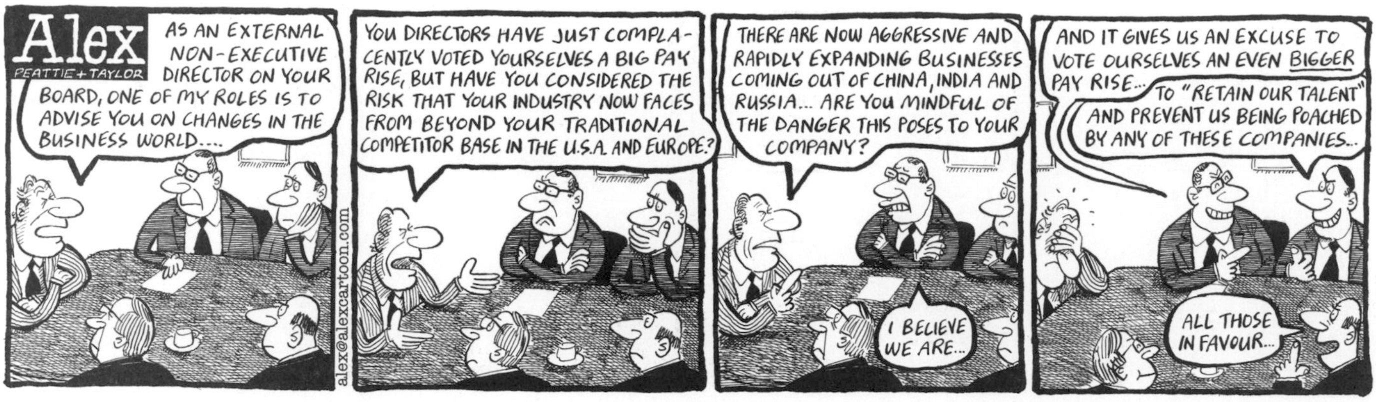
Alex
PEATTIE + TAYLOR
AS AN EXTERNAL NON-EXECUTIVE DIRECTOR ON YOUR BOARD, ONE OF MY ROLES IS TO ADVISE YOU ON CHANGES IN THE BUSINESS WORLD....
alex@alexcartoon.com
YOU DIRECTORS HAVE JUST COMPLACENTLY VOTED YOURSELVES A BIG PAY RISE, BUT HAVE YOU CONSIDERED THE RISK THAT YOUR INDUSTRY NOW FACES FROM BEYOND YOUR TRADITIONAL COMPETITOR BASE IN THE U.S.A. AND EUROPE?
THERE ARE NOW AGGRESSIVE AND RAPIDLY EXPANDING BUSINESSES COMING OUT OF CHINA, INDIA AND RUSSIA... ARE YOU MINDFUL OF THE DANGER THIS POSES TO YOUR COMPANY?
I BELIEVE WE ARE...
AND IT GIVES US AN EXCUSE TO VOTE OURSELVES AN EVEN BIGGER PAY RISE...
TO "RETAIN OUR TALENT" AND PREVENT US BEING POACHED BY ANY OF THESE COMPANIES...
ALL THOSE IN FAVOUR...

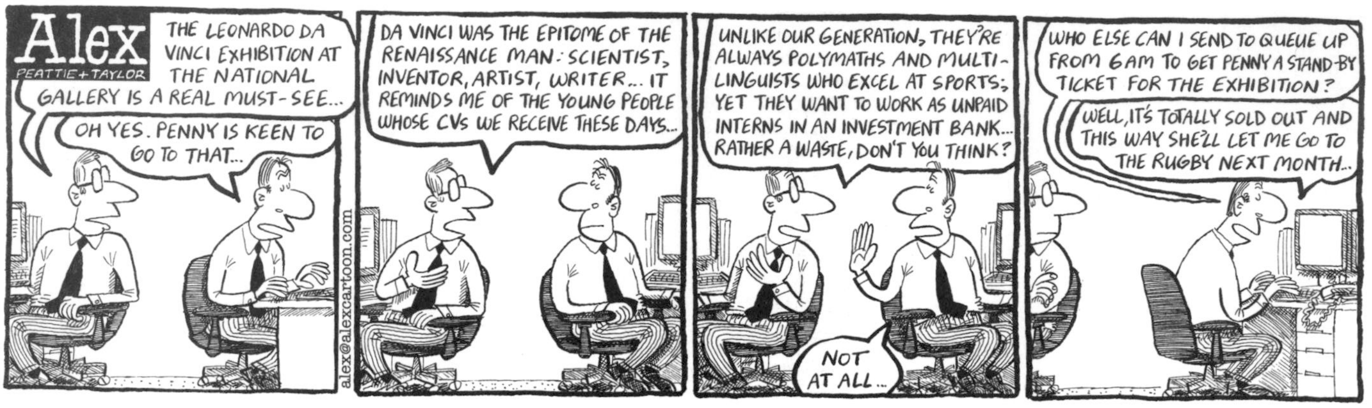
Alex
PEATTIE + TAYLOR
THE LEONARDO DA VINCI EXHIBITION AT THE NATIONAL GALLERY IS A REAL MUST-SEE...
OH YES. PENNY IS KEEN TO GO TO THAT...
alex@alexcartoon.com
DA VINCI WAS THE EPITOME OF THE RENAISSANCE MAN: SCIENTIST, INVENTOR, ARTIST, WRITER... IT REMINDS ME OF THE YOUNG PEOPLE WHOSE CVs WE RECEIVE THESE DAYS...
UNLIKE OUR GENERATION, THEY'RE ALWAYS POLYMATHS AND MULTI-LINGUISTS WHO EXCEL AT SPORTS; YET THEY WANT TO WORK AS UNPAID INTERNS IN AN INVESTMENT BANK... RATHER A WASTE, DON'T YOU THINK?
NOT AT ALL...
WHO ELSE CAN I SEND TO QUEUE UP FROM 6AM TO GET PENNY A STAND-BY TICKET FOR THE EXHIBITION?
WELL, IT'S TOTALLY SOLD OUT AND THIS WAY SHE'LL LET ME GO TO THE RUGBY NEXT MONTH...

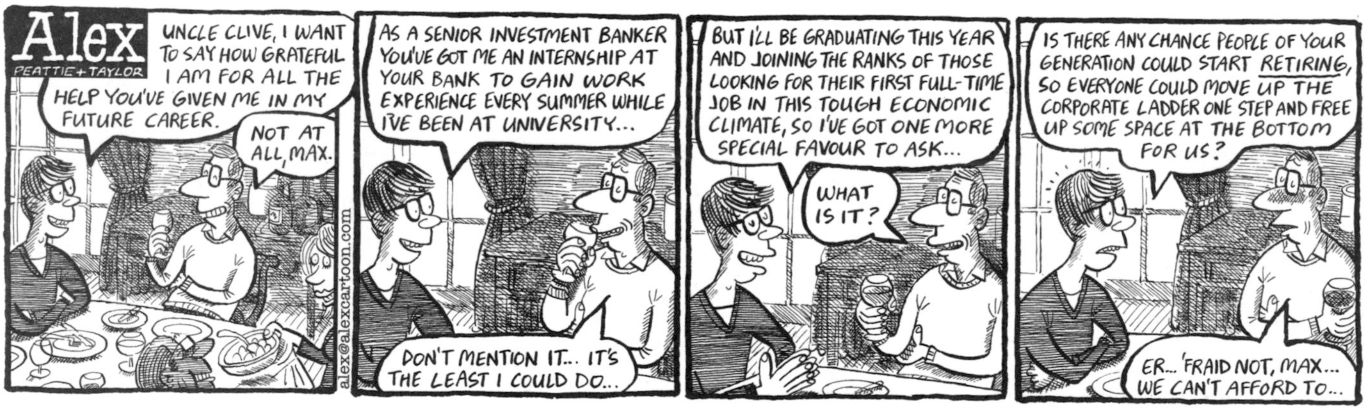
Alex
PEATTIE + TAYLOR
UNCLE CLIVE, I WANT TO SAY HOW GRATEFUL I AM FOR ALL THE HELP YOU'VE GIVEN ME IN MY FUTURE CAREER.
NOT AT ALL, MAX.
alex@alexcartoon.com
AS A SENIOR INVESTMENT BANKER YOU'VE GOT ME AN INTERNSHIP AT YOUR BANK TO GAIN WORK EXPERIENCE EVERY SUMMER WHILE I'VE BEEN AT UNIVERSITY...
DON'T MENTION IT... IT'S THE LEAST I COULD DO...
BUT I'LL BE GRADUATING THIS YEAR AND JOINING THE RANKS OF THOSE LOOKING FOR THEIR FIRST FULL-TIME JOB IN THIS TOUGH ECONOMIC CLIMATE, SO I'VE GOT ONE MORE SPECIAL FAVOUR TO ASK...
WHAT IS IT?
IS THERE ANY CHANCE PEOPLE OF YOUR GENERATION COULD START RETIRING, SO EVERYONE COULD MOVE UP THE CORPORATE LADDER ONE STEP AND FREE UP SOME SPACE AT THE BOTTOM FOR US?
ER... 'FRAID NOT, MAX... WE CAN'T AFFORD TO...

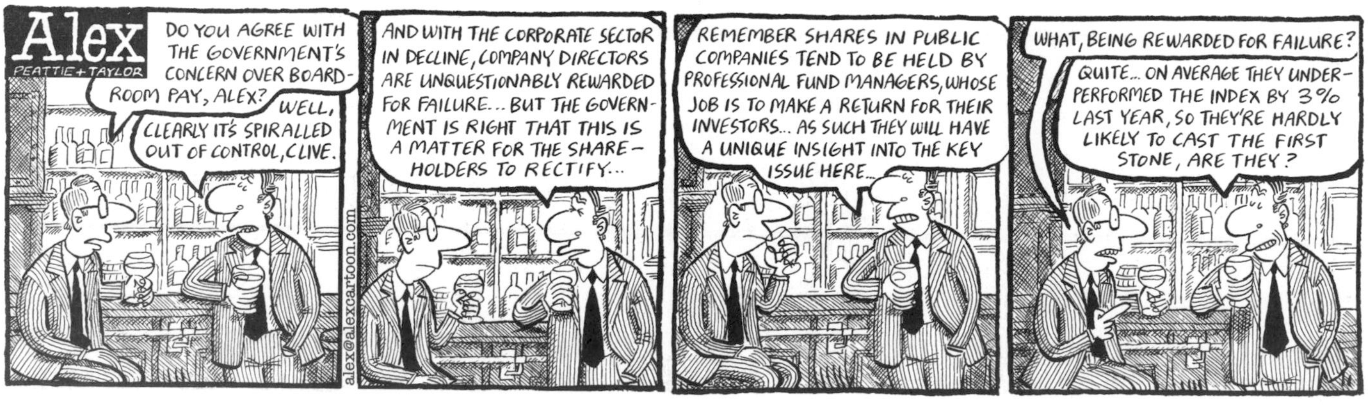
Alex
PEATTIE + TAYLOR
DO YOU AGREE WITH THE GOVERNMENT'S CONCERN OVER BOARDROOM PAY, ALEX?
WELL, CLEARLY IT'S SPIRALLED OUT OF CONTROL, CLIVE.
alex@alexcartoon.com
AND WITH THE CORPORATE SECTOR IN DECLINE, COMPANY DIRECTORS ARE UNQUESTIONABLY REWARDED FOR FAILURE... BUT THE GOVERNMENT IS RIGHT THAT THIS IS A MATTER FOR THE SHAREHOLDERS TO RECTIFY...
REMEMBER SHARES IN PUBLIC COMPANIES TEND TO BE HELD BY PROFESSIONAL FUND MANAGERS, WHOSE JOB IS TO MAKE A RETURN FOR THEIR INVESTORS... AS SUCH THEY WILL HAVE A UNIQUE INSIGHT INTO THE KEY ISSUE HERE...
WHAT, BEING REWARDED FOR FAILURE?
QUITE... ON AVERAGE THEY UNDERPERFORMED THE INDEX BY 3% LAST YEAR, SO THEY'RE HARDLY LIKELY TO CAST THE FIRST STONE, ARE THEY?

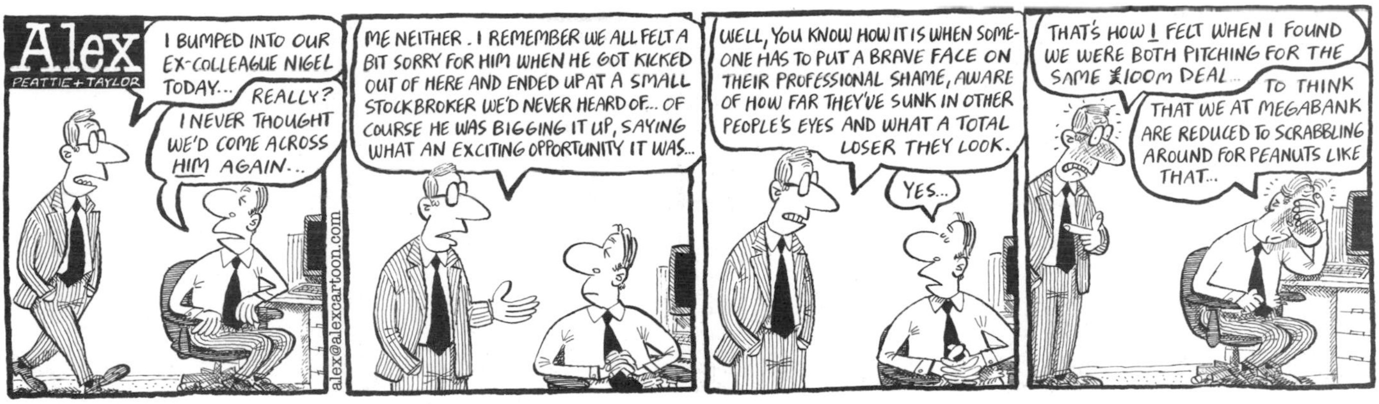
Alex
PEATTIE + TAYLOR
I BUMPED INTO OUR EX-COLLEAGUE NIGEL TODAY...
REALLY? I NEVER THOUGHT WE'D COME ACROSS HIM AGAIN...
alex@alexcartoon.com
ME NEITHER. I REMEMBER WE ALL FELT A BIT SORRY FOR HIM WHEN HE GOT KICKED OUT OF HERE AND ENDED UP AT A SMALL STOCKBROKER WE'D NEVER HEARD OF... OF COURSE HE WAS BIGGING IT UP, SAYING WHAT AN EXCITING OPPORTUNITY IT WAS...
WELL, YOU KNOW HOW IT IS WHEN SOMEONE HAS TO PUT A BRAVE FACE ON THEIR PROFESSIONAL SHAME, AWARE OF HOW FAR THEY'VE SUNK IN OTHER PEOPLE'S EYES AND WHAT A TOTAL LOSER THEY LOOK.
YES...
THAT'S HOW I FELT WHEN I FOUND WE WERE BOTH PITCHING FOR THE SAME ¥100M DEAL...
TO THINK THAT WE AT MEGABANK ARE REDUCED TO SCRABBLING AROUND FOR PEANUTS LIKE THAT...

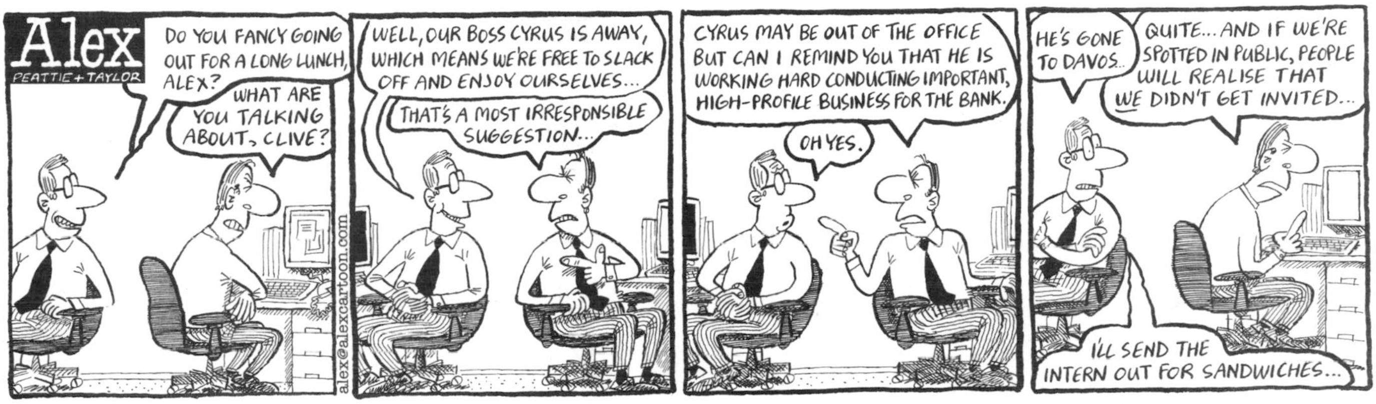
Alex
PEATTIE + TAYLOR
DO YOU FANCY GOING OUT FOR A LONG LUNCH, ALEX?
WHAT ARE YOU TALKING ABOUT, CLIVE?
alex@alexcartoon.com
WELL, OUR BOSS CYRUS IS AWAY, WHICH MEANS WE'RE FREE TO SLACK OFF AND ENJOY OURSELVES...
THAT'S A MOST IRRESPONSIBLE SUGGESTION...
CYRUS MAY BE OUT OF THE OFFICE BUT CAN I REMIND YOU THAT HE IS WORKING HARD CONDUCTING IMPORTANT, HIGH-PROFILE BUSINESS FOR THE BANK.
OH YES.
HE'S GONE TO DAVOS...
QUITE... AND IF WE'RE SPOTTED IN PUBLIC, PEOPLE WILL REALISE THAT WE DIDN'T GET INVITED...
I'LL SEND THE INTERN OUT FOR SANDWICHES...

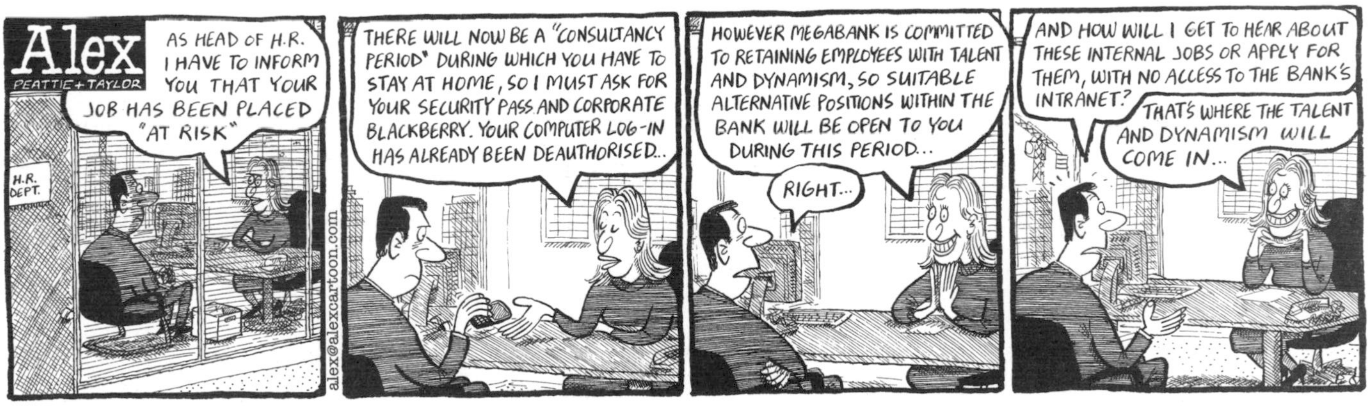
Alex
PEATTIE + TAYLOR
AS HEAD OF H.R. I HAVE TO INFORM YOU THAT YOUR JOB HAS BEEN PLACED "AT RISK"
H.R. DEPT.
alex@alexcartoon.com
THERE WILL NOW BE A "CONSULTANCY PERIOD" DURING WHICH YOU HAVE TO STAY AT HOME, SO I MUST ASK FOR YOUR SECURITY PASS AND CORPORATE BLACKBERRY. YOUR COMPUTER LOG-IN HAS ALREADY BEEN DEAUTHORISED...
HOWEVER MEGABANK IS COMMITTED TO RETAINING EMPLOYEES WITH TALENT AND DYNAMISM, SO SUITABLE ALTERNATIVE POSITIONS WITHIN THE BANK WILL BE OPEN TO YOU DURING THIS PERIOD...
RIGHT...
AND HOW WILL I GET TO HEAR ABOUT THESE INTERNAL JOBS OR APPLY FOR THEM, WITH NO ACCESS TO THE BANK'S INTRANET?
THAT'S WHERE THE TALENT AND DYNAMISM WILL COME IN...

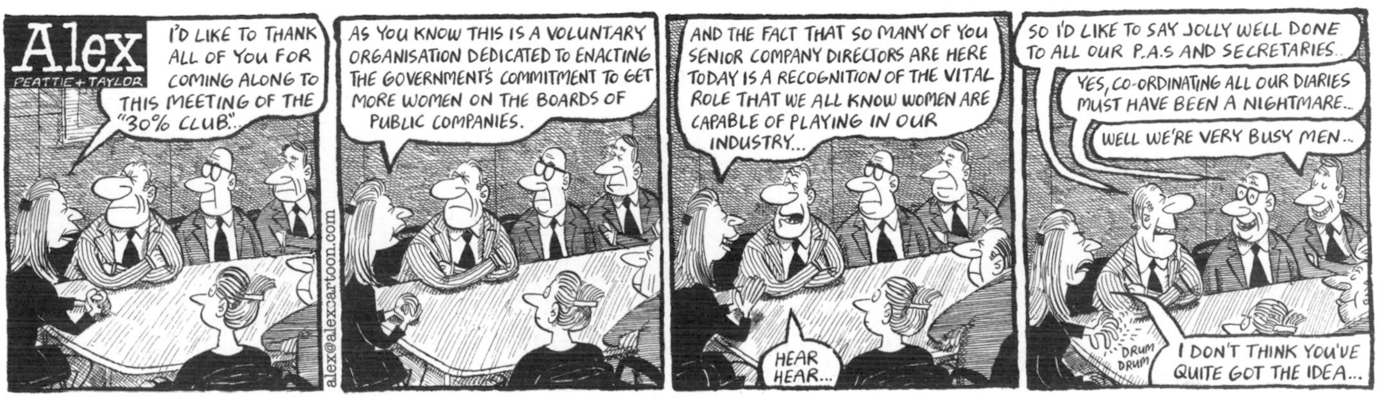
Alex
PEATTIE + TAYLOR
I'D LIKE TO THANK ALL OF YOU FOR COMING ALONG TO THIS MEETING OF THE "30% CLUB"...
alex@alexcartoon.com
AS YOU KNOW THIS IS A VOLUNTARY ORGANISATION DEDICATED TO ENACTING THE GOVERNMENT'S COMMITMENT TO GET MORE WOMEN ON THE BOARDS OF PUBLIC COMPANIES.
AND THE FACT THAT SO MANY OF YOU SENIOR COMPANY DIRECTORS ARE HERE TODAY IS A RECOGNITION OF THE VITAL ROLE THAT WE ALL KNOW WOMEN ARE CAPABLE OF PLAYING IN OUR INDUSTRY...
HEAR HEAR...
SO I'D LIKE TO SAY JOLLY WELL DONE TO ALL OUR P.A.S AND SECRETARIES...
YES, CO-ORDINATING ALL OUR DIARIES MUST HAVE BEEN A NIGHTMARE...
WELL WE'RE VERY BUSY MEN...
DRUM DRUM
I DON'T THINK YOU'VE QUITE GOT THE IDEA...

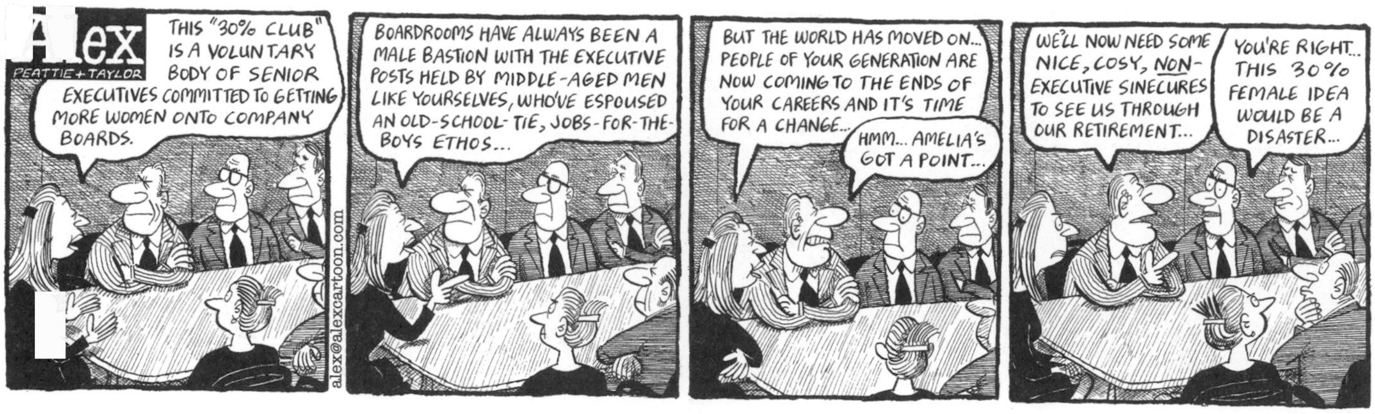
PEATTIE+TAYLOR
THIS "30% CLUB" IS A VOLUNTARY BODY OF SENIOR EXECUTIVES COMMITTED TO GETTING MORE WOMEN ONTO COMPANY BOARDS.
BOARDROOMS HAVE ALWAYS BEEN A MALE BASTION WITH THE EXECUTIVE POSTS HELD BY MIDDLE-AGED MEN LIKE YOURSELVES, WHO'VE ESPOUSED AN OLD-SCHOOL-TIE, JOBS-FOR-THE-BOYS ETHOS...
BUT THE WORLD HAS MOVED ON... PEOPLE OF YOUR GENERATION ARE NOW COMING TO THE ENDS OF YOUR CAREERS AND IT'S TIME FOR A CHANGE...
HMM... AMELIA'S GOT A POINT...
WE'LL NOW NEED SOME NICE, COSY, NON-EXECUTIVE SINECURES TO SEE US THROUGH OUR RETIREMENT...
YOU'RE RIGHT... THIS 30% FEMALE IDEA WOULD BE A DISASTER...
alex@alexcartoon.com

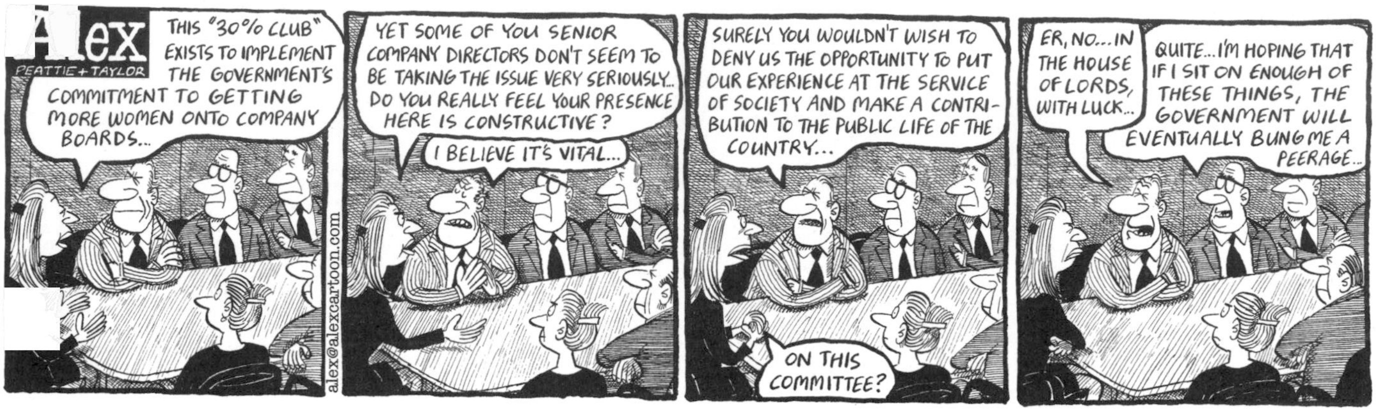
PEATTIE+TAYLOR
THIS "30% CLUB" EXISTS TO IMPLEMENT THE GOVERNMENT'S COMMITMENT TO GETTING MORE WOMEN ONTO COMPANY BOARDS...
YET SOME OF YOU SENIOR COMPANY DIRECTORS DON'T SEEM TO BE TAKING THE ISSUE VERY SERIOUSLY... DO YOU REALLY FEEL YOUR PRESENCE HERE IS CONSTRUCTIVE?
I BELIEVE IT'S VITAL...
SURELY YOU WOULDN'T WISH TO DENY US THE OPPORTUNITY TO PUT OUR EXPERIENCE AT THE SERVICE OF SOCIETY AND MAKE A CONTRIBUTION TO THE PUBLIC LIFE OF THE COUNTRY...
ON THIS COMMITTEE?
ER, NO... IN THE HOUSE OF LORDS, WITH LUCK...
QUITE... I'M HOPING THAT IF I SIT ON ENOUGH OF THESE THINGS, THE GOVERNMENT WILL EVENTUALLY BUNG ME A PEERAGE...
alex@alexcartoon.com

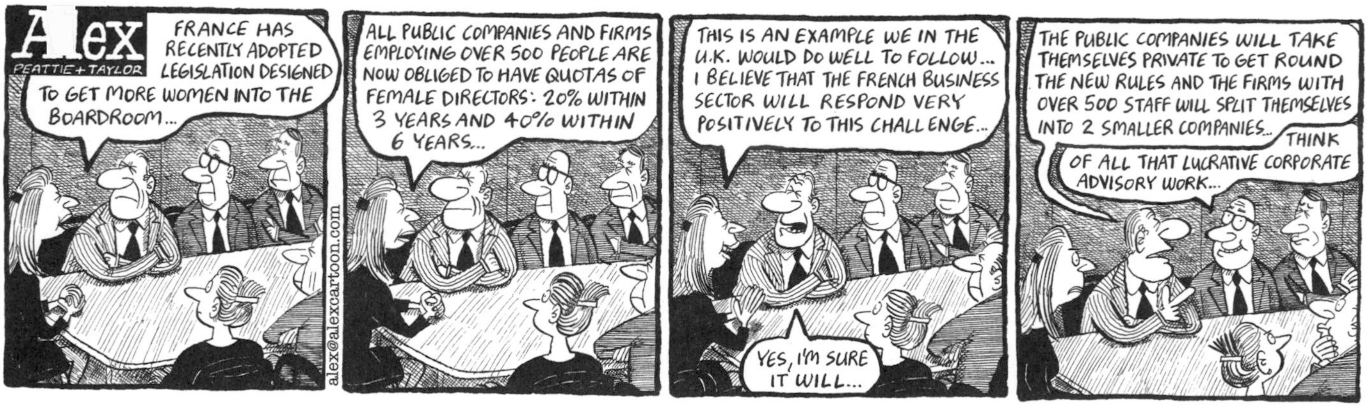
PEATTIE+TAYLOR
FRANCE HAS RECENTLY ADOPTED LEGISLATION DESIGNED TO GET MORE WOMEN INTO THE BOARDROOM...
ALL PUBLIC COMPANIES AND FIRMS EMPLOYING OVER 500 PEOPLE ARE NOW OBLIGED TO HAVE QUOTAS OF FEMALE DIRECTORS: 20% WITHIN 3 YEARS AND 40% WITHIN 6 YEARS...
THIS IS AN EXAMPLE WE IN THE U.K. WOULD DO WELL TO FOLLOW... I BELIEVE THAT THE FRENCH BUSINESS SECTOR WILL RESPOND VERY POSITIVELY TO THIS CHALLENGE...
YES, I'M SURE IT WILL...
THE PUBLIC COMPANIES WILL TAKE THEMSELVES PRIVATE TO GET ROUND THE NEW RULES AND THE FIRMS WITH OVER 500 STAFF WILL SPLIT THEMSELVES INTO 2 SMALLER COMPANIES...
THINK OF ALL THAT LUCRATIVE CORPORATE ADVISORY WORK...
alex@alexcartoon.com

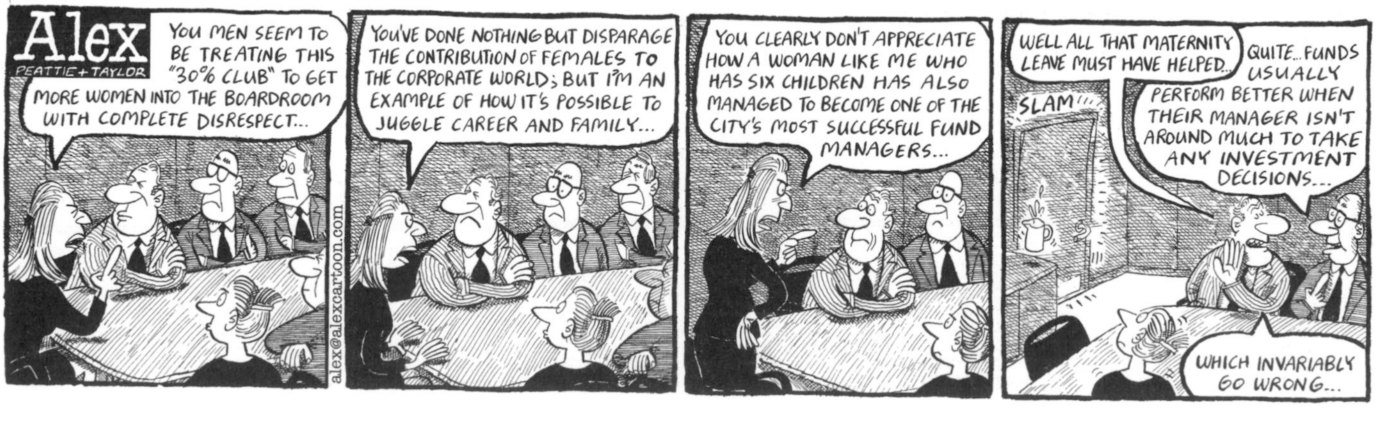
Alex
PEATTIE+TAYLOR
YOU MEN SEEM TO BE TREATING THIS "30% CLUB" TO GET MORE WOMEN INTO THE BOARDROOM WITH COMPLETE DISRESPECT...
YOU'VE DONE NOTHING BUT DISPARAGE THE CONTRIBUTION OF FEMALES TO THE CORPORATE WORLD; BUT I'M AN EXAMPLE OF HOW IT'S POSSIBLE TO JUGGLE CAREER AND FAMILY...
YOU CLEARLY DON'T APPRECIATE HOW A WOMAN LIKE ME WHO HAS SIX CHILDREN HAS ALSO MANAGED TO BECOME ONE OF THE CITY'S MOST SUCCESSFUL FUND MANAGERS...
WELL ALL THAT MATERNITY LEAVE MUST HAVE HELPED...
SLAM
QUITE... FUNDS USUALLY PERFORM BETTER WHEN THEIR MANAGER ISN'T AROUND MUCH TO TAKE ANY INVESTMENT DECISIONS...
WHICH INVARIABLY GO WRONG...
alex@alexcartoon.com

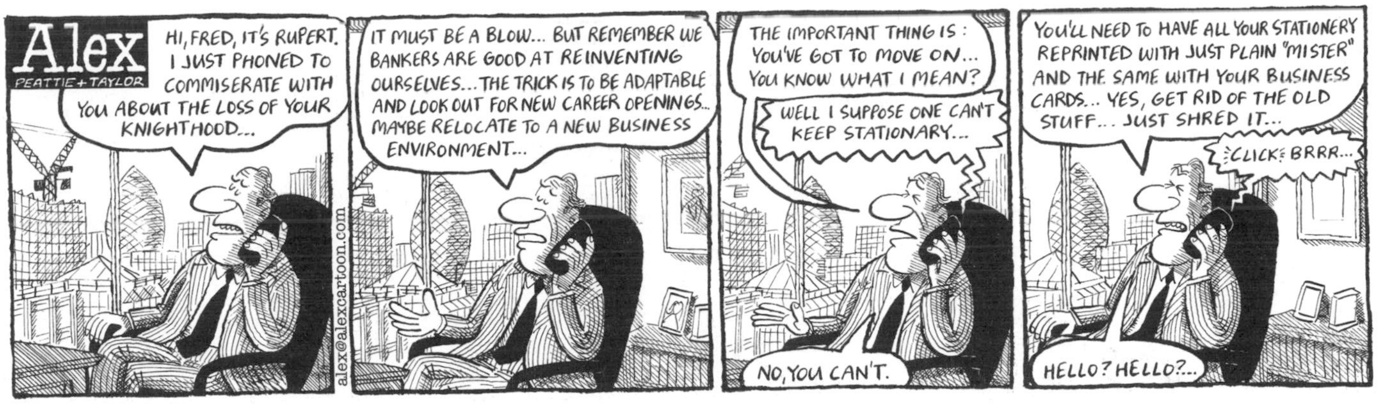
Alex
PEATTIE+TAYLOR
HI, FRED, IT'S RUPERT. I JUST PHONED TO COMMISERATE WITH YOU ABOUT THE LOSS OF YOUR KNIGHTHOOD...
alex@alexcartoon.com
IT MUST BE A BLOW... BUT REMEMBER WE BANKERS ARE GOOD AT REINVENTING OURSELVES... THE TRICK IS TO BE ADAPTABLE AND LOOK OUT FOR NEW CAREER OPENINGS... MAYBE RELOCATE TO A NEW BUSINESS ENVIRONMENT...
THE IMPORTANT THING IS: YOU'VE GOT TO MOVE ON... YOU KNOW WHAT I MEAN?
WELL I SUPPOSE ONE CAN'T KEEP STATIONARY...
NO, YOU CAN'T.
YOU'LL NEED TO HAVE ALL YOUR STATIONERY REPRINTED WITH JUST PLAIN "MISTER" AND THE SAME WITH YOUR BUSINESS CARDS... YES, GET RID OF THE OLD STUFF... JUST SHRED IT...
CLICK BRRR...
HELLO? HELLO?...

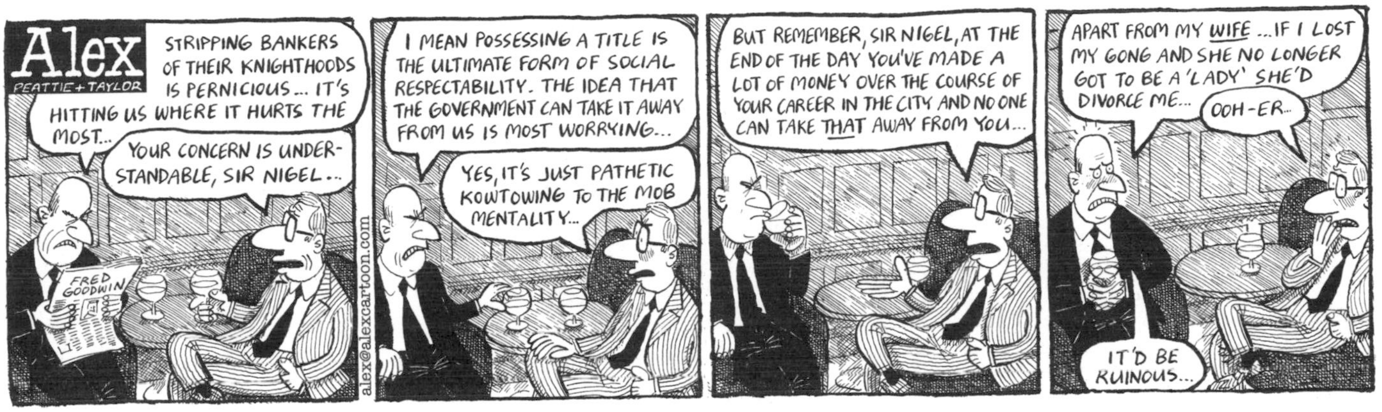
Alex
PEATTIE+TAYLOR
STRIPPING BANKERS OF THEIR KNIGHTHOODS IS PERNICIOUS... IT'S HITTING US WHERE IT HURTS THE MOST...
YOUR CONCERN IS UNDERSTANDABLE, SIR NIGEL...
FRED GOODWIN
alex@alexcartoon.com
I MEAN POSSESSING A TITLE IS THE ULTIMATE FORM OF SOCIAL RESPECTABILITY. THE IDEA THAT THE GOVERNMENT CAN TAKE IT AWAY FROM US IS MOST WORRYING...
YES, IT'S JUST PATHETIC KOWTOWING TO THE MOB MENTALITY...
BUT REMEMBER, SIR NIGEL, AT THE END OF THE DAY YOU'VE MADE A LOT OF MONEY OVER THE COURSE OF YOUR CAREER IN THE CITY AND NO ONE CAN TAKE THAT AWAY FROM YOU...
APART FROM MY WIFE ...IF I LOST MY GONG AND SHE NO LONGER GOT TO BE A 'LADY' SHE'D DIVORCE ME...
OOH-ER...
IT'D BE RUINOUS...

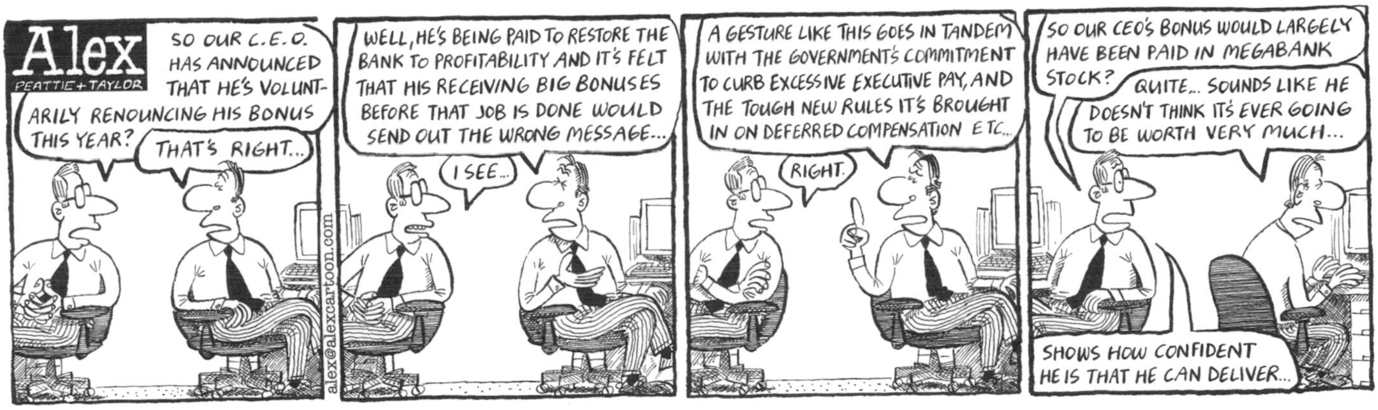
Alex
PEATTIE+TAYLOR
SO OUR C.E.O. HAS ANNOUNCED THAT HE'S VOLUNTARILY RENOUNCING HIS BONUS THIS YEAR?
THAT'S RIGHT...
alex@alexcartoon.com
WELL, HE'S BEING PAID TO RESTORE THE BANK TO PROFITABILITY AND IT'S FELT THAT HIS RECEIVING BIG BONUSES BEFORE THAT JOB IS DONE WOULD SEND OUT THE WRONG MESSAGE...
I SEE...
A GESTURE LIKE THIS GOES IN TANDEM WITH THE GOVERNMENT'S COMMITMENT TO CURB EXCESSIVE EXECUTIVE PAY, AND THE TOUGH NEW RULES IT'S BROUGHT IN ON DEFERRED COMPENSATION ETC...
RIGHT.
SO OUR CEO'S BONUS WOULD LARGELY HAVE BEEN PAID IN MEGABANK STOCK?
QUITE... SOUNDS LIKE HE DOESN'T THINK IT'S EVER GOING TO BE WORTH VERY MUCH...
SHOWS HOW CONFIDENT HE IS THAT HE CAN DELIVER...

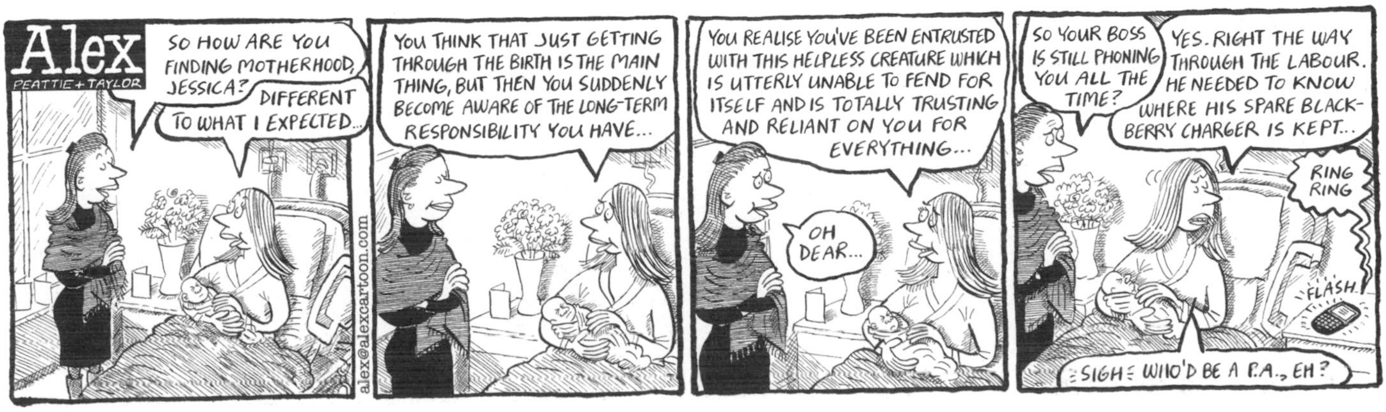
Alex
PEATTIE+TAYLOR
SO HOW ARE YOU FINDING MOTHERHOOD, JESSICA?
DIFFERENT TO WHAT I EXPECTED...
alex@alexcartoon.com
YOU THINK THAT JUST GETTING THROUGH THE BIRTH IS THE MAIN THING, BUT THEN YOU SUDDENLY BECOME AWARE OF THE LONG-TERM RESPONSIBILITY YOU HAVE...
YOU REALISE YOU'VE BEEN ENTRUSTED WITH THIS HELPLESS CREATURE WHICH IS UTTERLY UNABLE TO FEND FOR ITSELF AND IS TOTALLY TRUSTING AND RELIANT ON YOU FOR EVERYTHING...
OH DEAR...
SO YOUR BOSS IS STILL PHONING YOU ALL THE TIME?
YES. RIGHT THE WAY THROUGH THE LABOUR. HE NEEDED TO KNOW WHERE HIS SPARE BLACKBERRY CHARGER IS KEPT...
RING RING
FLASH
SIGH WHO'D BE A P.A., EH?

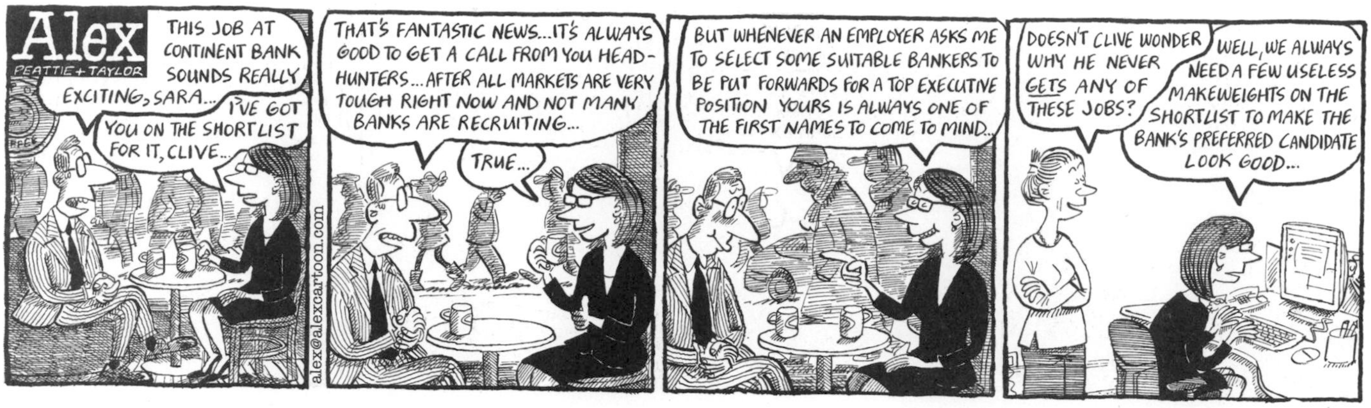
Alex
PEATTIE+TAYLOR
THIS JOB AT CONTINENT BANK SOUNDS REALLY EXCITING, SARA...
I'VE GOT YOU ON THE SHORTLIST FOR IT, CLIVE...
THAT'S FANTASTIC NEWS... IT'S ALWAYS GOOD TO GET A CALL FROM YOU HEAD-HUNTERS... AFTER ALL MARKETS ARE VERY TOUGH RIGHT NOW AND NOT MANY BANKS ARE RECRUITING...
TRUE...
alex@alexcartoon.com
BUT WHENEVER AN EMPLOYER ASKS ME TO SELECT SOME SUITABLE BANKERS TO BE PUT FORWARDS FOR A TOP EXECUTIVE POSITION YOURS IS ALWAYS ONE OF THE FIRST NAMES TO COME TO MIND...
DOESN'T CLIVE WONDER WHY HE NEVER GETS ANY OF THESE JOBS?
WELL, WE ALWAYS NEED A FEW USELESS MAKEWEIGHTS ON THE SHORTLIST TO MAKE THE BANK'S PREFERRED CANDIDATE LOOK GOOD...

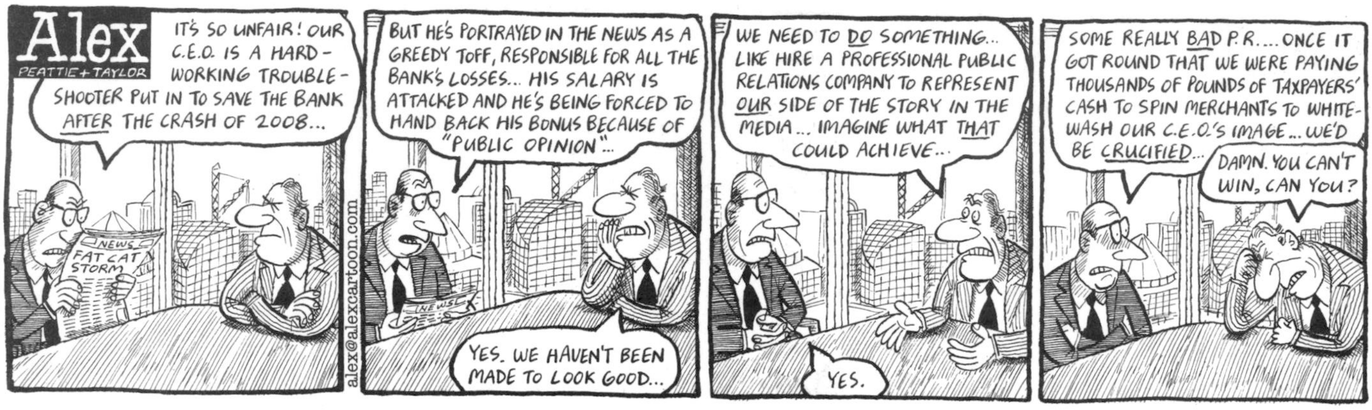
Alex
PEATTIE+TAYLOR
IT'S SO UNFAIR! OUR C.E.O. IS A HARD-WORKING TROUBLE-SHOOTER PUT IN TO SAVE THE BANK AFTER THE CRASH OF 2008...
NEWS
FAT CAT STORM
alex@alexcartoon.com
BUT HE'S PORTRAYED IN THE NEWS AS A GREEDY TOFF, RESPONSIBLE FOR ALL THE BANK'S LOSSES... HIS SALARY IS ATTACKED AND HE'S BEING FORCED TO HAND BACK HIS BONUS BECAUSE OF "PUBLIC OPINION"...
YES. WE HAVEN'T BEEN MADE TO LOOK GOOD...
WE NEED TO DO SOMETHING... LIKE HIRE A PROFESSIONAL PUBLIC RELATIONS COMPANY TO REPRESENT OUR SIDE OF THE STORY IN THE MEDIA... IMAGINE WHAT THAT COULD ACHIEVE...
YES.
SOME REALLY BAD P.R.... ONCE IT GOT ROUND THAT WE WERE PAYING THOUSANDS OF POUNDS OF TAXPAYERS' CASH TO SPIN MERCHANTS TO WHITE-WASH OUR C.E.O.'S IMAGE... WE'D BE CRUCIFIED...
DAMN. YOU CAN'T WIN, CAN YOU?

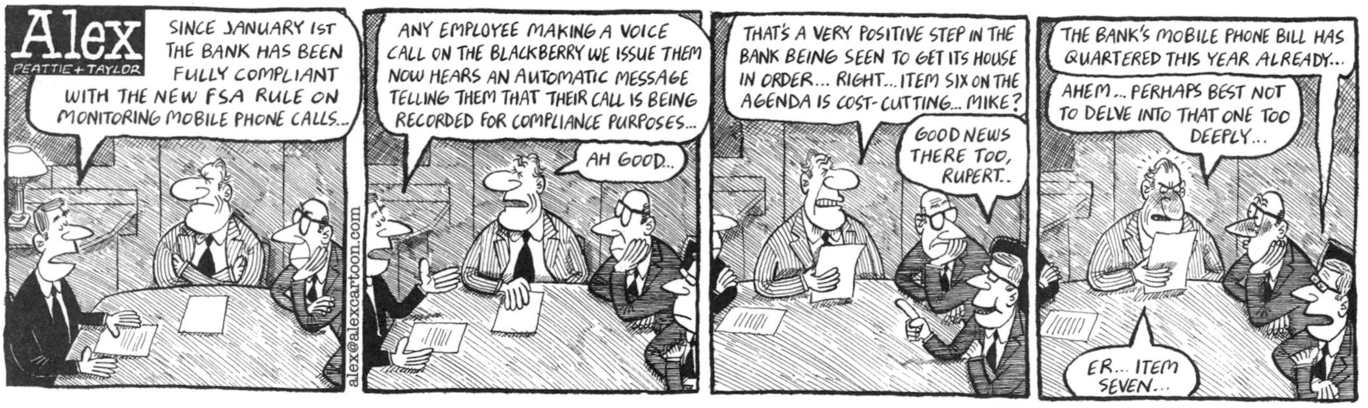
Alex
PEATTIE+TAYLOR
SINCE JANUARY 1ST THE BANK HAS BEEN FULLY COMPLIANT WITH THE NEW FSA RULE ON MONITORING MOBILE PHONE CALLS...
alex@alexcartoon.com
ANY EMPLOYEE MAKING A VOICE CALL ON THE BLACKBERRY WE ISSUE THEM NOW HEARS AN AUTOMATIC MESSAGE TELLING THEM THAT THEIR CALL IS BEING RECORDED FOR COMPLIANCE PURPOSES...
AH GOOD..
THAT'S A VERY POSITIVE STEP IN THE BANK BEING SEEN TO GET ITS HOUSE IN ORDER... RIGHT... ITEM SIX ON THE AGENDA IS COST-CUTTING... MIKE?
GOOD NEWS THERE TOO, RUPERT..
THE BANK'S MOBILE PHONE BILL HAS QUARTERED THIS YEAR ALREADY...
AHEM... PERHAPS BEST NOT TO DELVE INTO THAT ONE TOO DEEPLY...
ER... ITEM SEVEN...

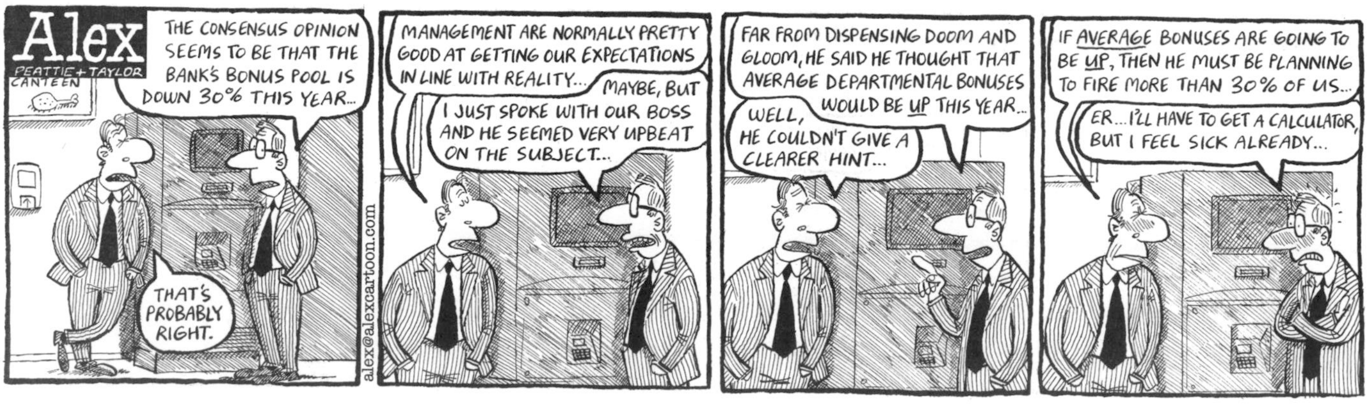
Alex
PEATTIE+TAYLOR
CANTEEN
THE CONSENSUS OPINION SEEMS TO BE THAT THE BANK'S BONUS POOL IS DOWN 30% THIS YEAR...
THAT'S PROBABLY RIGHT.
alex@alexcartoon.com
MANAGEMENT ARE NORMALLY PRETTY GOOD AT GETTING OUR EXPECTATIONS IN LINE WITH REALITY...
MAYBE, BUT I JUST SPOKE WITH OUR BOSS AND HE SEEMED VERY UPBEAT ON THE SUBJECT...
FAR FROM DISPENSING DOOM AND GLOOM, HE SAID HE THOUGHT THAT AVERAGE DEPARTMENTAL BONUSES WOULD BE UP THIS YEAR...
WELL, HE COULDN'T GIVE A CLEARER HINT...
IF AVERAGE BONUSES ARE GOING TO BE UP, THEN HE MUST BE PLANNING TO FIRE MORE THAN 30% OF US...
ER... I'LL HAVE TO GET A CALCULATOR, BUT I FEEL SICK ALREADY...

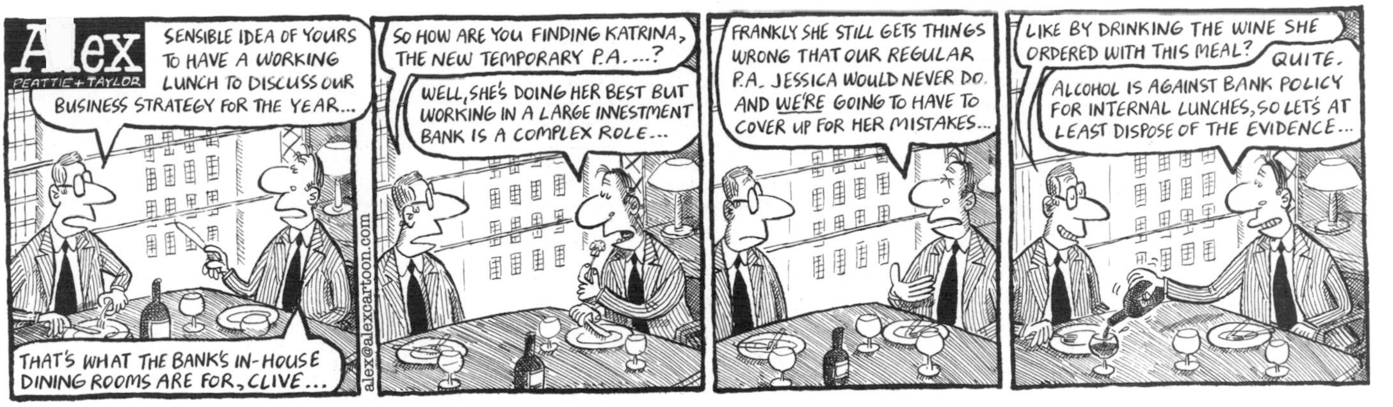
Alex
PEATTIE + TAYLOR
SENSIBLE IDEA OF YOURS TO HAVE A WORKING LUNCH TO DISCUSS OUR BUSINESS STRATEGY FOR THE YEAR...
THAT'S WHAT THE BANK'S IN-HOUSE DINING ROOMS ARE FOR, CLIVE...
alex@alexcartoon.com
SO HOW ARE YOU FINDING KATRINA, THE NEW TEMPORARY P.A. ...?
WELL, SHE'S DOING HER BEST BUT WORKING IN A LARGE INVESTMENT BANK IS A COMPLEX ROLE...
FRANKLY SHE STILL GETS THINGS WRONG THAT OUR REGULAR P.A. JESSICA WOULD NEVER DO. AND WE'RE GOING TO HAVE TO COVER UP FOR HER MISTAKES...
LIKE BY DRINKING THE WINE SHE ORDERED WITH THIS MEAL?
QUITE.
ALCOHOL IS AGAINST BANK POLICY FOR INTERNAL LUNCHES, SO LET'S AT LEAST DISPOSE OF THE EVIDENCE...

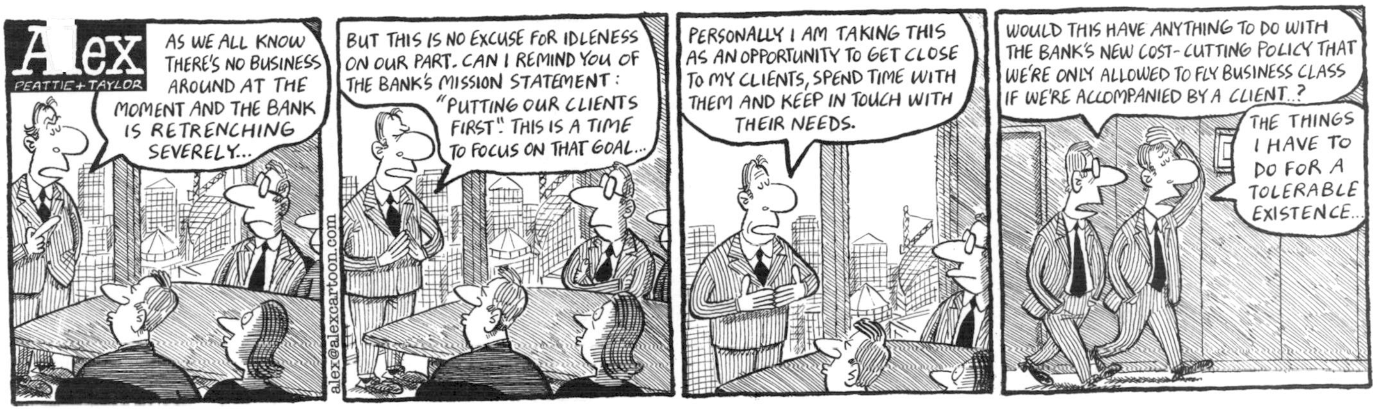
Alex
PEATTIE + TAYLOR
AS WE ALL KNOW THERE'S NO BUSINESS AROUND AT THE MOMENT AND THE BANK IS RETRENCHING SEVERELY...
alex@alexcartoon.com
BUT THIS IS NO EXCUSE FOR IDLENESS ON OUR PART. CAN I REMIND YOU OF THE BANK'S MISSION STATEMENT: "PUTTING OUR CLIENTS FIRST". THIS IS A TIME TO FOCUS ON THAT GOAL...
PERSONALLY I AM TAKING THIS AS AN OPPORTUNITY TO GET CLOSE TO MY CLIENTS, SPEND TIME WITH THEM AND KEEP IN TOUCH WITH THEIR NEEDS.
WOULD THIS HAVE ANYTHING TO DO WITH THE BANK'S NEW COST-CUTTING POLICY THAT WE'RE ONLY ALLOWED TO FLY BUSINESS CLASS IF WE'RE ACCOMPANIED BY A CLIENT..?
THE THINGS I HAVE TO DO FOR A TOLERABLE EXISTENCE...

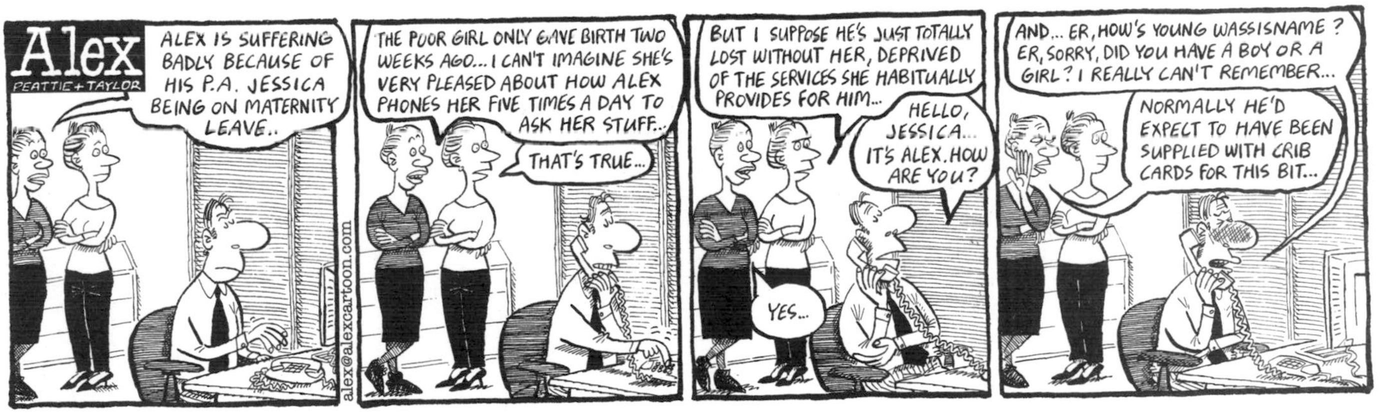
Alex
PEATTIE + TAYLOR
ALEX IS SUFFERING BADLY BECAUSE OF HIS P.A. JESSICA BEING ON MATERNITY LEAVE..
alex@alexcartoon.com
THE POOR GIRL ONLY GAVE BIRTH TWO WEEKS AGO... I CAN'T IMAGINE SHE'S VERY PLEASED ABOUT HOW ALEX PHONES HER FIVE TIMES A DAY TO ASK HER STUFF...
THAT'S TRUE...
BUT I SUPPOSE HE'S JUST TOTALLY LOST WITHOUT HER, DEPRIVED OF THE SERVICES SHE HABITUALLY PROVIDES FOR HIM...
HELLO, JESSICA... IT'S ALEX. HOW ARE YOU?
YES...
AND... ER, HOW'S YOUNG WASSISNAME? ER, SORRY, DID YOU HAVE A BOY OR A GIRL? I REALLY CAN'T REMEMBER...
NORMALLY HE'D EXPECT TO HAVE BEEN SUPPLIED WITH CRIB CARDS FOR THIS BIT...

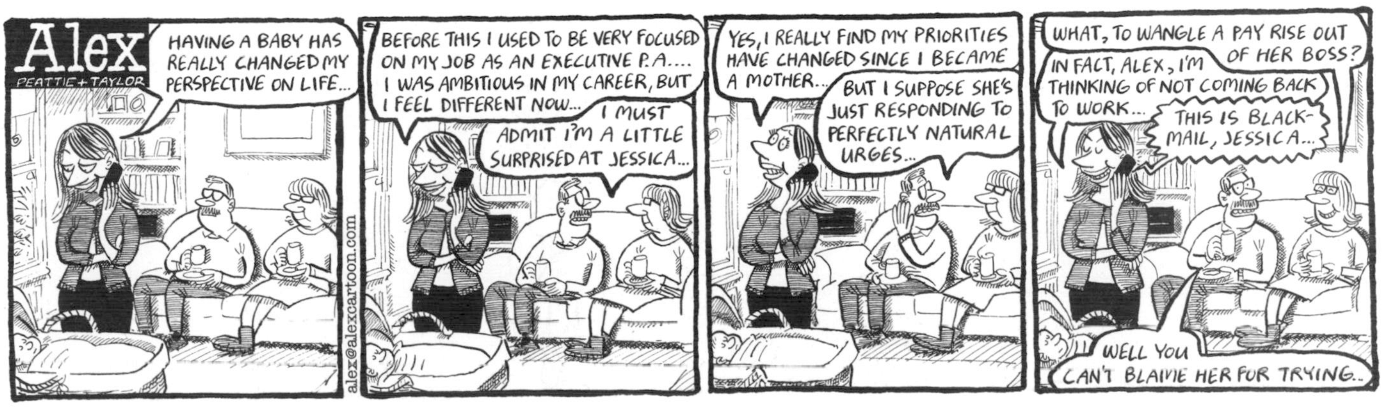
Alex
PEATTIE + TAYLOR
HAVING A BABY HAS REALLY CHANGED MY PERSPECTIVE ON LIFE...
alex@alexcartoon.com
BEFORE THIS I USED TO BE VERY FOCUSED ON MY JOB AS AN EXECUTIVE P.A.... I WAS AMBITIOUS IN MY CAREER, BUT I FEEL DIFFERENT NOW...
I MUST ADMIT I'M A LITTLE SURPRISED AT JESSICA...
YES, I REALLY FIND MY PRIORITIES HAVE CHANGED SINCE I BECAME A MOTHER...
BUT I SUPPOSE SHE'S JUST RESPONDING TO PERFECTLY NATURAL URGES...
IN FACT, ALEX, I'M THINKING OF NOT COMING BACK TO WORK...
WHAT, TO WANGLE A PAY RISE OUT OF HER BOSS?
THIS IS BLACKMAIL, JESSICA...
WELL YOU CAN'T BLAME HER FOR TRYING..

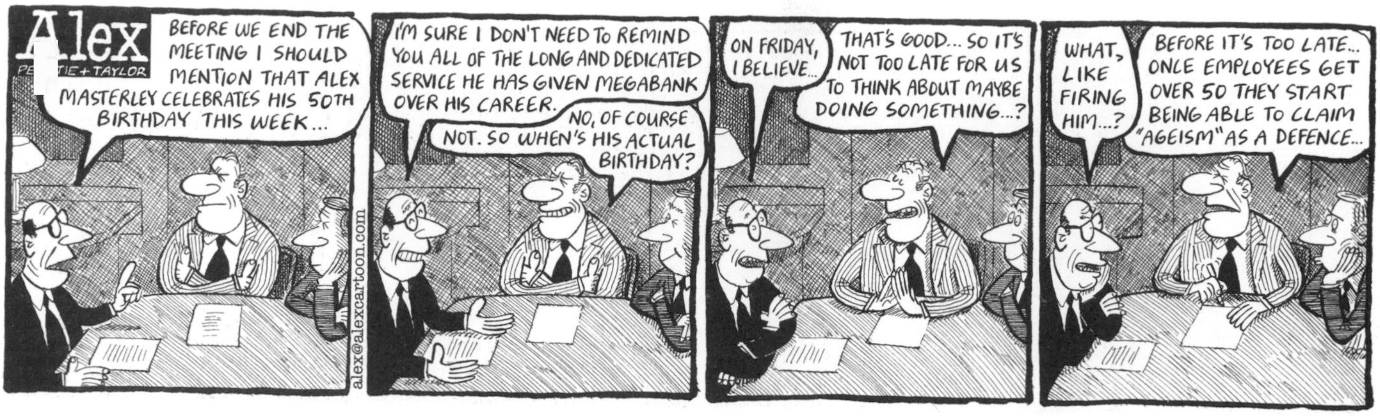
Alex
PEATTIE + TAYLOR
BEFORE WE END THE MEETING I SHOULD MENTION THAT ALEX MASTERLEY CELEBRATES HIS 50TH BIRTHDAY THIS WEEK...
I'M SURE I DON'T NEED TO REMIND YOU ALL OF THE LONG AND DEDICATED SERVICE HE HAS GIVEN MEGABANK OVER HIS CAREER.
NO, OF COURSE NOT. SO WHEN'S HIS ACTUAL BIRTHDAY?
ON FRIDAY, I BELIEVE...
THAT'S GOOD... SO IT'S NOT TOO LATE FOR US TO THINK ABOUT MAYBE DOING SOMETHING...?
WHAT, LIKE FIRING HIM...?
BEFORE IT'S TOO LATE... ONCE EMPLOYEES GET OVER 50 THEY START BEING ABLE TO CLAIM "AGEISM" AS A DEFENCE...
alex@alexcartoon.com

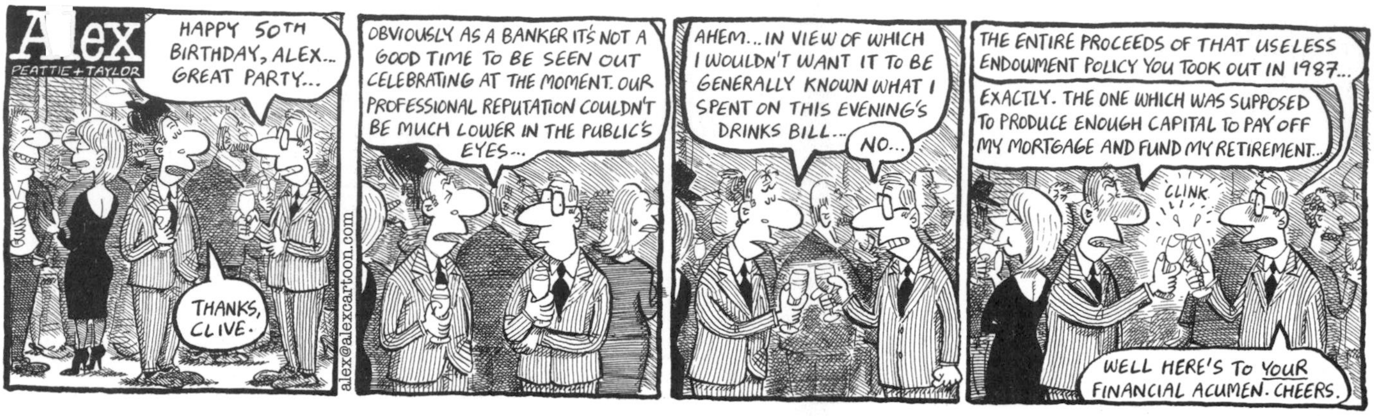
Alex
PEATTIE + TAYLOR
HAPPY 50TH BIRTHDAY, ALEX... GREAT PARTY...
THANKS, CLIVE.
OBVIOUSLY AS A BANKER IT'S NOT A GOOD TIME TO BE SEEN OUT CELEBRATING AT THE MOMENT. OUR PROFESSIONAL REPUTATION COULDN'T BE MUCH LOWER IN THE PUBLIC'S EYES...
AHEM... IN VIEW OF WHICH I WOULDN'T WANT IT TO BE GENERALLY KNOWN WHAT I SPENT ON THIS EVENING'S DRINKS BILL...
NO...
THE ENTIRE PROCEEDS OF THAT USELESS ENDOWMENT POLICY YOU TOOK OUT IN 1987...
EXACTLY. THE ONE WHICH WAS SUPPOSED TO PRODUCE ENOUGH CAPITAL TO PAY OFF MY MORTGAGE AND FUND MY RETIREMENT...
CLINK
WELL HERE'S TO YOUR FINANCIAL ACUMEN. CHEERS.
alex@alexcartoon.com

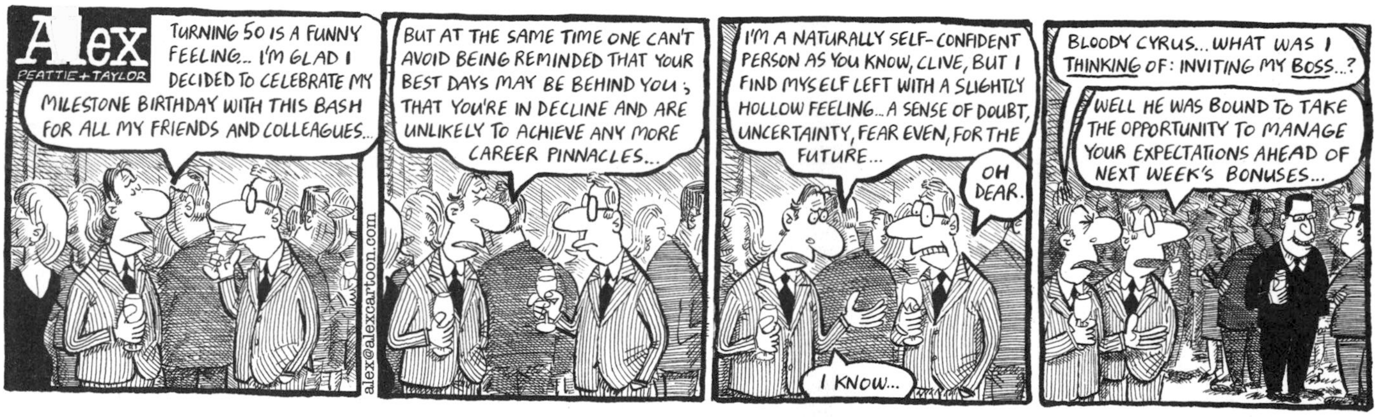
Alex
PEATTIE + TAYLOR
TURNING 50 IS A FUNNY FEELING... I'M GLAD I DECIDED TO CELEBRATE MY MILESTONE BIRTHDAY WITH THIS BASH FOR ALL MY FRIENDS AND COLLEAGUES...
BUT AT THE SAME TIME ONE CAN'T AVOID BEING REMINDED THAT YOUR BEST DAYS MAY BE BEHIND YOU; THAT YOU'RE IN DECLINE AND ARE UNLIKELY TO ACHIEVE ANY MORE CAREER PINNACLES...
I'M A NATURALLY SELF-CONFIDENT PERSON AS YOU KNOW, CLIVE, BUT I FIND MYSELF LEFT WITH A SLIGHTLY HOLLOW FEELING... A SENSE OF DOUBT, UNCERTAINTY, FEAR EVEN, FOR THE FUTURE...
OH DEAR.
I KNOW...
BLOODY CYRUS... WHAT WAS I THINKING OF: INVITING MY BOSS...?
WELL HE WAS BOUND TO TAKE THE OPPORTUNITY TO MANAGE YOUR EXPECTATIONS AHEAD OF NEXT WEEK'S BONUSES...
alex@alexcartoon.com

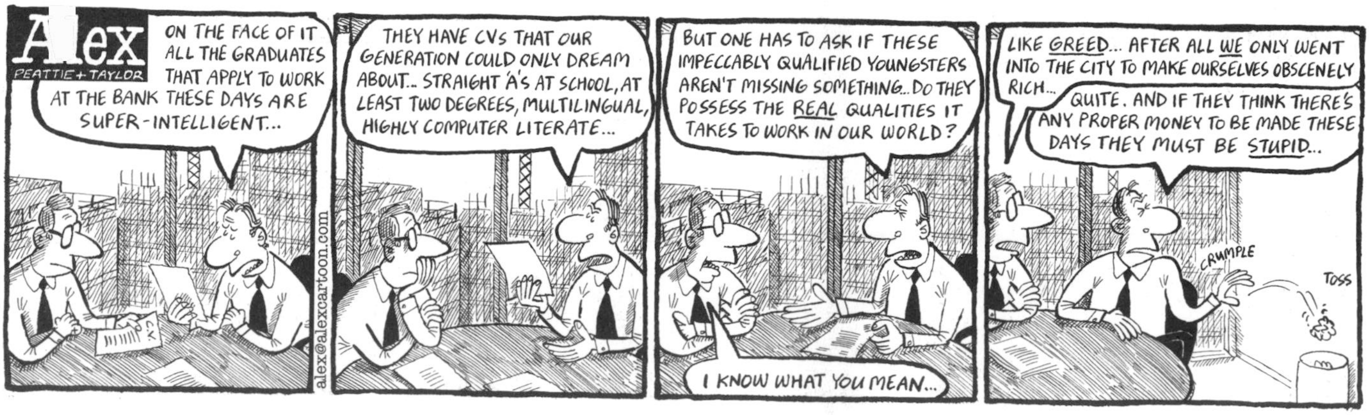
Alex
PEATTIE + TAYLOR
ON THE FACE OF IT ALL THE GRADUATES THAT APPLY TO WORK AT THE BANK THESE DAYS ARE SUPER-INTELLIGENT...
THEY HAVE CVs THAT OUR GENERATION COULD ONLY DREAM ABOUT... STRAIGHT A'S AT SCHOOL, AT LEAST TWO DEGREES, MULTILINGUAL, HIGHLY COMPUTER LITERATE...
BUT ONE HAS TO ASK IF THESE IMPECCABLY QUALIFIED YOUNGSTERS AREN'T MISSING SOMETHING... DO THEY POSSESS THE REAL QUALITIES IT TAKES TO WORK IN OUR WORLD?
I KNOW WHAT YOU MEAN...
LIKE GREED... AFTER ALL WE ONLY WENT INTO THE CITY TO MAKE OURSELVES OBSCENELY RICH...
QUITE. AND IF THEY THINK THERE'S ANY PROPER MONEY TO BE MADE THESE DAYS THEY MUST BE STUPID...
CRUMPLE
TOSS
alex@alexcartoon.com

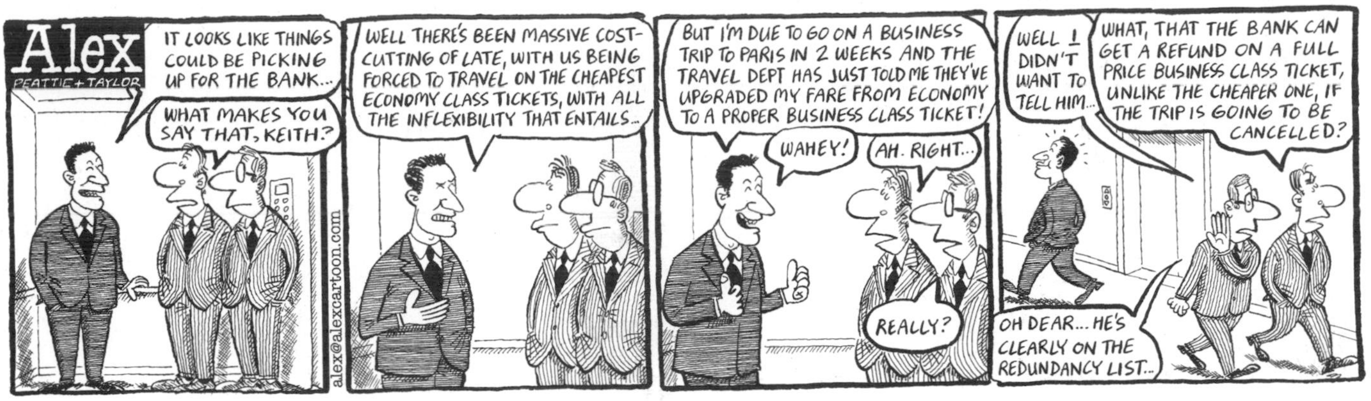
Alex
PEATTIE + TAYLOR
IT LOOKS LIKE THINGS COULD BE PICKING UP FOR THE BANK...
WHAT MAKES YOU SAY THAT, KEITH?
alex@alexcartoon.com
WELL THERE'S BEEN MASSIVE COST-CUTTING OF LATE, WITH US BEING FORCED TO TRAVEL ON THE CHEAPEST ECONOMY CLASS TICKETS, WITH ALL THE INFLEXIBILITY THAT ENTAILS...
BUT I'M DUE TO GO ON A BUSINESS TRIP TO PARIS IN 2 WEEKS AND THE TRAVEL DEPT HAS JUST TOLD ME THEY'VE UPGRADED MY FARE FROM ECONOMY TO A PROPER BUSINESS CLASS TICKET!
WAHEY!
AH. RIGHT...
REALLY?
WELL I DIDN'T WANT TO TELL HIM...
WHAT, THAT THE BANK CAN GET A REFUND ON A FULL PRICE BUSINESS CLASS TICKET, UNLIKE THE CHEAPER ONE, IF THE TRIP IS GOING TO BE CANCELLED?
OH DEAR... HE'S CLEARLY ON THE REDUNDANCY LIST...

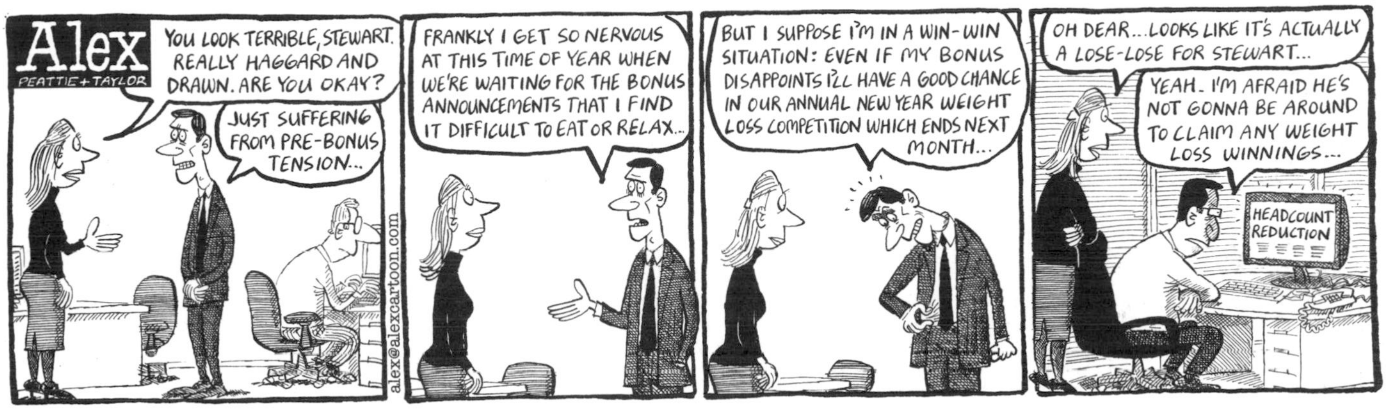
Alex
PEATTIE + TAYLOR
YOU LOOK TERRIBLE, STEWART. REALLY HAGGARD AND DRAWN. ARE YOU OKAY?
JUST SUFFERING FROM PRE-BONUS TENSION...
alex@alexcartoon.com
FRANKLY I GET SO NERVOUS AT THIS TIME OF YEAR WHEN WE'RE WAITING FOR THE BONUS ANNOUNCEMENTS THAT I FIND IT DIFFICULT TO EAT OR RELAX...
BUT I SUPPOSE I'M IN A WIN-WIN SITUATION: EVEN IF MY BONUS DISAPPOINTS I'LL HAVE A GOOD CHANCE IN OUR ANNUAL NEW YEAR WEIGHT LOSS COMPETITION WHICH ENDS NEXT MONTH...
OH DEAR... LOOKS LIKE IT'S ACTUALLY A LOSE-LOSE FOR STEWART...
YEAH. I'M AFRAID HE'S NOT GONNA BE AROUND TO CLAIM ANY WEIGHT LOSS WINNINGS...
HEADCOUNT REDUCTION

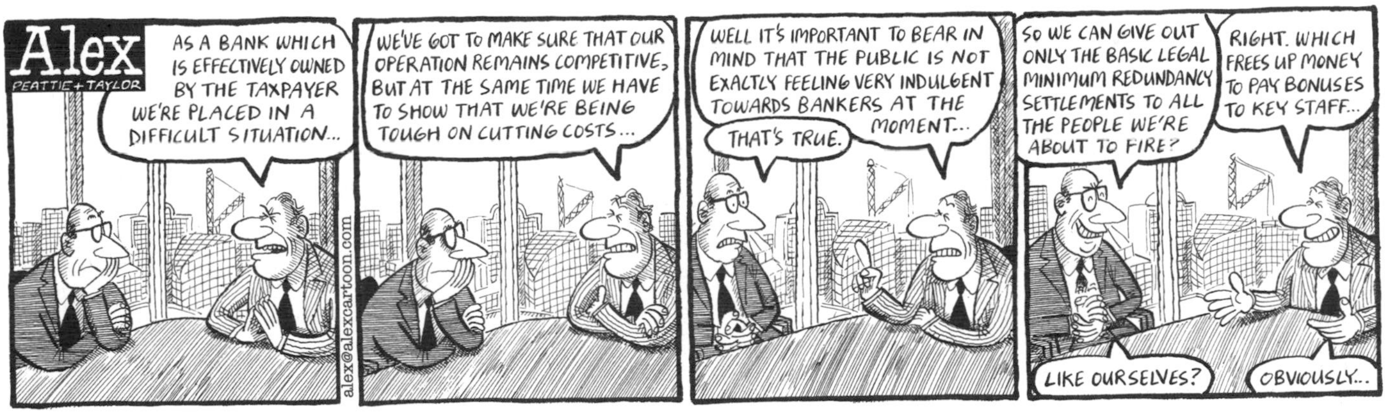
Alex
PEATTIE + TAYLOR
AS A BANK WHICH IS EFFECTIVELY OWNED BY THE TAXPAYER WE'RE PLACED IN A DIFFICULT SITUATION...
alex@alexcartoon.com
WE'VE GOT TO MAKE SURE THAT OUR OPERATION REMAINS COMPETITIVE, BUT AT THE SAME TIME WE HAVE TO SHOW THAT WE'RE BEING TOUGH ON CUTTING COSTS...
WELL IT'S IMPORTANT TO BEAR IN MIND THAT THE PUBLIC IS NOT EXACTLY FEELING VERY INDULGENT TOWARDS BANKERS AT THE MOMENT...
THAT'S TRUE.
SO WE CAN GIVE OUT ONLY THE BASIC LEGAL MINIMUM REDUNDANCY SETTLEMENTS TO ALL THE PEOPLE WE'RE ABOUT TO FIRE?
RIGHT. WHICH FREES UP MONEY TO PAY BONUSES TO KEY STAFF...
LIKE OURSELVES?
OBVIOUSLY...

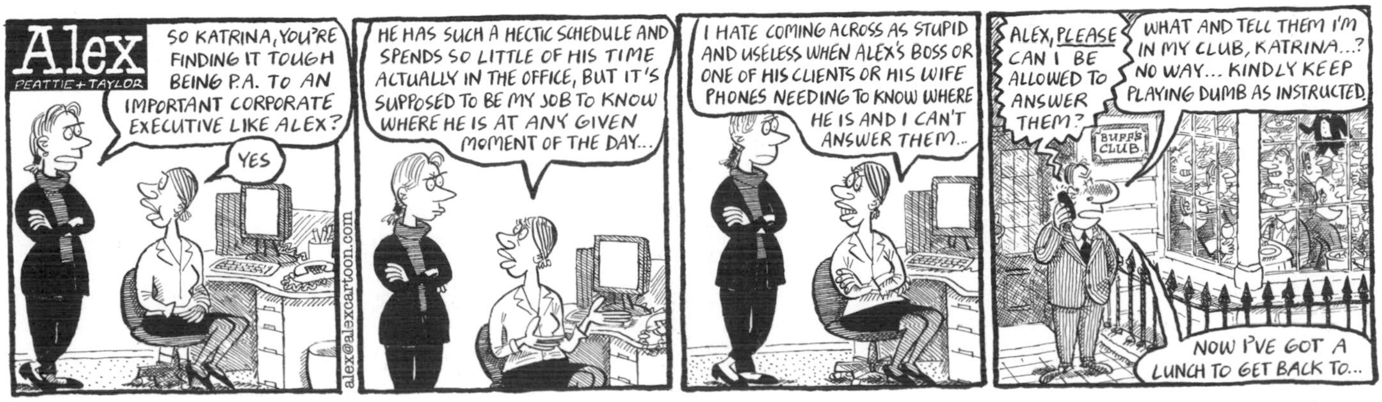
Alex
PEATTIE + TAYLOR
SO KATRINA, YOU'RE FINDING IT TOUGH BEING P.A. TO AN IMPORTANT CORPORATE EXECUTIVE LIKE ALEX?
YES
alex@alexcartoon.com
HE HAS SUCH A HECTIC SCHEDULE AND SPENDS SO LITTLE OF HIS TIME ACTUALLY IN THE OFFICE, BUT IT'S SUPPOSED TO BE MY JOB TO KNOW WHERE HE IS AT ANY GIVEN MOMENT OF THE DAY...
I HATE COMING ACROSS AS STUPID AND USELESS WHEN ALEX'S BOSS OR ONE OF HIS CLIENTS OR HIS WIFE PHONES NEEDING TO KNOW WHERE HE IS AND I CAN'T ANSWER THEM...
ALEX, PLEASE CAN I BE ALLOWED TO ANSWER THEM?
WHAT AND TELL THEM I'M IN MY CLUB, KATRINA...? NO WAY... KINDLY KEEP PLAYING DUMB AS INSTRUCTED
BUFFS CLUB
NOW I'VE GOT A LUNCH TO GET BACK TO...

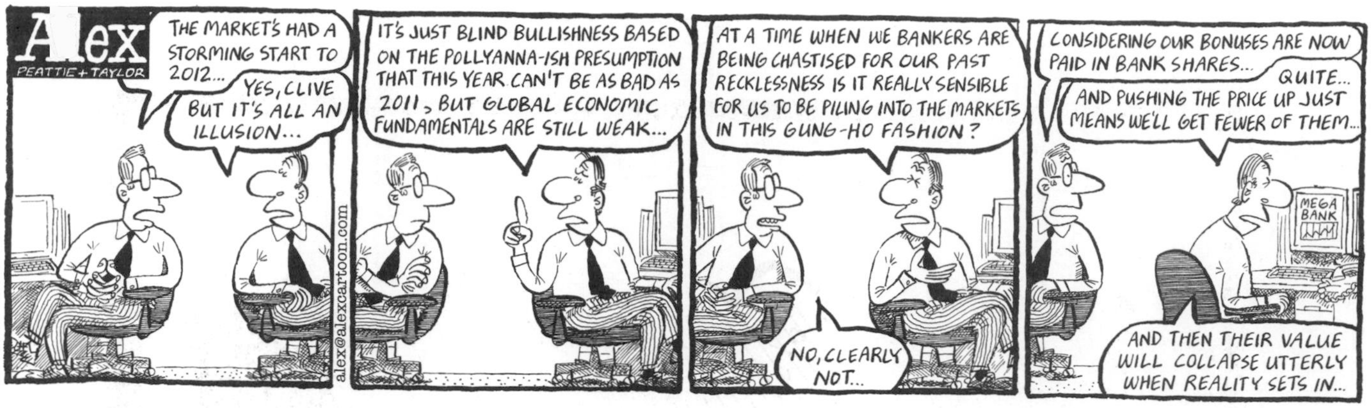
Alex
PEATTIE + TAYLOR
THE MARKET'S HAD A STORMING START TO 2012...
YES, CLIVE BUT IT'S ALL AN ILLUSION...
IT'S JUST BLIND BULLISHNESS BASED ON THE POLLYANNA-ISH PRESUMPTION THAT THIS YEAR CAN'T BE AS BAD AS 2011, BUT GLOBAL ECONOMIC FUNDAMENTALS ARE STILL WEAK...
alex@alexcartoon.com
AT A TIME WHEN WE BANKERS ARE BEING CHASTISED FOR OUR PAST RECKLESSNESS IS IT REALLY SENSIBLE FOR US TO BE PILING INTO THE MARKETS IN THIS GUNG-HO FASHION?
NO, CLEARLY NOT...
CONSIDERING OUR BONUSES ARE NOW PAID IN BANK SHARES...
QUITE... AND PUSHING THE PRICE UP JUST MEANS WE'LL GET FEWER OF THEM...
MEGA BANK
AND THEN THEIR VALUE WILL COLLAPSE UTTERLY WHEN REALITY SETS IN...

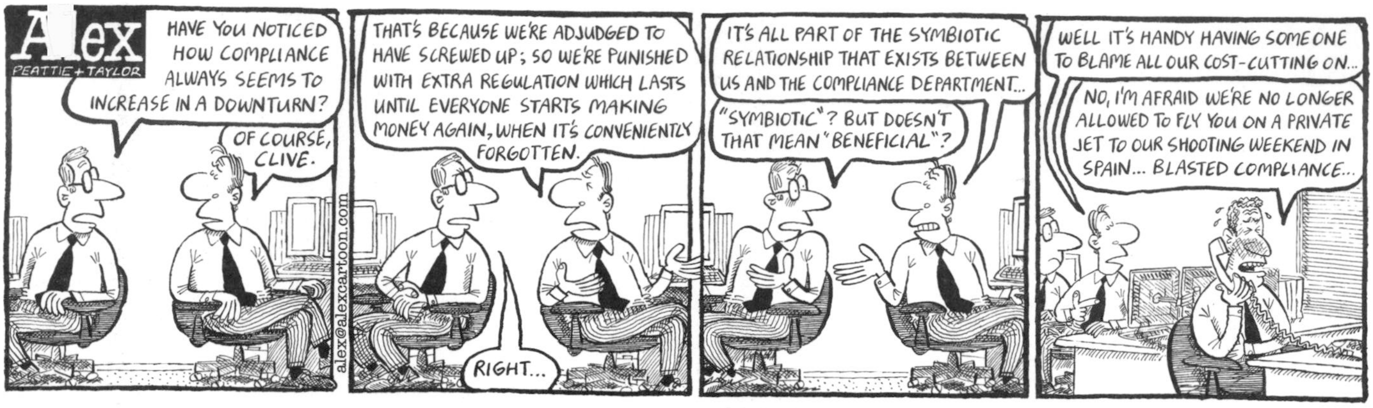
Alex
PEATTIE + TAYLOR
HAVE YOU NOTICED HOW COMPLIANCE ALWAYS SEEMS TO INCREASE IN A DOWNTURN?
OF COURSE, CLIVE.
THAT'S BECAUSE WE'RE ADJUDGED TO HAVE SCREWED UP; SO WE'RE PUNISHED WITH EXTRA REGULATION WHICH LASTS UNTIL EVERYONE STARTS MAKING MONEY AGAIN, WHEN IT'S CONVENIENTLY FORGOTTEN.
alex@alexcartoon.com
RIGHT...
IT'S ALL PART OF THE SYMBIOTIC RELATIONSHIP THAT EXISTS BETWEEN US AND THE COMPLIANCE DEPARTMENT...
"SYMBIOTIC"? BUT DOESN'T THAT MEAN "BENEFICIAL"?
WELL IT'S HANDY HAVING SOME ONE TO BLAME ALL OUR COST-CUTTING ON...
NO, I'M AFRAID WE'RE NO LONGER ALLOWED TO FLY YOU ON A PRIVATE JET TO OUR SHOOTING WEEKEND IN SPAIN... BLASTED COMPLIANCE...

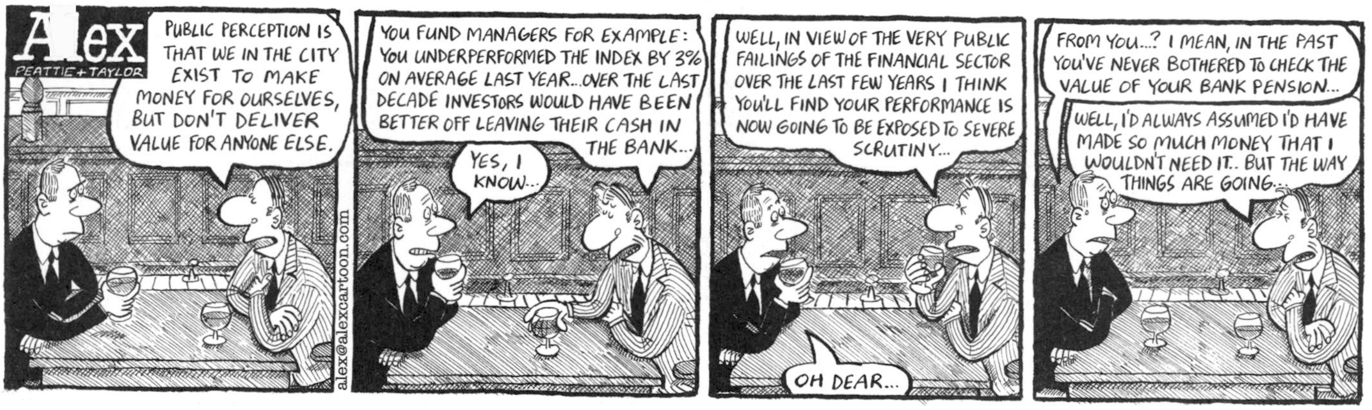
Alex
PEATTIE + TAYLOR
PUBLIC PERCEPTION IS THAT WE IN THE CITY EXIST TO MAKE MONEY FOR OURSELVES, BUT DON'T DELIVER VALUE FOR ANYONE ELSE.
YOU FUND MANAGERS FOR EXAMPLE: YOU UNDERPERFORMED THE INDEX BY 3% ON AVERAGE LAST YEAR...OVER THE LAST DECADE INVESTORS WOULD HAVE BEEN BETTER OFF LEAVING THEIR CASH IN THE BANK...
YES, I KNOW...
alex@alexcartoon.com
WELL, IN VIEW OF THE VERY PUBLIC FAILINGS OF THE FINANCIAL SECTOR OVER THE LAST FEW YEARS I THINK YOU'LL FIND YOUR PERFORMANCE IS NOW GOING TO BE EXPOSED TO SEVERE SCRUTINY...
OH DEAR...
FROM YOU...? I MEAN, IN THE PAST YOU'VE NEVER BOTHERED TO CHECK THE VALUE OF YOUR BANK PENSION...
WELL, I'D ALWAYS ASSUMED I'D HAVE MADE SO MUCH MONEY THAT I WOULDN'T NEED IT.. BUT THE WAY THINGS ARE GOING...

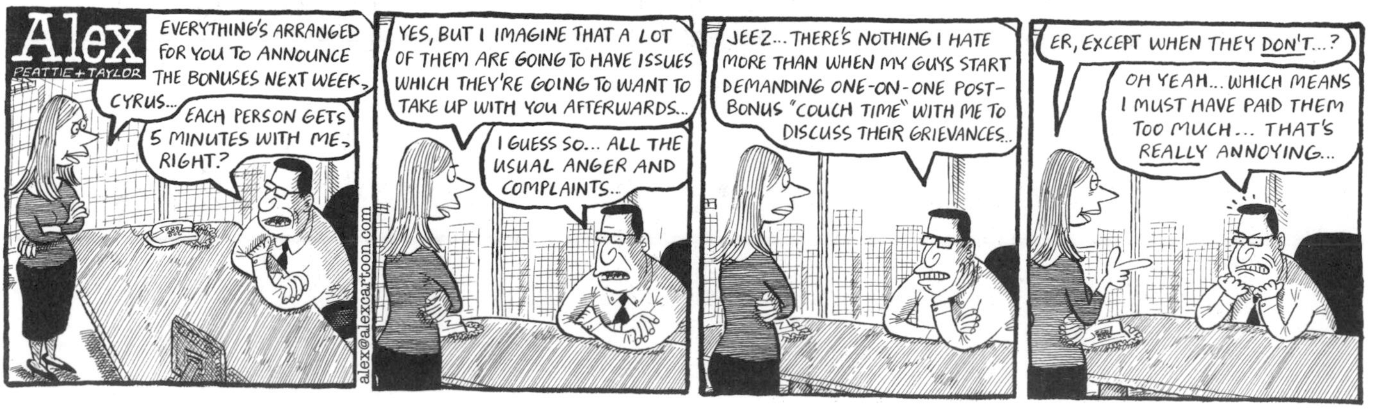
Alex
PEATTIE + TAYLOR
EVERYTHING'S ARRANGED FOR YOU TO ANNOUNCE THE BONUSES NEXT WEEK, CYRUS...
EACH PERSON GETS 5 MINUTES WITH ME, RIGHT?
YES, BUT I IMAGINE THAT A LOT OF THEM ARE GOING TO HAVE ISSUES WHICH THEY'RE GOING TO WANT TO TAKE UP WITH YOU AFTERWARDS...
I GUESS SO... ALL THE USUAL ANGER AND COMPLAINTS...
alex@alexcartoon.com
JEEZ... THERE'S NOTHING I HATE MORE THAN WHEN MY GUYS START DEMANDING ONE-ON-ONE POST-BONUS "COUCH TIME" WITH ME TO DISCUSS THEIR GRIEVANCES...
ER, EXCEPT WHEN THEY DON'T...?
OH YEAH... WHICH MEANS I MUST HAVE PAID THEM TOO MUCH... THAT'S REALLY ANNOYING...

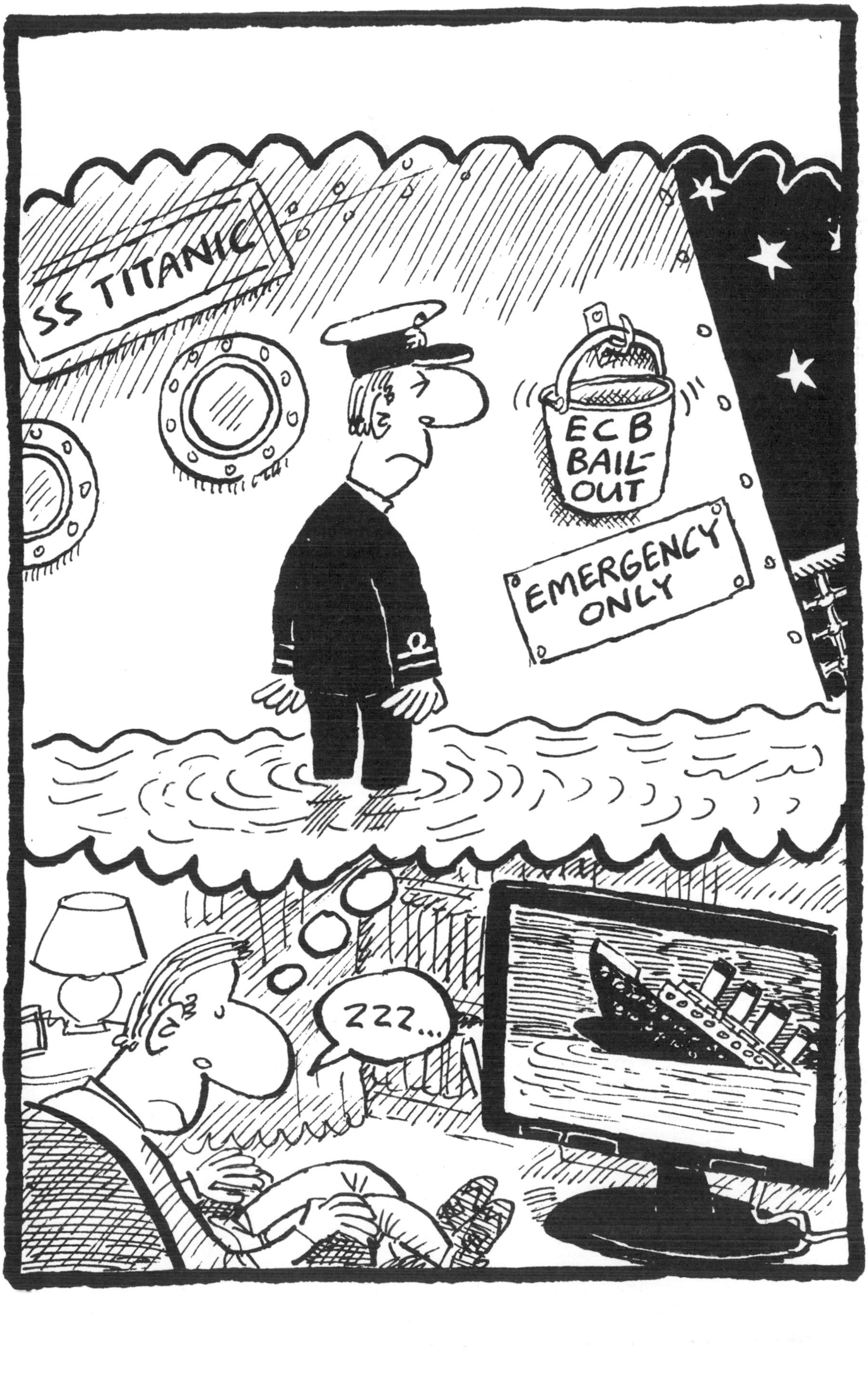
SS TITANIC
ECB BAIL-OUT
EMERGENCY ONLY
ZZZ...

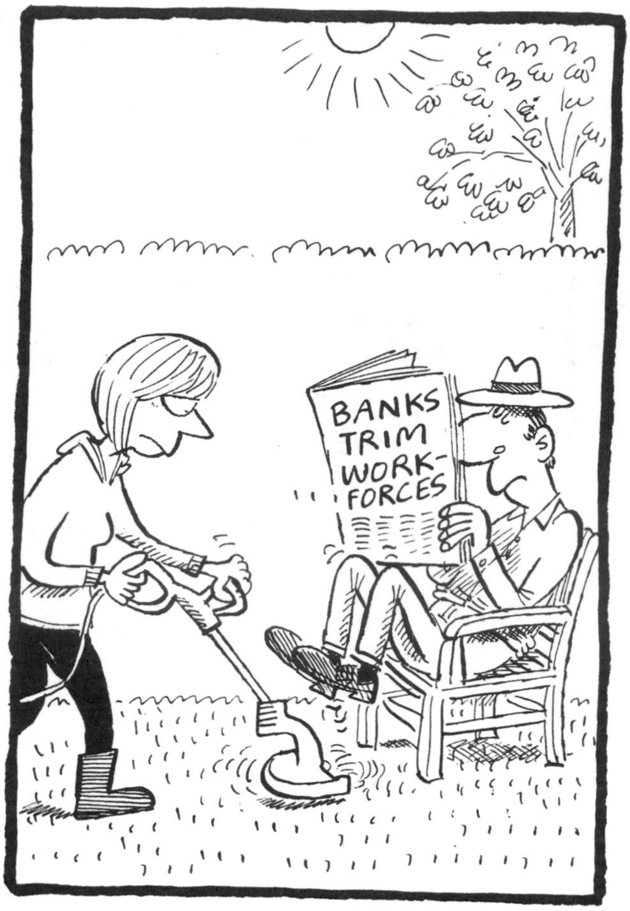
BANKS TRIM WORK-FORCES

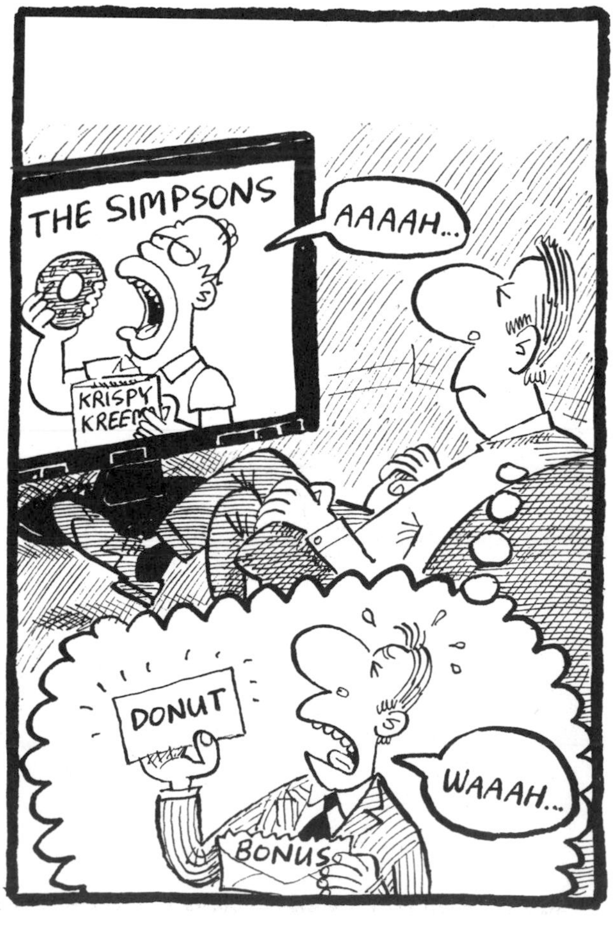
THE SIMPSONS
AAAAH...
KRISPY KREEM
DONUT
WAAAH...
BONUS

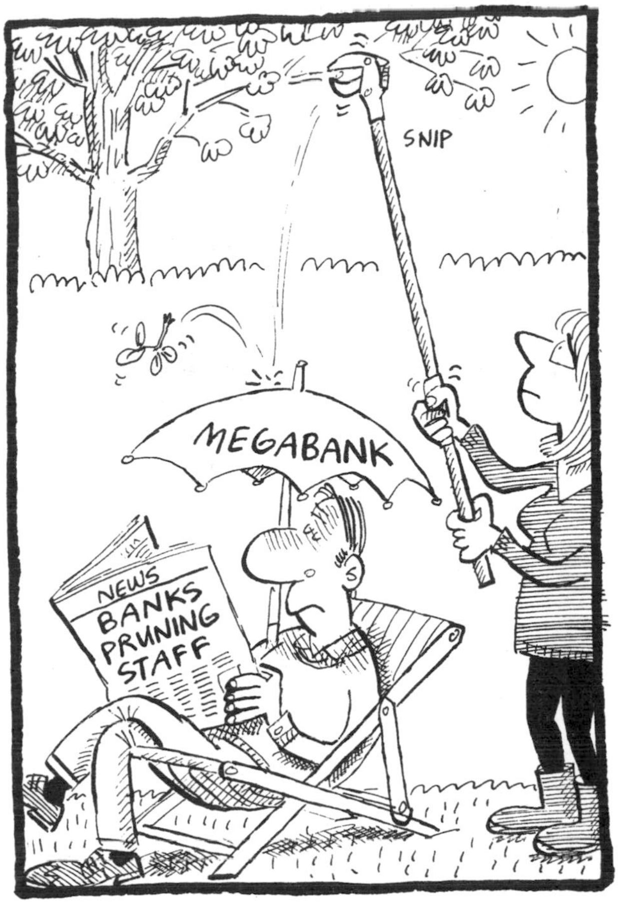
SNIP
MEGABANK
NEWS
BANKS PRUNING STAFF

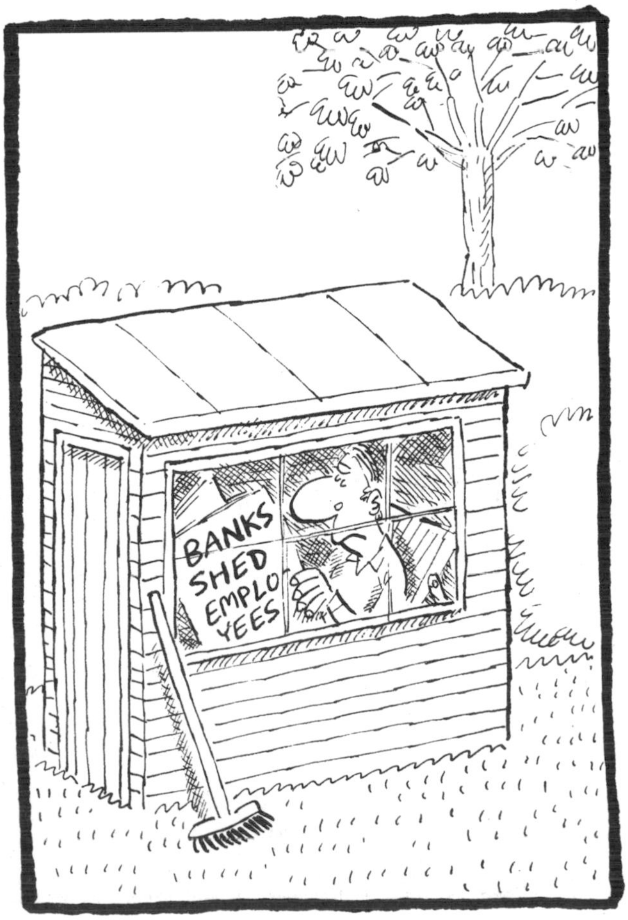
BANKS SHED EMPLOYEES

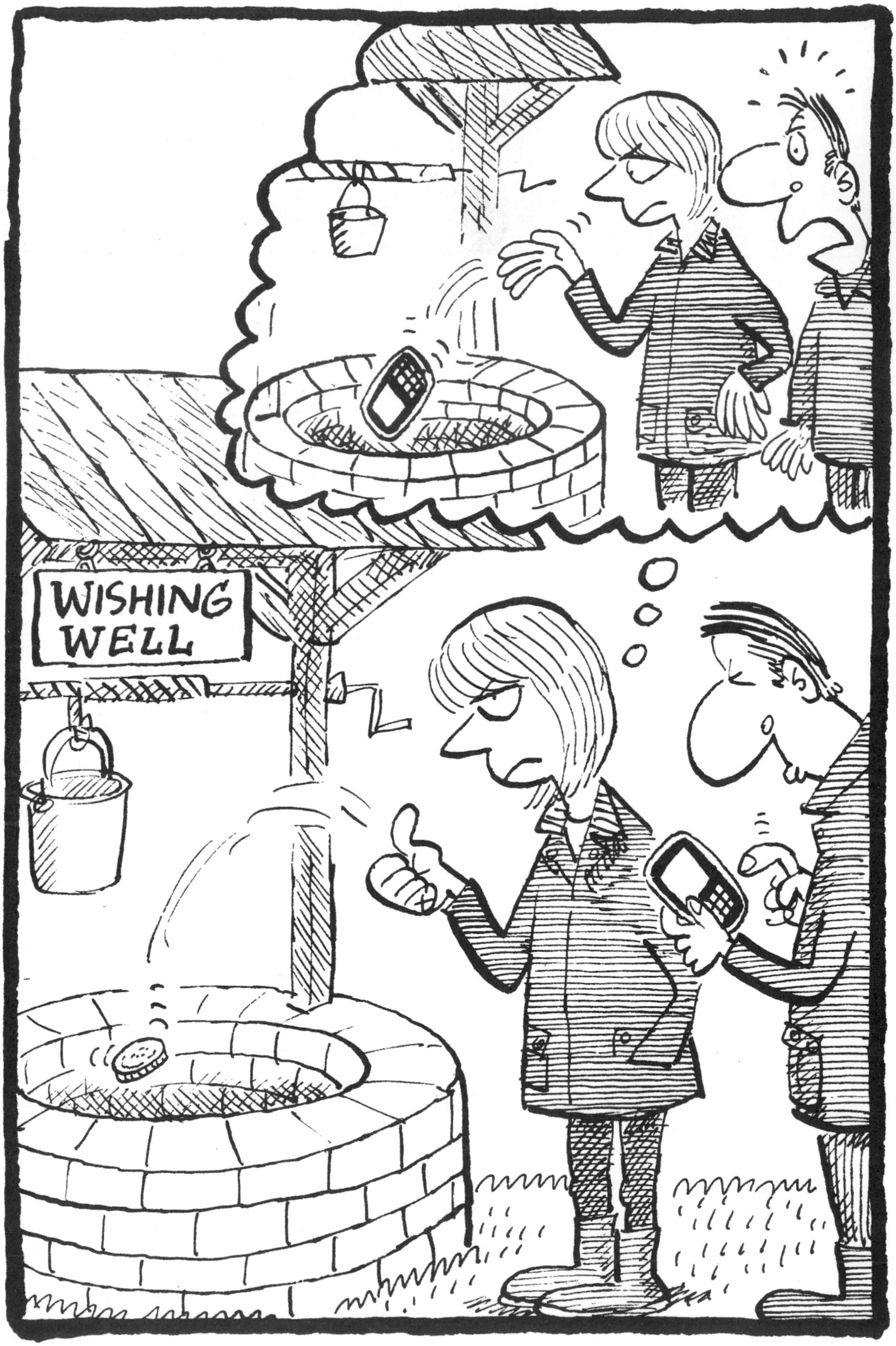
WISHING WELL

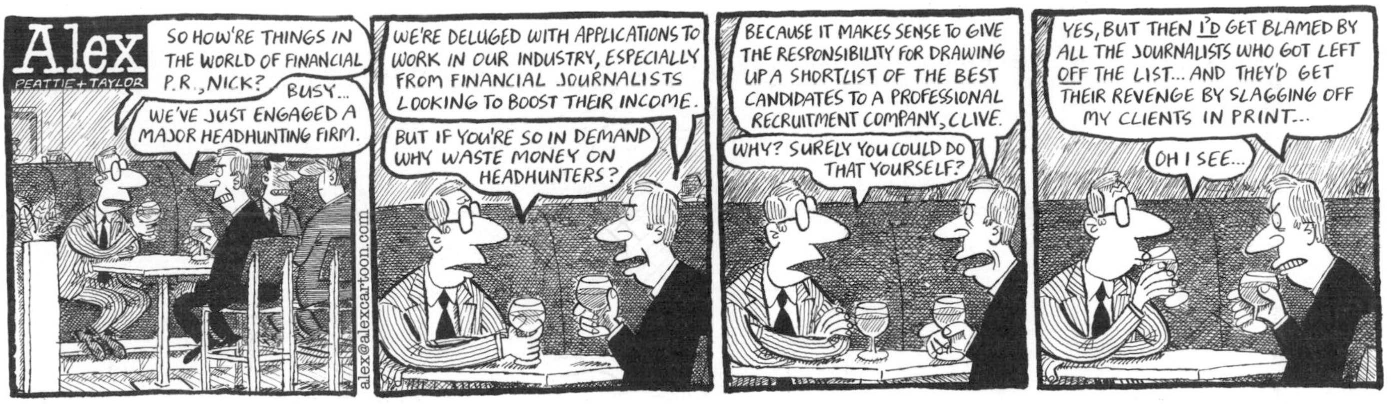
Alex
PEATTIE + TAYLOR
SO HOW'RE THINGS IN THE WORLD OF FINANCIAL P.R., NICK?
BUSY... WE'VE JUST ENGAGED A MAJOR HEADHUNTING FIRM.
alex@alexcartoon.com
WE'RE DELUGED WITH APPLICATIONS TO WORK IN OUR INDUSTRY, ESPECIALLY FROM FINANCIAL JOURNALISTS LOOKING TO BOOST THEIR INCOME.
BUT IF YOU'RE SO IN DEMAND WHY WASTE MONEY ON HEADHUNTERS?
BECAUSE IT MAKES SENSE TO GIVE THE RESPONSIBILITY FOR DRAWING UP A SHORTLIST OF THE BEST CANDIDATES TO A PROFESSIONAL RECRUITMENT COMPANY, CLIVE.
WHY? SURELY YOU COULD DO THAT YOURSELF?
YES, BUT THEN I'D GET BLAMED BY ALL THE JOURNALISTS WHO GOT LEFT OFF THE LIST... AND THEY'D GET THEIR REVENGE BY SLAGGING OFF MY CLIENTS IN PRINT...
OH I SEE...

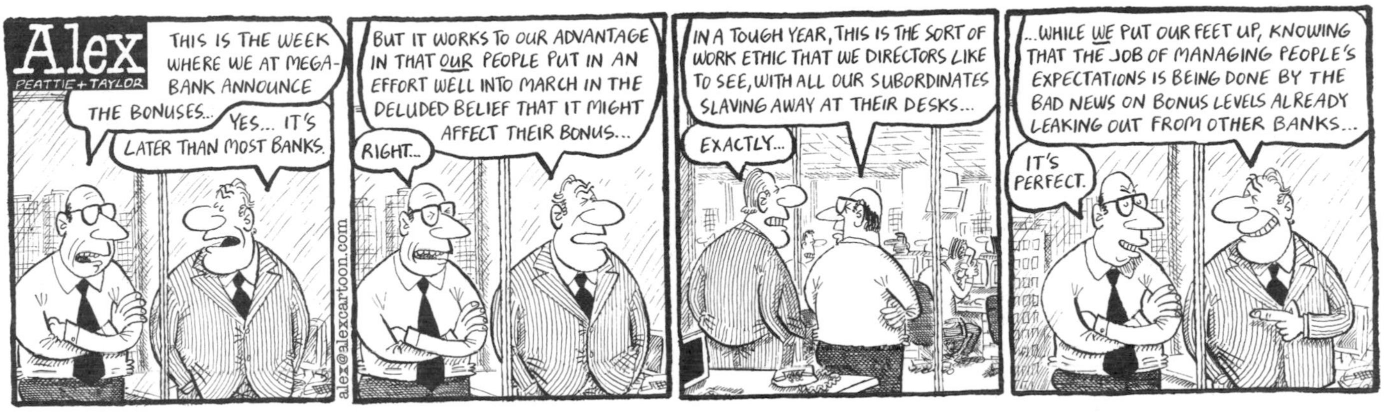
Alex
PEATTIE + TAYLOR
THIS IS THE WEEK WHERE WE AT MEGA-BANK ANNOUNCE THE BONUSES...
YES... IT'S LATER THAN MOST BANKS.
alex@alexcartoon.com
BUT IT WORKS TO OUR ADVANTAGE IN THAT OUR PEOPLE PUT IN AN EFFORT WELL INTO MARCH IN THE DELUDED BELIEF THAT IT MIGHT AFFECT THEIR BONUS...
RIGHT...
IN A TOUGH YEAR, THIS IS THE SORT OF WORK ETHIC THAT WE DIRECTORS LIKE TO SEE, WITH ALL OUR SUBORDINATES SLAVING AWAY AT THEIR DESKS...
EXACTLY...
...WHILE WE PUT OUR FEET UP, KNOWING THAT THE JOB OF MANAGING PEOPLE'S EXPECTATIONS IS BEING DONE BY THE BAD NEWS ON BONUS LEVELS ALREADY LEAKING OUT FROM OTHER BANKS...
IT'S PERFECT.

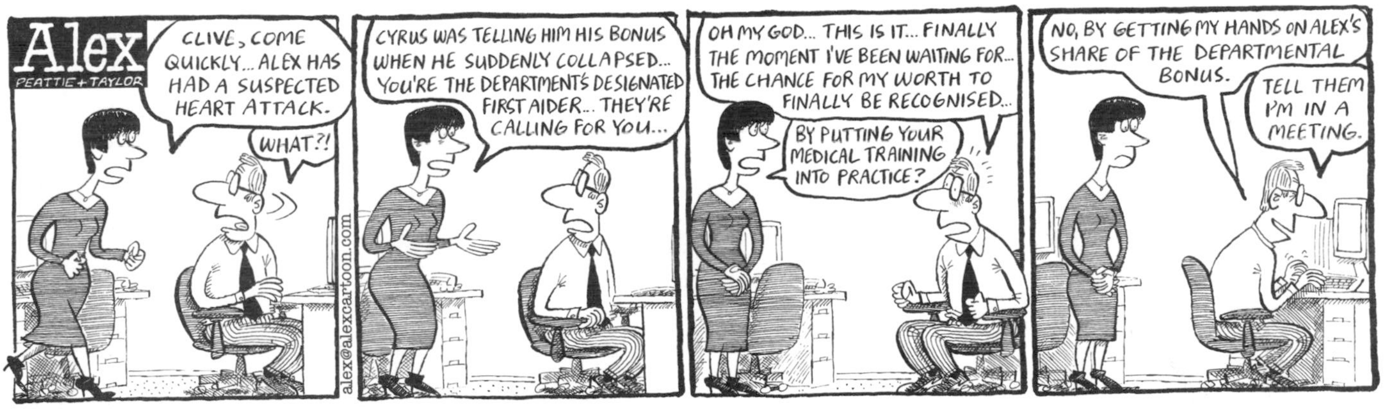
Alex
PEATTIE + TAYLOR
CLIVE, COME QUICKLY... ALEX HAS HAD A SUSPECTED HEART ATTACK.
WHAT?!
alex@alexcartoon.com
CYRUS WAS TELLING HIM HIS BONUS WHEN HE SUDDENLY COLLAPSED... YOU'RE THE DEPARTMENT'S DESIGNATED FIRST AIDER... THEY'RE CALLING FOR YOU...
OH MY GOD... THIS IS IT... FINALLY THE MOMENT I'VE BEEN WAITING FOR... THE CHANCE FOR MY WORTH TO FINALLY BE RECOGNISED...
BY PUTTING YOUR MEDICAL TRAINING INTO PRACTICE?
NO, BY GETTING MY HANDS ON ALEX'S SHARE OF THE DEPARTMENTAL BONUS.
TELL THEM I'M IN A MEETING.

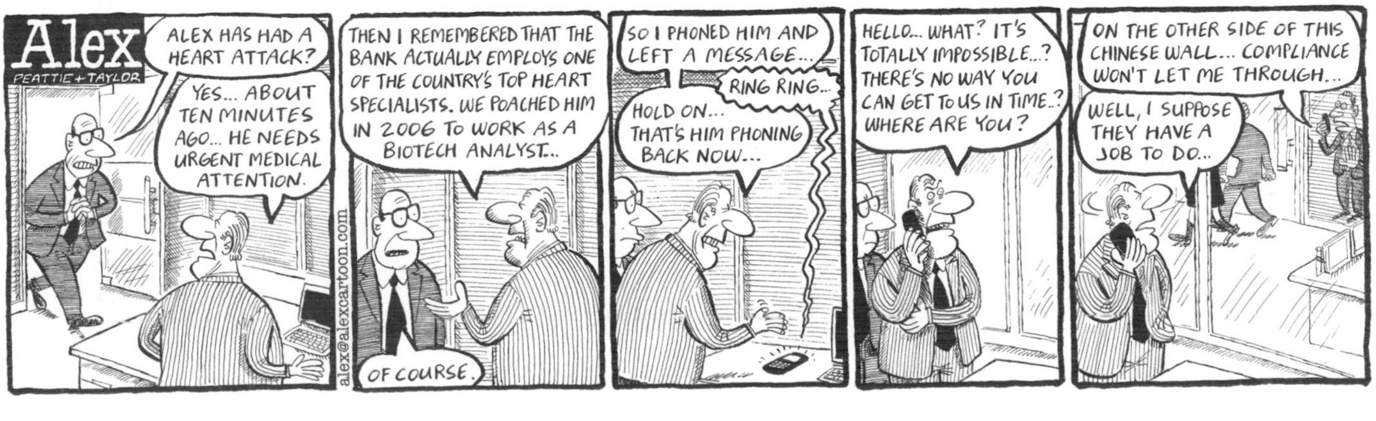
Alex
PEATTIE + TAYLOR
ALEX HAS HAD A HEART ATTACK?
YES... ABOUT TEN MINUTES AGO... HE NEEDS URGENT MEDICAL ATTENTION.
alex@alexcartoon.com
THEN I REMEMBERED THAT THE BANK ACTUALLY EMPLOYS ONE OF THE COUNTRY'S TOP HEART SPECIALISTS. WE POACHED HIM IN 2006 TO WORK AS A BIOTECH ANALYST...
OF COURSE.
SO I PHONED HIM AND LEFT A MESSAGE...
RING RING...
HOLD ON... THAT'S HIM PHONING BACK NOW...
HELLO... WHAT? IT'S TOTALLY IMPOSSIBLE...? THERE'S NO WAY YOU CAN GET TO US IN TIME..? WHERE ARE YOU?
ON THE OTHER SIDE OF THIS CHINESE WALL... COMPLIANCE WON'T LET ME THROUGH...
WELL, I SUPPOSE THEY HAVE A JOB TO DO...

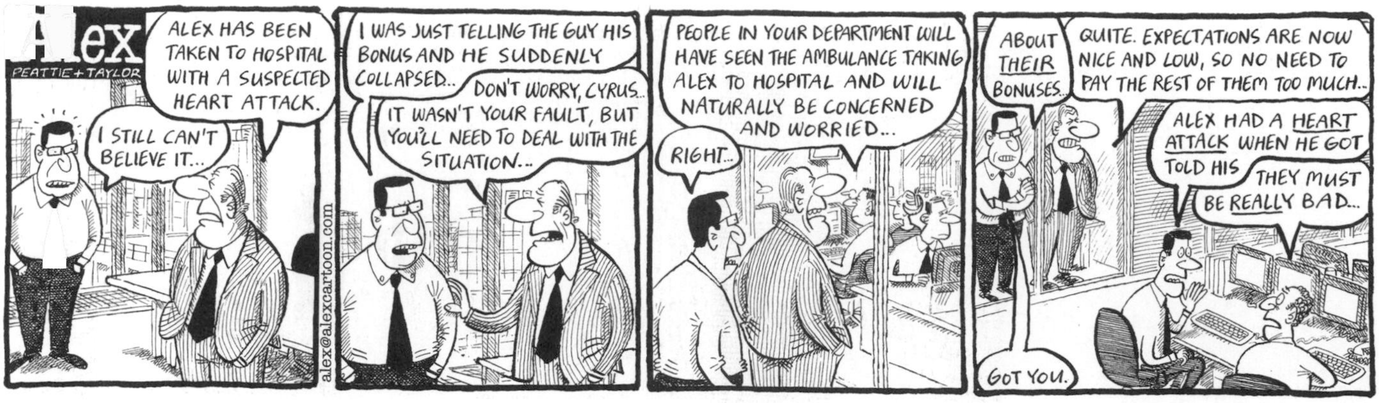
Alex
PEATTIE + TAYLOR
ALEX HAS BEEN TAKEN TO HOSPITAL WITH A SUSPECTED HEART ATTACK.
I STILL CAN'T BELIEVE IT...
I WAS JUST TELLING THE GUY HIS BONUS AND HE SUDDENLY COLLAPSED...
DON'T WORRY, CYRUS.. IT WASN'T YOUR FAULT, BUT YOU'LL NEED TO DEAL WITH THE SITUATION...
alex@alexcartoon.com
PEOPLE IN YOUR DEPARTMENT WILL HAVE SEEN THE AMBULANCE TAKING ALEX TO HOSPITAL AND WILL NATURALLY BE CONCERNED AND WORRIED...
RIGHT...
ABOUT THEIR BONUSES.
QUITE. EXPECTATIONS ARE NOW NICE AND LOW, SO NO NEED TO PAY THE REST OF THEM TOO MUCH..
ALEX HAD A HEART ATTACK WHEN HE GOT TOLD HIS
THEY MUST BE REALLY BAD...
GOT YOU.

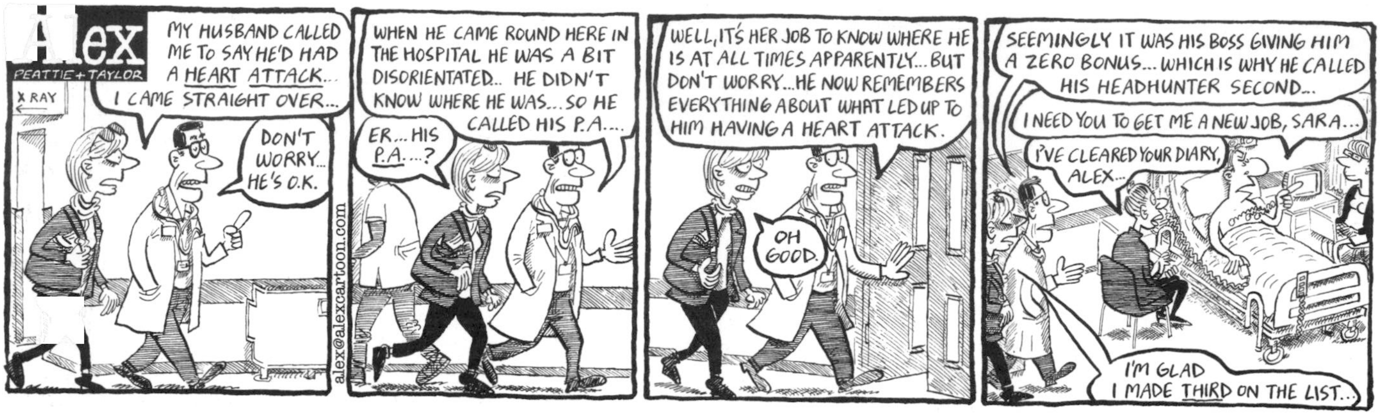
Alex
PEATTIE + TAYLOR
MY HUSBAND CALLED ME TO SAY HE'D HAD A HEART ATTACK... I CAME STRAIGHT OVER...
X RAY
DON'T WORRY... HE'S O.K.
alex@alexcartoon.com
WHEN HE CAME ROUND HERE IN THE HOSPITAL HE WAS A BIT DISORIENTATED... HE DIDN'T KNOW WHERE HE WAS... SO HE CALLED HIS P.A....
ER... HIS P.A. ...?
WELL, IT'S HER JOB TO KNOW WHERE HE IS AT ALL TIMES APPARENTLY... BUT DON'T WORRY... HE NOW REMEMBERS EVERYTHING ABOUT WHAT LED UP TO HIM HAVING A HEART ATTACK.
OH GOOD.
SEEMINGLY IT WAS HIS BOSS GIVING HIM A ZERO BONUS... WHICH IS WHY HE CALLED HIS HEADHUNTER SECOND...
I NEED YOU TO GET ME A NEW JOB, SARA...
I'VE CLEARED YOUR DIARY, ALEX...
I'M GLAD I MADE THIRD ON THE LIST...

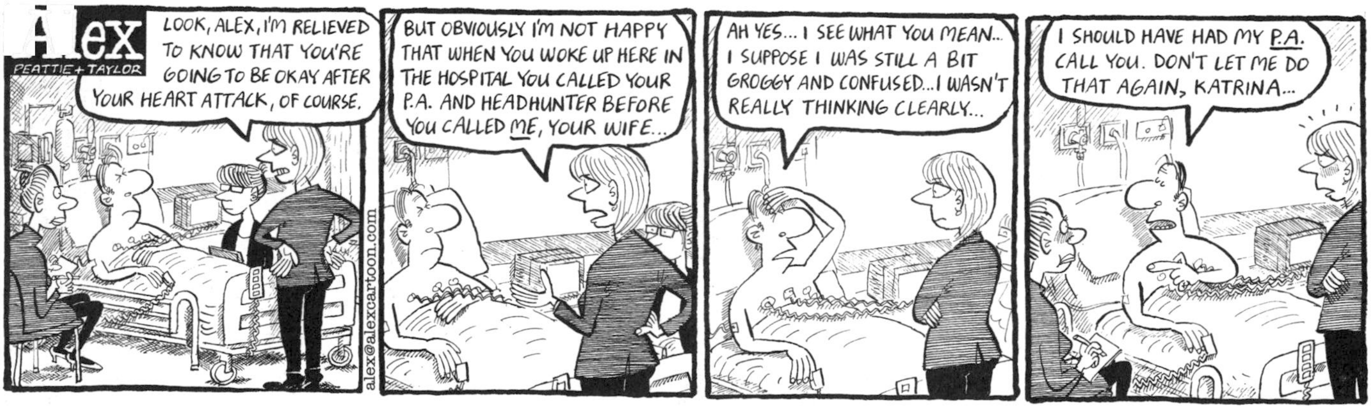
Alex
PEATTIE + TAYLOR
LOOK, ALEX, I'M RELIEVED TO KNOW THAT YOU'RE GOING TO BE OKAY AFTER YOUR HEART ATTACK, OF COURSE.
alex@alexcartoon.com
BUT OBVIOUSLY I'M NOT HAPPY THAT WHEN YOU WOKE UP HERE IN THE HOSPITAL YOU CALLED YOUR P.A. AND HEADHUNTER BEFORE YOU CALLED ME, YOUR WIFE...
AH YES... I SEE WHAT YOU MEAN... I SUPPOSE I WAS STILL A BIT GROGGY AND CONFUSED... I WASN'T REALLY THINKING CLEARLY...
I SHOULD HAVE HAD MY P.A. CALL YOU. DON'T LET ME DO THAT AGAIN, KATRINA...

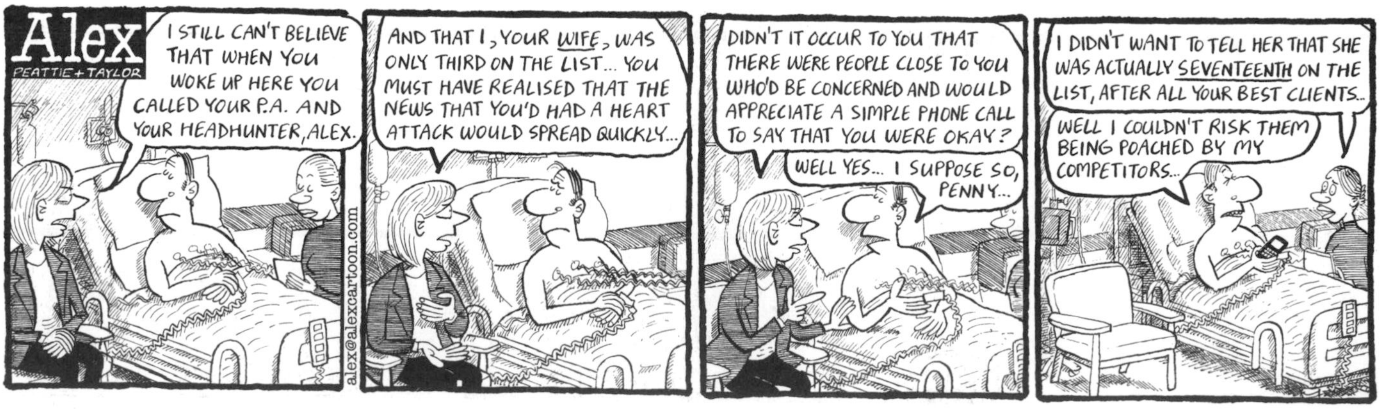
Alex
PEATTIE + TAYLOR
I STILL CAN'T BELIEVE THAT WHEN YOU WOKE UP HERE YOU CALLED YOUR P.A. AND YOUR HEADHUNTER, ALEX.
alex@alexcartoon.com
AND THAT I, YOUR WIFE, WAS ONLY THIRD ON THE LIST... YOU MUST HAVE REALISED THAT THE NEWS THAT YOU'D HAD A HEART ATTACK WOULD SPREAD QUICKLY...
DIDN'T IT OCCUR TO YOU THAT THERE WERE PEOPLE CLOSE TO YOU WHO'D BE CONCERNED AND WOULD APPRECIATE A SIMPLE PHONE CALL TO SAY THAT YOU WERE OKAY?
WELL YES... I SUPPOSE SO, PENNY...
I DIDN'T WANT TO TELL HER THAT SHE WAS ACTUALLY SEVENTEENTH ON THE LIST, AFTER ALL YOUR BEST CLIENTS...
WELL I COULDN'T RISK THEM BEING POACHED BY MY COMPETITORS...

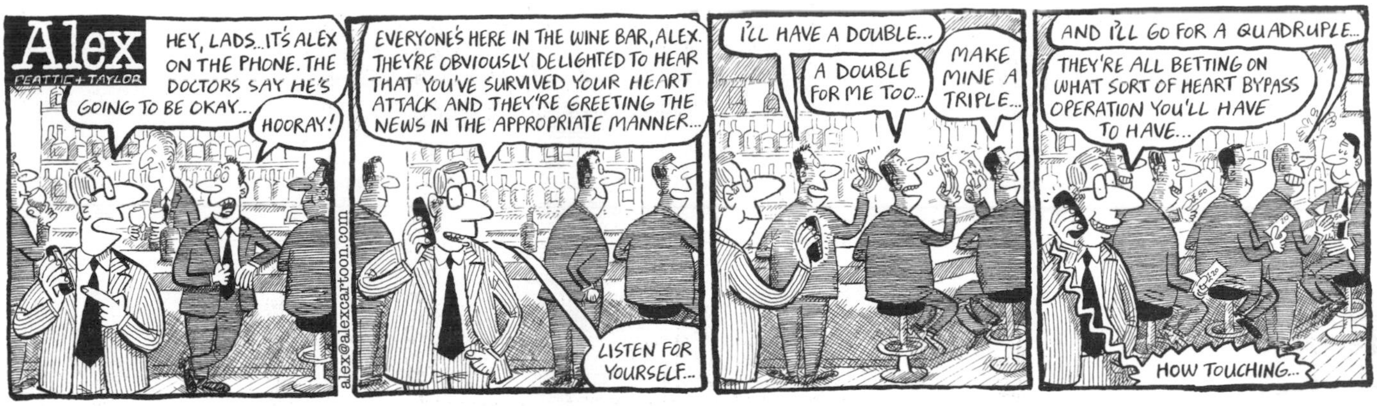
Alex
PEATTIE + TAYLOR
HEY, LADS...IT'S ALEX ON THE PHONE. THE DOCTORS SAY HE'S GOING TO BE OKAY...
HOORAY!
alex@alexcartoon.com
EVERYONE'S HERE IN THE WINE BAR, ALEX. THEY'RE OBVIOUSLY DELIGHTED TO HEAR THAT YOU'VE SURVIVED YOUR HEART ATTACK AND THEY'RE GREETING THE NEWS IN THE APPROPRIATE MANNER...
LISTEN FOR YOURSELF...
I'LL HAVE A DOUBLE...
A DOUBLE FOR ME TOO...
MAKE MINE A TRIPLE...
AND I'LL GO FOR A QUADRUPLE...
THEY'RE ALL BETTING ON WHAT SORT OF HEART BYPASS OPERATION YOU'LL HAVE TO HAVE...
HOW TOUCHING...

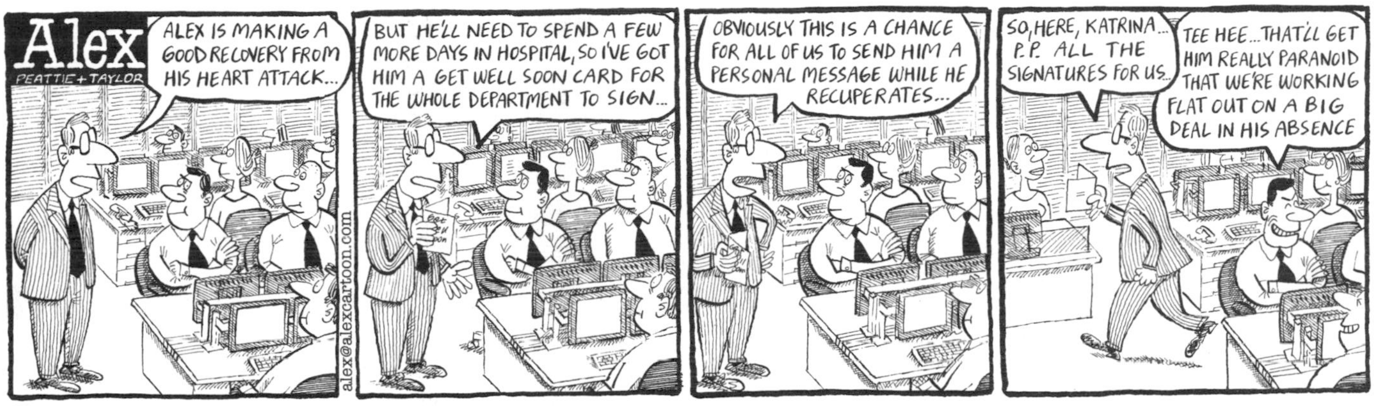
Alex
PEATTIE + TAYLOR
ALEX IS MAKING A GOOD RECOVERY FROM HIS HEART ATTACK...
alex@alexcartoon.com
BUT HE'LL NEED TO SPEND A FEW MORE DAYS IN HOSPITAL, SO I'VE GOT HIM A GET WELL SOON CARD FOR THE WHOLE DEPARTMENT TO SIGN...
OBVIOUSLY THIS IS A CHANCE FOR ALL OF US TO SEND HIM A PERSONAL MESSAGE WHILE HE RECUPERATES...
SO, HERE, KATRINA... P.P. ALL THE SIGNATURES FOR US...
TEE HEE...THAT'LL GET HIM REALLY PARANOID THAT WE'RE WORKING FLAT OUT ON A BIG DEAL IN HIS ABSENCE

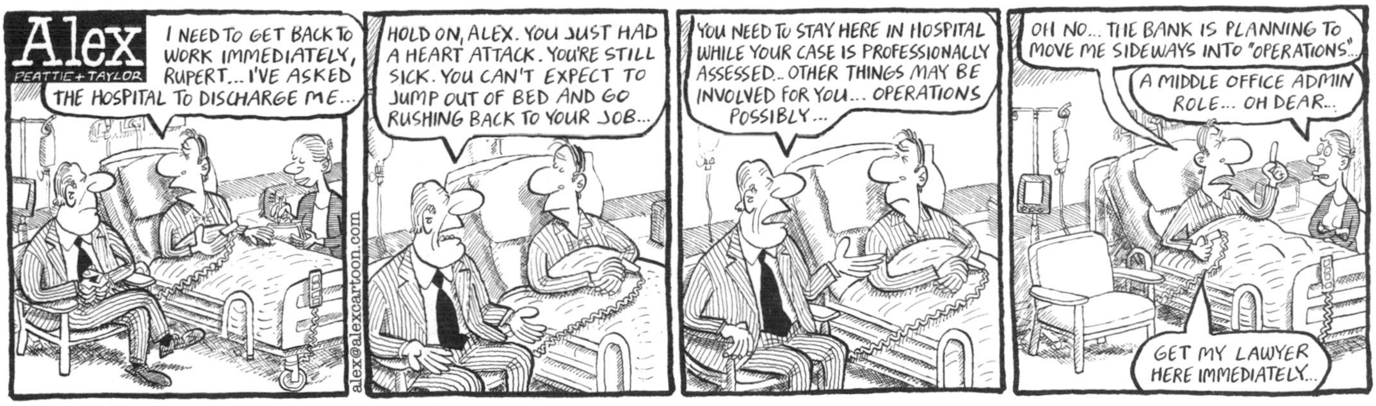
Alex
PEATTIE + TAYLOR
I NEED TO GET BACK TO WORK IMMEDIATELY, RUPERT... I'VE ASKED THE HOSPITAL TO DISCHARGE ME...
alex@alexcartoon.com
HOLD ON, ALEX. YOU JUST HAD A HEART ATTACK. YOU'RE STILL SICK. YOU CAN'T EXPECT TO JUMP OUT OF BED AND GO RUSHING BACK TO YOUR JOB...
YOU NEED TO STAY HERE IN HOSPITAL WHILE YOUR CASE IS PROFESSIONALLY ASSESSED... OTHER THINGS MAY BE INVOLVED FOR YOU... OPERATIONS POSSIBLY...
OH NO... THE BANK IS PLANNING TO MOVE ME SIDEWAYS INTO "OPERATIONS"...
A MIDDLE OFFICE ADMIN ROLE... OH DEAR...
GET MY LAWYER HERE IMMEDIATELY...

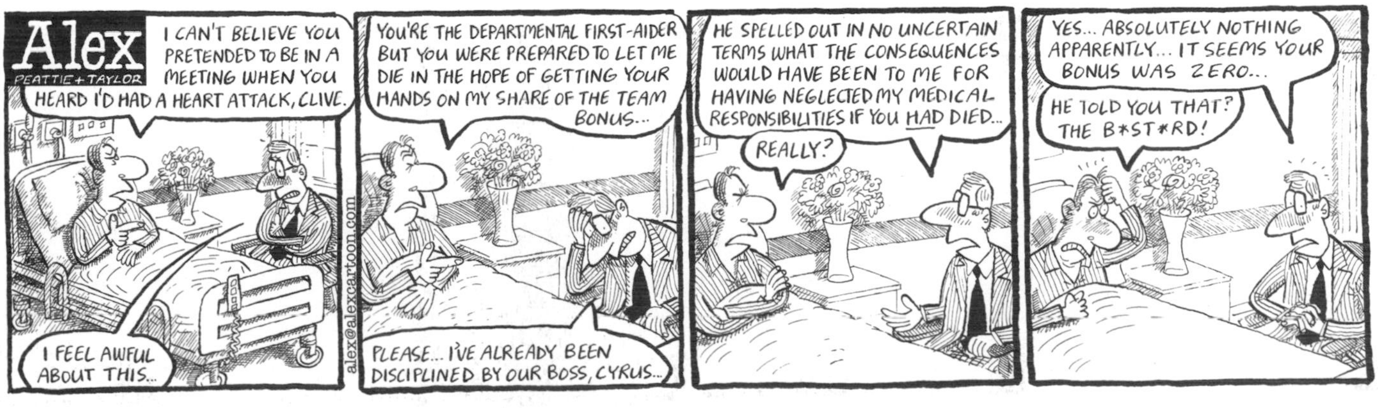
Alex
PEATTIE + TAYLOR
I CAN'T BELIEVE YOU PRETENDED TO BE IN A MEETING WHEN YOU HEARD I'D HAD A HEART ATTACK, CLIVE.
I FEEL AWFUL ABOUT THIS...
alex@alexcartoon.com
YOU'RE THE DEPARTMENTAL FIRST-AIDER BUT YOU WERE PREPARED TO LET ME DIE IN THE HOPE OF GETTING YOUR HANDS ON MY SHARE OF THE TEAM BONUS...
PLEASE... I'VE ALREADY BEEN DISCIPLINED BY OUR BOSS, CYRUS...
HE SPELLED OUT IN NO UNCERTAIN TERMS WHAT THE CONSEQUENCES WOULD HAVE BEEN TO ME FOR HAVING NEGLECTED MY MEDICAL RESPONSIBILITIES IF YOU HAD DIED...
REALLY?
YES... ABSOLUTELY NOTHING APPARENTLY... IT SEEMS YOUR BONUS WAS ZERO...
HE TOLD YOU THAT? THE B*ST*RD!

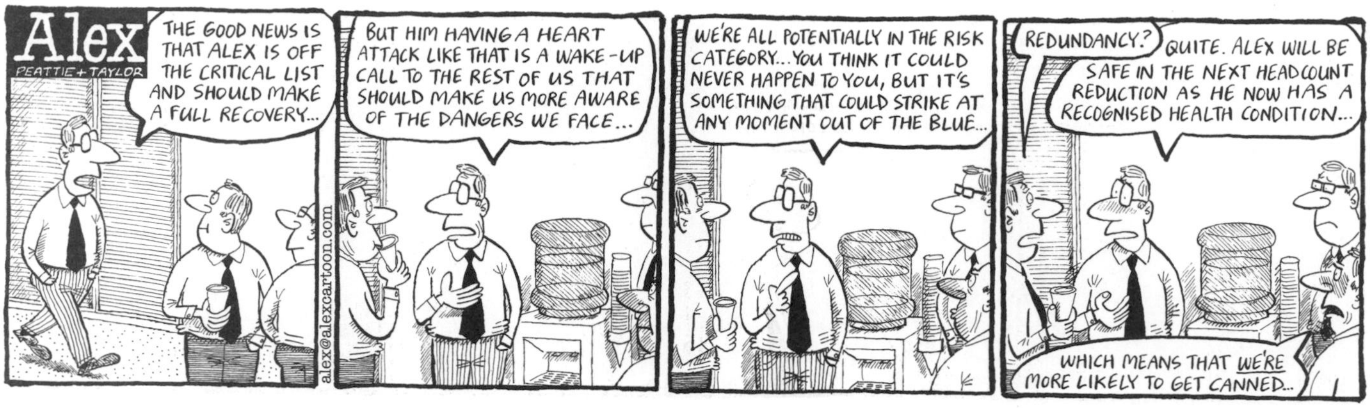
Alex
PEATTIE + TAYLOR
THE GOOD NEWS IS THAT ALEX IS OFF THE CRITICAL LIST AND SHOULD MAKE A FULL RECOVERY...
alex@alexcartoon.com
BUT HIM HAVING A HEART ATTACK LIKE THAT IS A WAKE-UP CALL TO THE REST OF US THAT SHOULD MAKE US MORE AWARE OF THE DANGERS WE FACE...
WE'RE ALL POTENTIALLY IN THE RISK CATEGORY... YOU THINK IT COULD NEVER HAPPEN TO YOU, BUT IT'S SOMETHING THAT COULD STRIKE AT ANY MOMENT OUT OF THE BLUE...
REDUNDANCY?
QUITE. ALEX WILL BE SAFE IN THE NEXT HEADCOUNT REDUCTION AS HE NOW HAS A RECOGNISED HEALTH CONDITION...
WHICH MEANS THAT WE'RE MORE LIKELY TO GET CANNED...

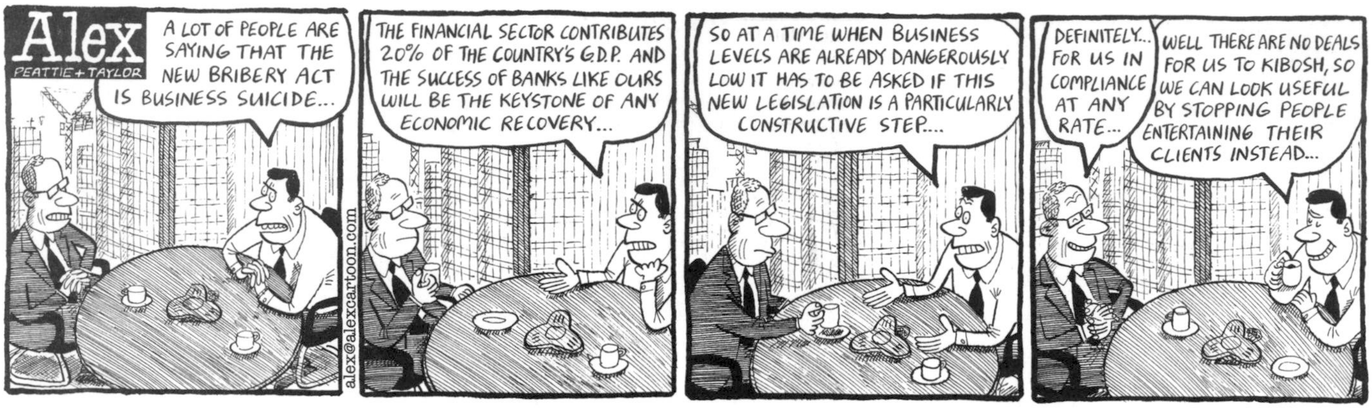
Alex
PEATTIE + TAYLOR
A LOT OF PEOPLE ARE SAYING THAT THE NEW BRIBERY ACT IS BUSINESS SUICIDE...
alex@alexcartoon.com
THE FINANCIAL SECTOR CONTRIBUTES 20% OF THE COUNTRY'S G.D.P. AND THE SUCCESS OF BANKS LIKE OURS WILL BE THE KEYSTONE OF ANY ECONOMIC RECOVERY...
SO AT A TIME WHEN BUSINESS LEVELS ARE ALREADY DANGEROUSLY LOW IT HAS TO BE ASKED IF THIS NEW LEGISLATION IS A PARTICULARLY CONSTRUCTIVE STEP...
DEFINITELY... FOR US IN COMPLIANCE AT ANY RATE...
WELL THERE ARE NO DEALS FOR US TO KIBOSH, SO WE CAN LOOK USEFUL BY STOPPING PEOPLE ENTERTAINING THEIR CLIENTS INSTEAD...

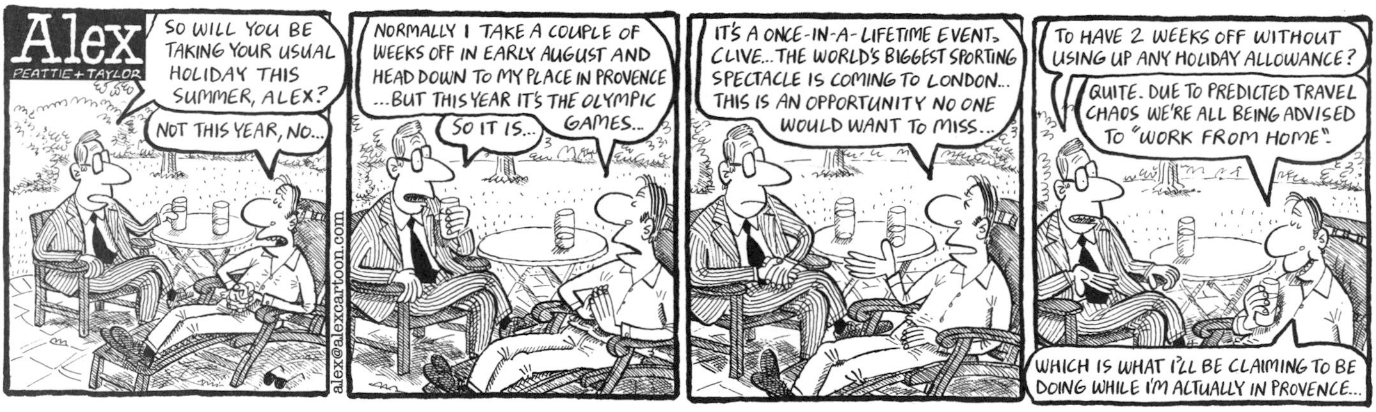
Alex
PEATTIE + TAYLOR
SO WILL YOU BE TAKING YOUR USUAL HOLIDAY THIS SUMMER, ALEX?
NOT THIS YEAR, NO...
alex@alexcartoon.com
NORMALLY I TAKE A COUPLE OF WEEKS OFF IN EARLY AUGUST AND HEAD DOWN TO MY PLACE IN PROVENCE ...BUT THIS YEAR IT'S THE OLYMPIC GAMES...
SO IT IS...
IT'S A ONCE-IN-A-LIFETIME EVENT, CLIVE... THE WORLD'S BIGGEST SPORTING SPECTACLE IS COMING TO LONDON... THIS IS AN OPPORTUNITY NO ONE WOULD WANT TO MISS...
TO HAVE 2 WEEKS OFF WITHOUT USING UP ANY HOLIDAY ALLOWANCE?
QUITE. DUE TO PREDICTED TRAVEL CHAOS WE'RE ALL BEING ADVISED TO "WORK FROM HOME".
WHICH IS WHAT I'LL BE CLAIMING TO BE DOING WHILE I'M ACTUALLY IN PROVENCE...

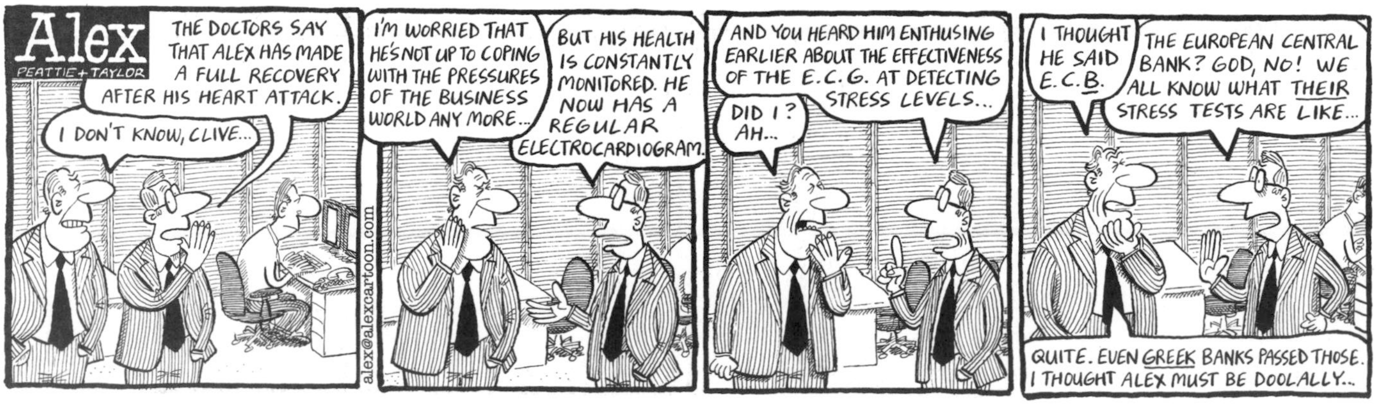
Alex
PEATTIE + TAYLOR
THE DOCTORS SAY THAT ALEX HAS MADE A FULL RECOVERY AFTER HIS HEART ATTACK.
I DON'T KNOW, CLIVE...
alex@alexcartoon.com
I'M WORRIED THAT HE'S NOT UP TO COPING WITH THE PRESSURES OF THE BUSINESS WORLD ANY MORE...
BUT HIS HEALTH IS CONSTANTLY MONITORED. HE NOW HAS A REGULAR ELECTROCARDIOGRAM.
AND YOU HEARD HIM ENTHUSING EARLIER ABOUT THE EFFECTIVENESS OF THE E.C.G. AT DETECTING STRESS LEVELS...
DID I? AH...
I THOUGHT HE SAID E.C.B.
THE EUROPEAN CENTRAL BANK? GOD, NO! WE ALL KNOW WHAT THEIR STRESS TESTS ARE LIKE...
QUITE. EVEN GREEK BANKS PASSED THOSE. I THOUGHT ALEX MUST BE DOOLALLY...

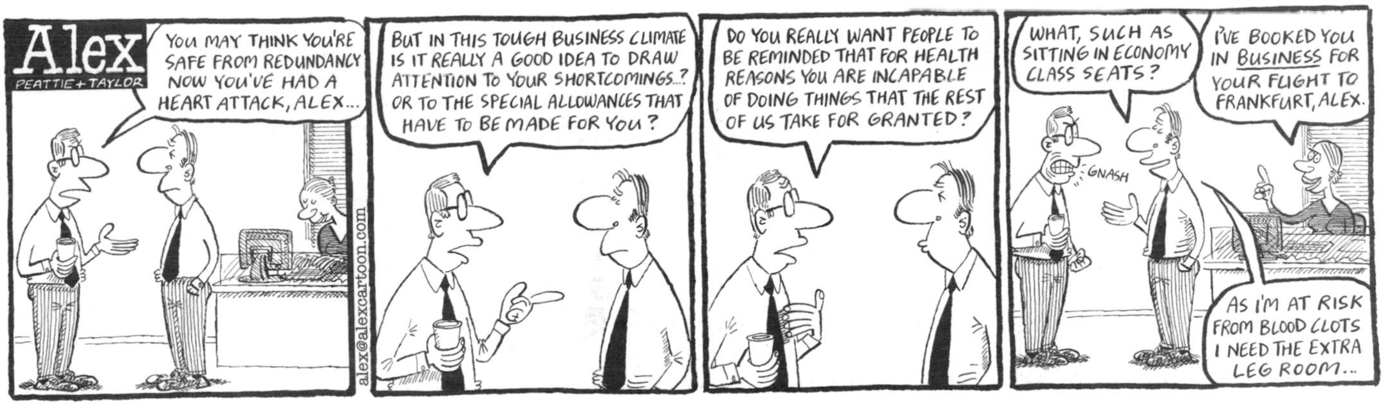
Alex
PEATTIE+TAYLOR
YOU MAY THINK YOU'RE SAFE FROM REDUNDANCY NOW YOU'VE HAD A HEART ATTACK, ALEX...
alex@alexcartoon.com
BUT IN THIS TOUGH BUSINESS CLIMATE IS IT REALLY A GOOD IDEA TO DRAW ATTENTION TO YOUR SHORTCOMINGS..? OR TO THE SPECIAL ALLOWANCES THAT HAVE TO BE MADE FOR YOU?
DO YOU REALLY WANT PEOPLE TO BE REMINDED THAT FOR HEALTH REASONS YOU ARE INCAPABLE OF DOING THINGS THAT THE REST OF US TAKE FOR GRANTED?
WHAT, SUCH AS SITTING IN ECONOMY CLASS SEATS?
GNASH
I'VE BOOKED YOU IN BUSINESS FOR YOUR FLIGHT TO FRANKFURT, ALEX.
AS I'M AT RISK FROM BLOOD CLOTS I NEED THE EXTRA LEG ROOM...

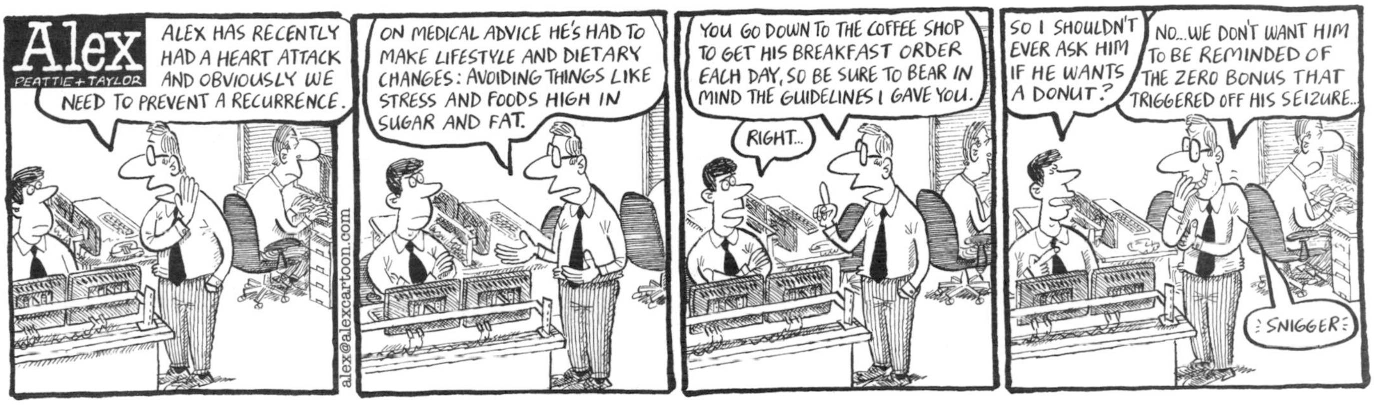
Alex
PEATTIE+TAYLOR
ALEX HAS RECENTLY HAD A HEART ATTACK AND OBVIOUSLY WE NEED TO PREVENT A RECURRENCE.
alex@alexcartoon.com
ON MEDICAL ADVICE HE'S HAD TO MAKE LIFESTYLE AND DIETARY CHANGES: AVOIDING THINGS LIKE STRESS AND FOODS HIGH IN SUGAR AND FAT.
YOU GO DOWN TO THE COFFEE SHOP TO GET HIS BREAKFAST ORDER EACH DAY, SO BE SURE TO BEAR IN MIND THE GUIDELINES I GAVE YOU.
RIGHT...
SO I SHOULDN'T EVER ASK HIM IF HE WANTS A DONUT?
NO...WE DON'T WANT HIM TO BE REMINDED OF THE ZERO BONUS THAT TRIGGERED OFF HIS SEIZURE...
SNIGGER

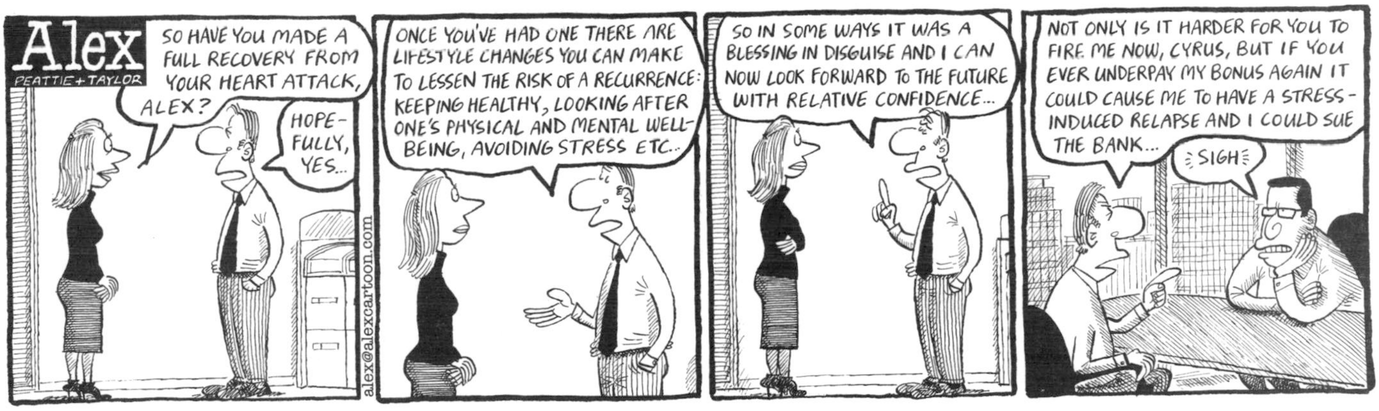
Alex
PEATTIE+TAYLOR
SO HAVE YOU MADE A FULL RECOVERY FROM YOUR HEART ATTACK, ALEX?
HOPE-FULLY, YES...
alex@alexcartoon.com
ONCE YOU'VE HAD ONE THERE ARE LIFESTYLE CHANGES YOU CAN MAKE TO LESSEN THE RISK OF A RECURRENCE: KEEPING HEALTHY, LOOKING AFTER ONE'S PHYSICAL AND MENTAL WELL-BEING, AVOIDING STRESS ETC...
SO IN SOME WAYS IT WAS A BLESSING IN DISGUISE AND I CAN NOW LOOK FORWARD TO THE FUTURE WITH RELATIVE CONFIDENCE...
NOT ONLY IS IT HARDER FOR YOU TO FIRE ME NOW, CYRUS, BUT IF YOU EVER UNDERPAY MY BONUS AGAIN IT COULD CAUSE ME TO HAVE A STRESS-INDUCED RELAPSE AND I COULD SUE THE BANK...
SIGH

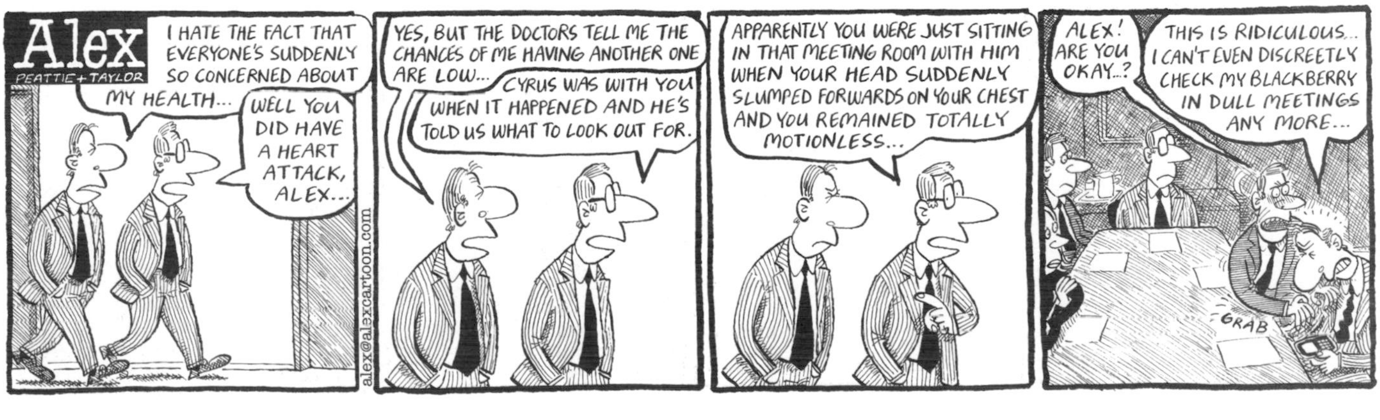
Alex
PEATTIE+TAYLOR
I HATE THE FACT THAT EVERYONE'S SUDDENLY SO CONCERNED ABOUT MY HEALTH...
WELL YOU DID HAVE A HEART ATTACK, ALEX...
alex@alexcartoon.com
YES, BUT THE DOCTORS TELL ME THE CHANCES OF ME HAVING ANOTHER ONE ARE LOW...
CYRUS WAS WITH YOU WHEN IT HAPPENED AND HE'S TOLD US WHAT TO LOOK OUT FOR.
APPARENTLY YOU WERE JUST SITTING IN THAT MEETING ROOM WITH HIM WHEN YOUR HEAD SUDDENLY SLUMPED FORWARDS ON YOUR CHEST AND YOU REMAINED TOTALLY MOTIONLESS...
ALEX! ARE YOU OKAY..?
THIS IS RIDICULOUS... I CAN'T EVEN DISCREETLY CHECK MY BLACKBERRY IN DULL MEETINGS ANY MORE...
GRAB

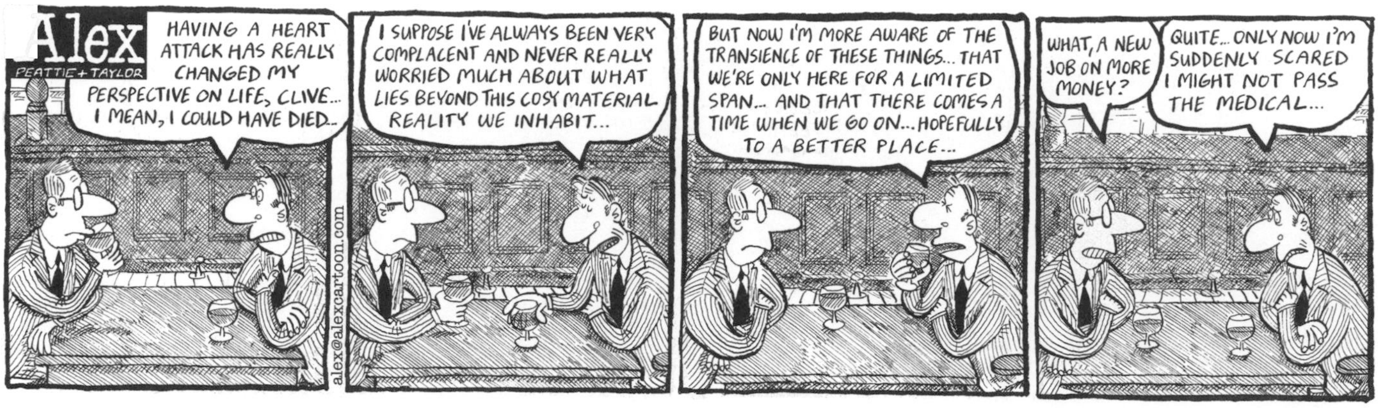
Alex
PEATTIE + TAYLOR
HAVING A HEART ATTACK HAS REALLY CHANGED MY PERSPECTIVE ON LIFE, CLIVE... I MEAN, I COULD HAVE DIED...
I SUPPOSE I'VE ALWAYS BEEN VERY COMPLACENT AND NEVER REALLY WORRIED MUCH ABOUT WHAT LIES BEYOND THIS COSY MATERIAL REALITY WE INHABIT...
alex@alexcartoon.com
BUT NOW I'M MORE AWARE OF THE TRANSIENCE OF THESE THINGS... THAT WE'RE ONLY HERE FOR A LIMITED SPAN... AND THAT THERE COMES A TIME WHEN WE GO ON... HOPEFULLY TO A BETTER PLACE...
WHAT, A NEW JOB ON MORE MONEY?
QUITE... ONLY NOW I'M SUDDENLY SCARED I MIGHT NOT PASS THE MEDICAL...

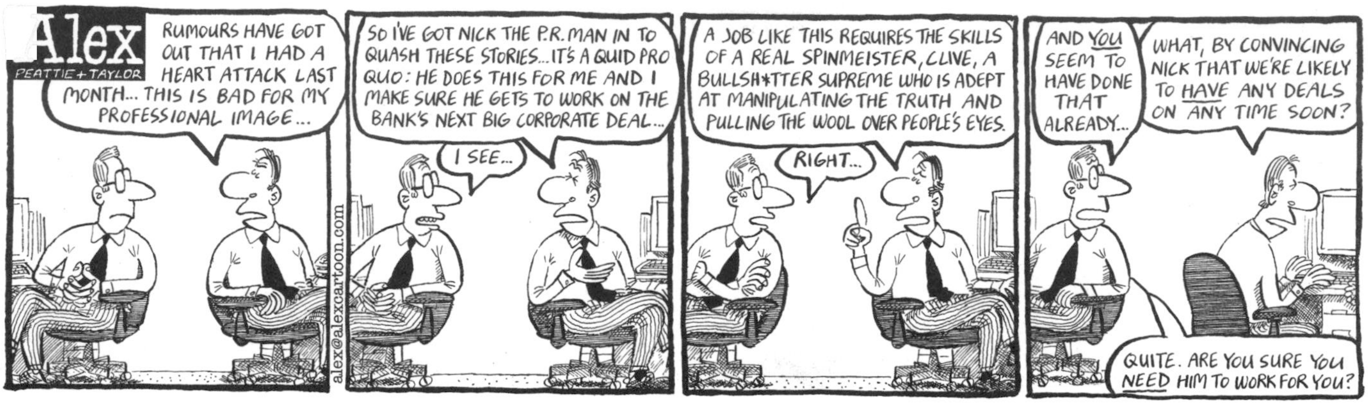
Alex
PEATTIE + TAYLOR
RUMOURS HAVE GOT OUT THAT I HAD A HEART ATTACK LAST MONTH... THIS IS BAD FOR MY PROFESSIONAL IMAGE...
SO I'VE GOT NICK THE P.R. MAN IN TO QUASH THESE STORIES... IT'S A QUID PRO QUO: HE DOES THIS FOR ME AND I MAKE SURE HE GETS TO WORK ON THE BANK'S NEXT BIG CORPORATE DEAL...
I SEE...
alex@alexcartoon.com
A JOB LIKE THIS REQUIRES THE SKILLS OF A REAL SPINMEISTER, CLIVE, A BULLSH*TTER SUPREME WHO IS ADEPT AT MANIPULATING THE TRUTH AND PULLING THE WOOL OVER PEOPLE'S EYES.
RIGHT...
AND YOU SEEM TO HAVE DONE THAT ALREADY...
WHAT, BY CONVINCING NICK THAT WE'RE LIKELY TO HAVE ANY DEALS ON ANY TIME SOON?
QUITE. ARE YOU SURE YOU NEED HIM TO WORK FOR YOU?

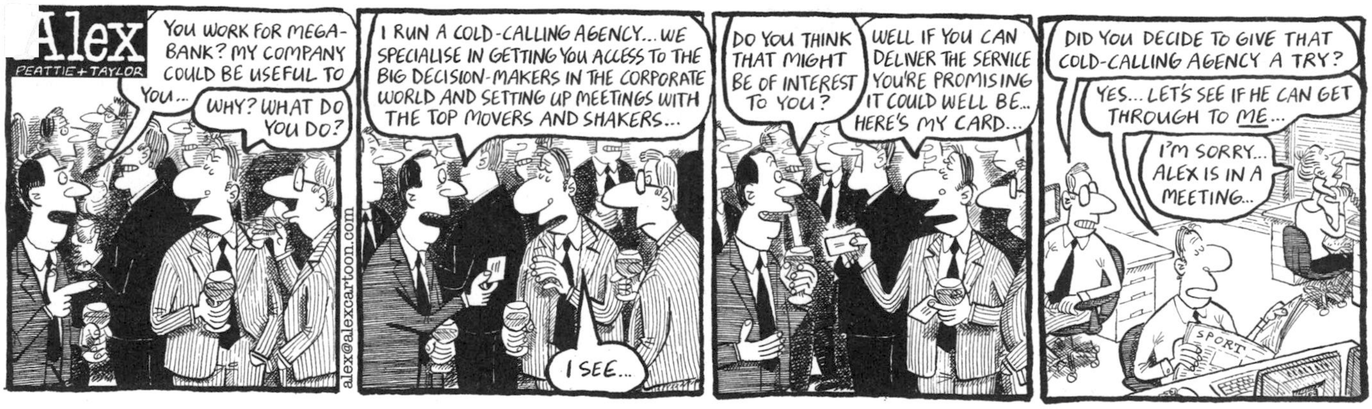
Alex
PEATTIE + TAYLOR
YOU WORK FOR MEGA-BANK? MY COMPANY COULD BE USEFUL TO YOU...
WHY? WHAT DO YOU DO?
alex@alexcartoon.com
I RUN A COLD-CALLING AGENCY... WE SPECIALISE IN GETTING YOU ACCESS TO THE BIG DECISION-MAKERS IN THE CORPORATE WORLD AND SETTING UP MEETINGS WITH THE TOP MOVERS AND SHAKERS...
I SEE...
DO YOU THINK THAT MIGHT BE OF INTEREST TO YOU?
WELL IF YOU CAN DELIVER THE SERVICE YOU'RE PROMISING IT COULD WELL BE... HERE'S MY CARD...
DID YOU DECIDE TO GIVE THAT COLD-CALLING AGENCY A TRY?
YES... LET'S SEE IF HE CAN GET THROUGH TO ME...
I'M SORRY... ALEX IS IN A MEETING...
SPORT

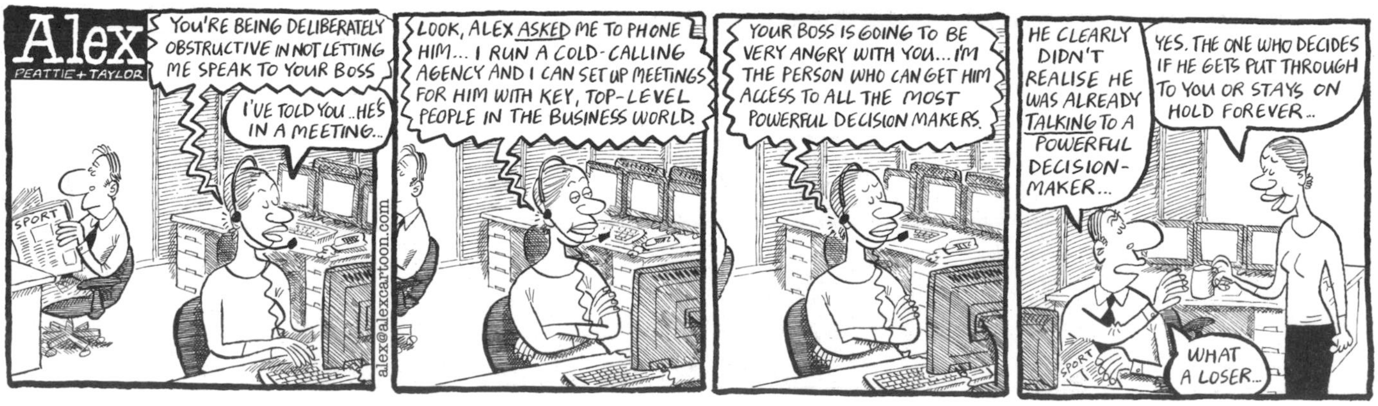
Alex
PEATTIE + TAYLOR
YOU'RE BEING DELIBERATELY OBSTRUCTIVE IN NOT LETTING ME SPEAK TO YOUR BOSS
I'VE TOLD YOU... HE'S IN A MEETING...
SPORT
alex@alexcartoon.com
LOOK, ALEX ASKED ME TO PHONE HIM... I RUN A COLD-CALLING AGENCY AND I CAN SET UP MEETINGS FOR HIM WITH KEY, TOP-LEVEL PEOPLE IN THE BUSINESS WORLD.
YOUR BOSS IS GOING TO BE VERY ANGRY WITH YOU... I'M THE PERSON WHO CAN GET HIM ACCESS TO ALL THE MOST POWERFUL DECISION MAKERS.
HE CLEARLY DIDN'T REALISE HE WAS ALREADY TALKING TO A POWERFUL DECISION-MAKER...
YES. THE ONE WHO DECIDES IF HE GETS PUT THROUGH TO YOU OR STAYS ON HOLD FOREVER...
SPORT
WHAT A LOSER...

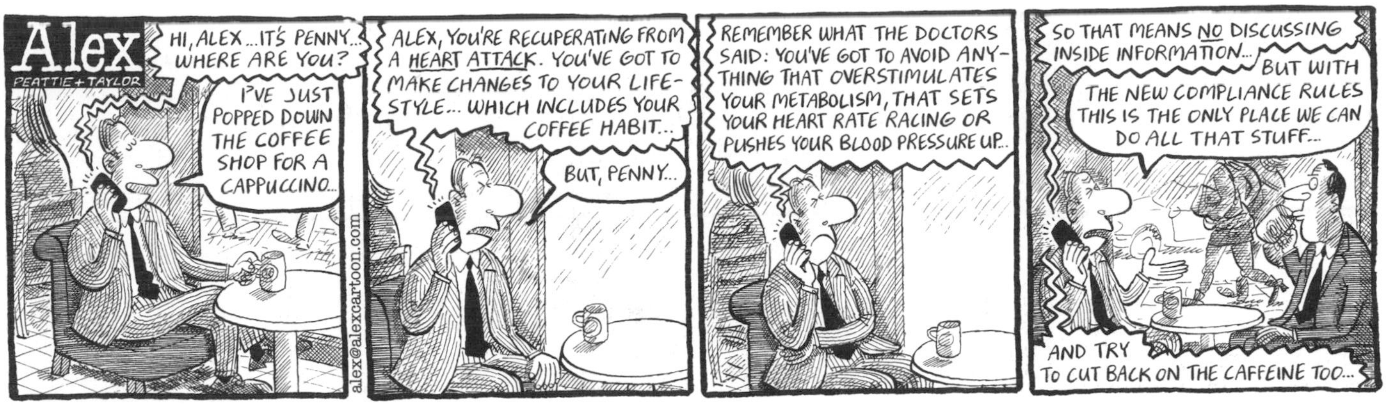
Alex
PEATTIE + TAYLOR
HI, ALEX... IT'S PENNY... WHERE ARE YOU?
I'VE JUST POPPED DOWN THE COFFEE SHOP FOR A CAPPUCCINO...
alex@alexcartoon.com
ALEX, YOU'RE RECUPERATING FROM A HEART ATTACK. YOU'VE GOT TO MAKE CHANGES TO YOUR LIFE-STYLE... WHICH INCLUDES YOUR COFFEE HABIT...
BUT, PENNY...
REMEMBER WHAT THE DOCTORS SAID: YOU'VE GOT TO AVOID ANY-THING THAT OVERSTIMULATES YOUR METABOLISM, THAT SETS YOUR HEART RATE RACING OR PUSHES YOUR BLOOD PRESSURE UP...
SO THAT MEANS NO DISCUSSING INSIDE INFORMATION...
BUT WITH THE NEW COMPLIANCE RULES THIS IS THE ONLY PLACE WE CAN DO ALL THAT STUFF...
AND TRY TO CUT BACK ON THE CAFFEINE TOO...

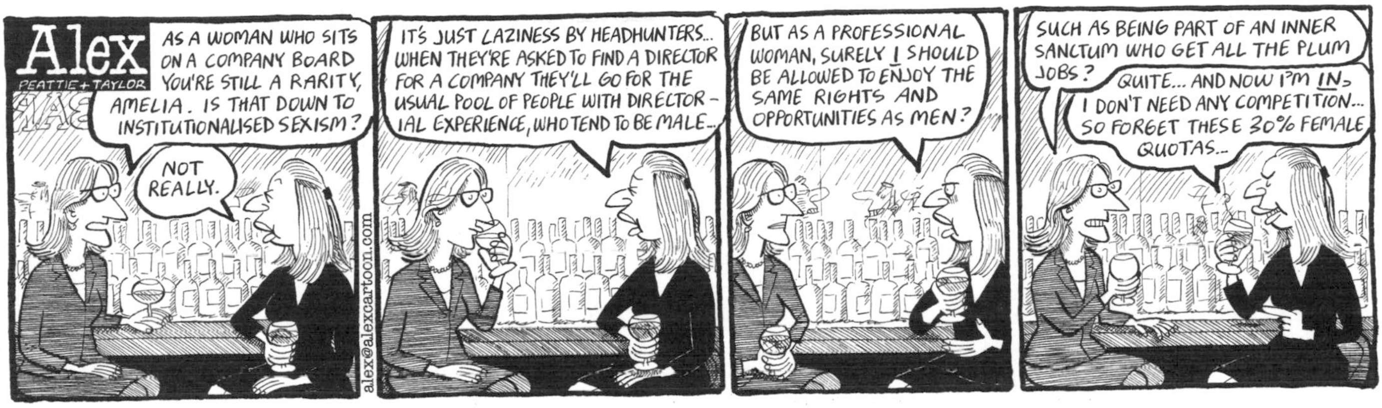
Alex
PEATTIE + TAYLOR
AS A WOMAN WHO SITS ON A COMPANY BOARD YOU'RE STILL A RARITY, AMELIA. IS THAT DOWN TO INSTITUTIONALISED SEXISM?
NOT REALLY.
alex@alexcartoon.com
IT'S JUST LAZINESS BY HEADHUNTERS... WHEN THEY'RE ASKED TO FIND A DIRECTOR FOR A COMPANY THEY'LL GO FOR THE USUAL POOL OF PEOPLE WITH DIRECTOR-IAL EXPERIENCE, WHO TEND TO BE MALE...
BUT AS A PROFESSIONAL WOMAN, SURELY I SHOULD BE ALLOWED TO ENJOY THE SAME RIGHTS AND OPPORTUNITIES AS MEN?
SUCH AS BEING PART OF AN INNER SANCTUM WHO GET ALL THE PLUM JOBS?
QUITE... AND NOW I'M IN, I DON'T NEED ANY COMPETITION... SO FORGET THESE 30% FEMALE QUOTAS...

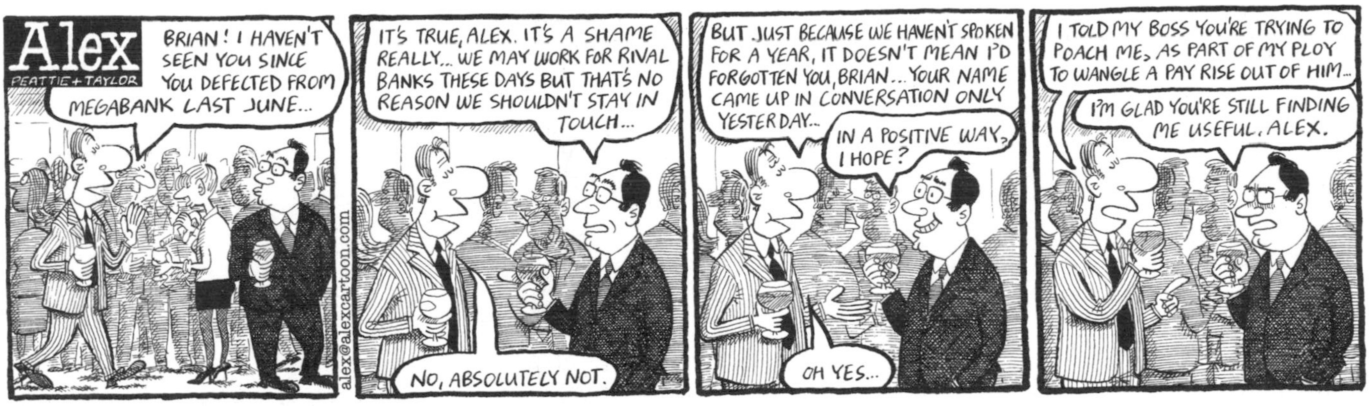
Alex
PEATTIE + TAYLOR
BRIAN! I HAVEN'T SEEN YOU SINCE YOU DEFECTED FROM MEGABANK LAST JUNE...
alex@alexcartoon.com
IT'S TRUE, ALEX. IT'S A SHAME REALLY... WE MAY WORK FOR RIVAL BANKS THESE DAYS BUT THAT'S NO REASON WE SHOULDN'T STAY IN TOUCH...
NO, ABSOLUTELY NOT.
BUT JUST BECAUSE WE HAVEN'T SPOKEN FOR A YEAR, IT DOESN'T MEAN I'D FORGOTTEN YOU, BRIAN... YOUR NAME CAME UP IN CONVERSATION ONLY YESTERDAY...
IN A POSITIVE WAY, I HOPE?
OH YES...
I TOLD MY BOSS YOU'RE TRYING TO POACH ME, AS PART OF MY PLOY TO WANGLE A PAY RISE OUT OF HIM...
I'M GLAD YOU'RE STILL FINDING ME USEFUL, ALEX.

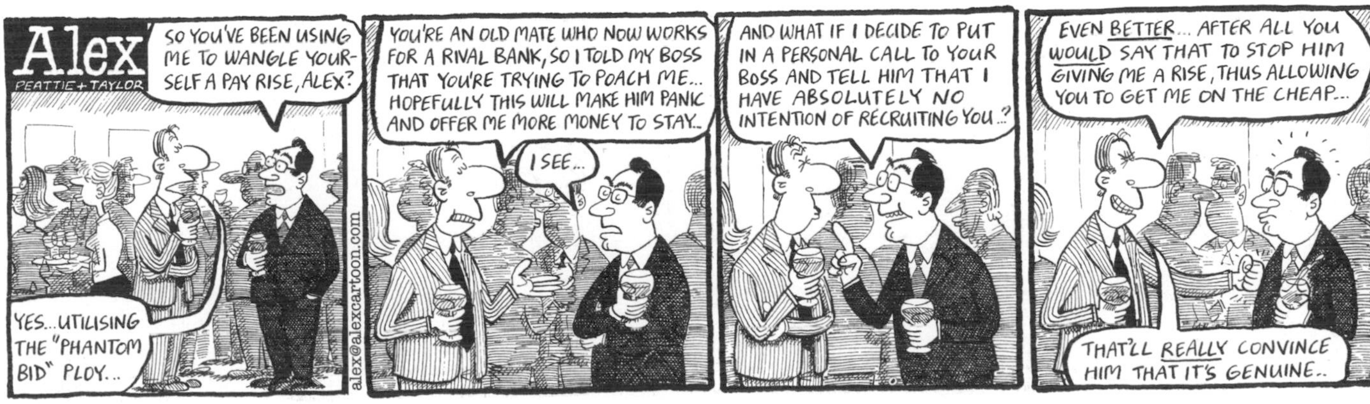
Alex
PEATTIE + TAYLOR
SO YOU'VE BEEN USING ME TO WANGLE YOUR-SELF A PAY RISE, ALEX?
YES... UTILISING THE "PHANTOM BID" PLOY...
alex@alexcartoon.com
YOU'RE AN OLD MATE WHO NOW WORKS FOR A RIVAL BANK, SO I TOLD MY BOSS THAT YOU'RE TRYING TO POACH ME... HOPEFULLY THIS WILL MAKE HIM PANIC AND OFFER ME MORE MONEY TO STAY...
I SEE...
AND WHAT IF I DECIDE TO PUT IN A PERSONAL CALL TO YOUR BOSS AND TELL HIM THAT I HAVE ABSOLUTELY NO INTENTION OF RECRUITING YOU...?
EVEN BETTER... AFTER ALL YOU WOULD SAY THAT TO STOP HIM GIVING ME A RISE, THUS ALLOWING YOU TO GET ME ON THE CHEAP...
THAT'LL REALLY CONVINCE HIM THAT IT'S GENUINE...

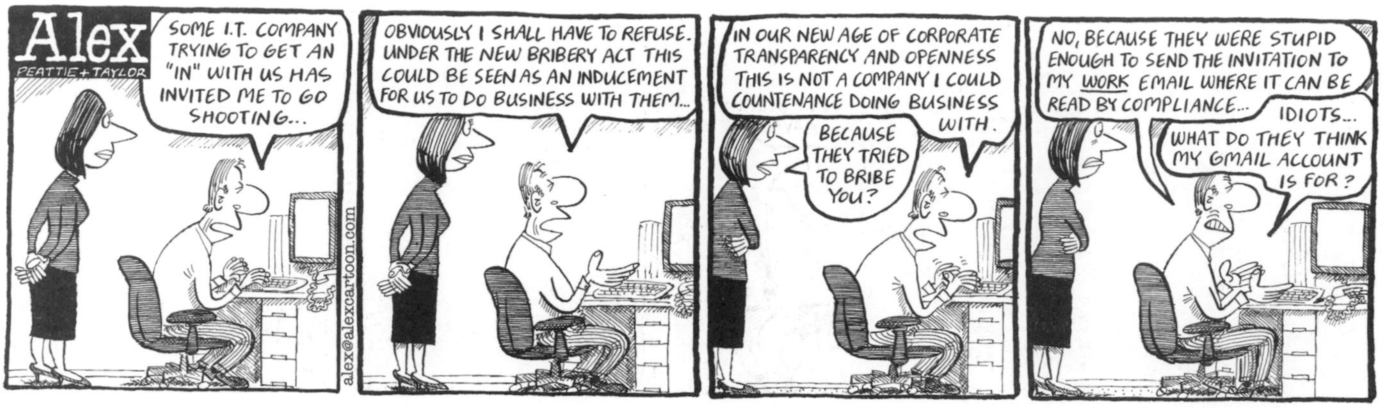
Alex
PEATTIE+TAYLOR
SOME I.T. COMPANY TRYING TO GET AN "IN" WITH US HAS INVITED ME TO GO SHOOTING...
alex@alexcartoon.com
OBVIOUSLY I SHALL HAVE TO REFUSE. UNDER THE NEW BRIBERY ACT THIS COULD BE SEEN AS AN INDUCEMENT FOR US TO DO BUSINESS WITH THEM...
IN OUR NEW AGE OF CORPORATE TRANSPARENCY AND OPENNESS THIS IS NOT A COMPANY I COULD COUNTENANCE DOING BUSINESS WITH.
BECAUSE THEY TRIED TO BRIBE YOU?
NO, BECAUSE THEY WERE STUPID ENOUGH TO SEND THE INVITATION TO MY WORK EMAIL WHERE IT CAN BE READ BY COMPLIANCE...
IDIOTS... WHAT DO THEY THINK MY GMAIL ACCOUNT IS FOR?

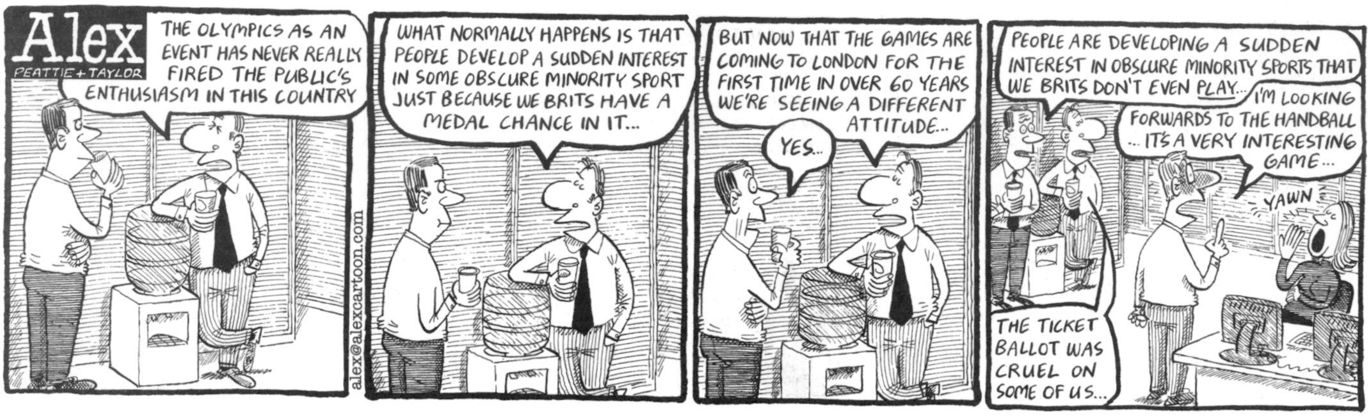
Alex
PEATTIE+TAYLOR
THE OLYMPICS AS AN EVENT HAS NEVER REALLY FIRED THE PUBLIC'S ENTHUSIASM IN THIS COUNTRY
alex@alexcartoon.com
WHAT NORMALLY HAPPENS IS THAT PEOPLE DEVELOP A SUDDEN INTEREST IN SOME OBSCURE MINORITY SPORT JUST BECAUSE WE BRITS HAVE A MEDAL CHANCE IN IT...
BUT NOW THAT THE GAMES ARE COMING TO LONDON FOR THE FIRST TIME IN OVER 60 YEARS WE'RE SEEING A DIFFERENT ATTITUDE...
YES...
PEOPLE ARE DEVELOPING A SUDDEN INTEREST IN OBSCURE MINORITY SPORTS THAT WE BRITS DON'T EVEN PLAY...
I'M LOOKING FORWARDS TO THE HANDBALL ... IT'S A VERY INTERESTING GAME...
YAWN
THE TICKET BALLOT WAS CRUEL ON SOME OF US...

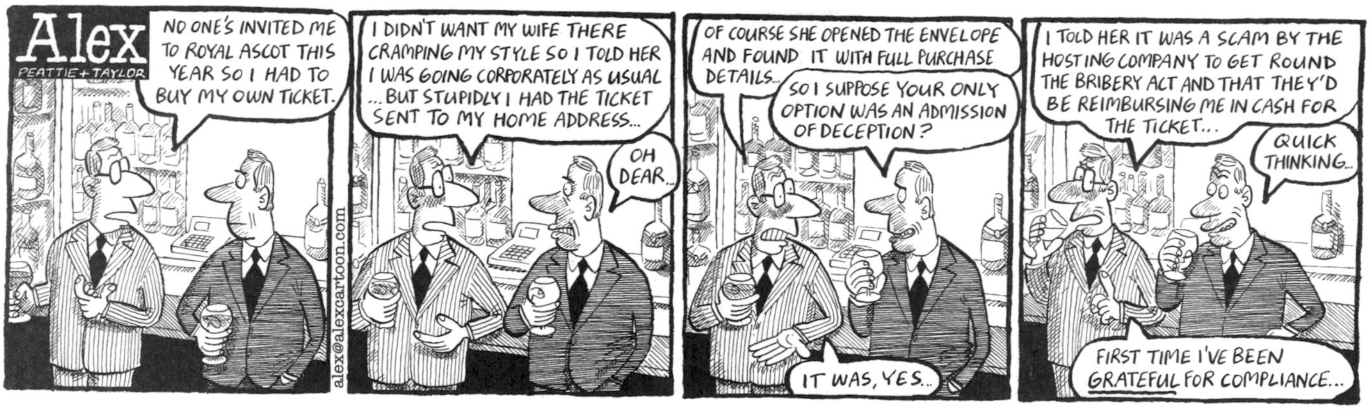
Alex
PEATTIE+TAYLOR
NO ONE'S INVITED ME TO ROYAL ASCOT THIS YEAR SO I HAD TO BUY MY OWN TICKET.
alex@alexcartoon.com
I DIDN'T WANT MY WIFE THERE CRAMPING MY STYLE SO I TOLD HER I WAS GOING CORPORATELY AS USUAL ...BUT STUPIDLY I HAD THE TICKET SENT TO MY HOME ADDRESS...
OH DEAR...
OF COURSE SHE OPENED THE ENVELOPE AND FOUND IT WITH FULL PURCHASE DETAILS...
SO I SUPPOSE YOUR ONLY OPTION WAS AN ADMISSION OF DECEPTION?
IT WAS, YES...
I TOLD HER IT WAS A SCAM BY THE HOSTING COMPANY TO GET ROUND THE BRIBERY ACT AND THAT THEY'D BE REIMBURSING ME IN CASH FOR THE TICKET...
QUICK THINKING...
FIRST TIME I'VE BEEN GRATEFUL FOR COMPLIANCE...

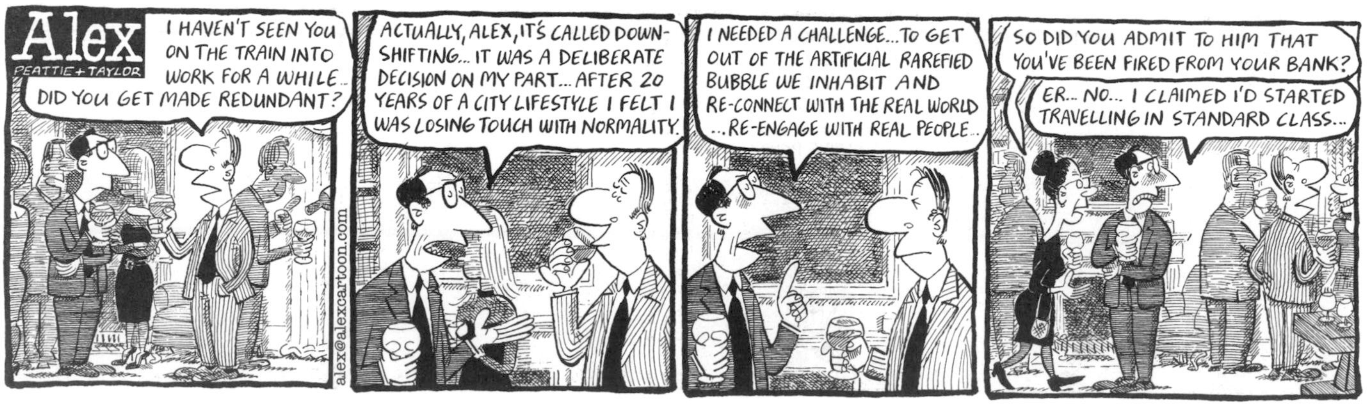
Alex
PEATTIE+TAYLOR
I HAVEN'T SEEN YOU ON THE TRAIN INTO WORK FOR A WHILE... DID YOU GET MADE REDUNDANT?
alex@alexcartoon.com
ACTUALLY, ALEX, IT'S CALLED DOWN-SHIFTING... IT WAS A DELIBERATE DECISION ON MY PART... AFTER 20 YEARS OF A CITY LIFESTYLE I FELT I WAS LOSING TOUCH WITH NORMALITY.
I NEEDED A CHALLENGE... TO GET OUT OF THE ARTIFICIAL RAREFIED BUBBLE WE INHABIT AND RE-CONNECT WITH THE REAL WORLD ...RE-ENGAGE WITH REAL PEOPLE...
SO DID YOU ADMIT TO HIM THAT YOU'VE BEEN FIRED FROM YOUR BANK?
ER... NO... I CLAIMED I'D STARTED TRAVELLING IN STANDARD CLASS...

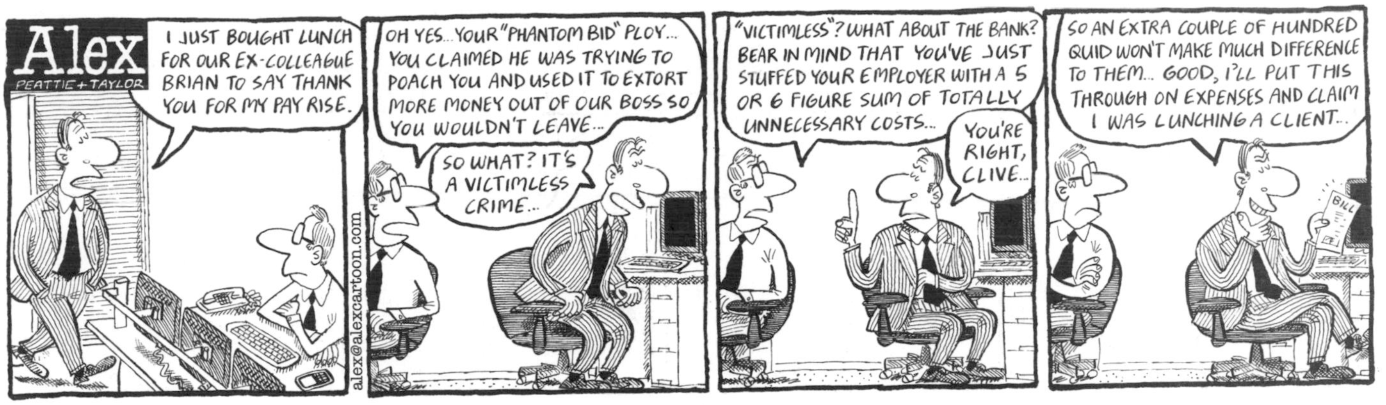
Alex
PEATTIE + TAYLOR
I JUST BOUGHT LUNCH FOR OUR EX-COLLEAGUE BRIAN TO SAY THANK YOU FOR MY PAY RISE.
OH YES... YOUR "PHANTOM BID" PLOY... YOU CLAIMED HE WAS TRYING TO POACH YOU AND USED IT TO EXTORT MORE MONEY OUT OF OUR BOSS SO YOU WOULDN'T LEAVE...
SO WHAT? IT'S A VICTIMLESS CRIME...
"VICTIMLESS"? WHAT ABOUT THE BANK? BEAR IN MIND THAT YOU'VE JUST STUFFED YOUR EMPLOYER WITH A 5 OR 6 FIGURE SUM OF TOTALLY UNNECESSARY COSTS...
YOU'RE RIGHT, CLIVE...
SO AN EXTRA COUPLE OF HUNDRED QUID WON'T MAKE MUCH DIFFERENCE TO THEM... GOOD, I'LL PUT THIS THROUGH ON EXPENSES AND CLAIM I WAS LUNCHING A CLIENT...
BILL
alex@alexcartoon.com

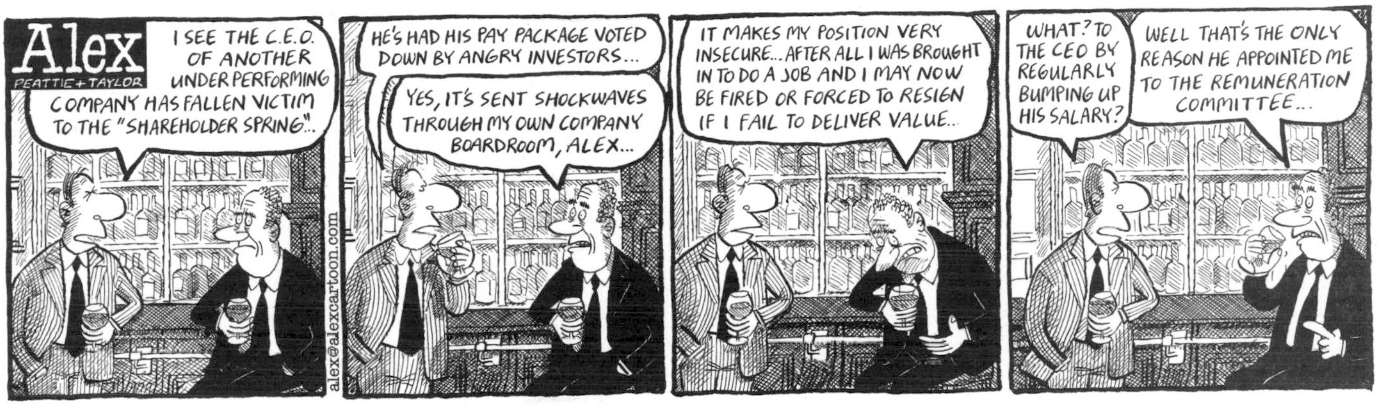
Alex
PEATTIE + TAYLOR
I SEE THE C.E.O. OF ANOTHER UNDER PERFORMING COMPANY HAS FALLEN VICTIM TO THE "SHAREHOLDER SPRING"...
HE'S HAD HIS PAY PACKAGE VOTED DOWN BY ANGRY INVESTORS...
YES, IT'S SENT SHOCKWAVES THROUGH MY OWN COMPANY BOARDROOM, ALEX...
IT MAKES MY POSITION VERY INSECURE... AFTER ALL I WAS BROUGHT IN TO DO A JOB AND I MAY NOW BE FIRED OR FORCED TO RESIGN IF I FAIL TO DELIVER VALUE...
WHAT? TO THE CEO BY REGULARLY BUMPING UP HIS SALARY?
WELL THAT'S THE ONLY REASON HE APPOINTED ME TO THE REMUNERATION COMMITTEE...
alex@alexcartoon.com

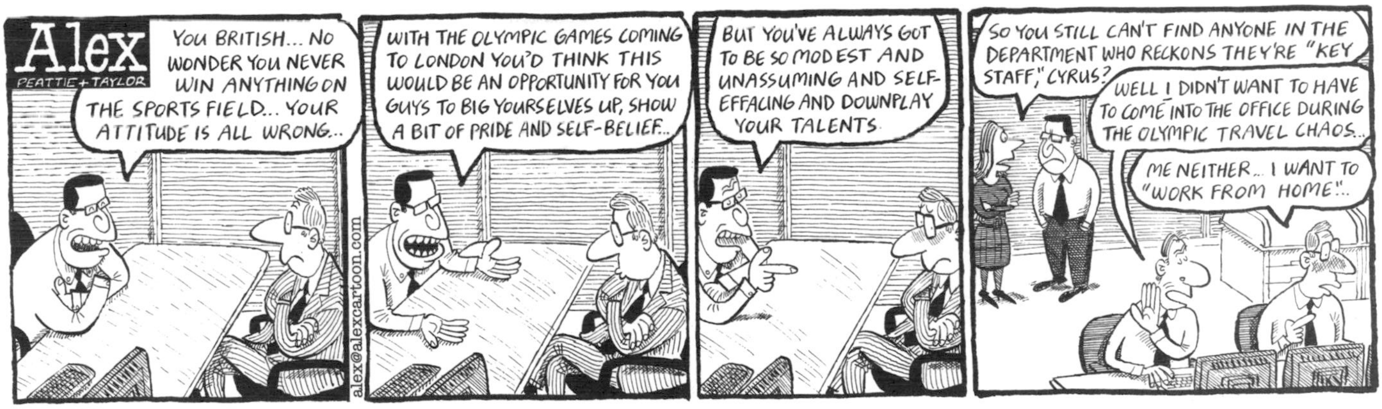
Alex
PEATTIE + TAYLOR
YOU BRITISH... NO WONDER YOU NEVER WIN ANYTHING ON THE SPORTS FIELD... YOUR ATTITUDE IS ALL WRONG...
WITH THE OLYMPIC GAMES COMING TO LONDON YOU'D THINK THIS WOULD BE AN OPPORTUNITY FOR YOU GUYS TO BIG YOURSELVES UP, SHOW A BIT OF PRIDE AND SELF-BELIEF...
BUT YOU'VE ALWAYS GOT TO BE SO MODEST AND UNASSUMING AND SELF-EFFACING AND DOWNPLAY YOUR TALENTS.
SO YOU STILL CAN'T FIND ANYONE IN THE DEPARTMENT WHO RECKONS THEY'RE "KEY STAFF," CYRUS?
WELL I DIDN'T WANT TO HAVE TO COME INTO THE OFFICE DURING THE OLYMPIC TRAVEL CHAOS...
ME NEITHER... I WANT TO "WORK FROM HOME"...
alex@alexcartoon.com

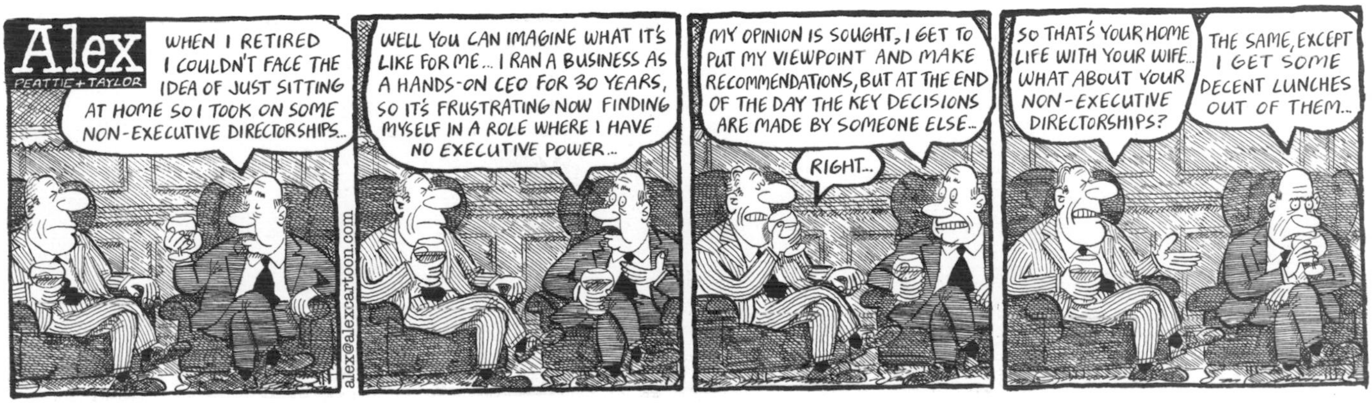
Alex
PEATTIE + TAYLOR
WHEN I RETIRED I COULDN'T FACE THE IDEA OF JUST SITTING AT HOME SO I TOOK ON SOME NON-EXECUTIVE DIRECTORSHIPS...
WELL YOU CAN IMAGINE WHAT IT'S LIKE FOR ME... I RAN A BUSINESS AS A HANDS-ON CEO FOR 30 YEARS, SO IT'S FRUSTRATING NOW FINDING MYSELF IN A ROLE WHERE I HAVE NO EXECUTIVE POWER...
MY OPINION IS SOUGHT, I GET TO PUT MY VIEWPOINT AND MAKE RECOMMENDATIONS, BUT AT THE END OF THE DAY THE KEY DECISIONS ARE MADE BY SOMEONE ELSE...
RIGHT...
SO THAT'S YOUR HOME LIFE WITH YOUR WIFE... WHAT ABOUT YOUR NON-EXECUTIVE DIRECTORSHIPS?
THE SAME, EXCEPT I GET SOME DECENT LUNCHES OUT OF THEM...
alex@alexcartoon.com

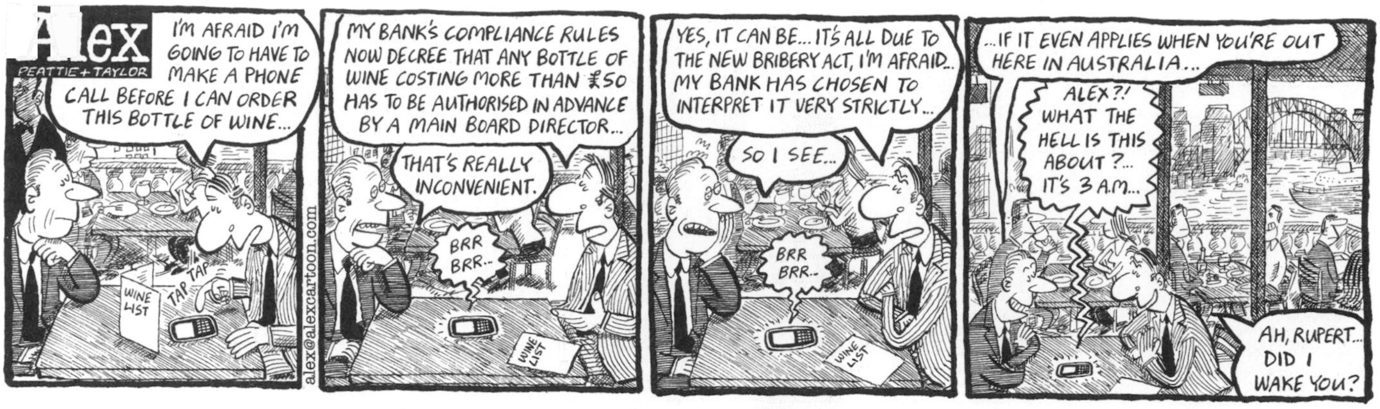
Alex
PEATTIE+TAYLOR
I'M AFRAID I'M GOING TO HAVE TO MAKE A PHONE CALL BEFORE I CAN ORDER THIS BOTTLE OF WINE...
TAP TAP
WINE LIST
alex@alexcartoon.com
MY BANK'S COMPLIANCE RULES NOW DECREE THAT ANY BOTTLE OF WINE COSTING MORE THAN £50 HAS TO BE AUTHORISED IN ADVANCE BY A MAIN BOARD DIRECTOR...
THAT'S REALLY INCONVENIENT.
BRR BRR...
WINE LIST
YES, IT CAN BE... IT'S ALL DUE TO THE NEW BRIBERY ACT, I'M AFRAID... MY BANK HAS CHOSEN TO INTERPRET IT VERY STRICTLY...
SO I SEE...
BRR BRR...
WINE LIST
...IF IT EVEN APPLIES WHEN YOU'RE OUT HERE IN AUSTRALIA...
ALEX?! WHAT THE HELL IS THIS ABOUT?... IT'S 3 A.M...
AH, RUPERT... DID I WAKE YOU?

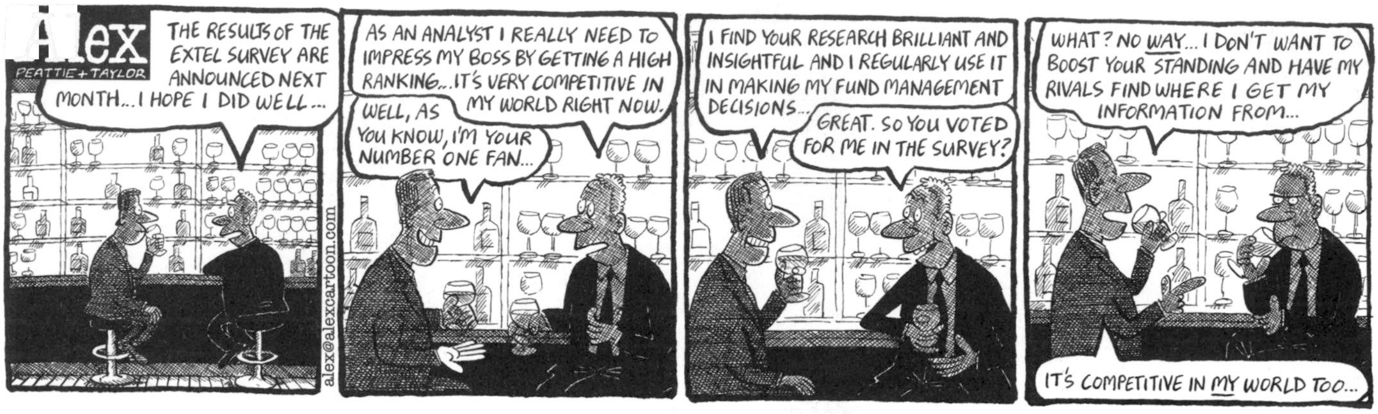
Alex
PEATTIE+TAYLOR
THE RESULTS OF THE EXTEL SURVEY ARE ANNOUNCED NEXT MONTH... I HOPE I DID WELL...
alex@alexcartoon.com
AS AN ANALYST I REALLY NEED TO IMPRESS MY BOSS BY GETTING A HIGH RANKING... IT'S VERY COMPETITIVE IN MY WORLD RIGHT NOW.
WELL, AS YOU KNOW, I'M YOUR NUMBER ONE FAN...
I FIND YOUR RESEARCH BRILLIANT AND INSIGHTFUL AND I REGULARLY USE IT IN MAKING MY FUND MANAGEMENT DECISIONS...
GREAT. SO YOU VOTED FOR ME IN THE SURVEY?
WHAT? NO WAY... I DON'T WANT TO BOOST YOUR STANDING AND HAVE MY RIVALS FIND WHERE I GET MY INFORMATION FROM...
IT'S COMPETITIVE IN MY WORLD TOO...

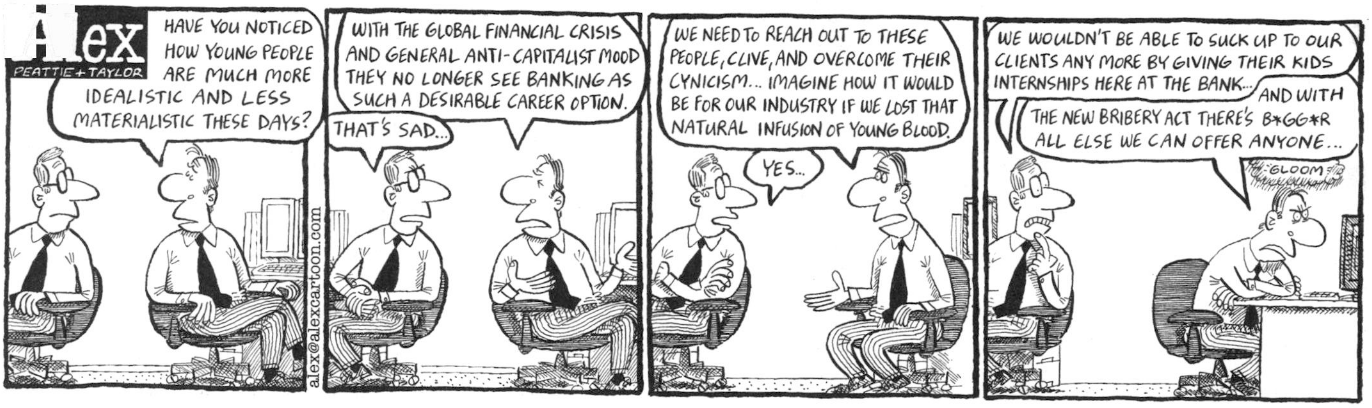
Alex
PEATTIE+TAYLOR
HAVE YOU NOTICED HOW YOUNG PEOPLE ARE MUCH MORE IDEALISTIC AND LESS MATERIALISTIC THESE DAYS?
alex@alexcartoon.com
WITH THE GLOBAL FINANCIAL CRISIS AND GENERAL ANTI-CAPITALIST MOOD THEY NO LONGER SEE BANKING AS SUCH A DESIRABLE CAREER OPTION.
THAT'S SAD...
WE NEED TO REACH OUT TO THESE PEOPLE, CLIVE, AND OVERCOME THEIR CYNICISM... IMAGINE HOW IT WOULD BE FOR OUR INDUSTRY IF WE LOST THAT NATURAL INFUSION OF YOUNG BLOOD.
YES...
WE WOULDN'T BE ABLE TO SUCK UP TO OUR CLIENTS ANY MORE BY GIVING THEIR KIDS INTERNSHIPS HERE AT THE BANK...
AND WITH THE NEW BRIBERY ACT THERE'S B*GG*R ALL ELSE WE CAN OFFER ANYONE...
GLOOM

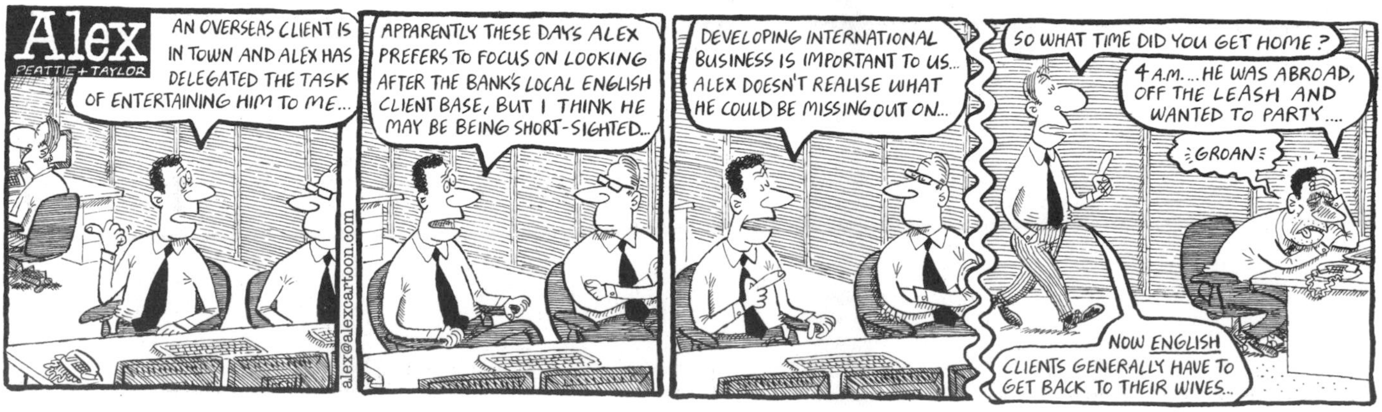
Alex
PEATTIE+TAYLOR
AN OVERSEAS CLIENT IS IN TOWN AND ALEX HAS DELEGATED THE TASK OF ENTERTAINING HIM TO ME...
alex@alexcartoon.com
APPARENTLY THESE DAYS ALEX PREFERS TO FOCUS ON LOOKING AFTER THE BANK'S LOCAL ENGLISH CLIENT BASE, BUT I THINK HE MAY BE BEING SHORT-SIGHTED...
DEVELOPING INTERNATIONAL BUSINESS IS IMPORTANT TO US... ALEX DOESN'T REALISE WHAT HE COULD BE MISSING OUT ON...
SO WHAT TIME DID YOU GET HOME?
4 A.M.... HE WAS ABROAD, OFF THE LEASH AND WANTED TO PARTY....
GROAN
NOW ENGLISH CLIENTS GENERALLY HAVE TO GET BACK TO THEIR WIVES...

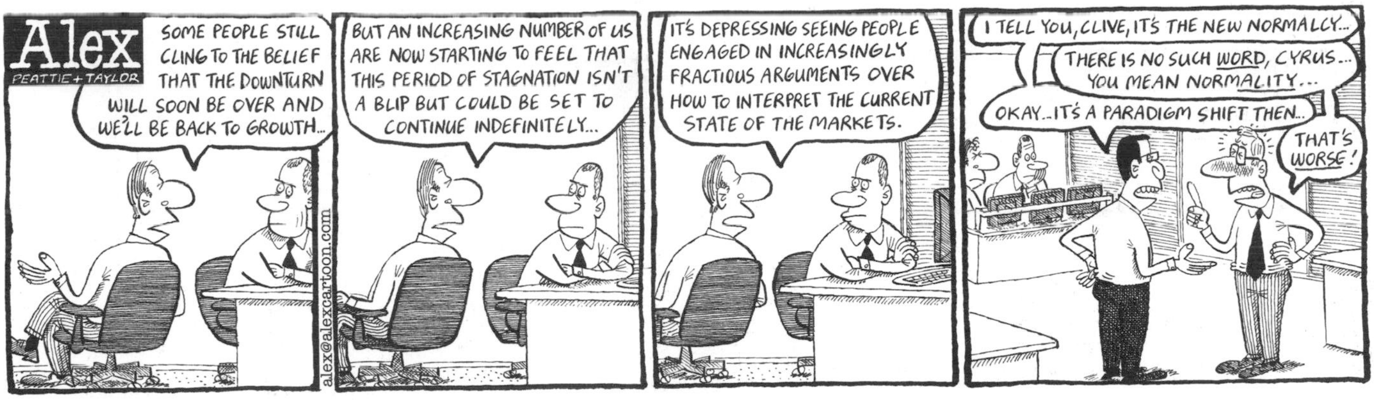

Alex
PEATTIE + TAYLOR
SOME PEOPLE STILL CLING TO THE BELIEF THAT THE DOWNTURN WILL SOON BE OVER AND WE'LL BE BACK TO GROWTH...
BUT AN INCREASING NUMBER OF US ARE NOW STARTING TO FEEL THAT THIS PERIOD OF STAGNATION ISN'T A BLIP BUT COULD BE SET TO CONTINUE INDEFINITELY...
alex@alexcartoon.com
IT'S DEPRESSING SEEING PEOPLE ENGAGED IN INCREASINGLY FRACTIOUS ARGUMENTS OVER HOW TO INTERPRET THE CURRENT STATE OF THE MARKETS.
I TELL YOU, CLIVE, IT'S THE NEW NORMALCY...
THERE IS NO SUCH WORD, CYRUS... YOU MEAN NORMALITY...
OKAY... IT'S A PARADIGM SHIFT THEN...
THAT'S WORSE!

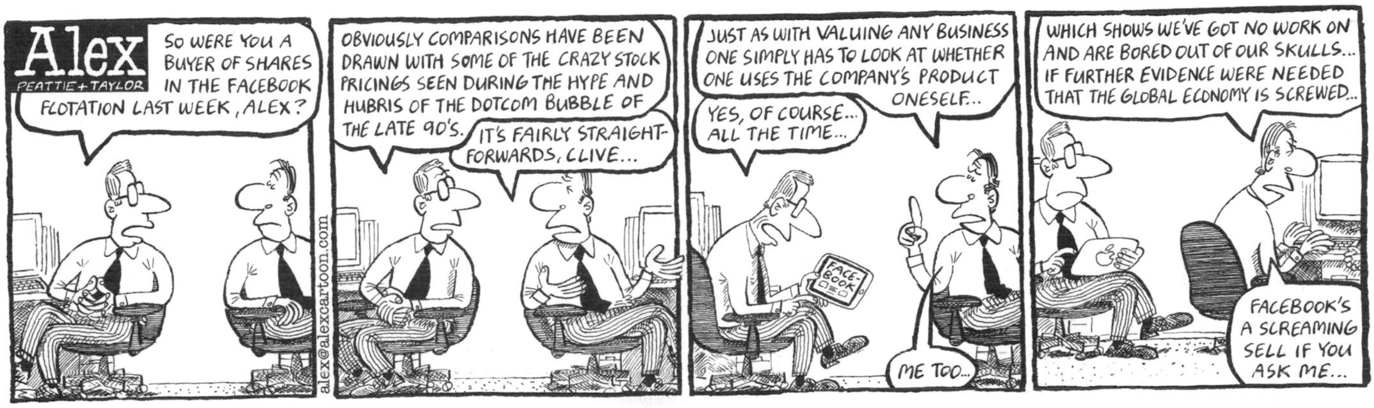

Alex
PEATTIE + TAYLOR
SO WERE YOU A BUYER OF SHARES IN THE FACEBOOK FLOTATION LAST WEEK, ALEX?
OBVIOUSLY COMPARISONS HAVE BEEN DRAWN WITH SOME OF THE CRAZY STOCK PRICINGS SEEN DURING THE HYPE AND HUBRIS OF THE DOTCOM BUBBLE OF THE LATE 90'S.
IT'S FAIRLY STRAIGHT-FORWARDS, CLIVE...
alex@alexcartoon.com
JUST AS WITH VALUING ANY BUSINESS ONE SIMPLY HAS TO LOOK AT WHETHER ONE USES THE COMPANY'S PRODUCT ONESELF...
YES, OF COURSE... ALL THE TIME...
FACE-BOOK
ME TOO...
WHICH SHOWS WE'VE GOT NO WORK ON AND ARE BORED OUT OF OUR SKULLS... IF FURTHER EVIDENCE WERE NEEDED THAT THE GLOBAL ECONOMY IS SCREWED...
FACEBOOK'S A SCREAMING SELL IF YOU ASK ME...

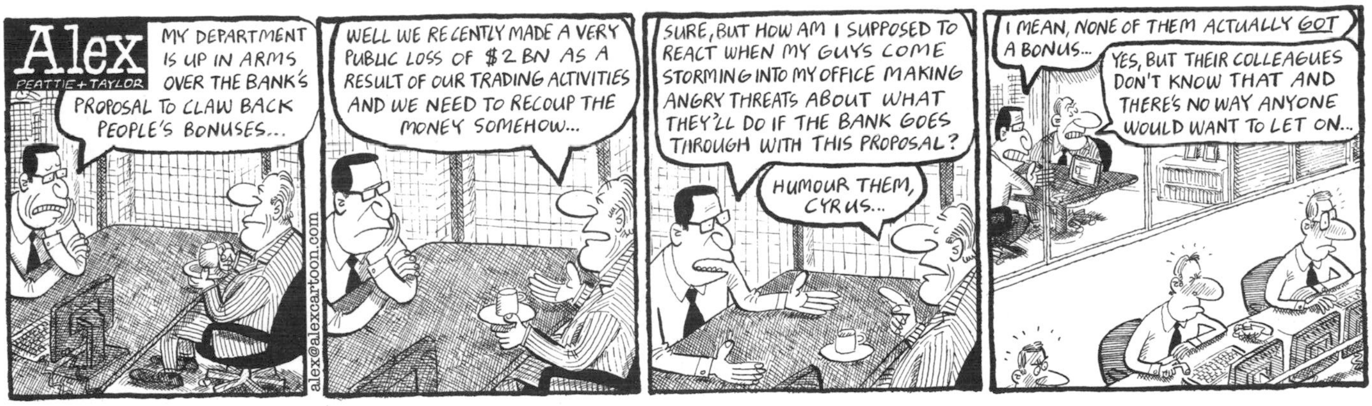

Alex
PEATTIE + TAYLOR
MY DEPARTMENT IS UP IN ARMS OVER THE BANK'S PROPOSAL TO CLAW BACK PEOPLE'S BONUSES...
WELL WE RECENTLY MADE A VERY PUBLIC LOSS OF $2 BN AS A RESULT OF OUR TRADING ACTIVITIES AND WE NEED TO RECOUP THE MONEY SOMEHOW...
alex@alexcartoon.com
SURE, BUT HOW AM I SUPPOSED TO REACT WHEN MY GUYS COME STORMING INTO MY OFFICE MAKING ANGRY THREATS ABOUT WHAT THEY'LL DO IF THE BANK GOES THROUGH WITH THIS PROPOSAL?
HUMOUR THEM, CYRUS...
I MEAN, NONE OF THEM ACTUALLY GOT A BONUS...
YES, BUT THEIR COLLEAGUES DON'T KNOW THAT AND THERE'S NO WAY ANYONE WOULD WANT TO LET ON...

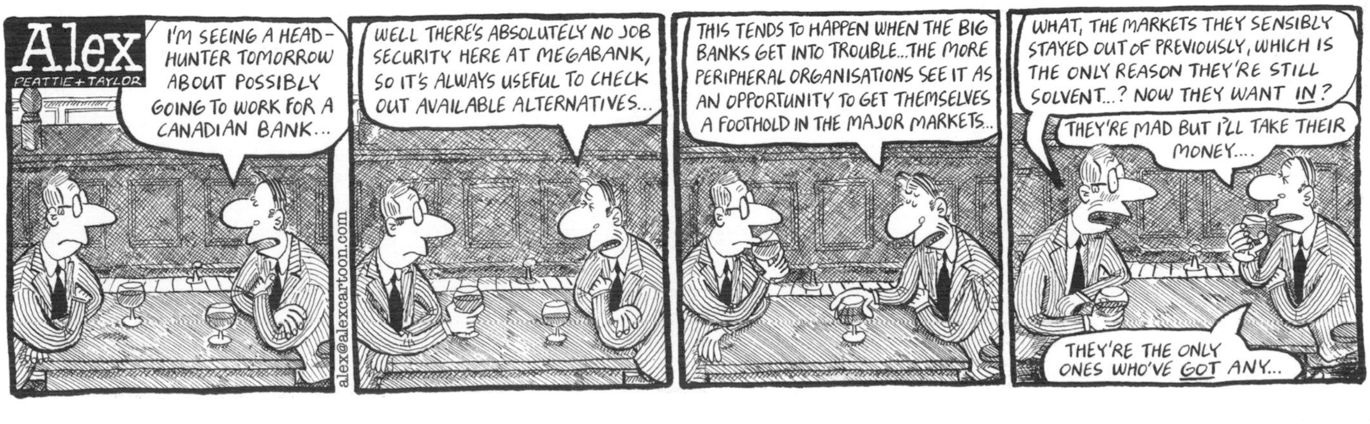

Alex
PEATTIE + TAYLOR
I'M SEEING A HEAD-HUNTER TOMORROW ABOUT POSSIBLY GOING TO WORK FOR A CANADIAN BANK...
WELL THERE'S ABSOLUTELY NO JOB SECURITY HERE AT MEGABANK, SO IT'S ALWAYS USEFUL TO CHECK OUT AVAILABLE ALTERNATIVES...
alex@alexcartoon.com
THIS TENDS TO HAPPEN WHEN THE BIG BANKS GET INTO TROUBLE... THE MORE PERIPHERAL ORGANISATIONS SEE IT AS AN OPPORTUNITY TO GET THEMSELVES A FOOTHOLD IN THE MAJOR MARKETS...
WHAT, THE MARKETS THEY SENSIBLY STAYED OUT OF PREVIOUSLY, WHICH IS THE ONLY REASON THEY'RE STILL SOLVENT...? NOW THEY WANT IN?
THEY'RE MAD BUT I'LL TAKE THEIR MONEY....
THEY'RE THE ONLY ONES WHO'VE GOT ANY...

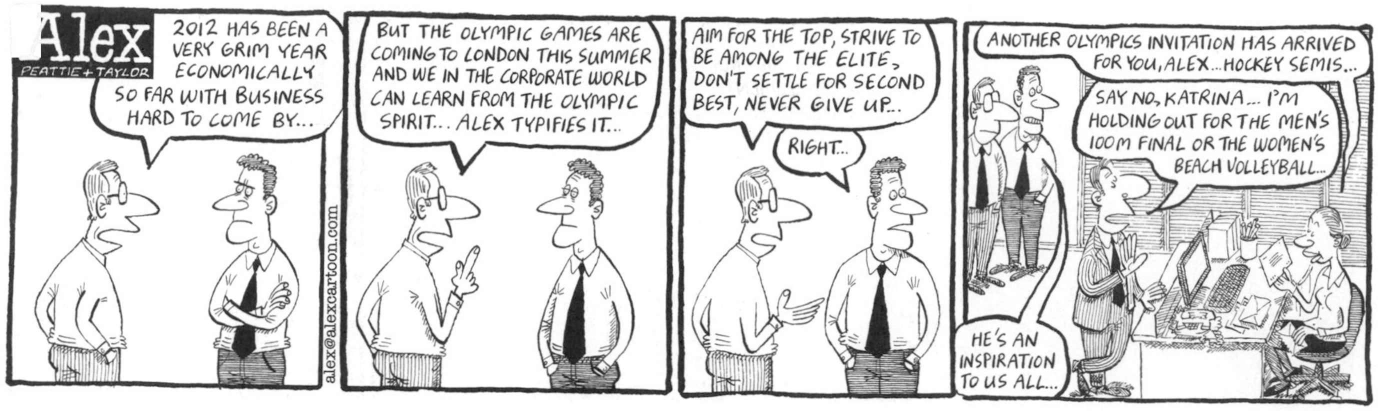
Alex
PEATTIE + TAYLOR
2012 HAS BEEN A VERY GRIM YEAR ECONOMICALLY SO FAR WITH BUSINESS HARD TO COME BY...
alex@alexcartoon.com
BUT THE OLYMPIC GAMES ARE COMING TO LONDON THIS SUMMER AND WE IN THE CORPORATE WORLD CAN LEARN FROM THE OLYMPIC SPIRIT... ALEX TYPIFIES IT...
AIM FOR THE TOP, STRIVE TO BE AMONG THE ELITE, DON'T SETTLE FOR SECOND BEST, NEVER GIVE UP...
RIGHT...
ANOTHER OLYMPICS INVITATION HAS ARRIVED FOR YOU, ALEX... HOCKEY SEMIS...
SAY NO, KATRINA... I'M HOLDING OUT FOR THE MEN'S 100M FINAL OR THE WOMEN'S BEACH VOLLEYBALL...
HE'S AN INSPIRATION TO US ALL...

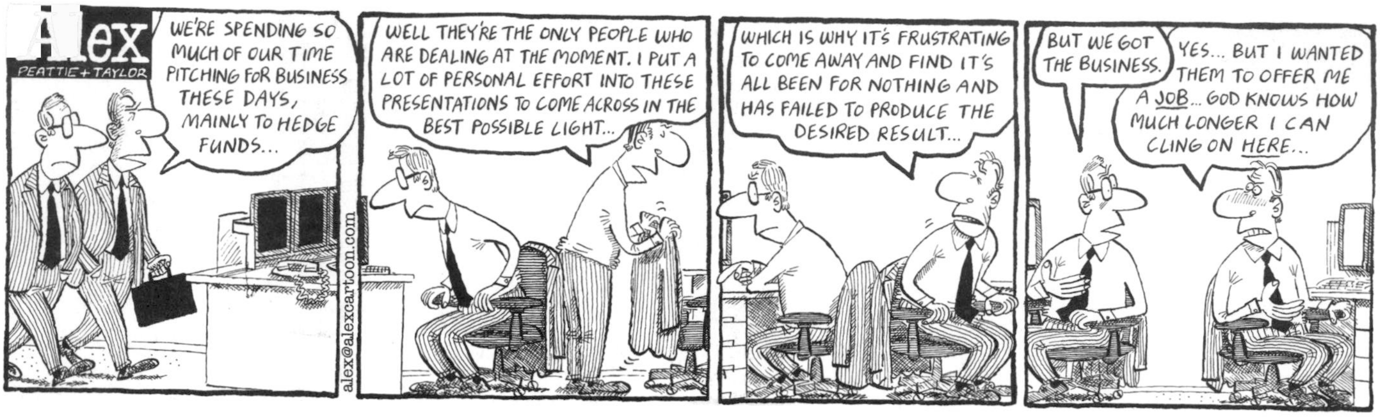
Alex
PEATTIE + TAYLOR
WE'RE SPENDING SO MUCH OF OUR TIME PITCHING FOR BUSINESS THESE DAYS, MAINLY TO HEDGE FUNDS...
alex@alexcartoon.com
WELL THEY'RE THE ONLY PEOPLE WHO ARE DEALING AT THE MOMENT. I PUT A LOT OF PERSONAL EFFORT INTO THESE PRESENTATIONS TO COME ACROSS IN THE BEST POSSIBLE LIGHT...
WHICH IS WHY IT'S FRUSTRATING TO COME AWAY AND FIND IT'S ALL BEEN FOR NOTHING AND HAS FAILED TO PRODUCE THE DESIRED RESULT...
BUT WE GOT THE BUSINESS.
YES... BUT I WANTED THEM TO OFFER ME A JOB... GOD KNOWS HOW MUCH LONGER I CAN CLING ON HERE...

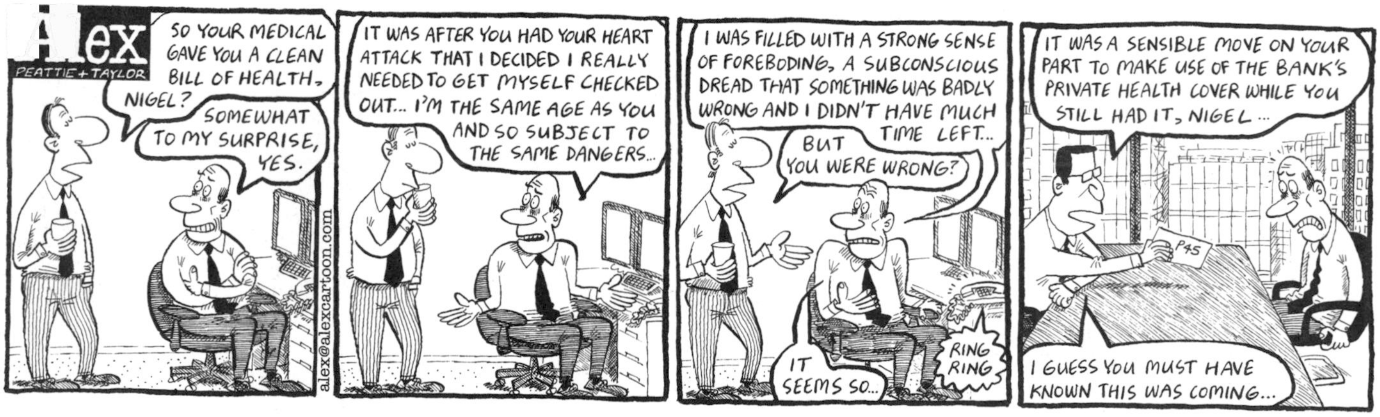
Alex
PEATTIE + TAYLOR
SO YOUR MEDICAL GAVE YOU A CLEAN BILL OF HEALTH, NIGEL?
SOMEWHAT TO MY SURPRISE, YES.
alex@alexcartoon.com
IT WAS AFTER YOU HAD YOUR HEART ATTACK THAT I DECIDED I REALLY NEEDED TO GET MYSELF CHECKED OUT... I'M THE SAME AGE AS YOU AND SO SUBJECT TO THE SAME DANGERS...
I WAS FILLED WITH A STRONG SENSE OF FOREBODING, A SUBCONSCIOUS DREAD THAT SOMETHING WAS BADLY WRONG AND I DIDN'T HAVE MUCH TIME LEFT...
BUT YOU WERE WRONG?
IT SEEMS SO...
RING RING
IT WAS A SENSIBLE MOVE ON YOUR PART TO MAKE USE OF THE BANK'S PRIVATE HEALTH COVER WHILE YOU STILL HAD IT, NIGEL...
P45
I GUESS YOU MUST HAVE KNOWN THIS WAS COMING...

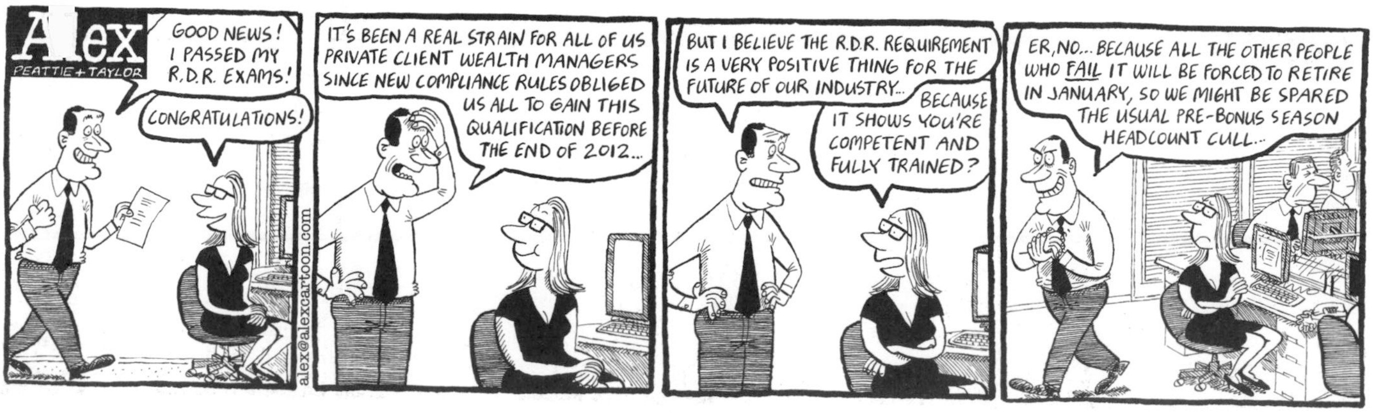
Alex
PEATTIE + TAYLOR
GOOD NEWS! I PASSED MY R.D.R. EXAMS!
CONGRATULATIONS!
alex@alexcartoon.com
IT'S BEEN A REAL STRAIN FOR ALL OF US PRIVATE CLIENT WEALTH MANAGERS SINCE NEW COMPLIANCE RULES OBLIGED US ALL TO GAIN THIS QUALIFICATION BEFORE THE END OF 2012...
BUT I BELIEVE THE R.D.R. REQUIREMENT IS A VERY POSITIVE THING FOR THE FUTURE OF OUR INDUSTRY...
BECAUSE IT SHOWS YOU'RE COMPETENT AND FULLY TRAINED?
ER, NO... BECAUSE ALL THE OTHER PEOPLE WHO FAIL IT WILL BE FORCED TO RETIRE IN JANUARY, SO WE MIGHT BE SPARED THE USUAL PRE-BONUS SEASON HEADCOUNT CULL...

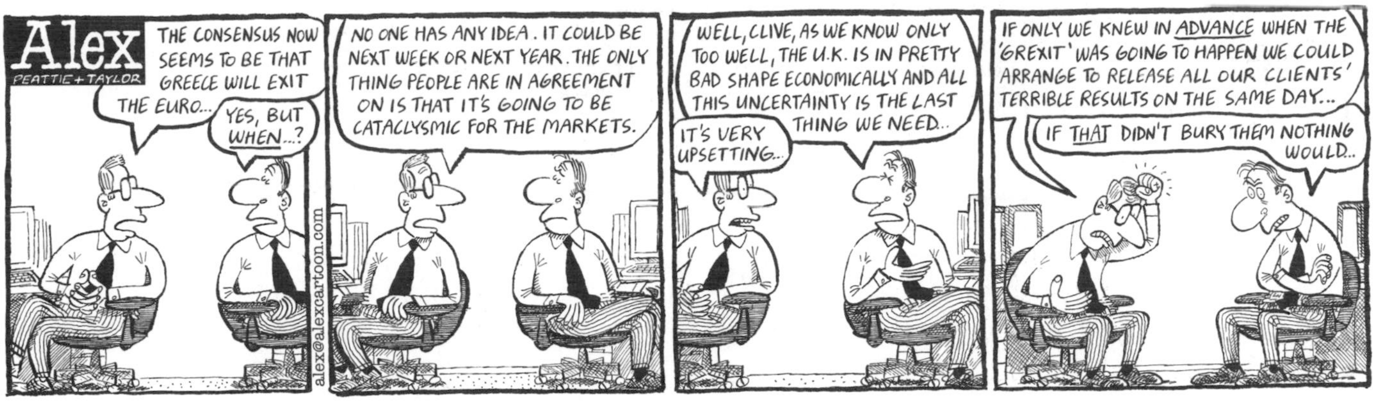
Alex
PEATTIE + TAYLOR
THE CONSENSUS NOW SEEMS TO BE THAT GREECE WILL EXIT THE EURO...
YES, BUT WHEN...?
alex@alexcartoon.com
NO ONE HAS ANY IDEA. IT COULD BE NEXT WEEK OR NEXT YEAR. THE ONLY THING PEOPLE ARE IN AGREEMENT ON IS THAT IT'S GOING TO BE CATACLYSMIC FOR THE MARKETS.
WELL, CLIVE, AS WE KNOW ONLY TOO WELL, THE U.K. IS IN PRETTY BAD SHAPE ECONOMICALLY AND ALL THIS UNCERTAINTY IS THE LAST THING WE NEED...
IT'S VERY UPSETTING...
IF ONLY WE KNEW IN ADVANCE WHEN THE 'GREXIT' WAS GOING TO HAPPEN WE COULD ARRANGE TO RELEASE ALL OUR CLIENTS' TERRIBLE RESULTS ON THE SAME DAY...
IF THAT DIDN'T BURY THEM NOTHING WOULD...

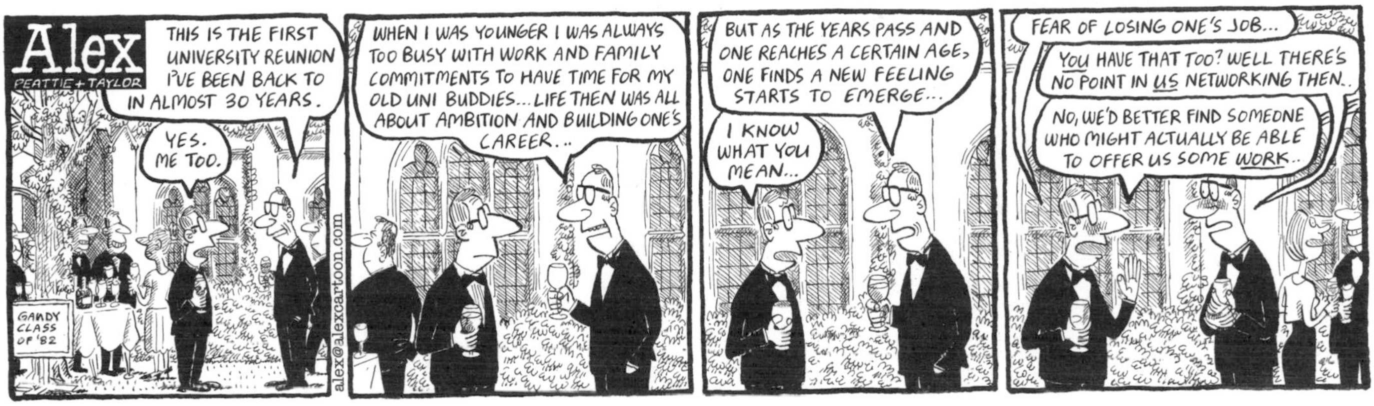
Alex
PEATTIE + TAYLOR
THIS IS THE FIRST UNIVERSITY REUNION I'VE BEEN BACK TO IN ALMOST 30 YEARS.
YES. ME TOO.
GAUDY CLASS OF '82
alex@alexcartoon.com
WHEN I WAS YOUNGER I WAS ALWAYS TOO BUSY WITH WORK AND FAMILY COMMITMENTS TO HAVE TIME FOR MY OLD UNI BUDDIES... LIFE THEN WAS ALL ABOUT AMBITION AND BUILDING ONE'S CAREER...
BUT AS THE YEARS PASS AND ONE REACHES A CERTAIN AGE, ONE FINDS A NEW FEELING STARTS TO EMERGE...
I KNOW WHAT YOU MEAN...
FEAR OF LOSING ONE'S JOB...
YOU HAVE THAT TOO? WELL THERE'S NO POINT IN US NETWORKING THEN..
NO, WE'D BETTER FIND SOMEONE WHO MIGHT ACTUALLY BE ABLE TO OFFER US SOME WORK..

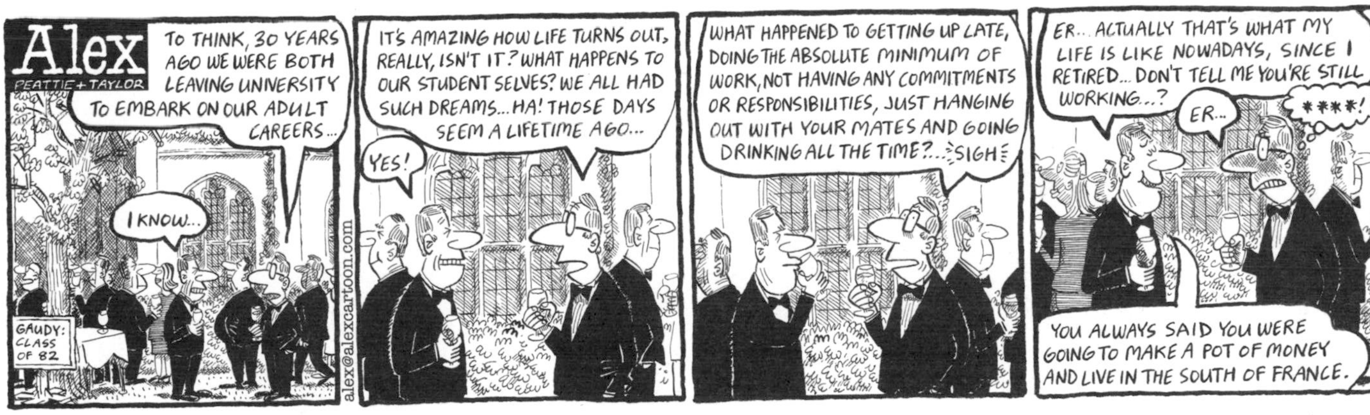
Alex
PEATTIE + TAYLOR
TO THINK, 30 YEARS AGO WE WERE BOTH LEAVING UNIVERSITY TO EMBARK ON OUR ADULT CAREERS...
I KNOW...
GAUDY: CLASS OF 82
alex@alexcartoon.com
IT'S AMAZING HOW LIFE TURNS OUT, REALLY, ISN'T IT? WHAT HAPPENS TO OUR STUDENT SELVES? WE ALL HAD SUCH DREAMS... HA! THOSE DAYS SEEM A LIFETIME AGO...
YES!
WHAT HAPPENED TO GETTING UP LATE, DOING THE ABSOLUTE MINIMUM OF WORK, NOT HAVING ANY COMMITMENTS OR RESPONSIBILITIES, JUST HANGING OUT WITH YOUR MATES AND GOING DRINKING ALL THE TIME?... SIGH
ER... ACTUALLY THAT'S WHAT MY LIFE IS LIKE NOWADAYS, SINCE I RETIRED... DON'T TELL ME YOU'RE STILL WORKING...?
ER...
****!
YOU ALWAYS SAID YOU WERE GOING TO MAKE A POT OF MONEY AND LIVE IN THE SOUTH OF FRANCE.

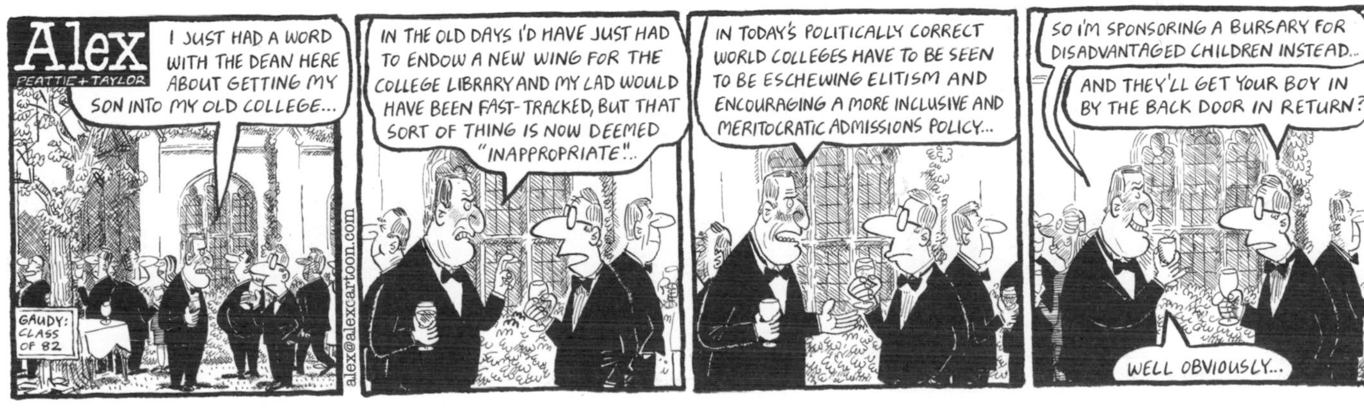
Alex
PEATTIE + TAYLOR
I JUST HAD A WORD WITH THE DEAN HERE ABOUT GETTING MY SON INTO MY OLD COLLEGE...
GAUDY: CLASS OF 82
alex@alexcartoon.com
IN THE OLD DAYS I'D HAVE JUST HAD TO ENDOW A NEW WING FOR THE COLLEGE LIBRARY AND MY LAD WOULD HAVE BEEN FAST-TRACKED, BUT THAT SORT OF THING IS NOW DEEMED "INAPPROPRIATE"...
IN TODAY'S POLITICALLY CORRECT WORLD COLLEGES HAVE TO BE SEEN TO BE ESCHEWING ELITISM AND ENCOURAGING A MORE INCLUSIVE AND MERITOCRATIC ADMISSIONS POLICY...
SO I'M SPONSORING A BURSARY FOR DISADVANTAGED CHILDREN INSTEAD...
AND THEY'LL GET YOUR BOY IN BY THE BACK DOOR IN RETURN?
WELL OBVIOUSLY...

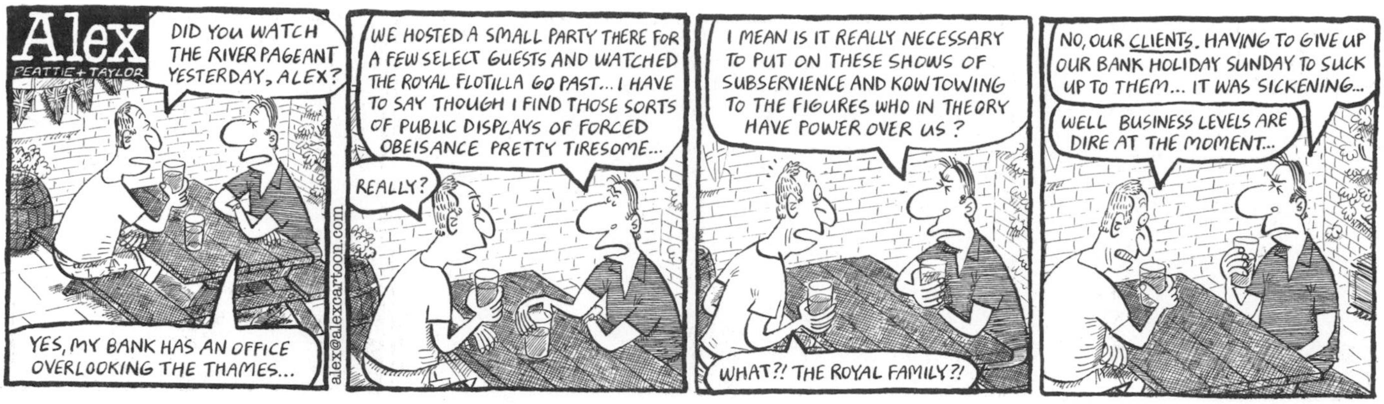
Alex
PEATTIE + TAYLOR
DID YOU WATCH THE RIVER PAGEANT YESTERDAY, ALEX?
YES, MY BANK HAS AN OFFICE OVERLOOKING THE THAMES...
alex@alexcartoon.com
WE HOSTED A SMALL PARTY THERE FOR A FEW SELECT GUESTS AND WATCHED THE ROYAL FLOTILLA GO PAST... I HAVE TO SAY THOUGH I FIND THOSE SORTS OF PUBLIC DISPLAYS OF FORCED OBEISANCE PRETTY TIRESOME...
REALLY?
I MEAN IS IT REALLY NECESSARY TO PUT ON THESE SHOWS OF SUBSERVIENCE AND KOWTOWING TO THE FIGURES WHO IN THEORY HAVE POWER OVER US?
WHAT?! THE ROYAL FAMILY?!
NO, OUR CLIENTS. HAVING TO GIVE UP OUR BANK HOLIDAY SUNDAY TO SUCK UP TO THEM... IT WAS SICKENING...
WELL BUSINESS LEVELS ARE DIRE AT THE MOMENT...

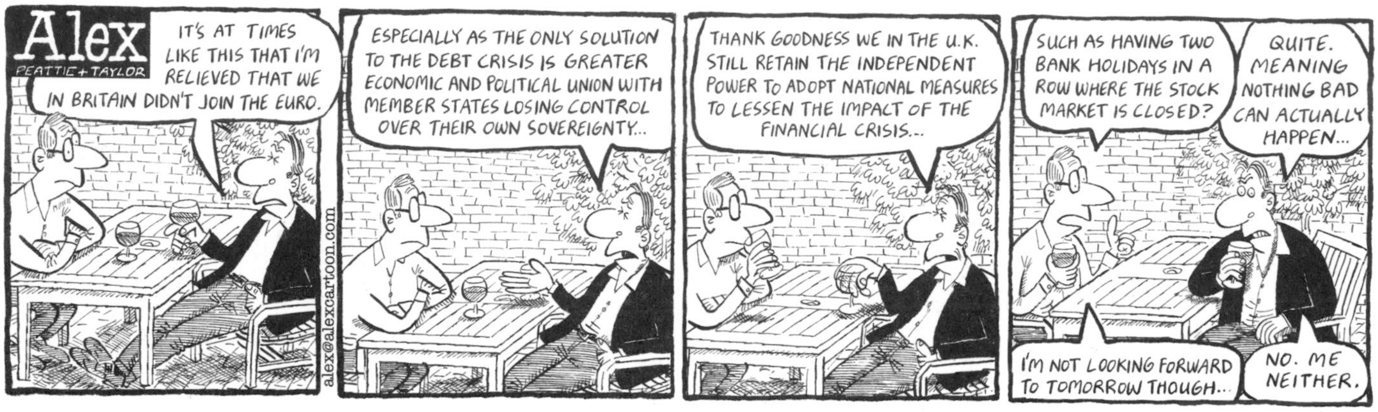
Alex
PEATTIE + TAYLOR
IT'S AT TIMES LIKE THIS THAT I'M RELIEVED THAT WE IN BRITAIN DIDN'T JOIN THE EURO.
alex@alexcartoon.com
ESPECIALLY AS THE ONLY SOLUTION TO THE DEBT CRISIS IS GREATER ECONOMIC AND POLITICAL UNION WITH MEMBER STATES LOSING CONTROL OVER THEIR OWN SOVEREIGNTY...
THANK GOODNESS WE IN THE U.K. STILL RETAIN THE INDEPENDENT POWER TO ADOPT NATIONAL MEASURES TO LESSEN THE IMPACT OF THE FINANCIAL CRISIS...
SUCH AS HAVING TWO BANK HOLIDAYS IN A ROW WHERE THE STOCK MARKET IS CLOSED?
QUITE. MEANING NOTHING BAD CAN ACTUALLY HAPPEN...
I'M NOT LOOKING FORWARD TO TOMORROW THOUGH...
NO. ME NEITHER.

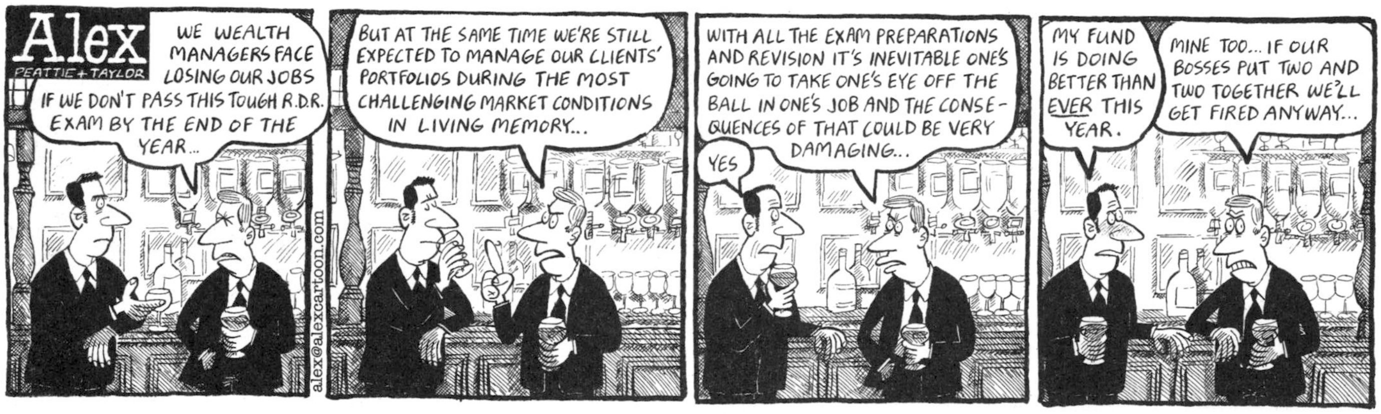
Alex
PEATTIE + TAYLOR
WE WEALTH MANAGERS FACE LOSING OUR JOBS IF WE DON'T PASS THIS TOUGH R.D.R. EXAM BY THE END OF THE YEAR...
alex@alexcartoon.com
BUT AT THE SAME TIME WE'RE STILL EXPECTED TO MANAGE OUR CLIENTS' PORTFOLIOS DURING THE MOST CHALLENGING MARKET CONDITIONS IN LIVING MEMORY...
WITH ALL THE EXAM PREPARATIONS AND REVISION IT'S INEVITABLE ONE'S GOING TO TAKE ONE'S EYE OFF THE BALL IN ONE'S JOB AND THE CONSEQUENCES OF THAT COULD BE VERY DAMAGING...
YES
MY FUND IS DOING BETTER THAN EVER THIS YEAR.
MINE TOO... IF OUR BOSSES PUT TWO AND TWO TOGETHER WE'LL GET FIRED ANYWAY...

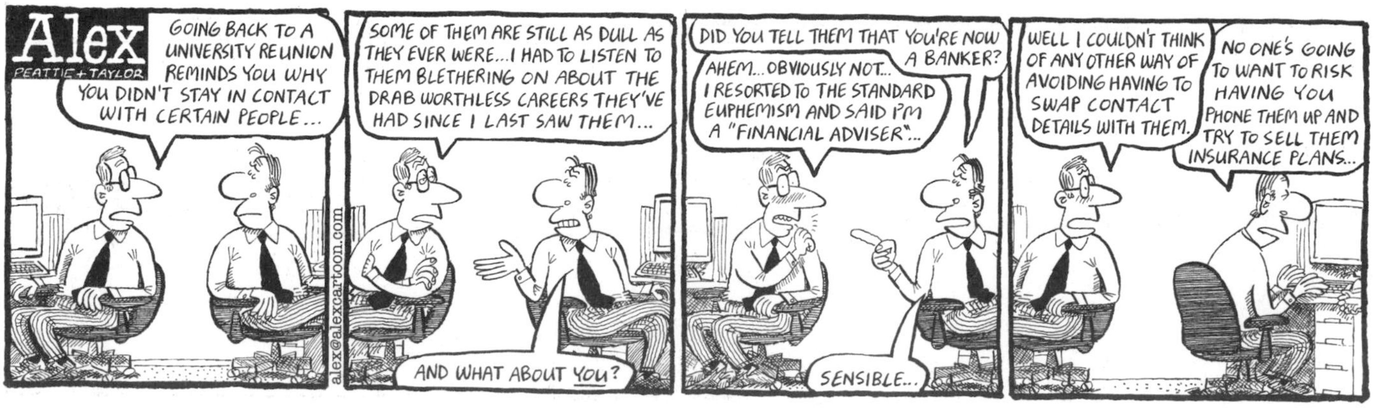
Alex
PEATTIE + TAYLOR
GOING BACK TO A UNIVERSITY REUNION REMINDS YOU WHY YOU DIDN'T STAY IN CONTACT WITH CERTAIN PEOPLE...
alex@alexcartoon.com
SOME OF THEM ARE STILL AS DULL AS THEY EVER WERE... I HAD TO LISTEN TO THEM BLETHERING ON ABOUT THE DRAB WORTHLESS CAREERS THEY'VE HAD SINCE I LAST SAW THEM...
AND WHAT ABOUT YOU?
DID YOU TELL THEM THAT YOU'RE NOW A BANKER?
AHEM... OBVIOUSLY NOT... I RESORTED TO THE STANDARD EUPHEMISM AND SAID I'M A "FINANCIAL ADVISER"...
SENSIBLE...
WELL I COULDN'T THINK OF ANY OTHER WAY OF AVOIDING HAVING TO SWAP CONTACT DETAILS WITH THEM.
NO ONE'S GOING TO WANT TO RISK HAVING YOU PHONE THEM UP AND TRY TO SELL THEM INSURANCE PLANS...

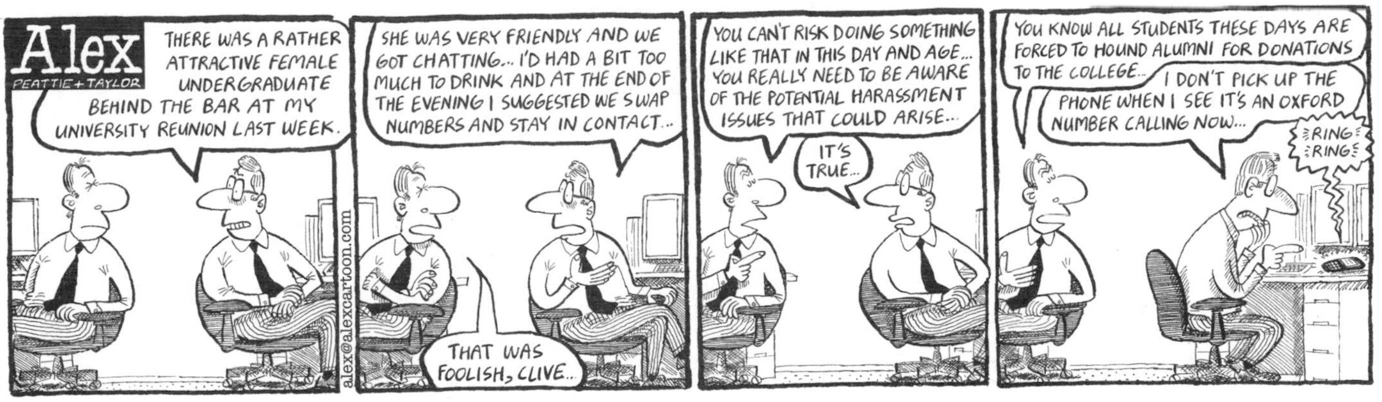
Alex
PEATTIE + TAYLOR
THERE WAS A RATHER ATTRACTIVE FEMALE UNDERGRADUATE BEHIND THE BAR AT MY UNIVERSITY REUNION LAST WEEK.
alex@alexcartoon.com
SHE WAS VERY FRIENDLY AND WE GOT CHATTING... I'D HAD A BIT TOO MUCH TO DRINK AND AT THE END OF THE EVENING I SUGGESTED WE SWAP NUMBERS AND STAY IN CONTACT...
THAT WAS FOOLISH, CLIVE...
YOU CAN'T RISK DOING SOMETHING LIKE THAT IN THIS DAY AND AGE... YOU REALLY NEED TO BE AWARE OF THE POTENTIAL HARASSMENT ISSUES THAT COULD ARISE...
IT'S TRUE...
YOU KNOW ALL STUDENTS THESE DAYS ARE FORCED TO HOUND ALUMNI FOR DONATIONS TO THE COLLEGE...
I DON'T PICK UP THE PHONE WHEN I SEE IT'S AN OXFORD NUMBER CALLING NOW...
RING RING

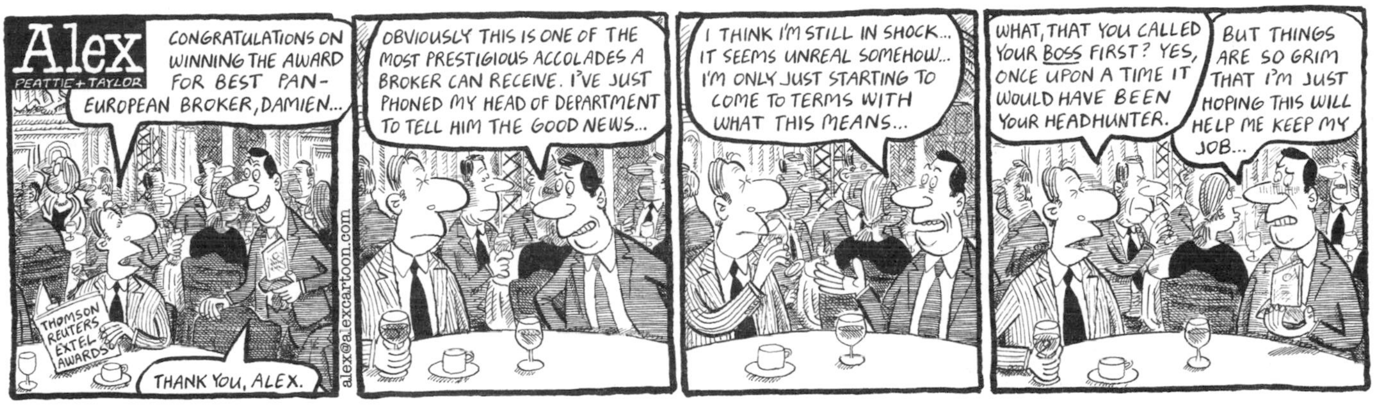
Alex
PEATTIE + TAYLOR
CONGRATULATIONS ON WINNING THE AWARD FOR BEST PAN-EUROPEAN BROKER, DAMIEN...
THOMSON REUTERS EXTEL AWARDS
THANK YOU, ALEX.
alex@alexcartoon.com
OBVIOUSLY THIS IS ONE OF THE MOST PRESTIGIOUS ACCOLADES A BROKER CAN RECEIVE. I'VE JUST PHONED MY HEAD OF DEPARTMENT TO TELL HIM THE GOOD NEWS...
I THINK I'M STILL IN SHOCK... IT SEEMS UNREAL SOMEHOW... I'M ONLY JUST STARTING TO COME TO TERMS WITH WHAT THIS MEANS...
WHAT, THAT YOU CALLED YOUR BOSS FIRST? YES, ONCE UPON A TIME IT WOULD HAVE BEEN YOUR HEADHUNTER.
BUT THINGS ARE SO GRIM THAT I'M JUST HOPING THIS WILL HELP ME KEEP MY JOB...

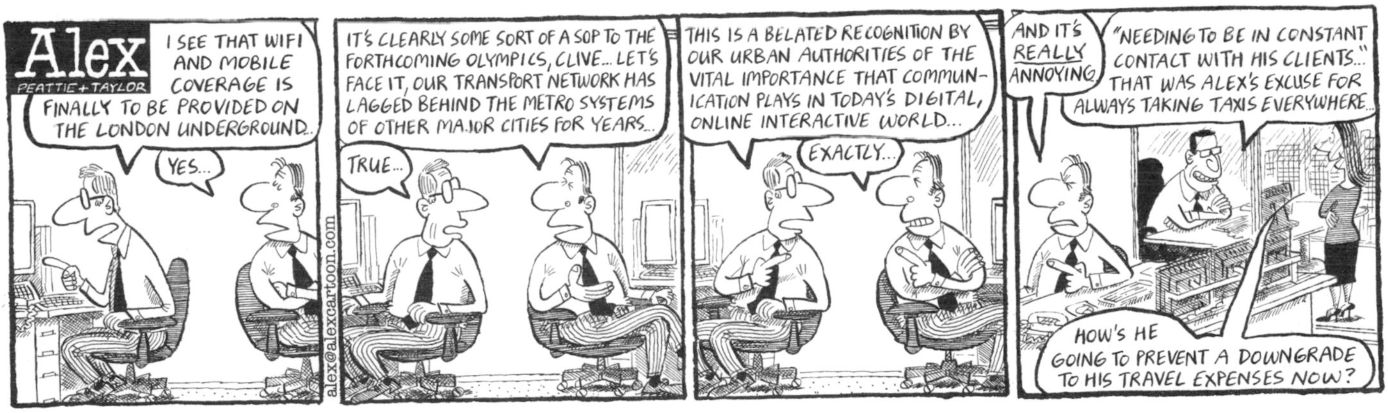
Alex
PEATTIE + TAYLOR
I SEE THAT WIFI AND MOBILE COVERAGE IS FINALLY TO BE PROVIDED ON THE LONDON UNDERGROUND...
YES...
alex@alexcartoon.com
IT'S CLEARLY SOME SORT OF A SOP TO THE FORTHCOMING OLYMPICS, CLIVE... LET'S FACE IT, OUR TRANSPORT NETWORK HAS LAGGED BEHIND THE METRO SYSTEMS OF OTHER MAJOR CITIES FOR YEARS...
TRUE...
THIS IS A BELATED RECOGNITION BY OUR URBAN AUTHORITIES OF THE VITAL IMPORTANCE THAT COMMUNICATION PLAYS IN TODAY'S DIGITAL, ONLINE INTERACTIVE WORLD...
EXACTLY...
AND IT'S REALLY ANNOYING.
"NEEDING TO BE IN CONSTANT CONTACT WITH HIS CLIENTS..." THAT WAS ALEX'S EXCUSE FOR ALWAYS TAKING TAXIS EVERYWHERE...
HOW'S HE GOING TO PREVENT A DOWNGRADE TO HIS TRAVEL EXPENSES NOW?

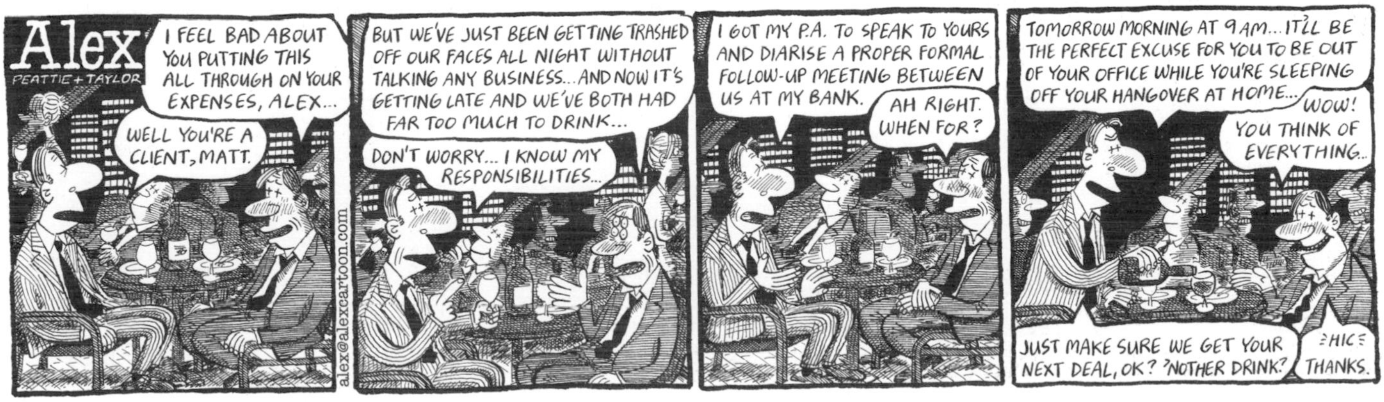
Alex
PEATTIE + TAYLOR
I FEEL BAD ABOUT YOU PUTTING THIS ALL THROUGH ON YOUR EXPENSES, ALEX...
WELL YOU'RE A CLIENT, MATT.
alex@alexcartoon.com
BUT WE'VE JUST BEEN GETTING TRASHED OFF OUR FACES ALL NIGHT WITHOUT TALKING ANY BUSINESS... AND NOW IT'S GETTING LATE AND WE'VE BOTH HAD FAR TOO MUCH TO DRINK...
DON'T WORRY... I KNOW MY RESPONSIBILITIES...
I GOT MY P.A. TO SPEAK TO YOURS AND DIARISE A PROPER FORMAL FOLLOW-UP MEETING BETWEEN US AT MY BANK.
AH RIGHT. WHEN FOR?
TOMORROW MORNING AT 9 AM... IT'LL BE THE PERFECT EXCUSE FOR YOU TO BE OUT OF YOUR OFFICE WHILE YOU'RE SLEEPING OFF YOUR HANGOVER AT HOME...
WOW! YOU THINK OF EVERYTHING...
JUST MAKE SURE WE GET YOUR NEXT DEAL, OK? 'NOTHER DRINK?
HIC
THANKS.

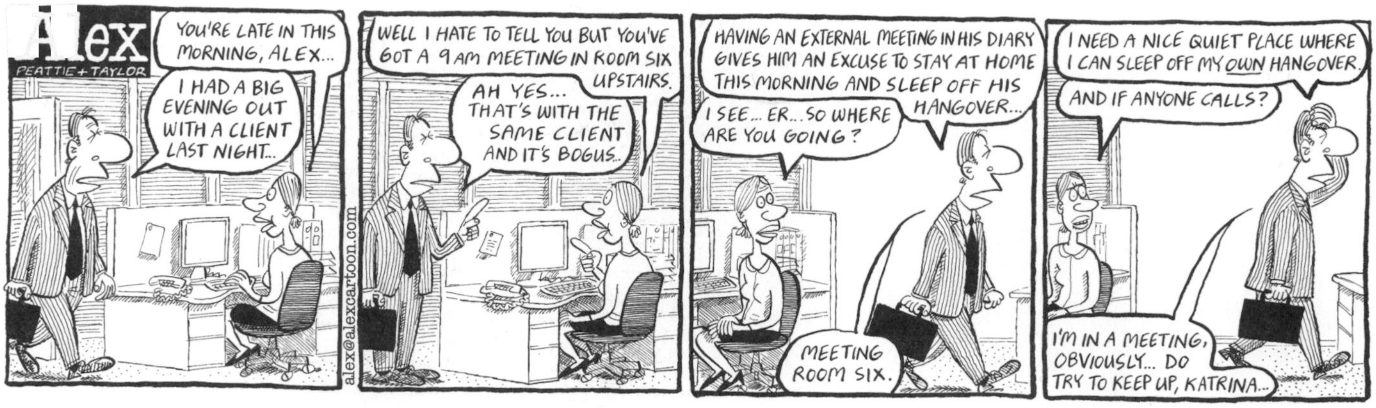
Alex
PEATTIE + TAYLOR
YOU'RE LATE IN THIS MORNING, ALEX...
I HAD A BIG EVENING OUT WITH A CLIENT LAST NIGHT...
alex@alexcartoon.com
WELL I HATE TO TELL YOU BUT YOU'VE GOT A 9 AM MEETING IN ROOM SIX UPSTAIRS.
AH YES... THAT'S WITH THE SAME CLIENT AND IT'S BOGUS...
HAVING AN EXTERNAL MEETING IN HIS DIARY GIVES HIM AN EXCUSE TO STAY AT HOME THIS MORNING AND SLEEP OFF HIS HANGOVER...
I SEE... ER... SO WHERE ARE YOU GOING?
MEETING ROOM SIX.
I NEED A NICE QUIET PLACE WHERE I CAN SLEEP OFF MY OWN HANGOVER.
AND IF ANYONE CALLS?
I'M IN A MEETING, OBVIOUSLY... DO TRY TO KEEP UP, KATRINA...

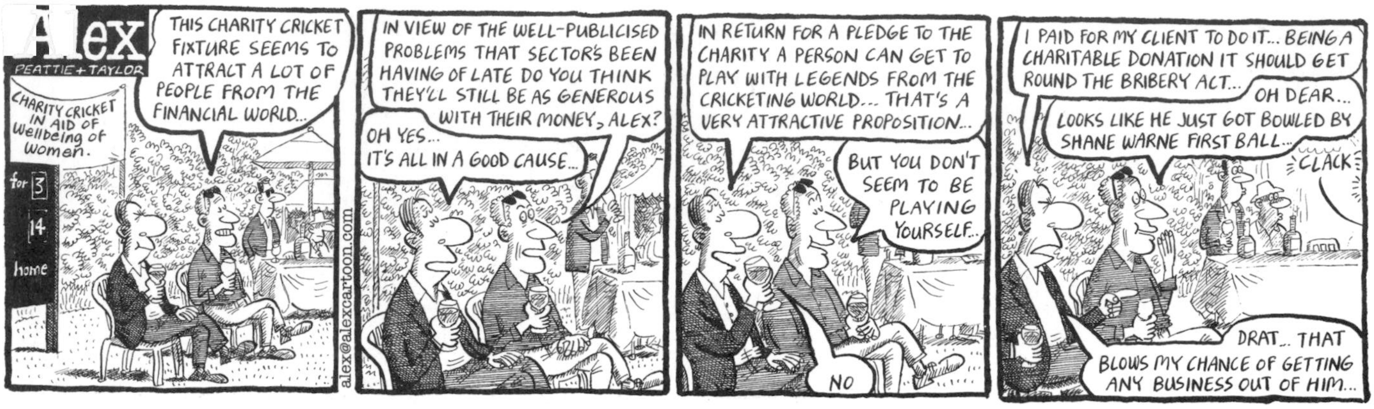
Alex
PEATTIE + TAYLOR
THIS CHARITY CRICKET FIXTURE SEEMS TO ATTRACT A LOT OF PEOPLE FROM THE FINANCIAL WORLD...
CHARITY CRICKET IN AID OF Wellbeing of Women.
for 3
14
home
alex@alexcartoon.com
IN VIEW OF THE WELL-PUBLICISED PROBLEMS THAT SECTOR'S BEEN HAVING OF LATE DO YOU THINK THEY'LL STILL BE AS GENEROUS WITH THEIR MONEY, ALEX?
OH YES... IT'S ALL IN A GOOD CAUSE...
IN RETURN FOR A PLEDGE TO THE CHARITY A PERSON CAN GET TO PLAY WITH LEGENDS FROM THE CRICKETING WORLD... THAT'S A VERY ATTRACTIVE PROPOSITION...
BUT YOU DON'T SEEM TO BE PLAYING YOURSELF...
NO
I PAID FOR MY CLIENT TO DO IT... BEING A CHARITABLE DONATION IT SHOULD GET ROUND THE BRIBERY ACT...
OH DEAR... LOOKS LIKE HE JUST GOT BOWLED BY SHANE WARNE FIRST BALL...
CLACK
DRAT... THAT BLOWS MY CHANCE OF GETTING ANY BUSINESS OUT OF HIM...

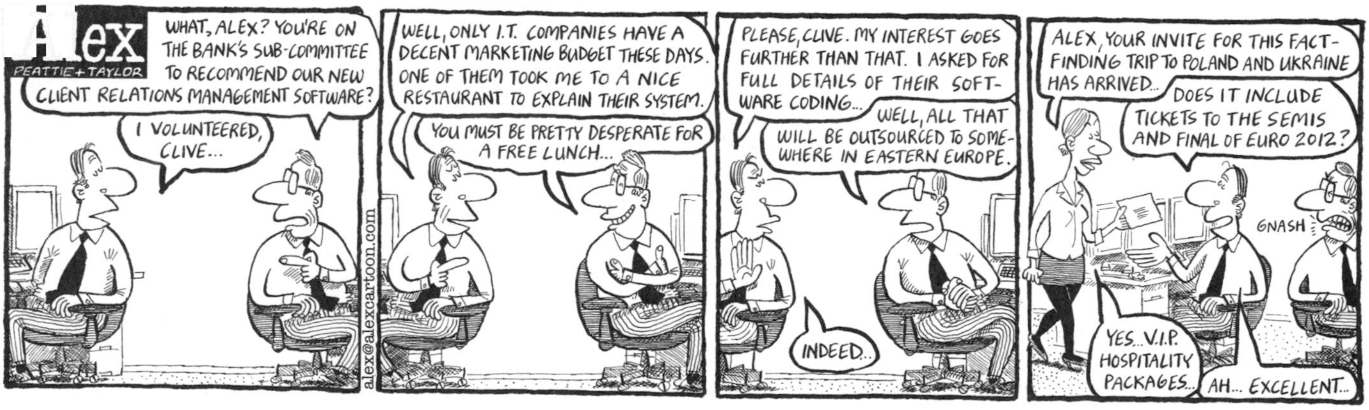
Alex
PEATTIE + TAYLOR
WHAT, ALEX? YOU'RE ON THE BANK'S SUB-COMMITTEE TO RECOMMEND OUR NEW CLIENT RELATIONS MANAGEMENT SOFTWARE?
I VOLUNTEERED, CLIVE...
alex@alexcartoon.com
WELL, ONLY I.T. COMPANIES HAVE A DECENT MARKETING BUDGET THESE DAYS. ONE OF THEM TOOK ME TO A NICE RESTAURANT TO EXPLAIN THEIR SYSTEM.
YOU MUST BE PRETTY DESPERATE FOR A FREE LUNCH...
PLEASE, CLIVE. MY INTEREST GOES FURTHER THAN THAT. I ASKED FOR FULL DETAILS OF THEIR SOFTWARE CODING...
WELL, ALL THAT WILL BE OUTSOURCED TO SOMEWHERE IN EASTERN EUROPE.
INDEED...
ALEX, YOUR INVITE FOR THIS FACT-FINDING TRIP TO POLAND AND UKRAINE HAS ARRIVED...
DOES IT INCLUDE TICKETS TO THE SEMIS AND FINAL OF EURO 2012?
GNASH
YES... V.I.P. HOSPITALITY PACKAGES...
AH... EXCELLENT...

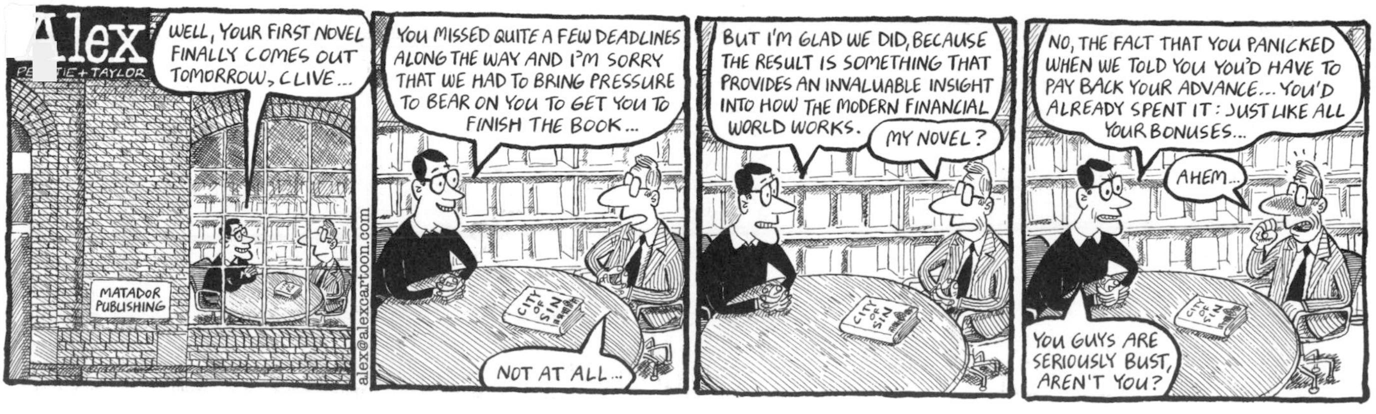
Alex
PEATTIE + TAYLOR
WELL, YOUR FIRST NOVEL FINALLY COMES OUT TOMORROW, CLIVE...
MATADOR PUBLISHING
alex@alexcartoon.com
YOU MISSED QUITE A FEW DEADLINES ALONG THE WAY AND I'M SORRY THAT WE HAD TO BRING PRESSURE TO BEAR ON YOU TO GET YOU TO FINISH THE BOOK...
CITY OF SIN
NOT AT ALL...
BUT I'M GLAD WE DID, BECAUSE THE RESULT IS SOMETHING THAT PROVIDES AN INVALUABLE INSIGHT INTO HOW THE MODERN FINANCIAL WORLD WORKS.
MY NOVEL?
NO, THE FACT THAT YOU PANICKED WHEN WE TOLD YOU YOU'D HAVE TO PAY BACK YOUR ADVANCE... YOU'D ALREADY SPENT IT: JUST LIKE ALL YOUR BONUSES...
AHEM...
YOU GUYS ARE SERIOUSLY BUST, AREN'T YOU?

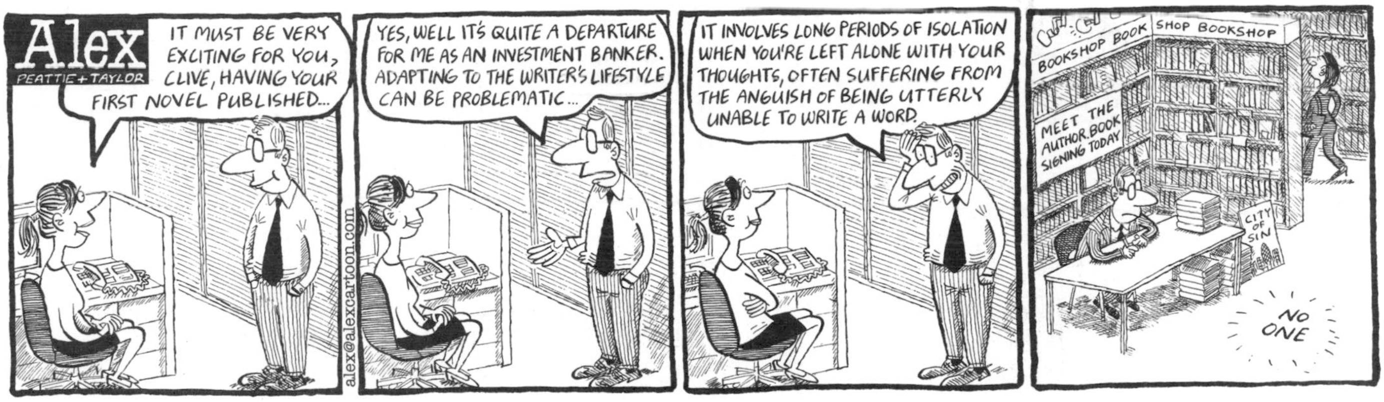
Alex
PEATTIE + TAYLOR
IT MUST BE VERY EXCITING FOR YOU, CLIVE, HAVING YOUR FIRST NOVEL PUBLISHED...
alex@alexcartoon.com
YES, WELL IT'S QUITE A DEPARTURE FOR ME AS AN INVESTMENT BANKER. ADAPTING TO THE WRITER'S LIFESTYLE CAN BE PROBLEMATIC...
IT INVOLVES LONG PERIODS OF ISOLATION WHEN YOU'RE LEFT ALONE WITH YOUR THOUGHTS, OFTEN SUFFERING FROM THE ANGUISH OF BEING UTTERLY UNABLE TO WRITE A WORD.
BOOKSHOP BOOK SHOP BOOKSHOP
MEET THE AUTHOR BOOK SIGNING TODAY
CITY OF SIN
NO ONE

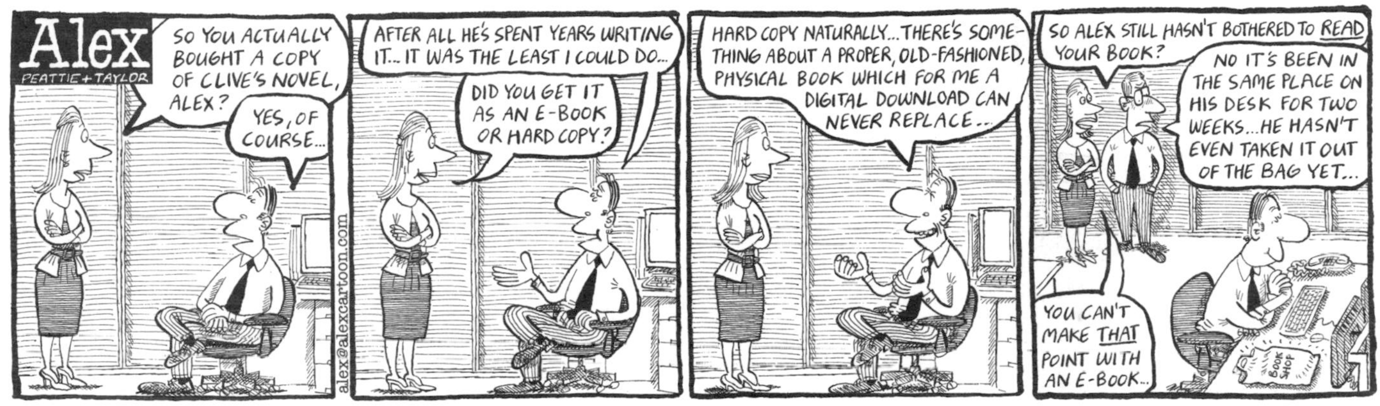
Alex
PEATTIE + TAYLOR
SO YOU ACTUALLY BOUGHT A COPY OF CLIVE'S NOVEL, ALEX?
YES, OF COURSE...
alex@alexcartoon.com
AFTER ALL HE'S SPENT YEARS WRITING IT... IT WAS THE LEAST I COULD DO...
DID YOU GET IT AS AN E-BOOK OR HARD COPY?
HARD COPY NATURALLY... THERE'S SOMETHING ABOUT A PROPER, OLD-FASHIONED, PHYSICAL BOOK WHICH FOR ME A DIGITAL DOWNLOAD CAN NEVER REPLACE...
SO ALEX STILL HASN'T BOTHERED TO READ YOUR BOOK?
NO IT'S BEEN IN THE SAME PLACE ON HIS DESK FOR TWO WEEKS... HE HASN'T EVEN TAKEN IT OUT OF THE BAG YET...
YOU CAN'T MAKE THAT POINT WITH AN E-BOOK...
BOOK SHOP

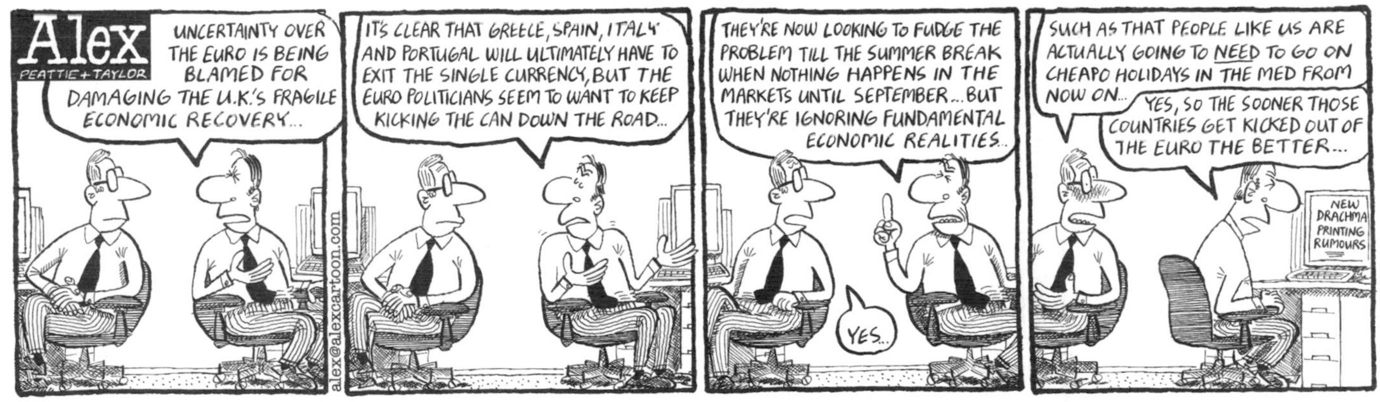
Alex
PEATTIE + TAYLOR
UNCERTAINTY OVER THE EURO IS BEING BLAMED FOR DAMAGING THE U.K.'S FRAGILE ECONOMIC RECOVERY...
alex@alexcartoon.com
IT'S CLEAR THAT GREECE, SPAIN, ITALY AND PORTUGAL WILL ULTIMATELY HAVE TO EXIT THE SINGLE CURRENCY, BUT THE EURO POLITICIANS SEEM TO WANT TO KEEP KICKING THE CAN DOWN THE ROAD...
THEY'RE NOW LOOKING TO FUDGE THE PROBLEM TILL THE SUMMER BREAK WHEN NOTHING HAPPENS IN THE MARKETS UNTIL SEPTEMBER... BUT THEY'RE IGNORING FUNDAMENTAL ECONOMIC REALITIES...
YES...
SUCH AS THAT PEOPLE LIKE US ARE ACTUALLY GOING TO NEED TO GO ON CHEAPO HOLIDAYS IN THE MED FROM NOW ON...
YES, SO THE SOONER THOSE COUNTRIES GET KICKED OUT OF THE EURO THE BETTER...
NEW DRACHMA PRINTING RUMOURS

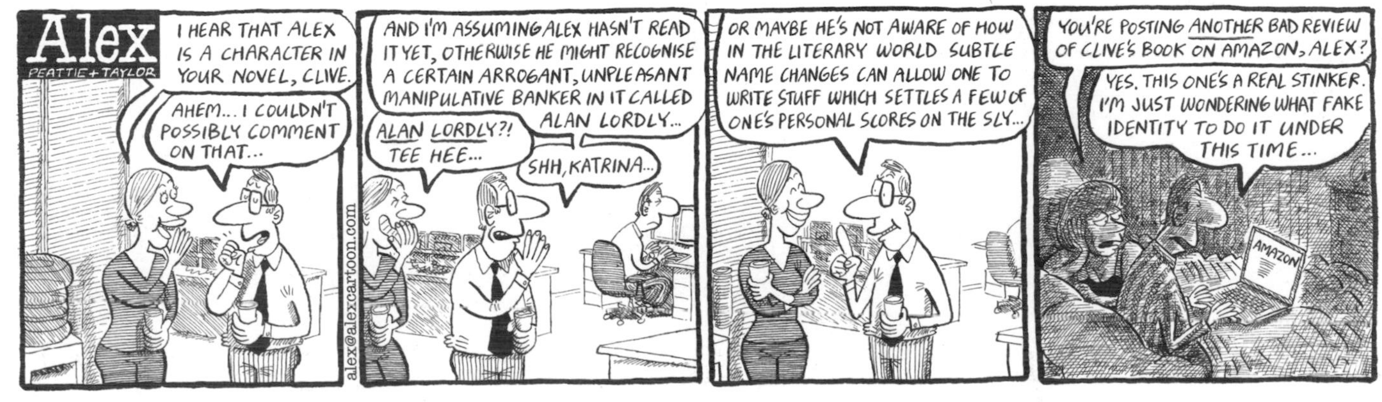
Alex
PEATTIE + TAYLOR
I HEAR THAT ALEX IS A CHARACTER IN YOUR NOVEL, CLIVE.
AHEM... I COULDN'T POSSIBLY COMMENT ON THAT...
alex@alexcartoon.com
AND I'M ASSUMING ALEX HASN'T READ IT YET, OTHERWISE HE MIGHT RECOGNISE A CERTAIN ARROGANT, UNPLEASANT MANIPULATIVE BANKER IN IT CALLED ALAN LORDLY...
ALAN LORDLY?! TEE HEE...
SHH, KATRINA...
OR MAYBE HE'S NOT AWARE OF HOW IN THE LITERARY WORLD SUBTLE NAME CHANGES CAN ALLOW ONE TO WRITE STUFF WHICH SETTLES A FEW OF ONE'S PERSONAL SCORES ON THE SLY...
YOU'RE POSTING ANOTHER BAD REVIEW OF CLIVE'S BOOK ON AMAZON, ALEX?
YES. THIS ONE'S A REAL STINKER. I'M JUST WONDERING WHAT FAKE IDENTITY TO DO IT UNDER THIS TIME...
AMAZON

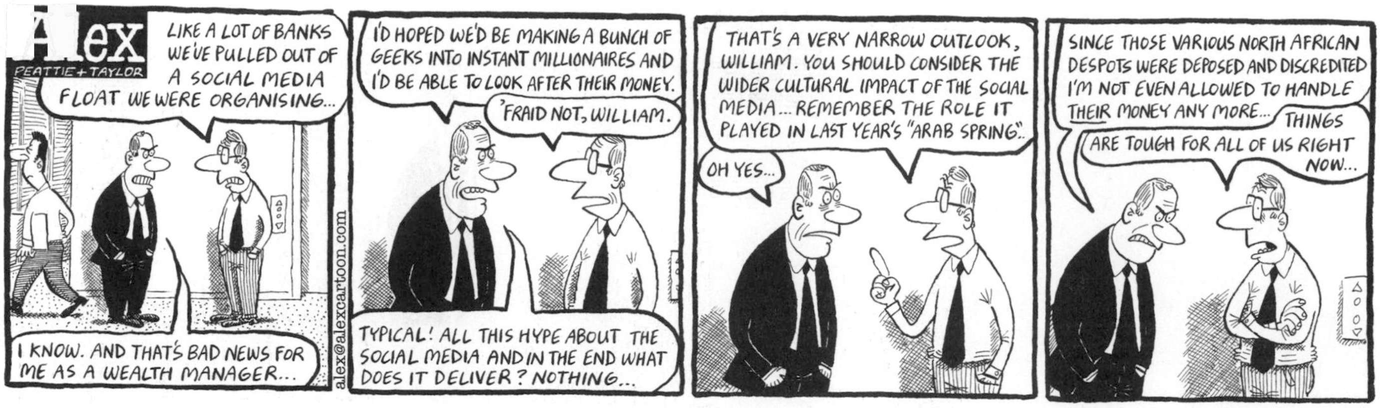
Alex
PEATTIE + TAYLOR
LIKE A LOT OF BANKS WE'VE PULLED OUT OF A SOCIAL MEDIA FLOAT WE WERE ORGANISING...
I KNOW. AND THAT'S BAD NEWS FOR ME AS A WEALTH MANAGER...
alex@alexcartoon.com
I'D HOPED WE'D BE MAKING A BUNCH OF GEEKS INTO INSTANT MILLIONAIRES AND I'D BE ABLE TO LOOK AFTER THEIR MONEY.
'FRAID NOT, WILLIAM.
TYPICAL! ALL THIS HYPE ABOUT THE SOCIAL MEDIA AND IN THE END WHAT DOES IT DELIVER? NOTHING...
THAT'S A VERY NARROW OUTLOOK, WILLIAM. YOU SHOULD CONSIDER THE WIDER CULTURAL IMPACT OF THE SOCIAL MEDIA... REMEMBER THE ROLE IT PLAYED IN LAST YEAR'S "ARAB SPRING".
OH YES...
SINCE THOSE VARIOUS NORTH AFRICAN DESPOTS WERE DEPOSED AND DISCREDITED I'M NOT EVEN ALLOWED TO HANDLE THEIR MONEY ANY MORE...
THINGS ARE TOUGH FOR ALL OF US RIGHT NOW...

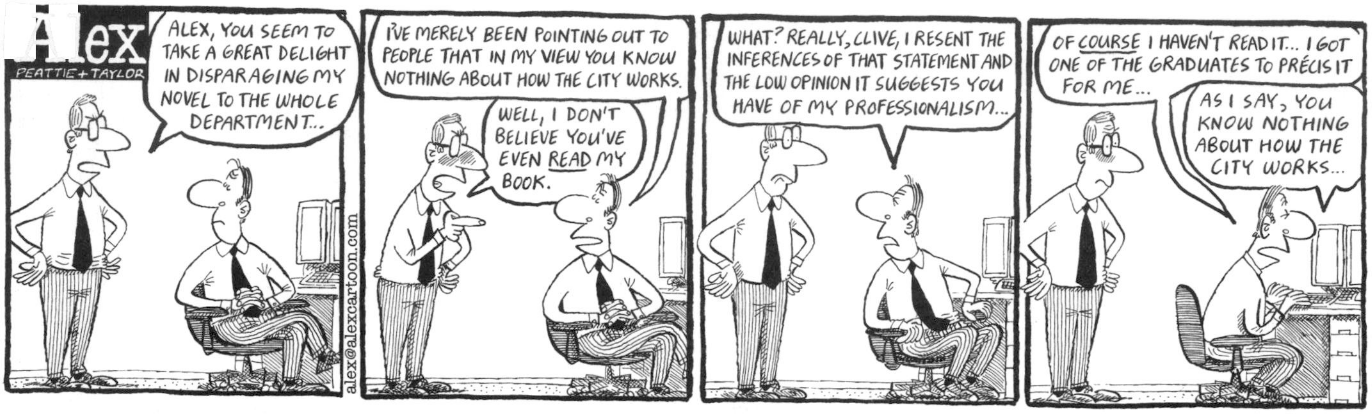
Alex
PEATTIE + TAYLOR
ALEX, YOU SEEM TO TAKE A GREAT DELIGHT IN DISPARAGING MY NOVEL TO THE WHOLE DEPARTMENT...
alex@alexcartoon.com
I'VE MERELY BEEN POINTING OUT TO PEOPLE THAT IN MY VIEW YOU KNOW NOTHING ABOUT HOW THE CITY WORKS.
WELL, I DON'T BELIEVE YOU'VE EVEN READ MY BOOK.
WHAT? REALLY, CLIVE, I RESENT THE INFERENCES OF THAT STATEMENT AND THE LOW OPINION IT SUGGESTS YOU HAVE OF MY PROFESSIONALISM...
OF COURSE I HAVEN'T READ IT... I GOT ONE OF THE GRADUATES TO PRÉCIS IT FOR ME...
AS I SAY, YOU KNOW NOTHING ABOUT HOW THE CITY WORKS...

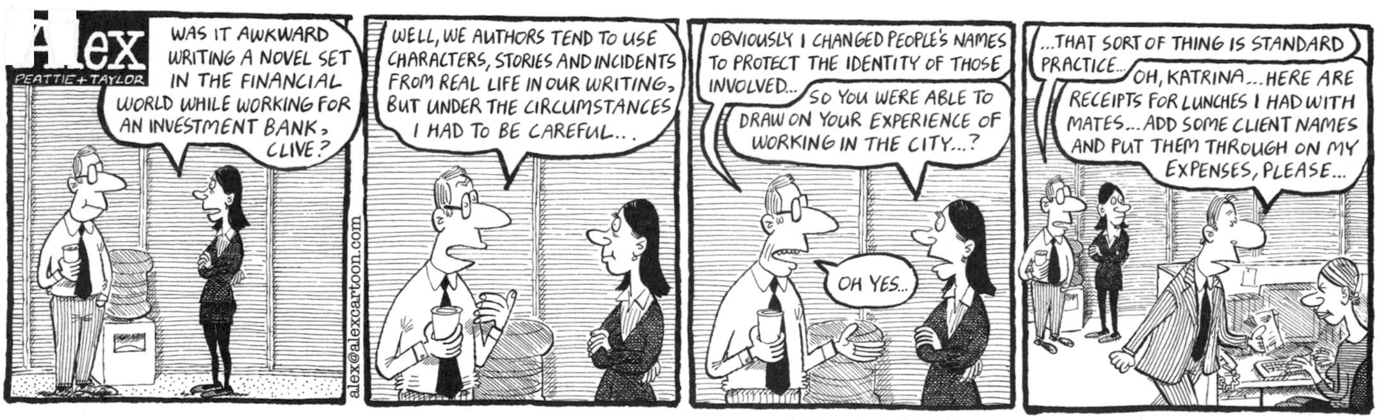
Alex
PEATTIE + TAYLOR
WAS IT AWKWARD WRITING A NOVEL SET IN THE FINANCIAL WORLD WHILE WORKING FOR AN INVESTMENT BANK, CLIVE?
alex@alexcartoon.com
WELL, WE AUTHORS TEND TO USE CHARACTERS, STORIES AND INCIDENTS FROM REAL LIFE IN OUR WRITING, BUT UNDER THE CIRCUMSTANCES I HAD TO BE CAREFUL...
OBVIOUSLY I CHANGED PEOPLE'S NAMES TO PROTECT THE IDENTITY OF THOSE INVOLVED...
SO YOU WERE ABLE TO DRAW ON YOUR EXPERIENCE OF WORKING IN THE CITY...?
OH YES...
...THAT SORT OF THING IS STANDARD PRACTICE...
OH, KATRINA... HERE ARE RECEIPTS FOR LUNCHES I HAD WITH MATES... ADD SOME CLIENT NAMES AND PUT THEM THROUGH ON MY EXPENSES, PLEASE...

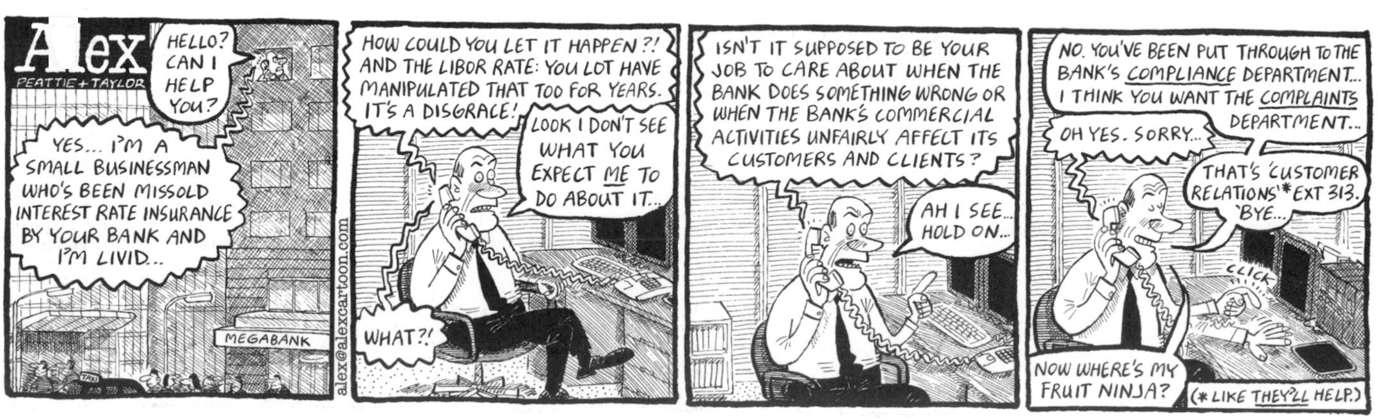
Alex
PEATTIE + TAYLOR
HELLO? CAN I HELP YOU?
YES... I'M A SMALL BUSINESSMAN WHO'S BEEN MISSOLD INTEREST RATE INSURANCE BY YOUR BANK AND I'M LIVID...
MEGABANK
alex@alexcartoon.com
HOW COULD YOU LET IT HAPPEN?! AND THE LIBOR RATE: YOU LOT HAVE MANIPULATED THAT TOO FOR YEARS. IT'S A DISGRACE!
LOOK I DON'T SEE WHAT YOU EXPECT ME TO DO ABOUT IT...
WHAT?!
ISN'T IT SUPPOSED TO BE YOUR JOB TO CARE ABOUT WHEN THE BANK DOES SOMETHING WRONG OR WHEN THE BANK'S COMMERCIAL ACTIVITIES UNFAIRLY AFFECT ITS CUSTOMERS AND CLIENTS?
AH I SEE... HOLD ON...
NO. YOU'VE BEEN PUT THROUGH TO THE BANK'S COMPLIANCE DEPARTMENT... I THINK YOU WANT THE COMPLAINTS DEPARTMENT...
OH YES. SORRY...
THAT'S 'CUSTOMER RELATIONS'* EXT 313. 'BYE...
CLICK
NOW WHERE'S MY FRUIT NINJA?
(* LIKE THEY'LL HELP.)

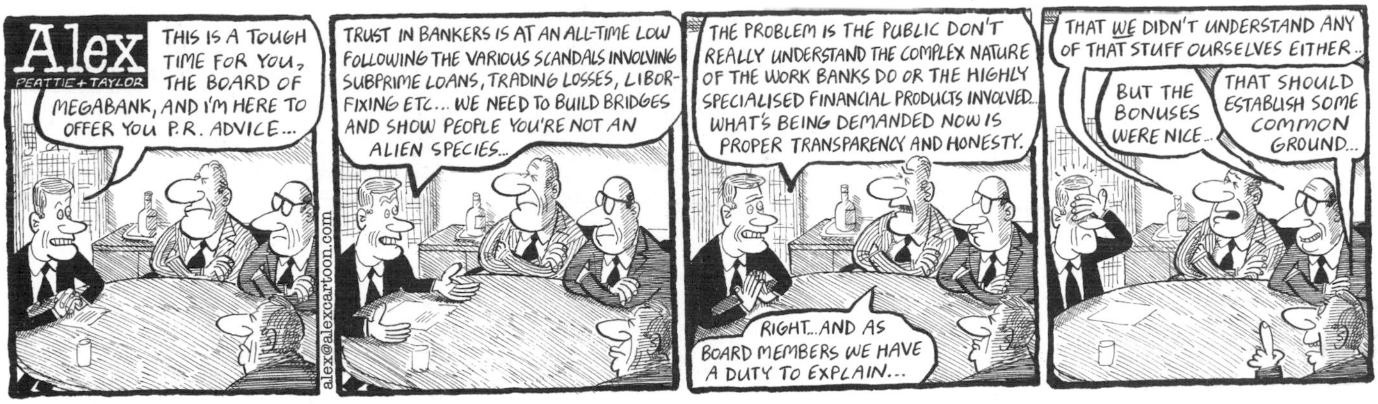
Alex
PEATTIE + TAYLOR
THIS IS A TOUGH TIME FOR YOU, THE BOARD OF MEGABANK, AND I'M HERE TO OFFER YOU P.R. ADVICE...
TRUST IN BANKERS IS AT AN ALL-TIME LOW FOLLOWING THE VARIOUS SCANDALS INVOLVING SUBPRIME LOANS, TRADING LOSSES, LIBOR-FIXING ETC... WE NEED TO BUILD BRIDGES AND SHOW PEOPLE YOU'RE NOT AN ALIEN SPECIES...
alex@alexcartoon.com
THE PROBLEM IS THE PUBLIC DON'T REALLY UNDERSTAND THE COMPLEX NATURE OF THE WORK BANKS DO OR THE HIGHLY SPECIALISED FINANCIAL PRODUCTS INVOLVED... WHAT'S BEING DEMANDED NOW IS PROPER TRANSPARENCY AND HONESTY.
RIGHT... AND AS BOARD MEMBERS WE HAVE A DUTY TO EXPLAIN...
THAT WE DIDN'T UNDERSTAND ANY OF THAT STUFF OURSELVES EITHER...
BUT THE BONUSES WERE NICE...
THAT SHOULD ESTABLISH SOME COMMON GROUND...

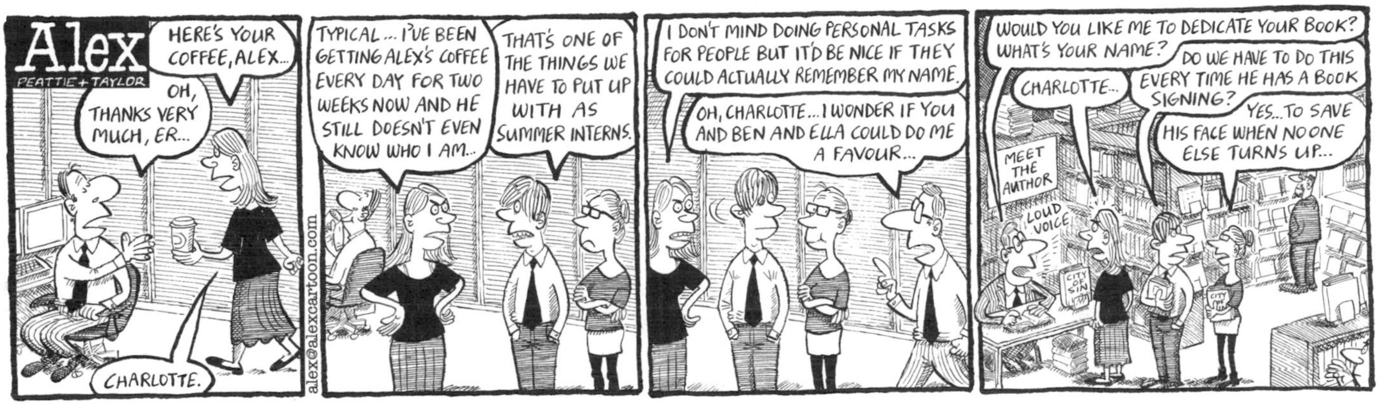
Alex
PEATTIE + TAYLOR
HERE'S YOUR COFFEE, ALEX...
OH, THANKS VERY MUCH, ER...
CHARLOTTE.
alex@alexcartoon.com
TYPICAL... I'VE BEEN GETTING ALEX'S COFFEE EVERY DAY FOR TWO WEEKS NOW AND HE STILL DOESN'T EVEN KNOW WHO I AM...
THAT'S ONE OF THE THINGS WE HAVE TO PUT UP WITH AS SUMMER INTERNS.
I DON'T MIND DOING PERSONAL TASKS FOR PEOPLE BUT IT'D BE NICE IF THEY COULD ACTUALLY REMEMBER MY NAME.
OH, CHARLOTTE... I WONDER IF YOU AND BEN AND ELLA COULD DO ME A FAVOUR...
WOULD YOU LIKE ME TO DEDICATE YOUR BOOK? WHAT'S YOUR NAME?
CHARLOTTE...
DO WE HAVE TO DO THIS EVERY TIME HE HAS A BOOK SIGNING?
YES... TO SAVE HIS FACE WHEN NO ONE ELSE TURNS UP...
MEET THE AUTHOR
LOUD VOICE
CITY OF SIN

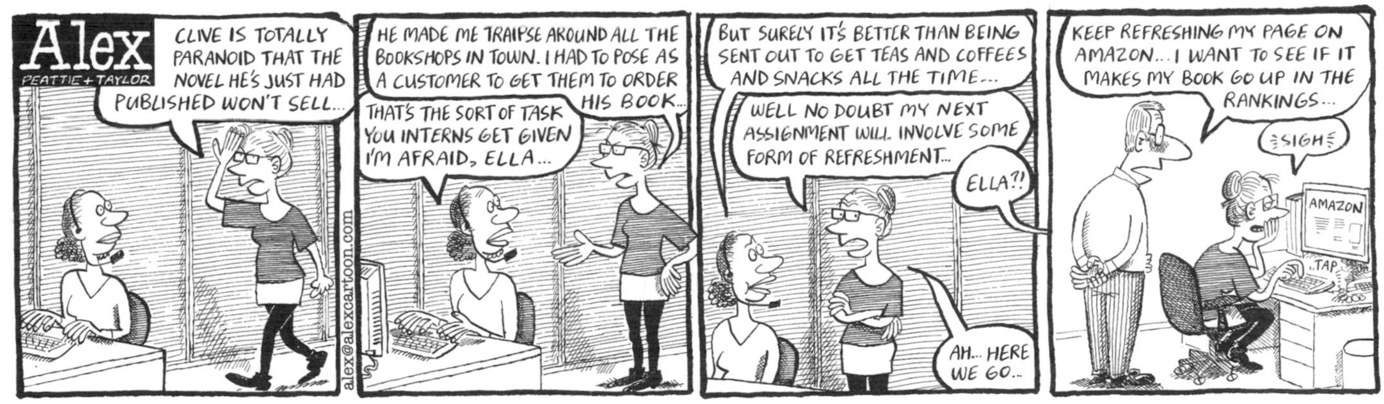
Alex
PEATTIE + TAYLOR
CLIVE IS TOTALLY PARANOID THAT THE NOVEL HE'S JUST HAD PUBLISHED WON'T SELL...
alex@alexcartoon.com
HE MADE ME TRAIPSE AROUND ALL THE BOOKSHOPS IN TOWN. I HAD TO POSE AS A CUSTOMER TO GET THEM TO ORDER HIS BOOK...
THAT'S THE SORT OF TASK YOU INTERNS GET GIVEN I'M AFRAID, ELLA...
BUT SURELY IT'S BETTER THAN BEING SENT OUT TO GET TEAS AND COFFEES AND SNACKS ALL THE TIME...
WELL NO DOUBT MY NEXT ASSIGNMENT WILL INVOLVE SOME FORM OF REFRESHMENT...
ELLA?!
AH... HERE WE GO...
KEEP REFRESHING MY PAGE ON AMAZON... I WANT TO SEE IF IT MAKES MY BOOK GO UP IN THE RANKINGS...
SIGH
AMAZON
TAP

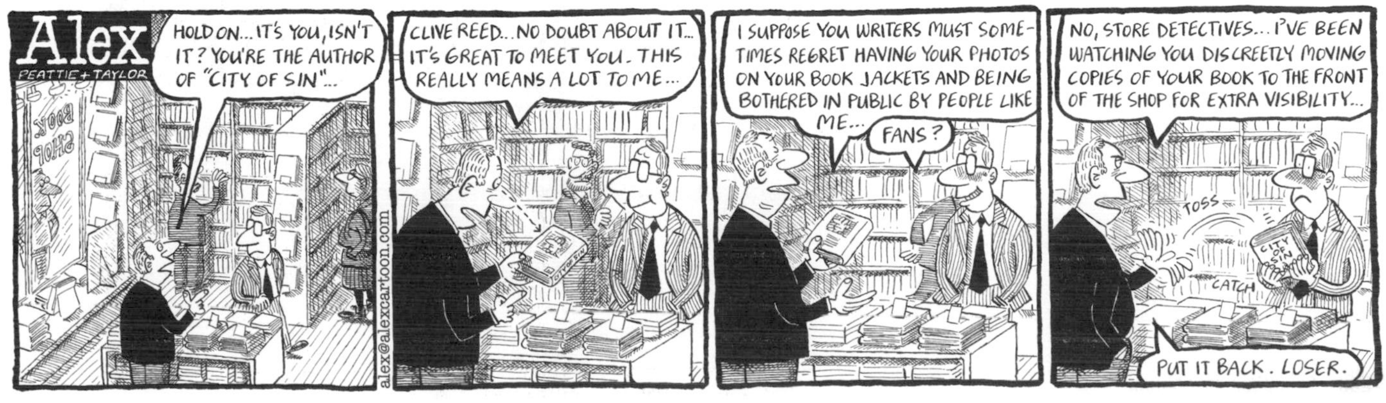
Alex
PEATTIE + TAYLOR
HOLD ON... IT'S YOU, ISN'T IT? YOU'RE THE AUTHOR OF "CITY OF SIN"...
alex@alexcartoon.com
CLIVE REED... NO DOUBT ABOUT IT... IT'S GREAT TO MEET YOU. THIS REALLY MEANS A LOT TO ME...
I SUPPOSE YOU WRITERS MUST SOMETIMES REGRET HAVING YOUR PHOTOS ON YOUR BOOK JACKETS AND BEING BOTHERED IN PUBLIC BY PEOPLE LIKE ME...
FANS?
NO, STORE DETECTIVES... I'VE BEEN WATCHING YOU DISCREETLY MOVING COPIES OF YOUR BOOK TO THE FRONT OF THE SHOP FOR EXTRA VISIBILITY...
TOSS
CATCH
CITY OF SIN
PUT IT BACK. LOSER.

ALEX AND CLIVE TOOK TIME OUT

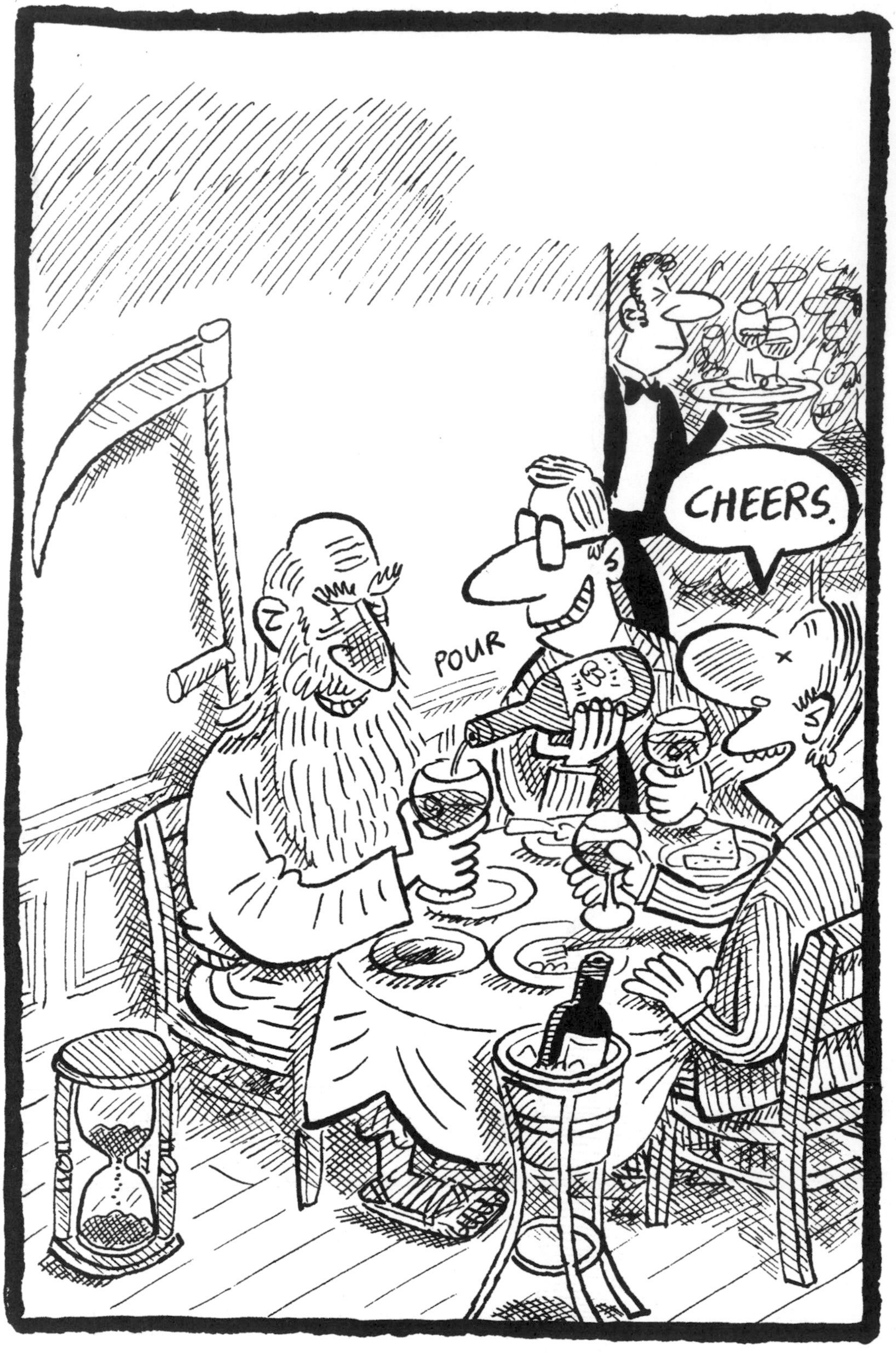
POUR
CHEERS.

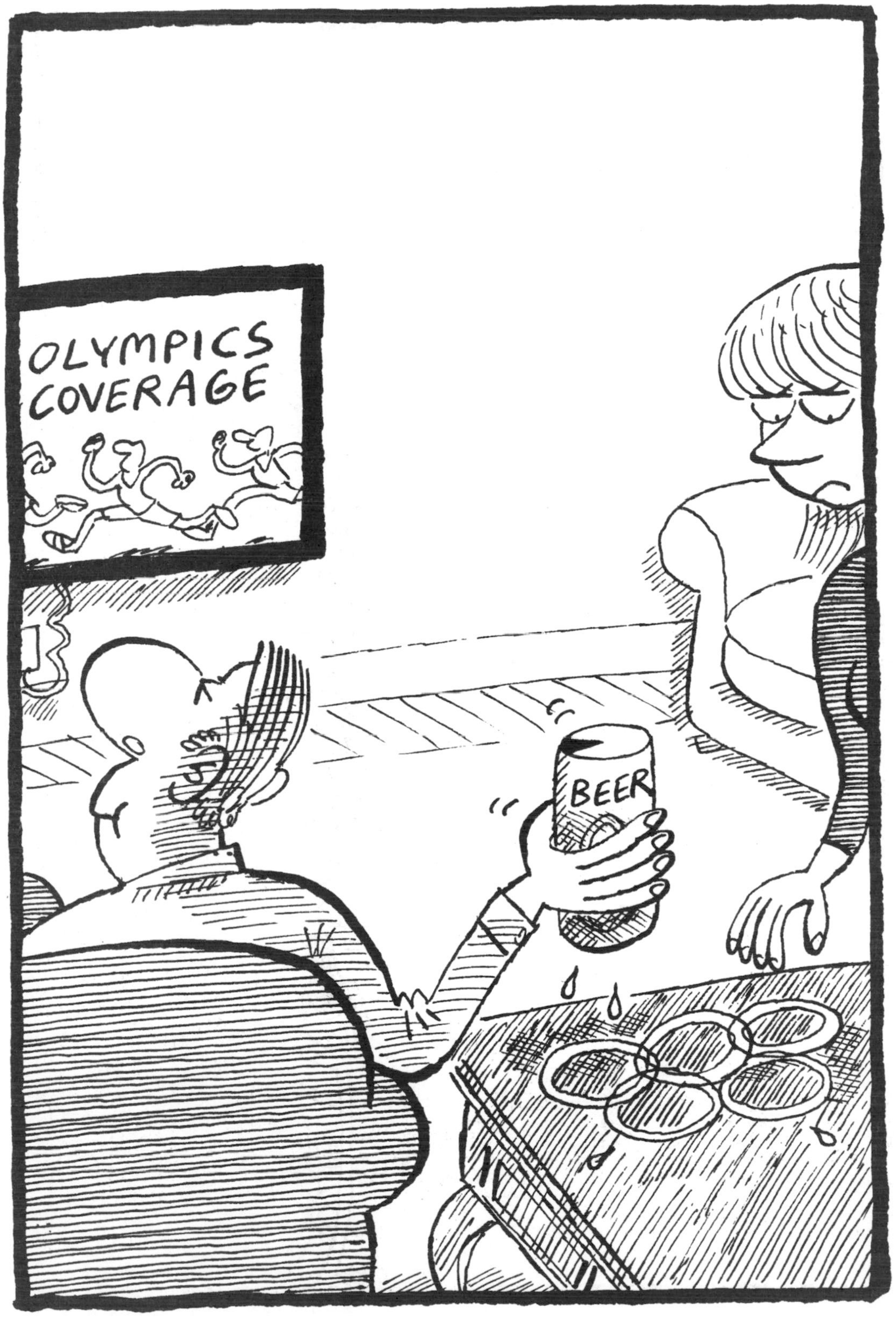
OLYMPICS COVERAGE
BEER

. . . TO WATCH THE OLYMPICS

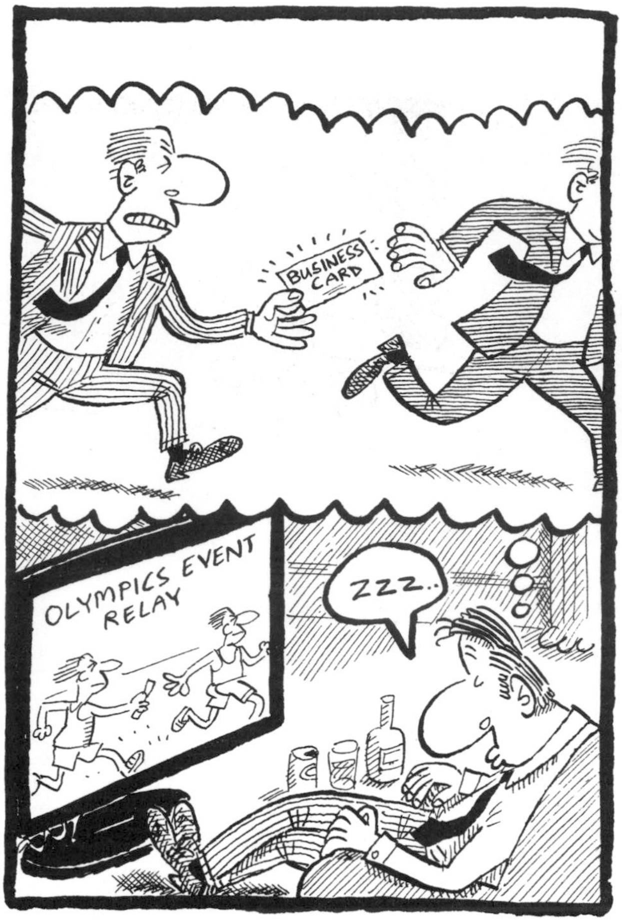
BUSINESS CARD
OLYMPICS EVENT RELAY
ZZZ..

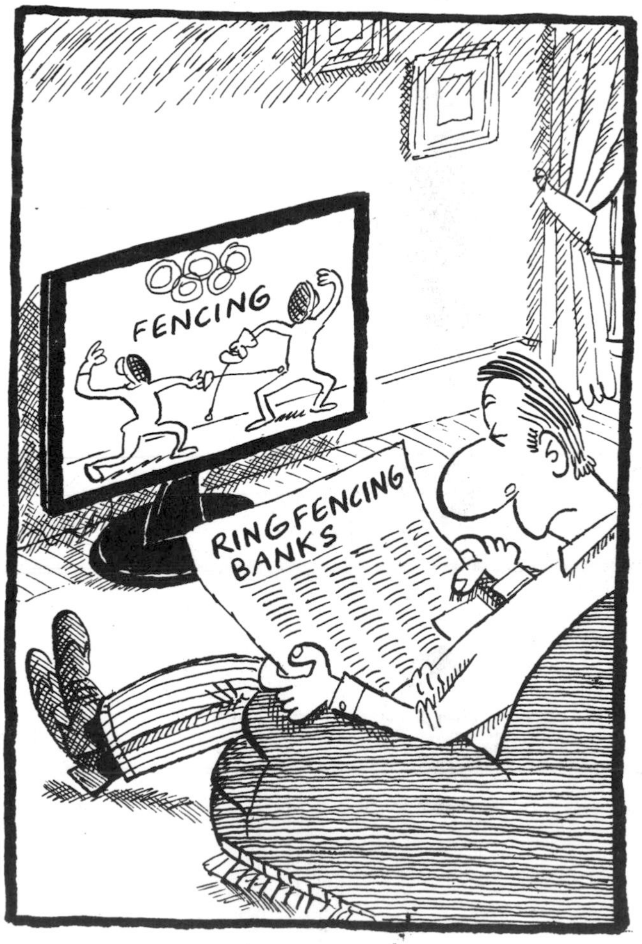
FENCING
RINGFENCING BANKS

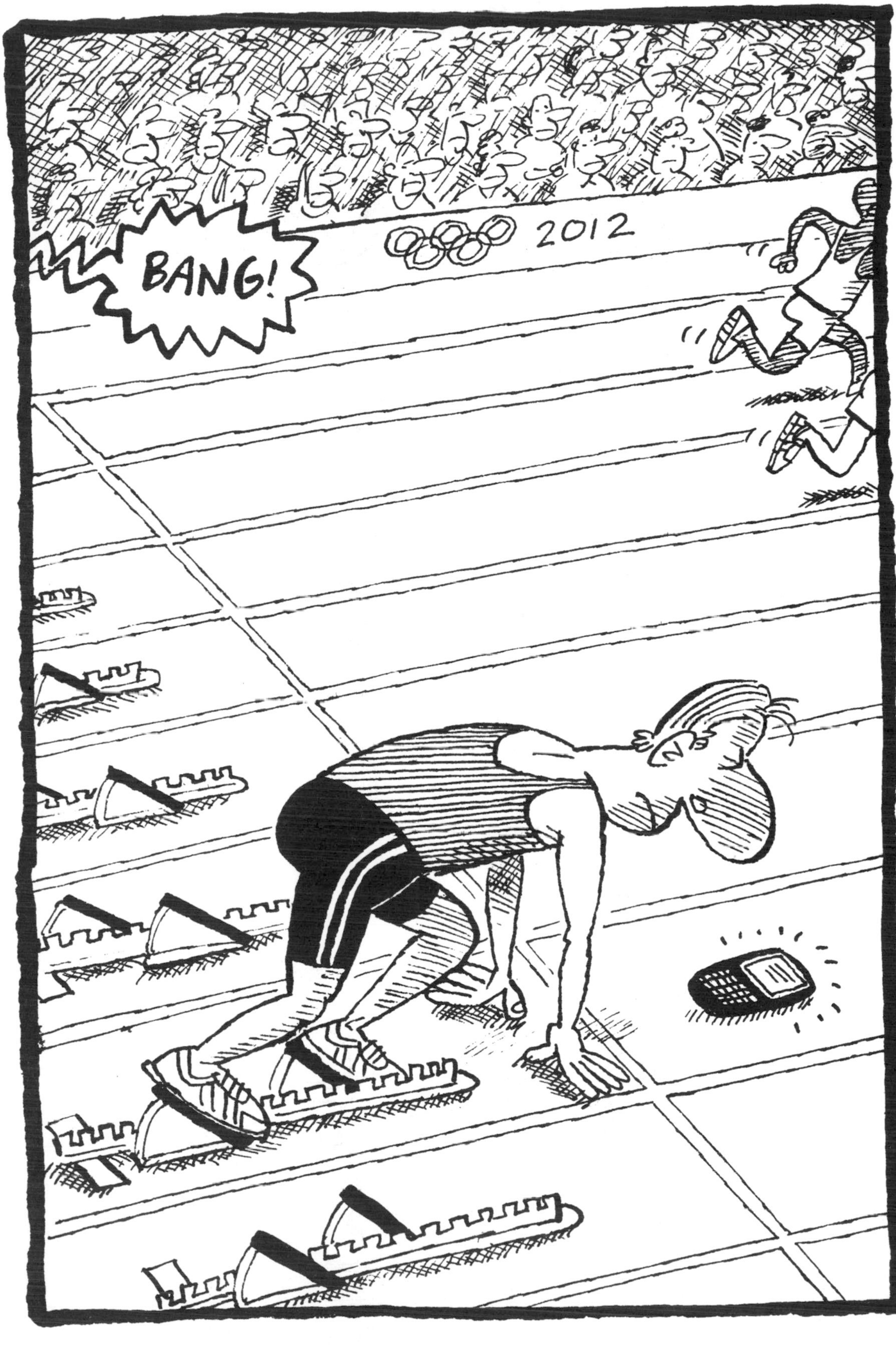
BANG!
2012

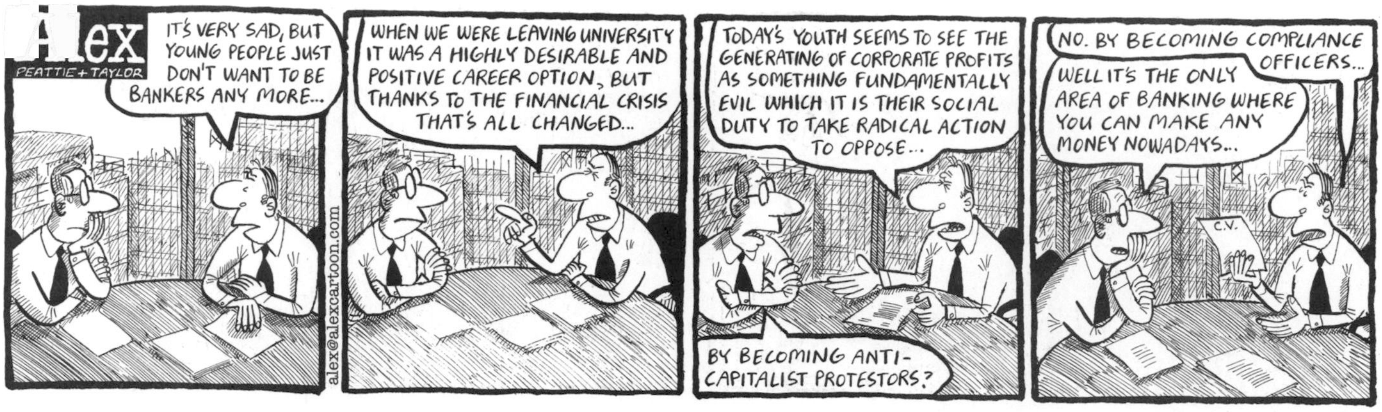
Alex
PEATTIE + TAYLOR
IT'S VERY SAD, BUT YOUNG PEOPLE JUST DON'T WANT TO BE BANKERS ANY MORE...
alex@alexcartoon.com
WHEN WE WERE LEAVING UNIVERSITY IT WAS A HIGHLY DESIRABLE AND POSITIVE CAREER OPTION, BUT THANKS TO THE FINANCIAL CRISIS THAT'S ALL CHANGED...
TODAY'S YOUTH SEEMS TO SEE THE GENERATING OF CORPORATE PROFITS AS SOMETHING FUNDAMENTALLY EVIL WHICH IT IS THEIR SOCIAL DUTY TO TAKE RADICAL ACTION TO OPPOSE...
BY BECOMING ANTI-CAPITALIST PROTESTORS?
NO. BY BECOMING COMPLIANCE OFFICERS...
WELL IT'S THE ONLY AREA OF BANKING WHERE YOU CAN MAKE ANY MONEY NOWADAYS...
C.V.

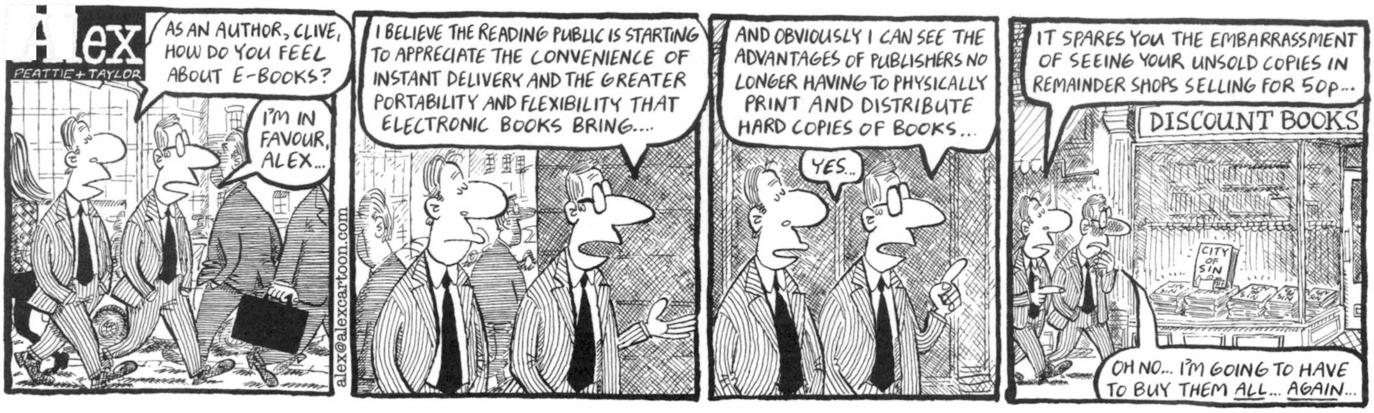
Alex
PEATTIE + TAYLOR
AS AN AUTHOR, CLIVE, HOW DO YOU FEEL ABOUT E-BOOKS?
I'M IN FAVOUR, ALEX...
alex@alexcartoon.com
I BELIEVE THE READING PUBLIC IS STARTING TO APPRECIATE THE CONVENIENCE OF INSTANT DELIVERY AND THE GREATER PORTABILITY AND FLEXIBILITY THAT ELECTRONIC BOOKS BRING....
AND OBVIOUSLY I CAN SEE THE ADVANTAGES OF PUBLISHERS NO LONGER HAVING TO PHYSICALLY PRINT AND DISTRIBUTE HARD COPIES OF BOOKS...
YES...
IT SPARES YOU THE EMBARRASSMENT OF SEEING YOUR UNSOLD COPIES IN REMAINDER SHOPS SELLING FOR 50p...
DISCOUNT BOOKS
CITY OF SIN
OH NO... I'M GOING TO HAVE TO BUY THEM ALL... AGAIN...

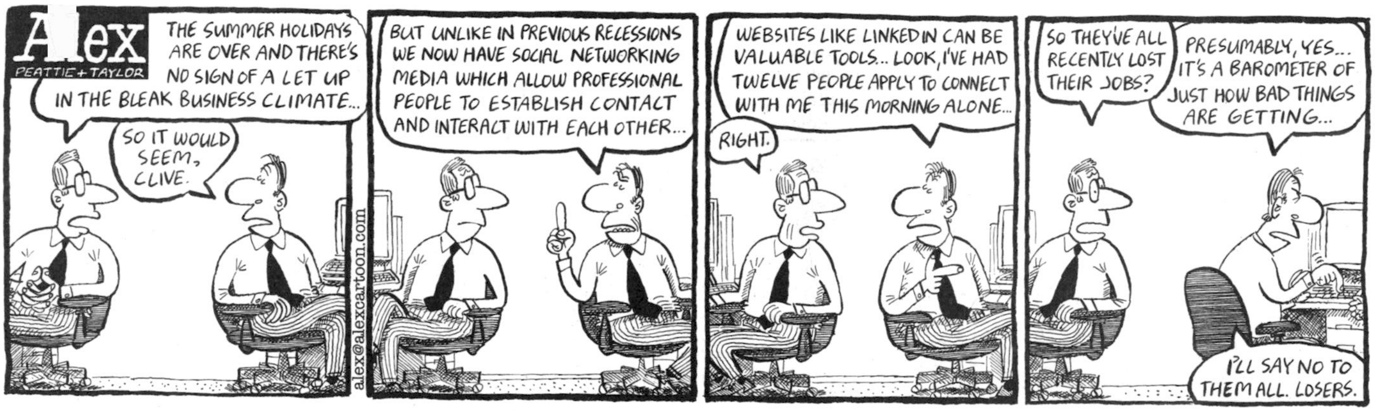
Alex
PEATTIE + TAYLOR
THE SUMMER HOLIDAYS ARE OVER AND THERE'S NO SIGN OF A LET UP IN THE BLEAK BUSINESS CLIMATE...
SO IT WOULD SEEM, CLIVE.
alex@alexcartoon.com
BUT UNLIKE IN PREVIOUS RECESSIONS WE NOW HAVE SOCIAL NETWORKING MEDIA WHICH ALLOW PROFESSIONAL PEOPLE TO ESTABLISH CONTACT AND INTERACT WITH EACH OTHER...
WEBSITES LIKE LINKEDIN CAN BE VALUABLE TOOLS... LOOK, I'VE HAD TWELVE PEOPLE APPLY TO CONNECT WITH ME THIS MORNING ALONE...
RIGHT.
SO THEY'VE ALL RECENTLY LOST THEIR JOBS?
PRESUMABLY, YES... IT'S A BAROMETER OF JUST HOW BAD THINGS ARE GETTING...
I'LL SAY NO TO THEM ALL. LOSERS.

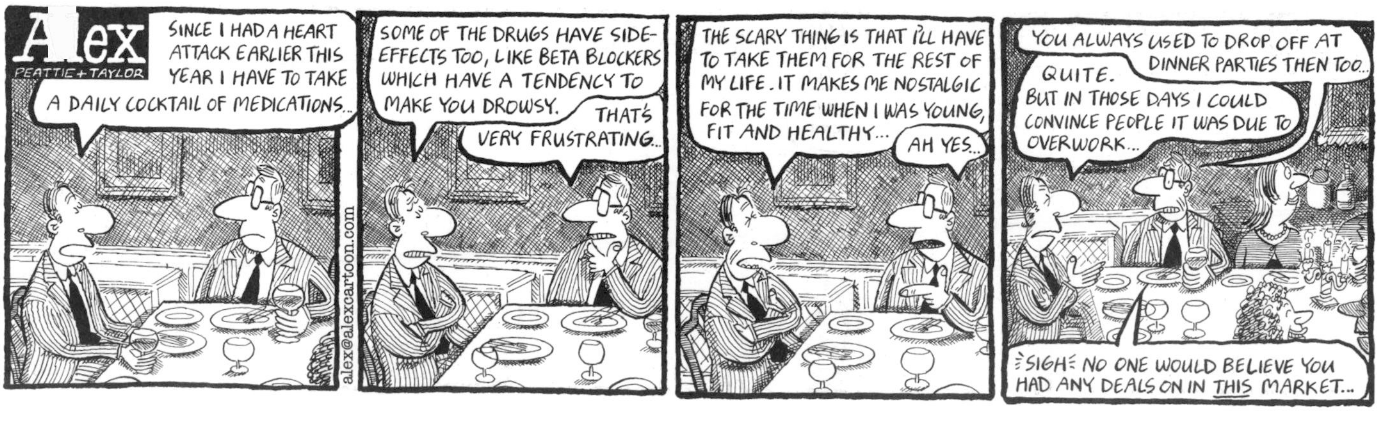
Alex
PEATTIE + TAYLOR
SINCE I HAD A HEART ATTACK EARLIER THIS YEAR I HAVE TO TAKE A DAILY COCKTAIL OF MEDICATIONS...
alex@alexcartoon.com
SOME OF THE DRUGS HAVE SIDE-EFFECTS TOO, LIKE BETA BLOCKERS WHICH HAVE A TENDENCY TO MAKE YOU DROWSY.
THAT'S VERY FRUSTRATING...
THE SCARY THING IS THAT I'LL HAVE TO TAKE THEM FOR THE REST OF MY LIFE. IT MAKES ME NOSTALGIC FOR THE TIME WHEN I WAS YOUNG, FIT AND HEALTHY...
AH YES...
YOU ALWAYS USED TO DROP OFF AT DINNER PARTIES THEN TOO...
QUITE. BUT IN THOSE DAYS I COULD CONVINCE PEOPLE IT WAS DUE TO OVERWORK...
SIGH NO ONE WOULD BELIEVE YOU HAD ANY DEALS ON IN THIS MARKET...

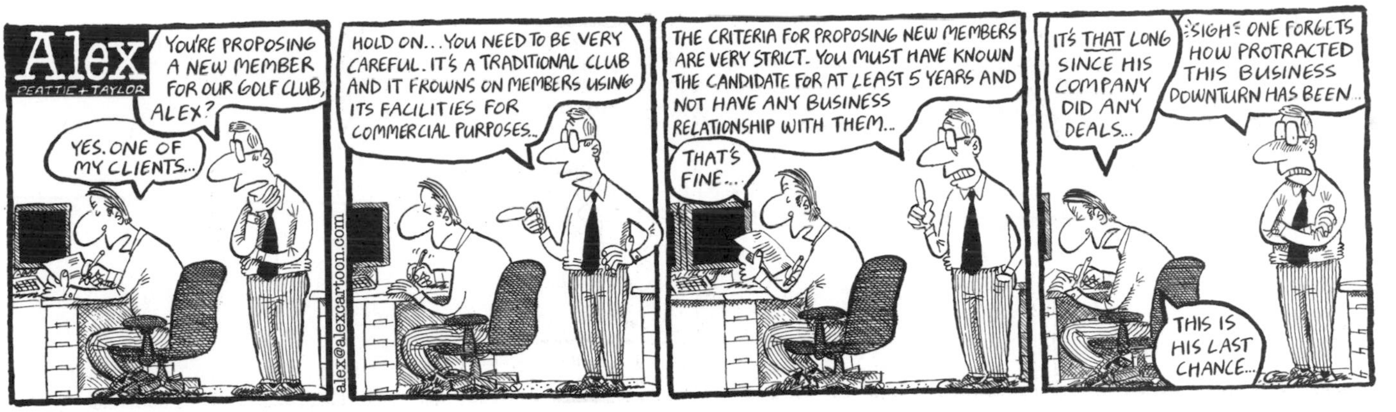
Alex
PEATTIE+TAYLOR
YOU'RE PROPOSING A NEW MEMBER FOR OUR GOLF CLUB, ALEX?
YES. ONE OF MY CLIENTS...
alex@alexcartoon.com
HOLD ON... YOU NEED TO BE VERY CAREFUL. IT'S A TRADITIONAL CLUB AND IT FROWNS ON MEMBERS USING ITS FACILITIES FOR COMMERCIAL PURPOSES...
THE CRITERIA FOR PROPOSING NEW MEMBERS ARE VERY STRICT. YOU MUST HAVE KNOWN THE CANDIDATE FOR AT LEAST 5 YEARS AND NOT HAVE ANY BUSINESS RELATIONSHIP WITH THEM...
THAT'S FINE...
IT'S THAT LONG SINCE HIS COMPANY DID ANY DEALS...
SIGH ONE FORGETS HOW PROTRACTED THIS BUSINESS DOWNTURN HAS BEEN...
THIS IS HIS LAST CHANCE...

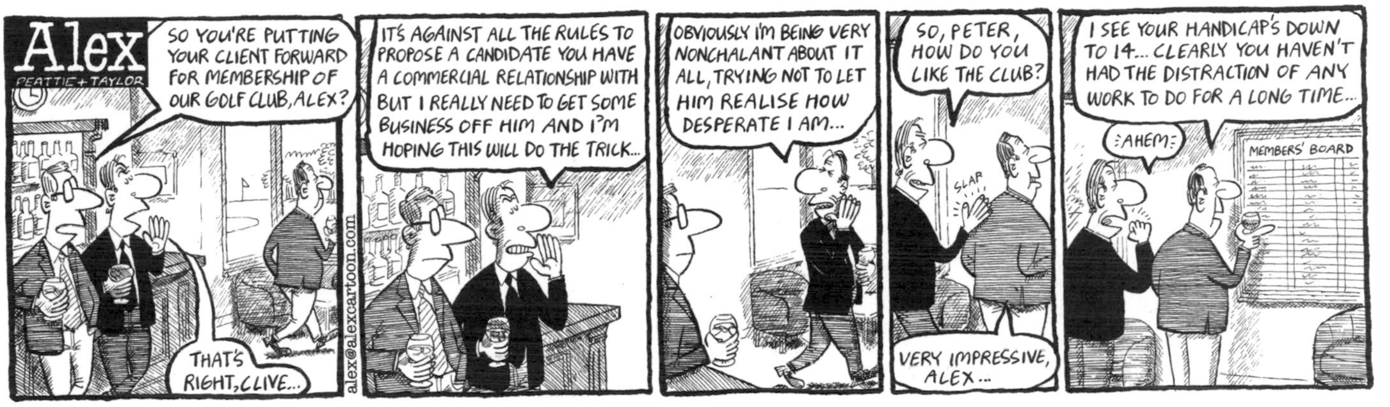
Alex
PEATTIE+TAYLOR
SO YOU'RE PUTTING YOUR CLIENT FORWARD FOR MEMBERSHIP OF OUR GOLF CLUB, ALEX?
THAT'S RIGHT, CLIVE...
alex@alexcartoon.com
IT'S AGAINST ALL THE RULES TO PROPOSE A CANDIDATE YOU HAVE A COMMERCIAL RELATIONSHIP WITH BUT I REALLY NEED TO GET SOME BUSINESS OFF HIM AND I'M HOPING THIS WILL DO THE TRICK...
OBVIOUSLY I'M BEING VERY NONCHALANT ABOUT IT ALL, TRYING NOT TO LET HIM REALISE HOW DESPERATE I AM...
SO, PETER, HOW DO YOU LIKE THE CLUB?
SLAP
VERY IMPRESSIVE, ALEX...
I SEE YOUR HANDICAP'S DOWN TO 14... CLEARLY YOU HAVEN'T HAD THE DISTRACTION OF ANY WORK TO DO FOR A LONG TIME...
AHEM
MEMBERS' BOARD

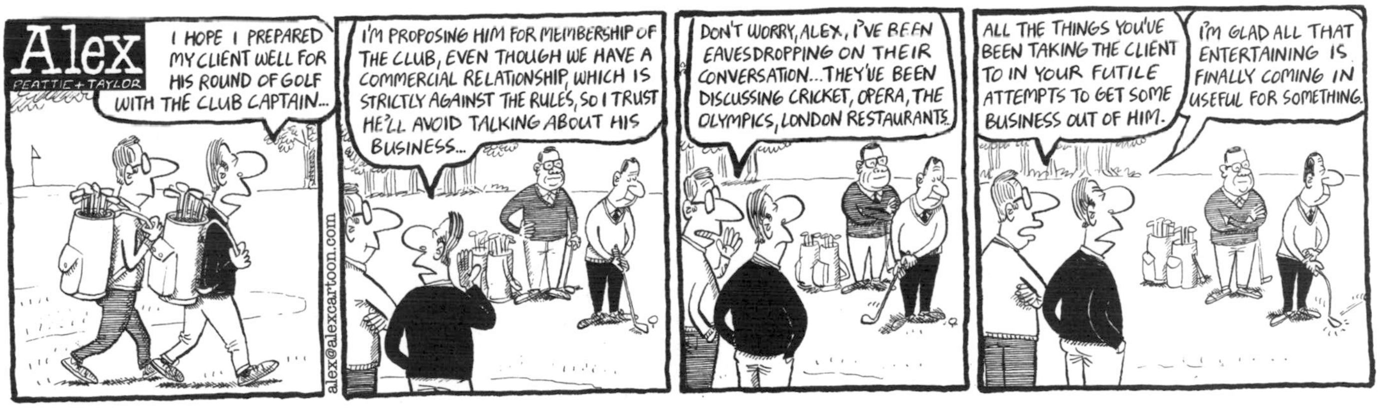
Alex
PEATTIE+TAYLOR
I HOPE I PREPARED MY CLIENT WELL FOR HIS ROUND OF GOLF WITH THE CLUB CAPTAIN...
alex@alexcartoon.com
I'M PROPOSING HIM FOR MEMBERSHIP OF THE CLUB, EVEN THOUGH WE HAVE A COMMERCIAL RELATIONSHIP, WHICH IS STRICTLY AGAINST THE RULES, SO I TRUST HE'LL AVOID TALKING ABOUT HIS BUSINESS...
DON'T WORRY, ALEX, I'VE BEEN EAVESDROPPING ON THEIR CONVERSATION... THEY'VE BEEN DISCUSSING CRICKET, OPERA, THE OLYMPICS, LONDON RESTAURANTS.
ALL THE THINGS YOU'VE BEEN TAKING THE CLIENT TO IN YOUR FUTILE ATTEMPTS TO GET SOME BUSINESS OUT OF HIM.
I'M GLAD ALL THAT ENTERTAINING IS FINALLY COMING IN USEFUL FOR SOMETHING.

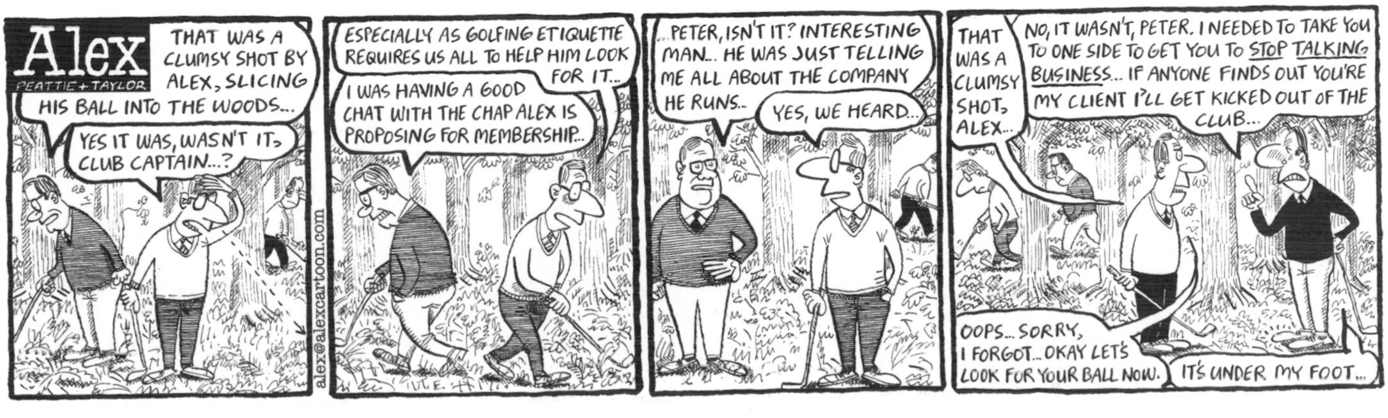
Alex
PEATTIE+TAYLOR
THAT WAS A CLUMSY SHOT BY ALEX, SLICING HIS BALL INTO THE WOODS...
YES IT WAS, WASN'T IT, CLUB CAPTAIN...?
alex@alexcartoon.com
ESPECIALLY AS GOLFING ETIQUETTE REQUIRES US ALL TO HELP HIM LOOK FOR IT...
I WAS HAVING A GOOD CHAT WITH THE CHAP ALEX IS PROPOSING FOR MEMBERSHIP...
...PETER, ISN'T IT? INTERESTING MAN... HE WAS JUST TELLING ME ALL ABOUT THE COMPANY HE RUNS...
YES, WE HEARD...
THAT WAS A CLUMSY SHOT, ALEX...
NO, IT WASN'T, PETER. I NEEDED TO TAKE YOU TO ONE SIDE TO GET YOU TO STOP TALKING BUSINESS... IF ANYONE FINDS OUT YOU'RE MY CLIENT I'LL GET KICKED OUT OF THE CLUB...
OOPS... SORRY, I FORGOT... OKAY LET'S LOOK FOR YOUR BALL NOW.
IT'S UNDER MY FOOT...

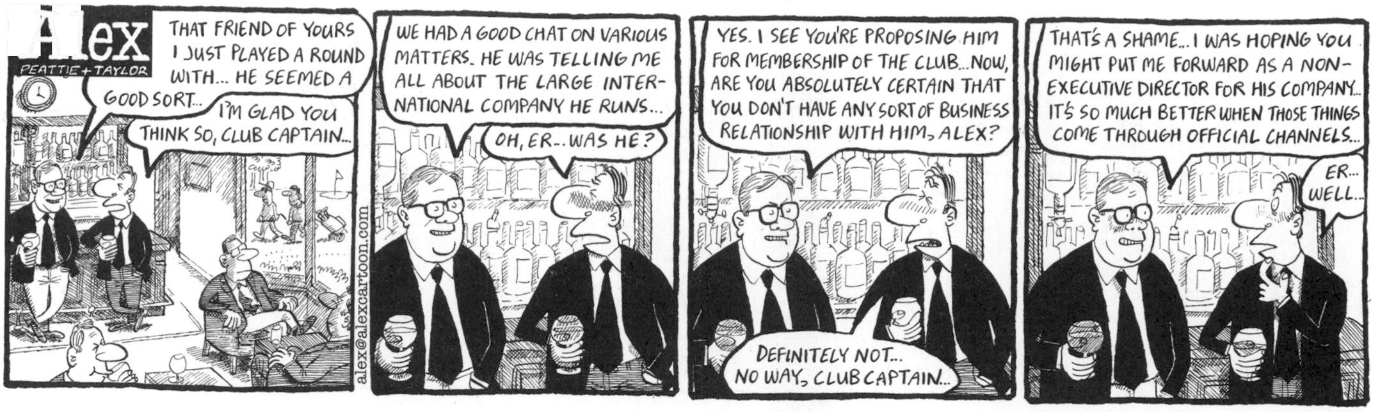
Alex
PEATTIE + TAYLOR
THAT FRIEND OF YOURS I JUST PLAYED A ROUND WITH... HE SEEMED A GOOD SORT...
I'M GLAD YOU THINK SO, CLUB CAPTAIN...
alex@alexcartoon.com
WE HAD A GOOD CHAT ON VARIOUS MATTERS. HE WAS TELLING ME ALL ABOUT THE LARGE INTERNATIONAL COMPANY HE RUNS...
OH, ER... WAS HE?
YES. I SEE YOU'RE PROPOSING HIM FOR MEMBERSHIP OF THE CLUB... NOW, ARE YOU ABSOLUTELY CERTAIN THAT YOU DON'T HAVE ANY SORT OF BUSINESS RELATIONSHIP WITH HIM, ALEX?
DEFINITELY NOT... NO WAY, CLUB CAPTAIN...
THAT'S A SHAME... I WAS HOPING YOU MIGHT PUT ME FORWARD AS A NON-EXECUTIVE DIRECTOR FOR HIS COMPANY... IT'S SO MUCH BETTER WHEN THOSE THINGS COME THROUGH OFFICIAL CHANNELS...
ER... WELL...

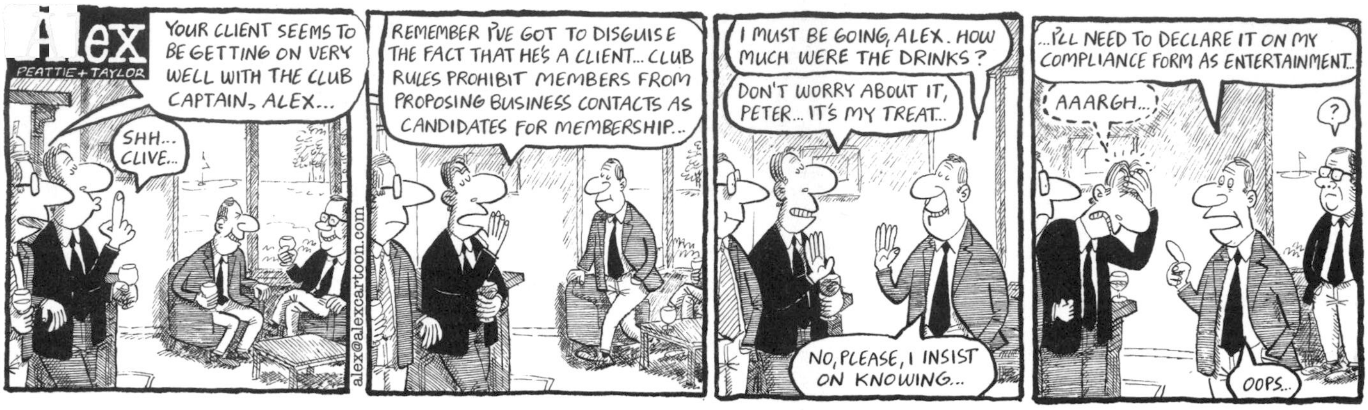
Alex
PEATTIE + TAYLOR
YOUR CLIENT SEEMS TO BE GETTING ON VERY WELL WITH THE CLUB CAPTAIN, ALEX...
SHH... CLIVE...
alex@alexcartoon.com
REMEMBER I'VE GOT TO DISGUISE THE FACT THAT HE'S A CLIENT... CLUB RULES PROHIBIT MEMBERS FROM PROPOSING BUSINESS CONTACTS AS CANDIDATES FOR MEMBERSHIP...
I MUST BE GOING, ALEX. HOW MUCH WERE THE DRINKS?
DON'T WORRY ABOUT IT, PETER... IT'S MY TREAT...
NO, PLEASE, I INSIST ON KNOWING...
...I'LL NEED TO DECLARE IT ON MY COMPLIANCE FORM AS ENTERTAINMENT...
AAARGH...
?
OOPS...

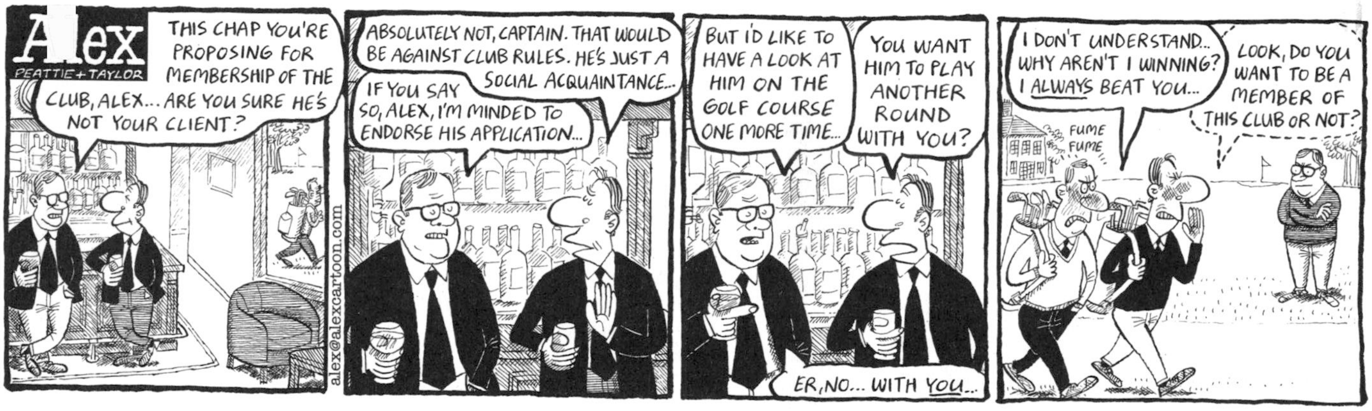
Alex
PEATTIE + TAYLOR
THIS CHAP YOU'RE PROPOSING FOR MEMBERSHIP OF THE CLUB, ALEX... ARE YOU SURE HE'S NOT YOUR CLIENT?
alex@alexcartoon.com
ABSOLUTELY NOT, CAPTAIN. THAT WOULD BE AGAINST CLUB RULES. HE'S JUST A SOCIAL ACQUAINTANCE...
IF YOU SAY SO, ALEX, I'M MINDED TO ENDORSE HIS APPLICATION...
BUT I'D LIKE TO HAVE A LOOK AT HIM ON THE GOLF COURSE ONE MORE TIME...
YOU WANT HIM TO PLAY ANOTHER ROUND WITH YOU?
ER, NO... WITH YOU...
I DON'T UNDERSTAND... WHY AREN'T I WINNING? I ALWAYS BEAT YOU...
FUME FUME
LOOK, DO YOU WANT TO BE A MEMBER OF THIS CLUB OR NOT?

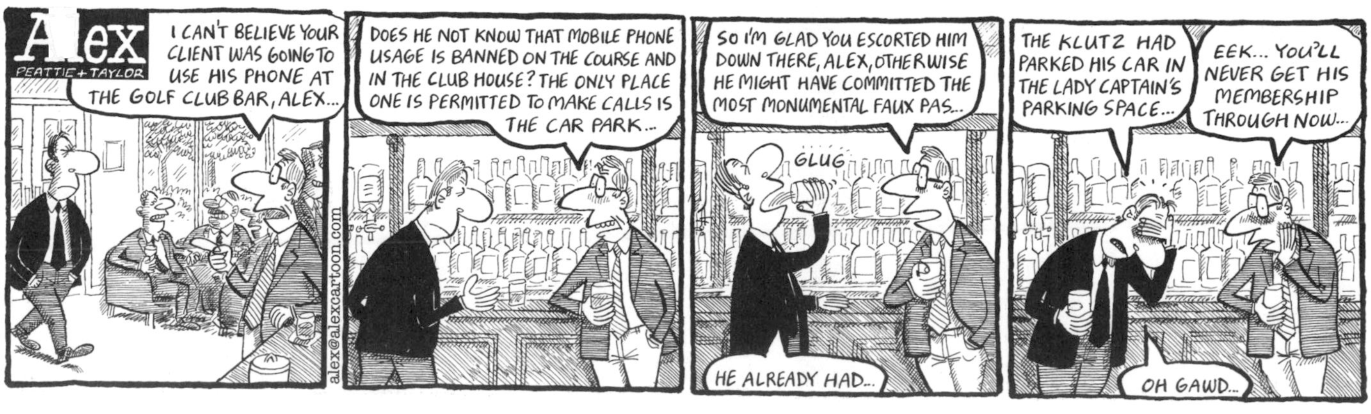
Alex
PEATTIE + TAYLOR
I CAN'T BELIEVE YOUR CLIENT WAS GOING TO USE HIS PHONE AT THE GOLF CLUB BAR, ALEX...
alex@alexcartoon.com
DOES HE NOT KNOW THAT MOBILE PHONE USAGE IS BANNED ON THE COURSE AND IN THE CLUB HOUSE? THE ONLY PLACE ONE IS PERMITTED TO MAKE CALLS IS THE CAR PARK...
SO I'M GLAD YOU ESCORTED HIM DOWN THERE, ALEX, OTHERWISE HE MIGHT HAVE COMMITTED THE MOST MONUMENTAL FAUX PAS...
GLUG
HE ALREADY HAD...
THE KLUTZ HAD PARKED HIS CAR IN THE LADY CAPTAIN'S PARKING SPACE...
EEK... YOU'LL NEVER GET HIS MEMBERSHIP THROUGH NOW...
OH GAWD...

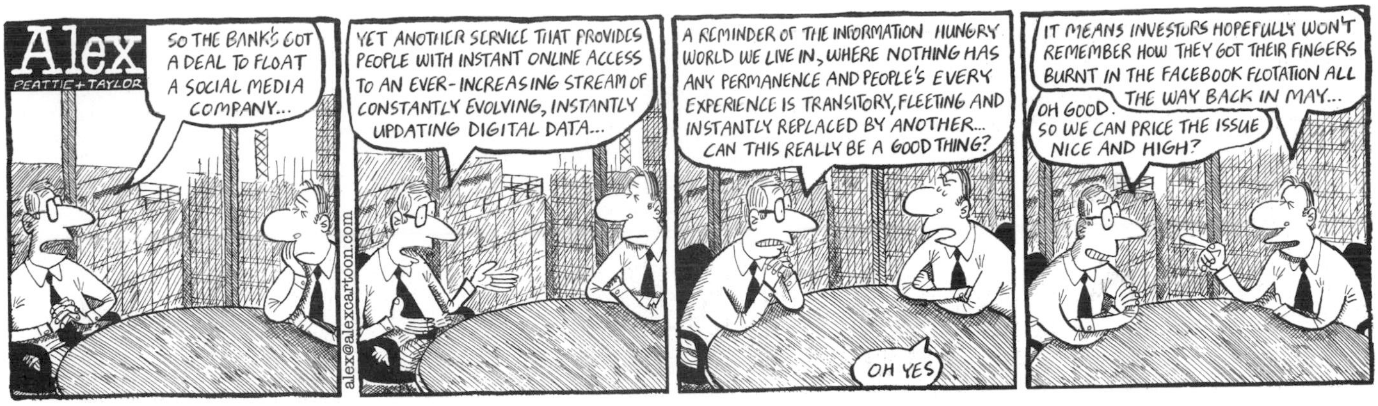
Alex
PEATTIE + TAYLOR
SO THE BANK'S GOT A DEAL TO FLOAT A SOCIAL MEDIA COMPANY...
alex@alexcartoon.com
YET ANOTHER SERVICE THAT PROVIDES PEOPLE WITH INSTANT ONLINE ACCESS TO AN EVER-INCREASING STREAM OF CONSTANTLY EVOLVING, INSTANTLY UPDATING DIGITAL DATA...
A REMINDER OF THE INFORMATION HUNGRY WORLD WE LIVE IN, WHERE NOTHING HAS ANY PERMANENCE AND PEOPLE'S EVERY EXPERIENCE IS TRANSITORY, FLEETING AND INSTANTLY REPLACED BY ANOTHER... CAN THIS REALLY BE A GOOD THING?
OH YES
IT MEANS INVESTORS HOPEFULLY WON'T REMEMBER HOW THEY GOT THEIR FINGERS BURNT IN THE FACEBOOK FLOTATION ALL THE WAY BACK IN MAY...
OH GOOD. SO WE CAN PRICE THE ISSUE NICE AND HIGH?

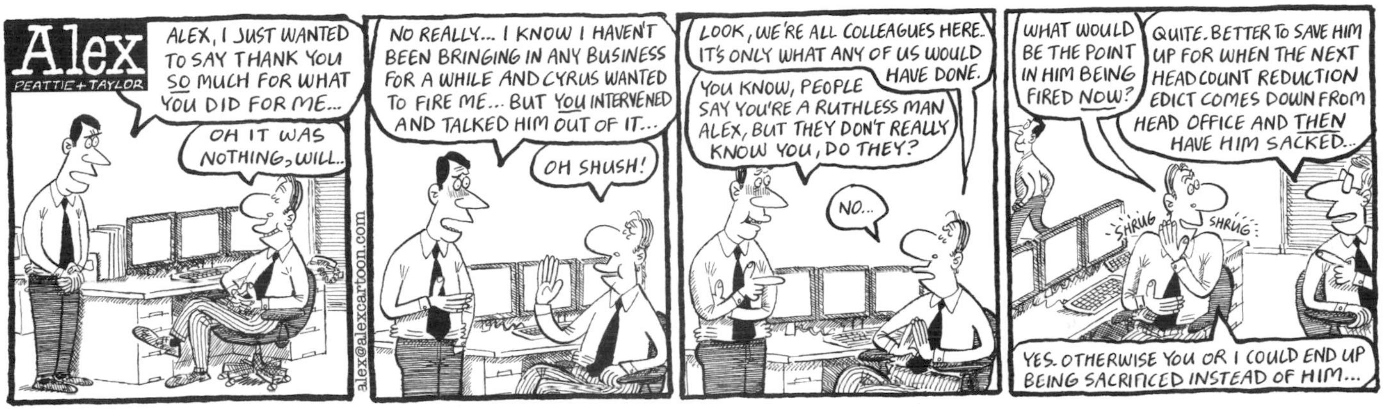
Alex
PEATTIE + TAYLOR
ALEX, I JUST WANTED TO SAY THANK YOU SO MUCH FOR WHAT YOU DID FOR ME...
OH IT WAS NOTHING, WILL..
alex@alexcartoon.com
NO REALLY... I KNOW I HAVEN'T BEEN BRINGING IN ANY BUSINESS FOR A WHILE AND CYRUS WANTED TO FIRE ME... BUT YOU INTERVENED AND TALKED HIM OUT OF IT...
OH SHUSH!
LOOK, WE'RE ALL COLLEAGUES HERE.. IT'S ONLY WHAT ANY OF US WOULD HAVE DONE.
YOU KNOW, PEOPLE SAY YOU'RE A RUTHLESS MAN ALEX, BUT THEY DON'T REALLY KNOW YOU, DO THEY?
NO...
WHAT WOULD BE THE POINT IN HIM BEING FIRED NOW?
QUITE. BETTER TO SAVE HIM UP FOR WHEN THE NEXT HEAD COUNT REDUCTION EDICT COMES DOWN FROM HEAD OFFICE AND THEN HAVE HIM SACKED...
SHRUG
SHRUG
YES. OTHERWISE YOU OR I COULD END UP BEING SACRIFICED INSTEAD OF HIM...

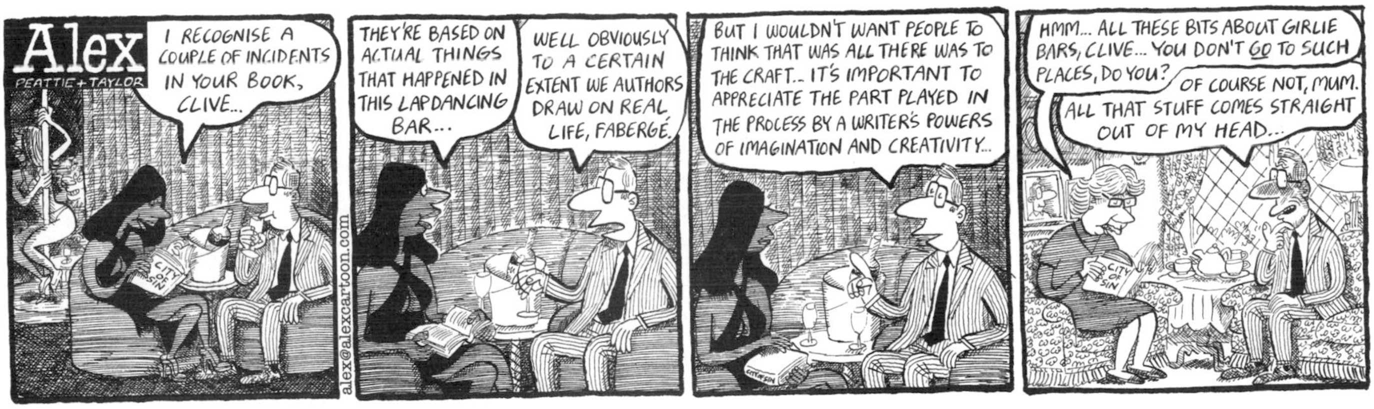
Alex
PEATTIE + TAYLOR
I RECOGNISE A COUPLE OF INCIDENTS IN YOUR BOOK, CLIVE...
alex@alexcartoon.com
THEY'RE BASED ON ACTUAL THINGS THAT HAPPENED IN THIS LAPDANCING BAR...
WELL OBVIOUSLY TO A CERTAIN EXTENT WE AUTHORS DRAW ON REAL LIFE, FABERGÉ.
BUT I WOULDN'T WANT PEOPLE TO THINK THAT WAS ALL THERE WAS TO THE CRAFT.. IT'S IMPORTANT TO APPRECIATE THE PART PLAYED IN THE PROCESS BY A WRITER'S POWERS OF IMAGINATION AND CREATIVITY...
HMM... ALL THESE BITS ABOUT GIRLIE BARS, CLIVE... YOU DON'T GO TO SUCH PLACES, DO YOU?
OF COURSE NOT, MUM. ALL THAT STUFF COMES STRAIGHT OUT OF MY HEAD...

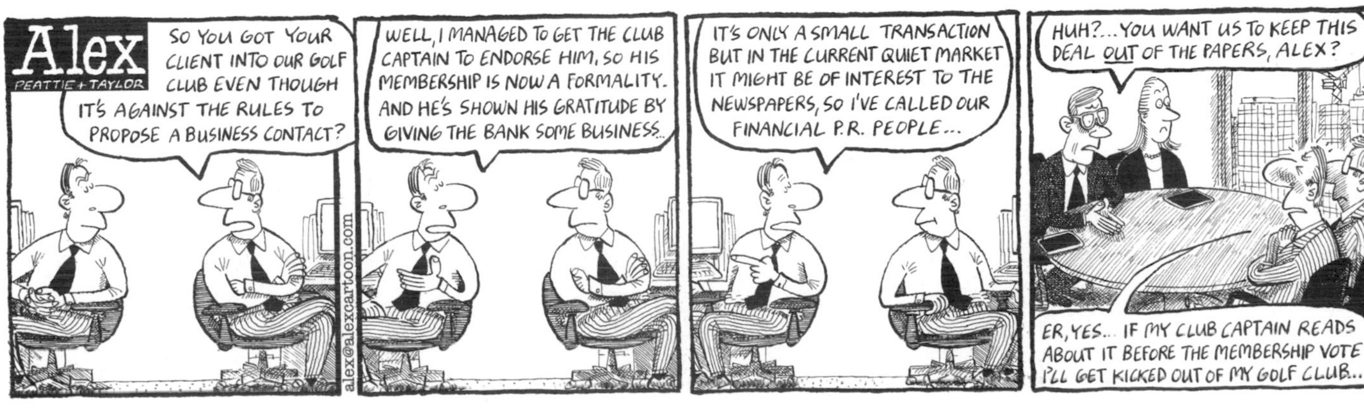
Alex
PEATTIE + TAYLOR
SO YOU GOT YOUR CLIENT INTO OUR GOLF CLUB EVEN THOUGH IT'S AGAINST THE RULES TO PROPOSE A BUSINESS CONTACT?
alex@alexcartoon.com
WELL, I MANAGED TO GET THE CLUB CAPTAIN TO ENDORSE HIM, SO HIS MEMBERSHIP IS NOW A FORMALITY. AND HE'S SHOWN HIS GRATITUDE BY GIVING THE BANK SOME BUSINESS...
IT'S ONLY A SMALL TRANSACTION BUT IN THE CURRENT QUIET MARKET IT MIGHT BE OF INTEREST TO THE NEWSPAPERS, SO I'VE CALLED OUR FINANCIAL P.R. PEOPLE...
HUH?... YOU WANT US TO KEEP THIS DEAL OUT OF THE PAPERS, ALEX?
ER, YES... IF MY CLUB CAPTAIN READS ABOUT IT BEFORE THE MEMBERSHIP VOTE I'LL GET KICKED OUT OF MY GOLF CLUB...

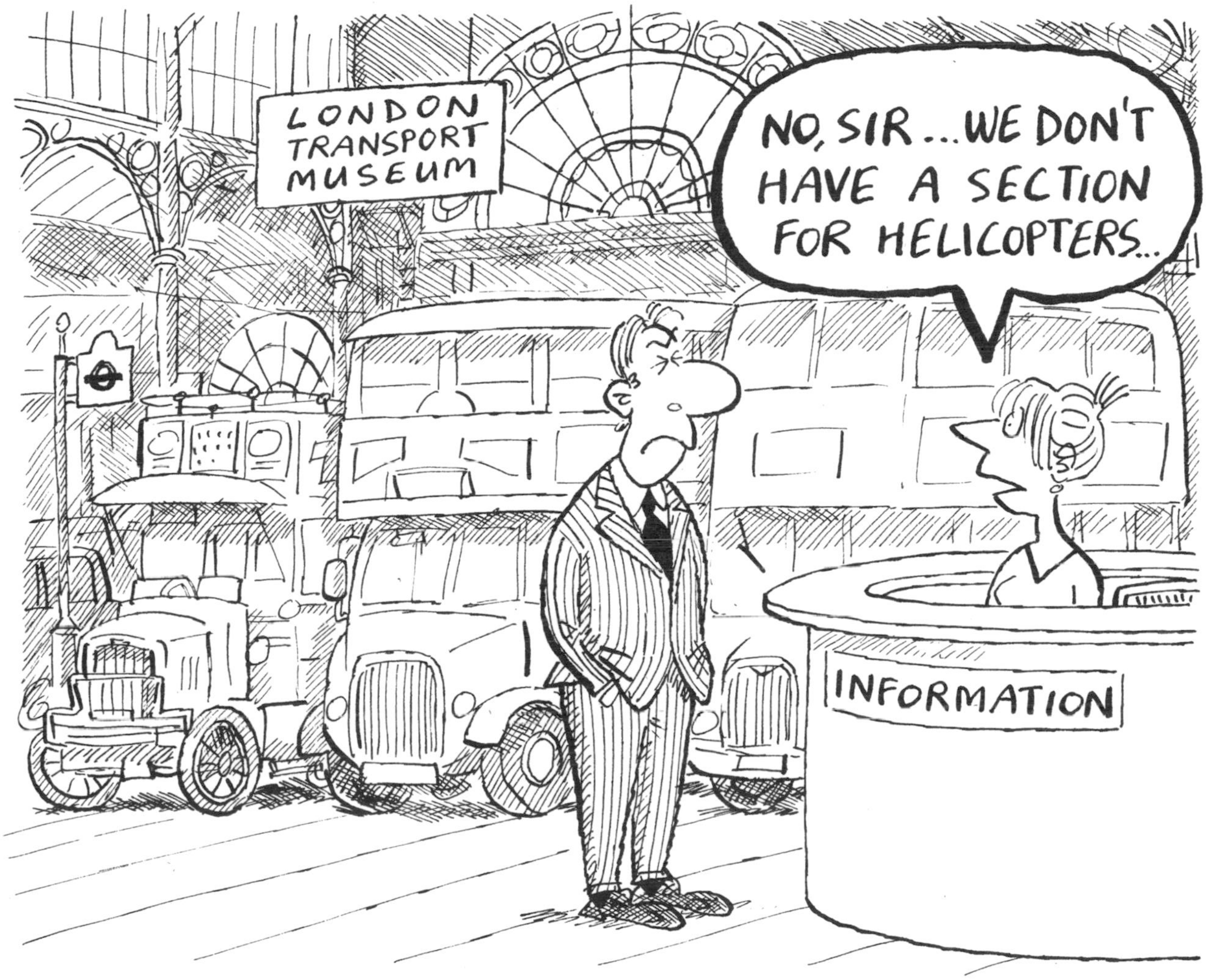
LONDON TRANSPORT MUSEUM
NO, SIR ... WE DON'T HAVE A SECTION FOR HELICOPTERS...
INFORMATION

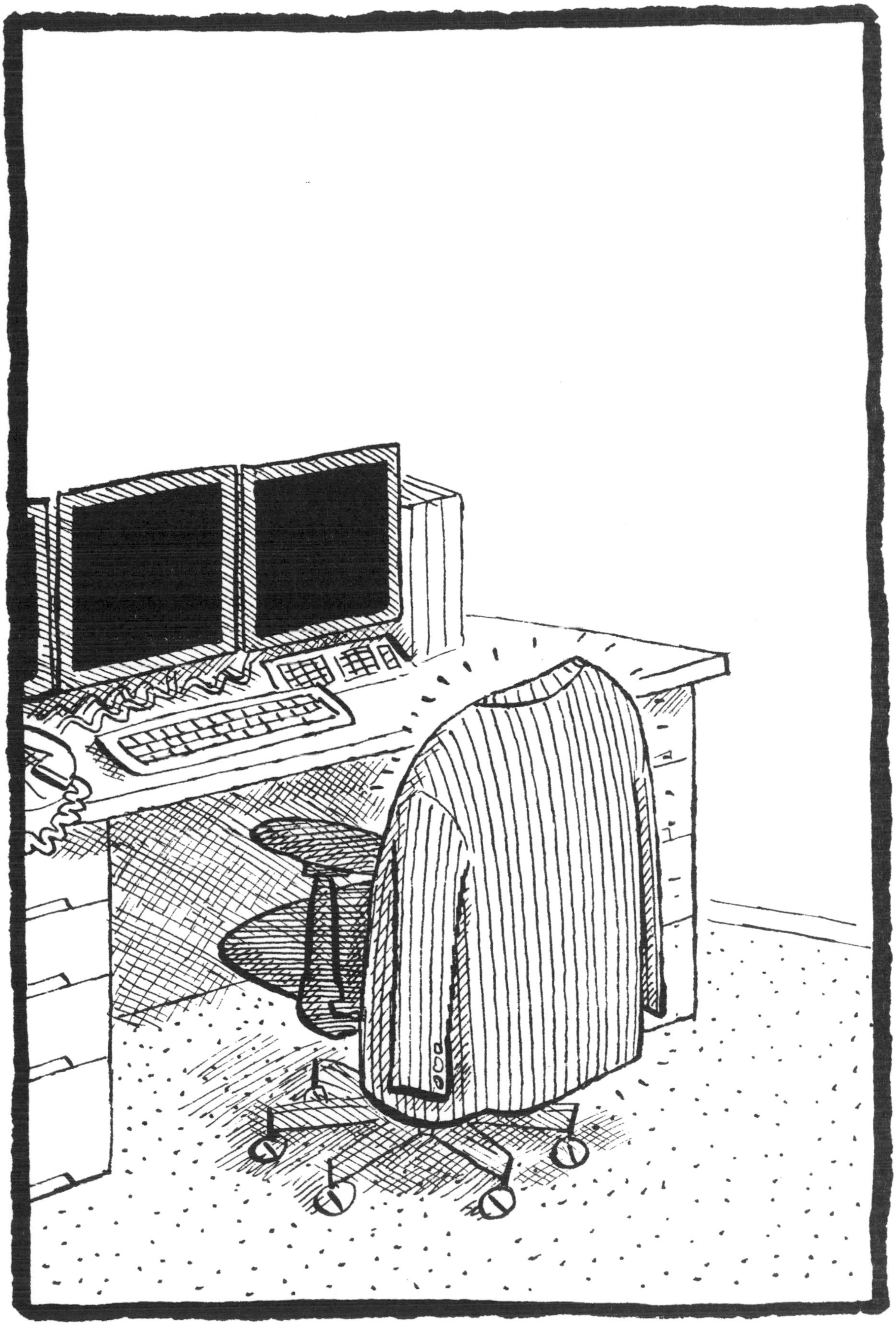

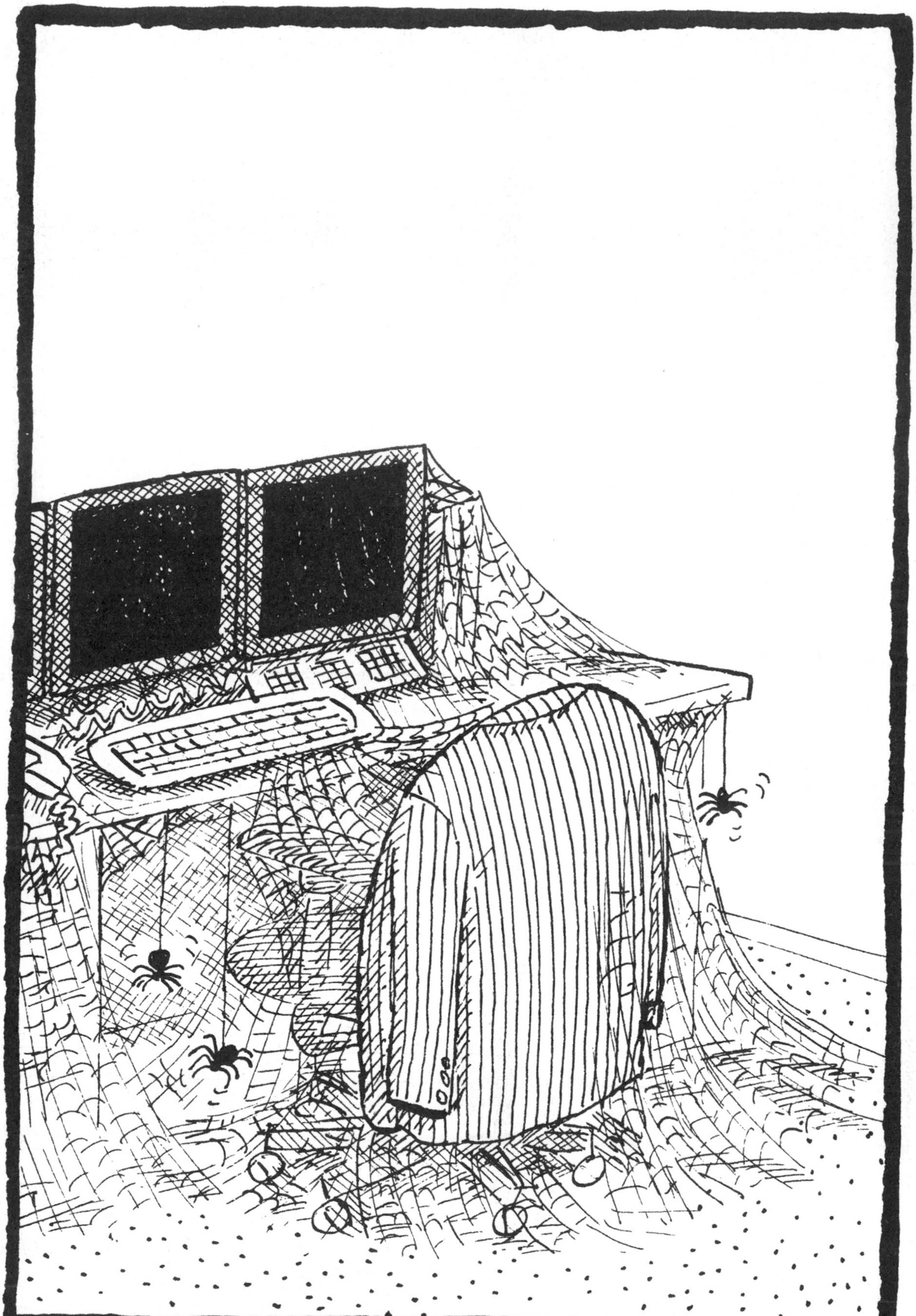

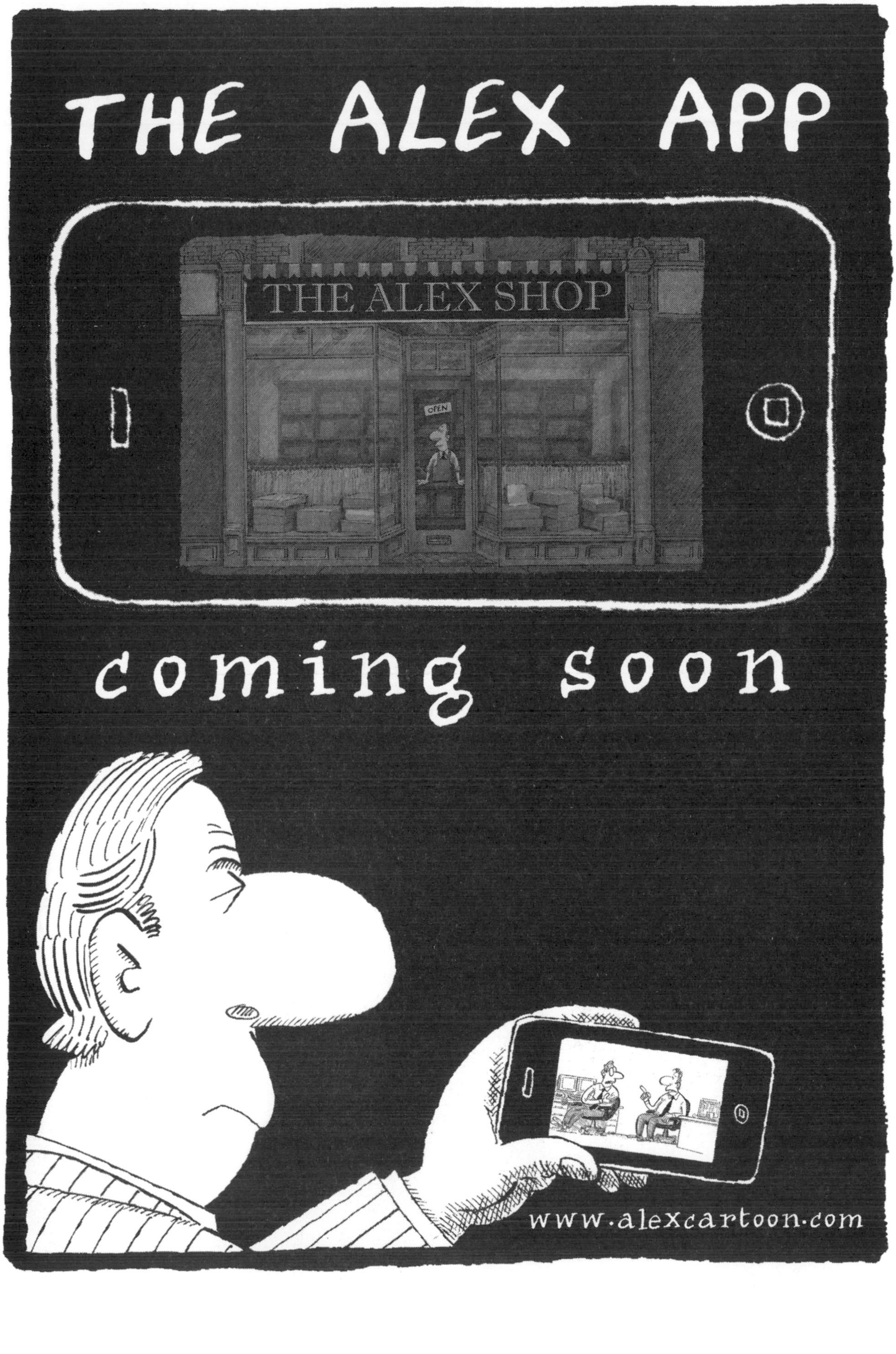
THE ALEX APP
THE ALEX SHOP
OPEN
coming soon
www.alexcartoon.com

Also available from Masterley Publishing

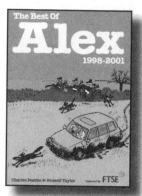

The Best Of
Alex
1998-2001
Charles Peattie & Russell Taylor
FTSE

The Best of Alex 1998 - 2001
Boom to bust via the dotcom bubble.

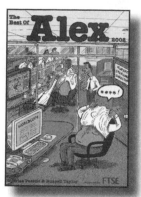

The Best Of
Alex
2002
FTSE

The Best of Alex 2002
Scandals rock the corporate world.

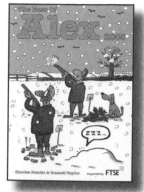

Alex
zzz..
FTSE

The Best of Alex 2003
Alex gets made redundant.

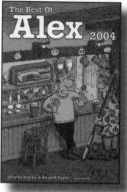

The Best Of
Alex
2004

The Best of Alex 2004
And gets his job back.

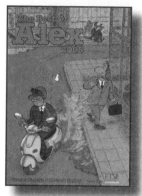

FTSE

The Best of Alex 2005
Alex has problems with the French.

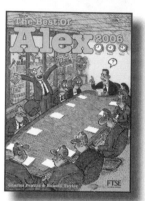

The Best Of
Alex
2006
FTSE

The Best of Alex 2006
Alex gets a new American boss.

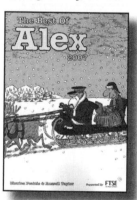

The Best Of
Alex
2007
FTSE

The Best of Alex 2007
Alex restructures Christmas.

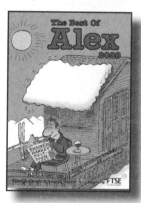

The Best Of
Alex
FTSE

The Best of Alex 2008
The credit crunch bites.

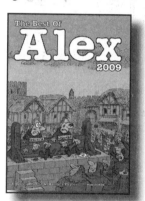

The Best Of
Alex
2009

The Best of Alex 2009
Global capitalism self-destructs.

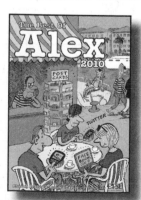

The Best Of
Alex
2010
POST CARDS
TWITTER

The Best of Alex 2010
But somehow lurches on.

The Best Of
Alex
2011
Charles Peattie & Russell Taylor

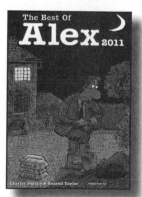

Best of Alex 2011
The financial crisis continues.

Celeb
The Original Gary Bloke From
PRIVATE EYE
Charles Peattie and Mark Warren

Celeb
Wrinkly rockstar Gary Bloke.

All books cost £9.99 plus p+p.
Cartoon originals and prints are also for sale. They measure 4 x 14 inches and are signed by the creators.
For further details on prices: **tel: 020 8374 1225 email: alex@alexcartoon.com web: www.alexcartoon.com**

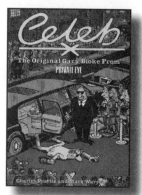